ROUTLEDGE LIBRARY EDITIONS: THE NINETEENTH-CENTURY NOVEL

Volume 1

BALZAC AND MUSIC

BALZAC AND MUSIC
Its Place and Meaning in His Life and Work

JEAN-PIERRE BARRICELLI

Routledge
Taylor & Francis Group
LONDON AND NEW YORK

First published in 1990 by Garland Publishing

This edition first published in 2016
by Routledge
2 Park Square, Milton Park, Abingdon, Oxon OX14 4RN

and by Routledge
711 Third Avenue, New York, NY 10017

Routledge is an imprint of the Taylor & Francis Group, an informa business

© 1990 Jean-Pierre Barricelli

All rights reserved. No part of this book may be reprinted or reproduced or utilised in any form or by any electronic, mechanical, or other means, now known or hereafter invented, including photocopying and recording, or in any information storage or retrieval system, without permission in writing from the publishers.

Trademark notice: Product or corporate names may be trademarks or registered trademarks, and are used only for identification and explanation without intent to infringe.

British Library Cataloguing in Publication Data
A catalogue record for this book is available from the British Library

ISBN: 978-1-138-67777-7 (Set)
ISBN: 978-1-315-55928-5 (Set) (ebk)
ISBN: 978-1-138-67040-2 (Volume 1) (hbk)
ISBN: 978-1-138-67042-6 (Volume 1) (pbk)
ISBN: 978-1-315-61764-0 (Volume 1) (ebk)

Publisher's Note
The publisher has gone to great lengths to ensure the quality of this reprint but points out that some imperfections in the original copies may be apparent.

Disclaimer
The publisher has made every effort to trace copyright holders and would welcome correspondence from those they have been unable to trace.

BALZAC and MUSIC
Its Place and Meaning in His Life and Work

Jean-Pierre Barricelli

GARLAND PUBLISHING
New York & London
1990

Copyright © 1990 by Jean-Pierre Barricelli
All Rights Reserved

Library of Congress Cataloging-in-Publication Data

Barricelli, Jean-Pierre.
Balzac and music: its place and meaning in his life and work/ Jean-Pierre Barricelli.
p. cm.—(Garland studies in comparative literature)
Includes bibliographical references.
ISBN 0-8240-0003-X (alk. paper)
1. Balzac, Honoré de, 1799–1850—Knowledge—Music. 2. Music—France—History—19th century. 3. Music and literature. I. Title. II. Series.
PQ2184.M8B37   1990
843'.7—dc20   90-34443

Printed on acid-free, 250-year-life paper.
Manufactured in the United States of America

To the Memory of my Mother

who saw me lovingly through my many Harvard years
that culminated in this work fittingly dedicated to her

[Balzac]

Neither to excuse him nor to revile him,
but to explain, to feel what he is,

                          Herder (on Shakespeare)

[Music]

This world of shapes and figures,
inexhaustibly rich in styles, national
characteristics, traditional values,
and charms of personality, historic
and individual variations of the ideal
beauty.

                          Mann (*Doktor Faustus*)

CONTENTS

Preface   xi
List of abbreviations   xiii

Introduction   1

Part One: Music In Balzac's Life and Time   7
    1. The Enticement of Sound   9
    2. Shallow Enchantments   29
    3. Celebrated Musician Friends   51
    4. An Otherwise Forgotten Teacher   68

Part Two: Debates, Premises, and Balzac's Comments   85
    5. From Beyond the Alps and Rhine   87
    6. Critical Estimates   96

Part Three: Balzac's Major Persuasions   121
    7. Religious Music: An Innate Affinity   123
    8. Beethoven: The Growth Of a Concept   133

Part Four: Balzac's Musical Tales and Their Implications   147
    9. *Gambara*: Preserving Idealism   149
   10. *Massimilla Doni*: Transcending Sensualism   173
   11. An Animating Psychology   188
   12. A Dynamic Philosophy   203

Appendix	225
1. Synopses Of the Operas	227
2. Musical Compositions Inspired By Balzac's Works	228
3. Auber's Music For the Romance in *Modeste Mignon*	230
Notes	231
Bibliography	269
Outline of the Chapters	289
Index	291

ILLUSTRATIONS

Portrait of Balzac	ii
Profile of Balzac	xvi
Caricature of Balzac	84
Gambara at the Panharmonicon	120
Massimilla Doni at the Fenice	146

PREFACE

No comprehensive study of Balzac and music exists; the subject is therefore as valid—and important—today as it was in 1953, when this Harvard doctoral dissertation, here revised and updated, was presented. Its purpose is now what it was then: to blend past scholarship on the question (whatever there is of it) with new perspectives and formulate an inclusive account of the novelist's relationship to the art. A few aspects have been investigated, sometimes with laudable depth, like religious music by Philippe Bertault, folkmusic by Julien Tiersot, some elements of musical aesthetics by Pierre Laubriet, and the Liszt biographical connection by Korwin-Piotrowska, and in 1964 Maurice Regard and Max Milner provided informative introductions for editions of Balzac's two musical novellas. Most other articles on the topic have tended to fall on the extreme ends of the critical spectrum, either overly laudatory or overly abusive of the novelist's range and ability in the field of music.

In Part I of the present study, I examine the contacts and experiences that shaped the musical side of Balzac's life—his friendships, teacher, and cultural milieu to which he may have contributed little musically but from which he garnered valuable and lasting impressions. Many of these impressions found their way into *La Comédie humaine* and other writings where he recorded, not without ingenuous enthusiasm at times, a myriad of critical and musicological opinions, factored by the polemics of the contesting Italian and German schools. These discussions in Part II prepare Part III, which is devoted to Balzac's two major—indeed, telling—persuasions that underscore his musical orientations and suggest a discerning sensibility: religious music and Beethoven. What, then, he says about the art psychologically, aesthetically, and philosophically—centered primarily around *Gambara* and *Massimilla Doni* and assessed in Part IV—needs to be taken seriously, even in its more commonplace stances, for it reveals the thinking, feeling, and imaginative Balzac at his best. Consistent with its nature, music serves to disclose his soul as it casts a very special light into multiple corners of his writings, and, by extension, into his personality and period.

For the sake of comprehensiveness, I have found it necessary to view, in more than one section of this study, a given passage of a novel from different perspectives. A quotation says different, though not contradictory, things in different contexts. The effect is that produced by mirrors placed at various angles with reference to the same object. The line of presentation shifts accordingly, each perspective hopefully investing the whole with an additional dimension of meaning. And in the process, I have seeded the text generously with references to the original source, in the knowledge that Balzac's own words are inevitably more convincing than my paraphrases.

Following the counsel of the publisher, I have translated these words—as, to be sure, all foreign quotations here—into English (the famous Italian caveat about betraying translators notwithstanding) in order to reach as broad an audience as possible. Garland Publishing's selection of this work for publication is both flattering and humbling, and I should be remiss not to express my gratitude. I am grateful, too, to the late Professor Leiv Flydal of Norway's Handelshøyskole, Direktor Hallvard S. Bakken and Audun Tvinnereim of the Library of the University of Bergen, and the Fulbright Commission in that beautiful land of *Séraphita*, for having created for me gracious opportunities which facilitated the revision of this text in 1962-63. And to my late and renowned academic mentor, Jean Seznec, who originally suggested a comprehensive study on Balzac and music to a fledgling scholar back around 1950, go my very special thanks and warm remembrance. *Si parva licet componere magnis*.

J-P. Barricelli

Riverside, California
1989

ABBREVIATIONS AND EDITIONS

From *La Comédie humaine*		Pléiade edition volume
A	*Adieu*	IX
AEF	*Autre étude de femme*	III
AR	*L'Auberge rouge*	IX
AS	*Albert Savarus*	I
B	*Béatrix*	II
BS	*Le Bal de Sceaux*	I
C	*Les Chouans*	VII
CA	*Le Cabinet des antiques*	IV
CB	*Histoire de la grandeur et de la décadence de César Birotteau*	V
CBe	*La Cousine Bette*	VI
CC	*Le Colonel Chabert*	II
CM	*Le Contrat de mariage*	III
CI	*Le Chef-d'oeuvre inconnu*	IX
CP	*Le Cousin Pons*	VI
CBS	*Les Comédiens sans le savoir*	VII
CT	*Le Curé de Tours*	III
CV	*Le Curé de village*	VIII
DA	*Le Député d'Arcis*	VII
DBM	*Un Drame au bord de la mer*	IX
DF	*Une double Famille*	I
DL	*La Duchesse de Langeais*	V
DR	*Les deux Rêves* (in *Sur Catherine de Médicis*)	X
DV	*Un Début dans la vie*	I
EG	*Eugénie Grandet*	III
EHC	*L'Envers de l'histoire contemporaine*	VII
ELV	*L'Elixir de longue vie*	X
EM	*L'Enfant maudit*	IX
Em	*Les Employés*	VI
F	*Ferragus*	V
FC	*Facino Cane*	VI

FE	*Une Fille d'Eve*	II
FM	*La fausse Maîtresse*	II
FTA	*La Femme de trente ans*	II
FYD	*La Fille aux yeux d'or*	V
G	*Gambara*	IX
H	*Honorine*	II
HA	*Un Homme d'affaires*	VI
I	*L'Interdiction*	III
IG	*L'illustre Gaudissart*	IV
IP	*Illusions perdues*	IV
JCF	*Jésus-Christ en Flandre*	IX
LL	*Louis Lambert*	X
LV	*Le Lys dans la vallée*	VIII
MA	*La Messe de l'athée*	II
MC	*Le Médecin de campagne*	VIII
MCo	*Maître Cornélius*	IX
MD	*Massimilla Doni*	IX
MF	*Madame Firmiani*	I
MJM	*Mémoires de deux jeunes mariées*	I
MM	*Modeste Mignon*	I
MN	*La Maison Nucingen*	V
MR	*Melmoth réconcilié*	IX
MuD	*La Muse du département*	IV
P	*Pierrette*	III
Pa	*Les Paysans*	VIII
PB	*Les petits Bourgeois*	VII
PC	*La Peau de chagrin*	IX
PCa	*Le Prêtre catholique*	XI
PG	*Le Père Goriot*	II
PM	*La Physiologie du mariage*	X
PMVC	*Petites misères de la vie conjugale*	X
R	*La Rabouilleuse*	III
RA	*La Recherche de l'Absolu*	IX
Ré	*Le Réquisitionnaire*	IX
S	*Séraphita*	X
Sa	*Sarrasine*	VI
SMC	*Splendeurs et misères des courtisanes*	V
SPC	*Les Secrets de la princesse de Cadignan*	V
UM	*Ursule Mirouët*	III

From the *OEuvres complètes* Club de l'Honnête homme edition volume

AAI	"Aventures administratives d'une idée heureuse"	16
ADB	"Les Amours de Deux Bêtes"	24
Art	"Des Artistes"	22

CD	"La Comédie du Diable"	22
CGH	"Code des gens honnêtes"	21
FJP	"Feuilleton des journaux politiques"	22
LP	"Lettre sur Paris"	22
ML	"De la mode in littérature"	22
TEM	"Traité des excitants modernes"	23
ThD	"Théorie de la démarche"	23
VC	"De la vie de château"	22
VPJ	"Voyage de Paris à Java"	23

From the early novels   **Editions**

AP	*Argow-le-Pirate*	Michel Lévy, 1868
Is	*L'Israélite*	Michel Lévy
JP	*Jane la pale*	Michel Lévy
St	*Sténie*	A. Prioult (Jouve), 1936
VA	*Le Vicaire des Ardennes*	Michel Lévy
WC	*Wann-Chlore*	Michel Lévy

From the correspondence   **Edition**

E	*Lettres à l'Etrangère*	M. Bouteron (Calmann-Lévy), 1899-1950

INTRODUCTION

During the "Journées Balzaciennes" at the University of Paris in 1950, the distinguished philologist Mario Roques observed that only a person of genuine musical sensibility could have devised a title so assonantly beautiful as *Le Lys dans la vallée*. The parenthetical nature of his statement notwithstanding, its implications are rich and remain worthy of scrutiny. That the novel was actually a translation of an 1820 English short story, *The Lily in the Valley*, which Countess Guidoboni had introduced to Honoré de Balzac, matters little. Many pages in the book reveal a musical vibrancy of style worthy of Chateaubriand, as for example the phrase that may be regarded as Balzac's own description of the novel: "ce poème en fleurs lumineuses qui bourdonne incessamment ses mélodies au coeur en y caressant des voluptés cachées, des espérances inavouées, des illusions qui s'enflamment et qui s'éteignent comme des fils de la Vierge par une nuit chaude" (LV 859): ("this poem of luminous flowers that hums its melodies constantly to the heart which it strokes with hidden desires, undisclosed hopes, illusions that catch fire and become extinguished like so many gossamers on a warm night").

Architecturally, we might make a case for music as it provides a framework for love in *Mémoires de deux jeunes mariées*, or as it punctuates the story of *Ferragus*. Its role is structural in the two climaxes in the affairs of César Birotteau (CB), and it becomes a pivotal experience that accompanies the rhythm of Antoinette de Navarrin's life (DL). Pierre Laubriet suggests that the beginning of the latter work is "a brilliant variation on the *Magnificat*: the rhythm of the sentences, broad and solemn at times or quick and jerky, or implacably monotonous; the tonality of the words, sparkling, sharp, and gliding, smothered and heavy; the images and ideas that brace this passage—all make it a page of music in prose."[1]

But no inference should be drawn about Balzac's musical talent. The attempt in *La Duchesse de Langeais* was not repeated. He lacked the musical abilities of a Hoffmann, or even a Rousseau or a Diderot, and was not conspicuously associated with music like his contemporaries Stendhal, Mazzini, and Nerval. No, Balzac confessed, "musically speaking I am nothing"[2]—an admission of unusual frankness made at the height of his melomania when he had finished one of his two musical *contes philosophiques* and all but finished the other.

That negative self-appraisal should not be accepted literally and may have represented only a turn of false modesty. Balzac spoke of the art of music often and with love. Weak in his historical and technical understanding of the art, he replaced understanding with imaginative response and perception, writing penetrating pages on composers, singers, instruments, and musical psychology, even philosophy. The question inspired by Professor Roques' remark is not whether Balzac was a musician, but rather what were the nature, the genuineness, and the intensity of his musical sensibility, and in what ways was that sensibility woven into his works.

Most of the accounts, ennobling or belittling, by the mere handful of critics who have considered Balzac's musical interest need serious emendation. There are those who read astounding foresights into his words, foresights that bear on extraneous modulation (independent of Beethoven), Wagnerian aesthetics, and the harmonic atonality of the twentieth century. Others scowl at his ostentatious pretentiousness and find him a follower of consecrated modes, a petulant dilettante who could enjoy only the frivolous scores of the Italian theatre of his day or the tingling "false jewelry"[3] of Meyerbeer, an untutored aficionado who accepted the works of Beethoven, Mozart, and the Italian classical school not on inner experience but on the faith of knowledgeable listeners or esteemed musician friends.

Théophile Gautier's assertion that Balzac "execrated"[4] music frequently provides the point of departure for those who would discard outright the novelist's opinions about the art. It is but a short step from there to consider him unsophisticated and incompetent. The reader of 1888 would find this summation by Louis de Fourcand:

> Do you think that Balzac really loved music? I seriously doubt it. Music is a diffuse, confused, and consequently inferior language. Balzac may have had something to do with it, but only accessorily and as an observer and

> pathologist, in order to show its effects on his character . . . .[5]

Sixty-three years later, Bernard Gavoty wrote: "Balzac's ideas on music were as simplistic and disarming as those of his contemporary men of letters"[6]; and the year before, Mme Maurice-Amour had declared: "Balzac's personal revelation is less imperative than the tyranny of fashion; Balzac bends or reacts under successive and contradictory influences. Balzac is not a musician: he perceives music through his ears alone, and is no authority in musical aesthetics."[7] In 1959, Herbert Hunt concluded that "Balzac's taste in music and his comprehension of music scarcely rise above the elementary."[8]

Opinions of kinder critics—Auguste Getteman, Fernand Baldensperger, Louis Laloy, Gabriel Rouchès, Camille Bellaigue—appeared mainly between 1903 and 1927.[9] While they may disagree among themselves and at times betray discomfort at the obvious incompleteness of Balzac's musical education, they converge in paying tribute to his imaginative genius, which sensed a future musical aesthetic in music (primarily Wagnerian), just as it sensed one in painting in *Le Chef-d'oeuvre inconnu*. E. R. Curtius in 1951 supported the tie with Wagner.[10] Omitting the Wagnerian argument, Thérèse Marix-Spire in 1954 was willing to credit Balzac with "correct and profound ideas about music,"[11] and others made brief but bold comparisons between Balzac and Debussy, Stravinsky, and Schönberg.

More recently, more sensible yet guarded statements have been made by Maurice Regard and Max Milner in their introductions to editions of *Gambara* and *Massimilla Doni* respectively, and by Pierre Laubriet in his long study entitled *L'Intelligence de l'art chez Balzac*.[12] Yet, viewing all critical opinion on the subject of Balzac and music in the aggregate, from Gautier to the present, the picture is as disjointed, disparate, conflicting, and contradictory as that of Machiavelli after four and a half centuries of scholarship on the Florentine Secretary.

A self-portrait by Balzac that forms part of a letter to Duchess d'Abrantès points ahead to the vagaries of future criticism:

> I harbor within my frame all possible incoherences and contrasts, and those who believe me vain, prodigal, bull-headed, frivolous, inconsistent, fatuous, negligent, lazy, unapplied, thoughtless, inconstant, talkative, tactless, uneducated, impolite, crotchety, and moody, are as correct as those

> who say that I am frugal, modest, courageous, tenacious, energetic, relaxed, hard-working, constant, taciturn, delicate, polite, and forever cheerful.[13]

Balzac could not have been more confounding—or more correct.

The difficulty in tracing his musical sensibility lies not solely in reconciling the problematic discussions in *Gambara* and *Massimilla Doni* but also in grouping alongside these discussions the scattered references to music that dot his other works and his correspondence. Something of a detective game is involved, an interlocking as in a puzzle of a phrase with a paragraph, a sentence with a page, in the hope of assembling a view more coherent than that given by his two musical tales alone. And if Emile Zola spoke correctly when he said that Balzac took to heart all the interests of his characters and identified himself with them, then it is proper to accept also the serious opinions of his Caprajas, Cataneos, Marcosinis, Schmuckes, and Modestes, however dissimilar these may be, as Balzac's own. If this consideration of the alternatives of his taste involves a running debate, at least both sides of each argument are voiced by Balzac himself, assuring us who note them an experience as rich as it is puzzling.

Music was not for Balzac merely another discipline to be added to his roster of intellectual conquests, nor an opportunity for pleasant distraction. His self-indulgent roaring exacerbated many a serious listener during a musical performance, but at the same time a less obstreperous side of him required that he surround himself with intimate melody and harmony. Like one of his biographers, Stefan Zweig, who sought spiritual comfort in what he called "Toscanini baths,"[14] Balzac felt the need on occasion for a music bath,[15] for what we may call a Euterpean therapy that recharged his limbs and soul, after which he could resume his orgy of work by candlestick and coffee-pot. He not only evoked music as a language of sentiment but also tried to establish it as the most complex, subtle, and suggestive of the arts. He perceived the art in both its philosophical and emotional contexts, correlating its intimate being with the psychological effects on individuals, relating its higher metaphysics to the physical world, and evolving through music relationships between idealism, art, and reality.

In all of this, Balzac both succeeded and failed. He appreciated not only the great and lasting but also the trivial and transient musical expressions of his time, and if some of his words define the practices of his era in an original way, others merely reflect standard definitions. His echoes, like his original utterances, are important. For although in his novels music is dwarfed quantitatively by such pervasive concerns as economics and sociology, law and love, it is no less central in its implications. When Balzac is profound or prescient, he displays his genius. When he is mistaken or self-contradictory, he betrays his struggle—that of a man untutored in the art writing about it not only because he had for a while a compulsive interest in music (and the expertise he imagined himself to have acquired flattered his vanity), but also because he was a professional novelist with an output and audience to maintain, and a vast social canvas to paint in the process. It is not alone what Balzac the amateur musicologist says about music that we must consider, but the uses to which Balzac the writer puts music, as theme, as material for analysis by his characters, as a mirror to reflect and color those characters, as a medium of communication among them, as a structure to pattern their emotional evolutions.

PART ONE

MUSIC IN BALZAC'S LIFE AND TIME

CHAPTER I

THE ENTICEMENT OF SOUND

The Formative Years [1799-1819]

"Here is the state of affairs you inquire about: FINE ARTS. I miss music! . . ."[1] So wrote Balzac at age twenty to his sister from his humble garret room on rue Lesdiguières, near the Arsénal in Paris. The reaction to such a deprivation may not have surprised Laure de Surville, with whom he had shared some musical experiences in and around his native Tours. Because the record of experiences like these is scanty, and because Laure sometimes yielded to the temptation of presenting her brother in the best light by retouching his correspondence here and there, some scholars might be justified in considering his complaint apocryphal.[2] Yet it remains none too clear what reason she could have had to insert this particular statement without similarly editing subsequent letters, where references to music are too thinly distributed to even suggest a musical temperament, if this was her intention.

If we look back to Balzac's younger years to Touraine, we find little to promote a stimulating awareness of music in him. His father, Bernard-François, a self-satisfied, talkative, joyful liver who had ridden high on the crest of both Revolution and Empire, occupied a position of municipal responsibility and found little time for serious music beyond the superficial requirements of convention. His mother, Anne Charlotte Laure Sallambier, a pious but ill-humored, viciously frugal woman, was beset by imaginary illnesses that benumbed the atmosphere and chilled any display of affection on the part of the four children, especially on that of Honoré. Flanked by the garrulousness of the one and the whining of the other, Balzac grew to regard his childhood as dreadful. Only sporadic instances of anecdotal interest can be salvaged from the otherwise musically barren setting in which he was raised.

The nurse and her gendarme husband who cared for him until the age of four allowed him no playmates and, more inconceivably, no playthings. His companion became his imagination. Little surprise, then, that two years later he delighted in running the bow over the strings of a small, wooden, red violin that someone had purchased for him at a local fair for twenty-five sous. "For hours and hours," wrote his sister, he would "grate" on that instrument, "and his radiant expression showed that he thought he was hearing melodies." If Laure, finally unnerved and much to his amazement, would ask him to stop the "charivari" because "that music would have moved Mouche (our house dog) to howls," he would look at her with his small, black eyes still spellbound by his delicious improvisations and say: "Don't you hear how pretty it is?"[3]

In another context, young Honoré experienced a different kind of musical sensation. On holidays, he and his sister used to accompany their mother to the cathedral of Saint-Gatien to hear high mass. A unisonous choir and an organ always accompanied the rite. The boy's curiosity quickly became fascination as the echoing sounds floated under the grey, Gothic vaults and heightened the mysteries of the service. However unconscious he may have been of the profound artistic and religious manifestations that surrounded him, his young mind was absorbing its first authentic musical impressions produced by what Bertault has called "the inexplicable phenomenon of spirituality" of holy music born of "the sober and monotonal hymn of the service." The boy endeavored to understand the Holy Office with the aid of "the secret of the magic influences that the chanting of priests and organ melodies possess."[4] The holy service provides the first clues to reveal whatever early affinity Balzac may have had for music, an affinity evidenced later by the place given to religious music in *La Comédie humaine*. For it was the spiritual element that was to draw him toward a preference for the "Prayer" from Rossini's *Mosè in Egitto*, for the organ as an instrument, for operatic tales of Biblical import such as Gambara's story of Mohammed, and for the sense of the superterrestrial in a Beethoven symphony.

But a mysterious shiver at the sound of liturgical chants, which no one noticed, and a toy violin which everyone decried, hardly suggested a musical talent to M. and Mme Balzac. The boarding school of the Oratorian Brothers at Vendôme, where the boy stayed for six years until he was fourteen, with its monastic discipline, gloomy towers, stuffy classrooms, and thrashings, was spiritually incarcerating. As he wrote autobiographically in *Louis Lambert*, had it not been for the library whose collection he perused with passion and dream, he might well have changed into a brute. Except for singing in the church choir for Sunday services, musical instruction found no place in the curriculum which, among similar items, included the nauseous *mensa-mensae-mensam* of Latin grammar. A Mozart sonata would have sounded incongruous in that Dickensian setting.

After leaving the Lycée, Balzac spent the next five years in Tours in various notarial studies and employments, neither fruitful nor uplifting to his way of thinking. Nor did he find the respectable legal career his parents envisioned for him tailored to his aspirations. Vendôme had reenforced his need to dream; Father Lefèbvre, his teacher, had remarked that Honoré had "more imagination than judgment."[5] And dream he did. A brilliant drama, he mused, would go farther in the direction of fame than a thorough legal brief. Music at this time served at best as a diversion. Even so, if his father took him to a concert every now and then, as an autobiographical reference in *La Peau de chagrin* would indicate, we are not permitted to infer that young Balzac craved the experience. If anything, it afforded him heterogeneous sensations, among which can be listed the crass, mock concerts improvised earlier by his Lycée comrades "in the room of master notary Passez's master clerk Janvier (rue du Temple)." As one of the group recorded, they met "for the purpose of making mad, enraged music (only quadrilles were performed) . . . Balzac and I were the audience."[6]

Yet, diversion notwithstanding, he did ask his parents' permission to study the piano, along with his sisters Laure and Laurence. "Le Songe de Rousseau," a popular ditty by J.-B. Cramer,[7] held his attention for some time, but his short, awkward fingers never permitted him to progress beyond it. The "*Songe*" represented his executorial accomplishment, and he retained for it throughout his life a fondness which, although artistically unwarranted, was sentimentally understandable.

Dancing, too, presented difficulties. Despite the lessons of a fine master of the Opéra, Honoré fretted every time he was called upon to execute a step. Self-conscious about his weight, his awkwardnesses prompted the young ladies to smile. After several embarrassing performances, during one of which he tripped and fell,[8] he not only terminated resolutely his lessons but stopped accompanying his family to dances as well.

Such failures the future novelist could blame on physical nature without too much humiliation. What they related to fundamentally, however, was more serious than he cared to admit: a faulty sense of rhythm. A glance at his generally unmanicured style of writing suffices to illustrate this, not to mention his flaccid attempts at poetry. Théophile Gautier once wrote: "Balzac, we must admit, never possessed the gift of poetry, or at least that of versification; his complex thinking always remained rebellious to rhythm. . . . He was always astonished to see us write verses and derive such pleasure from them."[9] (Not coincidentally, his instincts were always going to favor the unmetrical chants of liturgy over the metrical, consciously rhythmed lines of symphonies.) For this and other reasons, Balzac decided that it was not through "graces and drawing-room talents"[10] that he would distinguish himself and achieve his aspirations for independence and prominence. The imaginative observer conquers the world better than the tripping participant. In 1819, Balzac left for Paris, something of a literary Rastignac, poor and ingenuous, but ambitious and determined, as he so famously put it, to complete with the pen what Napoleon had begun with the sword.[11]

First Decade in Paris [1819-1829]

In the light of Balzac's youth, then, "I miss music" comes to signify something less than it promises. Surrounded by the dirty yellow walls of his garret room, what he missed, it seems, was the opportunity for distraction through music, for his friends' maniacal quadrilles at the sound of their own bellows, or for an occasional rendition of "Le Songe de Rousseau." His life was drab. Not that he was unable to tap his inner reserve of humor to counteract the depressing environment. His imaginative mind singularized everything down to the most uninviting particular, so that even the disturbing drafts, against which his imaginary valet "Myself" was powerless, reminded him of a famous flutist of his day: "Myself is lazy, clumsy, unforesighted. His master is hungry and thirsty; sometimes he has neither bread nor water to offer him; he is even incapable of protecting him from the wind which blows through the door and window, like Tulou into his flute, but less agreeably."[12] A desire to make some kind of music himself occupied his mind when he insisted on altering the very architecture of his room to make place for a piano, the same piano that will occupy Raphaël's attention in his own attic quarters (PC). Imagining Tulou was not enough. He wrote to Laure: "I beg to inform you, mademoiselle, that I am economizing in order to have a piano here; when mother and you will come to see me, you will find one. I have taken the measurements: it will fit by pushing back the walls, and if my landlord doesn't want to hear of this little expense, I shall add the money to the acquisition of the piano, and *Le Songe de Rousseau* will resound in my garret, where a need for dreams is generally felt."[13] Though nothing more than Cramer's ditty, it was more the dream and the idea of music that interested the budding writer than the composition itself.

And dreams became plans. Looking ahead to his future, Balzac's problem was not how to embark upon a career but how to rocket into fame. An opera libretto based on Byron's *The Corsair* was among the various philosophic, dramatic, poetic, novelistic, and also scientific projects he envisioned as a launching pad. During the Restoration, as during the July Monarchy later, librettists rose to enviable prominence as a result of the popularity of the lyric theatre. Balzac too might join the glamorous ranks, but neither in the manner of a de Jouy, whose mediocre libretto *La Vestale* had to be saved by the musical genius of Spontini after having been rejected by Boieldieu and Cherubini, nor in the "veterinarian"[14] manner of a Castil-Blaze whose pasticcio operas (rearranged dissections from Beethoven, Rossini, Meyerbeer, Mozart, Paesiello, Cimarosa, Guglielmi, Salieri, Farinelli, Grétry, Pucitta, Federici, Päer . . .) were merely adaptations of Regnard, Destouches, Collé, and Molière. Although he realized how much less essential good poetry was than a good subject that could be exploited musically with dramatic pathos, his primary interest lay more in the realization of a musical dream than in the royalties. Great as the temptation may have been to see his name fixed on the elegant programs of the Opéra or the Italiens, he did not care for expedients that catered to contemporary taste, and preferred to explore for something worthier and new. As it happened, his idea was too new, or so he thought. And in its novelty, the subject demanded an equally novel musical treatment, more than any contemporary composer could handle properly, so the dream dissipated shortly after hatching. Balzac announced to his sister that he was discarding the project: "I have definitely abandoned my comic opera. I cannot find a composer to suit me; besides, I must not write for current taste, but rather do like the Racines and Corneilles, like them work for posterity. . . . Anyway, the second act was weak, and the first was too brilliant with music. One must think and think in order to think."[15] "Too brilliant with music," added Laure in her commentary; "the character of that man is in those four words; he saw, he heard that opera . . ."[16] Was *Gambara* in the making as early as this?

His first work, as we know, turned out to be not an opera but a play, *Cromwell*. So many eyebrows were raised that it had to be buried in his drawer almost immediately. Perhaps at this point his honest determination yielded to unscrupulous ambition, for now he did as a novelist what he had refused to do as a librettist. Balzac's early novels represent a clear acquiescence to the siren of popular taste, to its spectral thrills and historical fetishes, and to the lure of lucrative royalties. For a while, he did not even hesitate before the taboo of plagiarism. Then with pricked conscience he sighed: "My attempts to free myself by the bold stroke of writing novels—and what novels! Oh, Laure, how pitifully have my glorious projects collapsed!"[17] But at least he had not affixed his name to the thrillers, having published them under various pseudonyms.

The necessities of ambition pushed aside musical pursuits, even "Le Songe de Rousseau." But at this point, more than drive he needed encouragement. In 1821 he was fortunate to meet Mme Laure de Berny—"La Dilecta," as he called her for the rest of his life—someone who could give him the affection and the self reliance he had always lacked as a "shy and timid" boy (PC 76) by turning into what Mme de Warens had become for Rousseau. (May we look forward to *Madame Firmiani* and *Le Lys dans la vallée*?) She also served to renew his exposure to music. Her grandfather and her father, *musicien ordinaire* of Louis XVI and private musician of Marie-Antoinette,[18] had both been harpists. Both of her daughters, Emma and Emmanuella, played the piano, one supposedly the harp also, and Laure de Berny herself sang with more than common ability. *Sténie* took shape during these years and reflects the emotional relationship between the writer and his patroness. The heroine, now Mme de Plancksey, writes to a friend about Job del Ryès' improvisations: "Several people had tears in their eyes, above all my mother and I—I who knew the secret of that harmony, I who was the text, the motive, and the object of those tears of the soul" (St 116). Much of what del Ryès plays in the novel during the musical evening in Tours, including the "Ranz des Suisses," clearly recalls experiences at Mme de Berny's. If Mme de Mortsauf was inspired by her, then even her speaking voice reflects La Dilecta's: "musical, [like] a continuous caress," and the affection she lavished possessed "the most skillful gradations of music" (LV 990, 981). As he wrote later, she was a mother, a friend, a family, a counsel; "she made the writer . . . , she created taste."[19] Little wonder that at this time music began to acquire a more sentimental, love-coated dimension. Baldensperger has described these years in his life as a period of "mounting musical awareness,"[20] a view which is borne out by the words he used in urging his sister to continue studying the piano: "Don't you have your piano playing to improve? Doesn't music possess the fortunate gift of calming the soul, of soothing it with a refreshing balm and of relieving the ills of life?"[21] In the spirit of Mme de Berny, Balzac sought to encourage Laure's musical interests.[22]

Gradually music, musicians, and musical references creep into his writings (St, VA, Sa, CD, JCF). *Sténie*'s Job del Ryès is a pianist—whose favorite piece is "Le Songe de Rousseau"![23] And in the partly autobiographical *La Peau de chagrin*, Raphaël will be a pianist, only more like del Ryès than like Balzac. Afterward, the young ladies dominate the field. The lineage begun by the earlier heroines Sténie (St) and Jane (JP), both of whom play the harp, extended later into *La Comédie humaine* proper with Antoinette de Langeais (DL), Ursule Mirouët (UM), Camille Maupin (B), and others. Harp, organ, piano, and voice are only the first reflections from a prism that will radiate many musical colors. Voice especially, the female voice: del Ryès himself had written to Vanhers how men can never attain "the sweet music of their intoxicating song" (St 131); therefore, we read in *La Physiologie du mariage*, France and Italy cater to them.

To be sure, social custom together with literary taste favored this artistic attribute in young ladies and heroines, considering it a mark of gentility and sensitivity, of proper breeding; Chateaubriand's Blanca and Musset's Lucie perpetuated a tradition in which we find, three centuries before, the celebrations of Cassandre by Ronsard, of Pernette by Scève, and of Louise by Pontus de Tyard. But Balzac's young ladies do not fit the poetic mold in the same way. They emerge more realistically from the context of his observations and glow with an inner light of their own, forsaking literature, we might say, in favor of life. After *Les Chouans*, Balzac could also count among his experiences visits to the glittering drawing rooms of high society, where musical sensibility and a lady's ability to sing or play an instrument counted. No doubt, the gracious melophiles of *La Comédie humaine* reflect the social pattern and no doubt, too, a good part of the author's interest in his sister's piano lessons stems from his awareness of this requisite. He often appreciated the pianistic talent of a Duchess d'Abrantès and the vocal charm of a Mme de Castries or a Countess Merlin during those famous receptions where music, along with elegant conversation, was the only pastime worthy of setting an aristocratic tone. The queens of this society—Mme Récamier, Sophie and Delphine Gay—were also music lovers and, on occasion, performers. Sophie wrote libretti; one, *Le Maître de chapelle*, had been set to music by Paër and produced in 1821. When the musical portion of the evening began, she would very carefully name both the author of the poem and the composer. During her Wednesdays on rue Laffite, her sister Delphine followed suit. Like her, Duchess de Rauzan was "given to the arts [and] did her 'little bit of painting and her little bit of music.'"[24] Mme de Duras, Mme Ancelot, Charles Nodier, Benjamin Constant would not open their doors unless some musical entertainment was available. The patronage of Princesses Belgiojoso and Czartoryska, and the accomplished singing talent of Countess Merlin, where Balzac circulated among musicians (Malibran, Lablache, Pasta, Rossini, Grassini, Rubini, Persiani) and other prominent contemporaries (Destutt de Tracy, Count Saint-Aulaire, Chateaubriand, Vicount Siméon, Duke Decazes, James de Rothschild), arranged veritable concerts in their homes. Having become a *visiteur assidu*, it did not take Balzac long to associate certain arias with certain personalities: "Don't we know that Madame de C. can only sing the finale of *Anna Bolena*, that Mademoiselle de J. fancies the air from *Norma*, and that Madame de N. always sings the cavatina from *La sonnambula* . . .?"[25] But whatever the gossip, the muses of the salons enriched Balzac's musical development.

When, at the age of twenty-seven, after several disastrous attempts at publishing, printing, and type casting, Balzac found himself in debt to the extent of 90,000 francs, he began his elephantine working schedule. Two years later, through the successes of the historical *Les Chouans* and of the piquant *La Physiologie du mariage*, he not only titillated the curiosity of Frenchmen with his versatility but also launched himself securely on the road to fame. Now there was little time for musical diversions, since publication deadlines had to be met and a vast social epic had to be shaped. In the process, he did not care to stop and distinguish between popular, passing musical vogues and serious, enduring aesthetic values. Barring Berlioz and a few like him, Balzac's generation was lured by sentimental lyrical romances and technical instrumental exhibitions, reserving only a polite nod for the more sober artistic expressions of symphonies and chamber concerts. Thus Balzac's musical heroines sang mostly the romances he heard in high society. Not exclusively, however. As the months elapsed, he added more names to his expanding list of salons: Mme Delphine de Girardin, at whose home he was exposed chiefly to Italian music and to romances, to some of which the hostess herself had furnished the lyrics; Mme Guidoboni-Visconti, at whose receptions (from 1834 onward), which resembled those of Mme de Castries, he applauded a number of instrumental virtuosos and famous vocalists; Ambassador Rodolphe Apponyi, who was visited often by Rossini and Meyerbeer and whose musical matinees in the Fall attracted the most cosmopolitan and artistic society in the capital; musicographer François Joseph Fétis and promoter Sébastien Erard, whose professional evenings in the presence of Liszt, Berlioz, and Chopin were more serious and commensurately less attended (by Balzac too). Here Balzac once met and heard the Genevan pianist Wolff.[26] We might also add the name of Countess Maffei, in Milan, at whose salon Balzac learned of the prodigious reputation of Paganini, a reputation which was confirmed when he listened to the violinist during one of painter Gérard's regular "Wednesdays," after which he exclaimed to his friend Berthoud: "What a fantastic tale!"[27] There, years later, he heard the famed signora Vigano, about whom he expatiated: "I idolize her singing," and there too he once congratulated la signora Grisi on her performance the night before in *La gazza ladra*.[28] Another favorite drawing room, and possibly the liveliest both conversationally and musically, was that of Countess Marie d'Agoult, whose dazzling attraction was her future lover, the virtuoso Franz Liszt. Still another was the one to which Balzac was introduced by Eugène Sue in 1830, that of the capricious, deceitful, stunning courtesan, Olympe Pélissier. Representing the ultimate in aristocratic refinement, her soirées drew composers from Berlioz to Auber and sparkled with the wit and joviality of her future husband, Gioacchino Rossini, who would sit at the keyboard and accompany any performer for the asking. Rossini was the unquestioned idol and rage

of the French capital. Everywhere Balzac turned, it was the master
from Pesaro who occupied the spotlight, and it was with him that the
novelist formed a close and abiding friendship. The composer's
disciples, Bellini and Donizetti, along with his vocal
interpreters—Rubini, Tamburini, Grisi, La Pasta, La Malibran—
sucked Balzac into the whirl of European-wide adulation for melodic
music, in which he was delighted to spin. The efforts of Fétis,
Erard, and others to counterbalance the Italian charm with German
sobriety were destined not to succeed for the time being. Yet,
however limited the doses, they did allow a different kind of music
to reach Balzac's ears; Weber, Mozart, Beethoven. His musical
formation was gaining in variety what it lacked in focus.

Great Musical Exaltations [1829-1837]

After 1830 Balzac experienced a number of musical enthusiasms.
We might look upon it as a period of concentrated apprenticeship
which filled many hours, indeed whole evenings, of his normal day.
He contributed articles on musical events to newspapers, and he
regularly sought performances where he would "digest" in leisure,
"because there one doesn't have to think or talk and it is enough
to look and listen."[29] He listened, took notes, learned, presumably
the more to understand and the better to love. The world of opera
in particular, according to the current vogue, claimed his
fashionable attentions . . . and his money. Thanks to the
extraordinary success of *La Peau de chagrin* in 1831, he could
indulge in the luxury of musical theatres. But the sincerity of his
new modes can be readily doubted in the light of the dandyism and
swagger that characterized his nightly visits to the Parisian opera
houses. Moreover, the most recent fan of the Opéra and the Théâtre
Italien had inserted a "de" in his name, enlarged his apartment at
1 rue Cassini, hired a real valet to replace the imaginary Myself,
and invested in a horse-driven carriage. He wanted to make certain
that all aristocratic circles were open to him in 1832, the year he
became a Royalist candidate. Everything, in short, was to converge
toward his new perception of himself. The tender entreaties of his
latest comforter and counselor, Mme Zulma Carraud, could not
disincline him from his life of pavonine elegance and waste. That
his appearances at the Opéra represented a form of extravagance, he
knew well, but despite his high esteem for Mme Carraud, he balked
at her advice. Temptation seduced even his Promethean will. The
decade 1830-1840, his period of most genuine musical experiences,
coincides paradoxically with his years of servitude to splendor.

All this he rationalized easily when he said that his debauch
was his work. Besides, between 1832 and 1833, he found another
reason to encourage his grand manner: the correspondence in feminine

handwriting which reached his box from remote Russia, mysteriously signed "L'Etrangère." The story is well known of his love by proxy with the Polish countess Eve Hanska, of their scattered meetings in Europe, and of their eventual marriage almost two decades later. The exotic contact with foreign aristocracy inspired Balzac to do more literarily with music, and he used it, too, to calm the Polish lady's jealousies of his popularity when, having just returned from a meeting with her in Switzerland, he assured her that nothing excited him except "music and travel."[30] Much of what he wrote to her seems calculated to impress his "faraway princess" with the happy musical experiences she could have in the French capital, if she cared to join him there. In 1834, he purchased a regular Monday-Wednesday-Friday evening subscription to the Opéra, where, he told her, he went to listen to music "voluptuously."[31]

The distant presence of "l'Etrangère" did not restrain Balzac's exhibitionistic behavior; more and more he betrayed a need to appear like his heroes de Marsay, Rubempré, de Trailles, Rastignac, Bixiou. . . . There were the white gloves, as his friend and publisher Edmond Werdet reported;[32] the blue suit with golden buttons specially made by one of the best metal engravers of Paris, Gosselin; the vest of white English quilting; the Venetian chain whose golden links were fashioned to his liking by the renowned jeweler Buisson; the black trousers with foot-straps; the meticulously polished leather ankle-boots; and the celebrated cane, whose golden, turquoise-incrusted hilt he further adorned with a chain of gold, a gift from Mme Hanska. In short, he was not Honoré Balzac or even Honoré de Balzac, but "le chevalier d'Entragues de Balzac" who spent no less than five hundred francs a month for a brougham bearing the d'Entragues coat of arms, just to drive him to the theatre. "Music, embossed golden canes, buttons, lorgnettes, are my only distractions," he told Mme Hanska[33] as he questionably coupled art and artifice. True to his nature, he coupled art and social observation too, although again ostentatiously: "Our Amphitryon," relates Gautier, "took us to the Italiens [though it was late and he and his friends were soporific with a heavy meal and good wines] in superb attire. . . . Balzac did not want to miss, he said, 'the descent down the staircase,' an eminently instructive spectacle, according to him."[34] Of course, they all fell asleep in the loge.

Extravagance is only a short step away from obnoxiousness. Along with six other gallants,[35] the "chevalier" rented yearly a box at the Opéra, the most disliked "infernal loge" that exacerbated Parisian audiences from 1833 to 1836. All relatively wealthy and carefree, some of the self-styled counts and barons wrote newspaper articles whose biting criticism of any singer who happened to displease them became notorious.[36] D'Entragues de Balzac, their senior, occupied the seat of honor in their midst. He would talk lustily of his novels, of the infatuation of women for his person, of his many conquests, of his illustriously noble ancestry, and of the performance in both fact and theory. Often other writers and friends, including the dethroned Duke of Brunswick, would come to exchange salty gossip and jokes with him, and more often the police commissioner would be summoned in order to dampen their obstreperous laughter. Spectators complained: "those young people knock over chairs with the slightest movement. . . . Their opinion on singing and dancing is heard out loud and elicits many a 'shh' from the audience."[37] Another spectator, a lady who had read *La Physiologie du mariage*, registered caustic surprise at the author's inattention: "Finally, Sir, if you wish to attend the opera on Monday and place yourself not facing the spectators as you always do, but vis-à-vis the stage. . ."[38] etc., etc.

But the "Loge of the Tigers,"[39] as Rossini supposedly had baptized it to distinguish it from the boxes of the fashionable London sharks or "Lions," was not altogether a display of factitious wealth for Balzac. For all the audible imposition of his presence upon the public, he ultimately reacted to the seductive presence of the art of sounds. What he wrote to Mme Hanska, that he was "plunged in music,"[40] rings with as much satisfaction as boastfulness. *Gambara* and *Massimilla Doni* were beginning to seethe in his mind, while in other works the Opéra was acquiring ever clearer delineations, the dividends of an alert documentation. As late as 1845, he will advise his fellow citizens, as he had once advised them how to build a harmonious city (MC), how and where to build an opera house. His concern lay in its financial administration, to be sure, but also in its *raison d'être*: "To occupy the mind agreeably, to flatter the two most avid and delicate senses, to recall your pleasures when you are old, to draw inspiration from it when you are middle-aged, to fuse in a few hours all the magnificence of poetry, the marvels of painting, the human grace and infinite richness of music, such is the goal of opera. It is definitely the spectacle in which civilization gathers all its forces. . . ."[41]

Under the Corinthian pilasters of the foyer or the plain pillars of a café, the "Tigers" frequently discussed and compared operas: *La gazza ladra*, *Mosè in Egitto*, *Semiramide*, *Guglielmo Tell*, *Otello*, *La sonnambula*, *Norma*, *I puritani*, *Les Huguenots*, *Robert le Diable*, *Fra Diavolo*, *Don Giovanni*, and possibly *Fidelio*. More important than technical considerations was the emotional experience these works provided Balzac, and the relaxation they afforded after long hours of writing. "Music, for me, is remembrance. To listen to music is to love better what one loves. It's to think voluptuously about one's secret voluptuousness, it's to live under the eyes whose fire one loves, it's to listen to the beloved voice. . . . I love with delight. My thought travels."[42]

Needless to say, to "love with delight," especially as a member of the d'Entragues peerage, meant incurring many more bills than those of which he had despaired in 1828 when he had cried to his sister that he was dazed and crippled with debts.[43] He sometimes tried "to drown [such] sorrows in torrents of harmony."[44] By 1834, Balzac was already informing Mme Hanska that his "tiger" friends annoyed him, that he seldom went now to the Opéra or that he went not at all, that he was forced to give up the box because it had become "a stall of 'tigers,'" and, a few months later, that he had abandoned everything for the sake of his work: "I have renounced all pleasures. No more Opéra, no more Italiens, no more of anything; just solitude and work."[45]

Again an overstatement of fact, presumably not to arouse in L'Etrangère unwelcome suspicions about his *modus vivendi*. Yet he retained a loge at the Italiens. And we know that he returned to the musical dramas—albeit less frequently and, to his credit, more soberly—and that he passed from the "Tigers" to Rossini's box where the composer's wife, Olympe Pélissier, reigned; then to a stall occupied by old family friends; and, at the Italiens, to the loge of the Viscontis. We also know that he did not abandon the Opéra once the Fall seasons began, and that he feted his friends, including Rossini, with Lucullan banquets. The fact that, in addition, he had set up secretly Countess Guidoboni-Visconti in Chaillot at this time, or that he shared a loge with her family at the Bouffons, may have made some of his expressions of austerity that much more desirable in order to elude the ranging eye of Eve Hanska. When he wrote to her: "If calumny, which respects nothing, demands it, I shall give up music too," he uttered an empty threat, though it may have served its immediate purpose. Especially effective must have sounded the sequel to the threat: "I was there surrounded by people who hurt me and were inconsiderate to me. I had to go elsewhere, and actually I didn't want Olympe's loge . . . ," or the obvious invitation to sympathy: "If I go to hear *Guglielmo Tell* or if I stay at home to weep in the corner by the fire, it doesn't matter in this place where so few words can be heard."[46]

Tracing the evolution of musical awareness in Balzac's life reveals the extent to which music gradually imposed itself as a need. His hedonism had a teleological side. He complained if he went to Italy and could not find music at La Scala, La Fenice, in Genoa, and in Bergamo.[47] He complained if he could visit the Italiens only twice a month, or, much worse, twice during a whole winter, because the Italiens represented "the sole pleasure I find in Paris" and because for him music was "more necessary than bread."[48] The truth is that for over six years he remained assiduous about his evenings of musical theatre. In 1843 he could still declare: "[Music] never tires me."[49] Laure de Surville asked herself with justification, therefore, "what more important place music would have had, from this time onward, if he had not been overwhelmed with financial problems."[50]

The years 1830 to 1836, then, mark a period of musical incubation as well as exaltation, during which a welter of badly assembled exposures, impressions, tastes, and prejudices leave the author of *La Comédie humaine* in a limbo between popular and professional opinion. As a result, we find many and straightforward references to music in his correspondence, but few and tentative references to it in what was destined for publication. In *Le Bal de Sceaux* (1830), for example, there is only a passing reflection of the prevailing Rossinian fervor when a young lady enters her room humming an air from *Il barbiere di Siviglia*; in *L'Elixir de longue vie* (1830), Mozart's harmonies are described as better suited to accompany great allegorical figures than Rossini's melodies; in *Le Chef-d'oeuvre inconnu* (1831), the gesture of a painter is compared with the sweep of an organist performing the "O Filii" at Easter; in *Le Colonel Chabert* (1832), a disaffected countess is likened to a singer during and after her performance; in *Le Père Goriot* (1835), one of the characters sings variations on Grétry's "O Richard, ô mon roi" and other songs; in *Un Drame an bord de la mer* (1835), the joy of a loving heart is likened to Mozart's "Andiamo mio ben"; in *Facino Cane* (1836), we are aware that the subject was suggested to the author when he met an old, blind violinist; in *La Messe de l'athée* (1836), great singers, like great actors and surgeons, are called heroes of a moment who increase the power of music tenfold by their performance; and in *Le Cabinet des antiques* (1836), the quality of a painter's brush is claimed to possess the communicative magnetism of Paganini's bow. This random list of examples does not even tease our curiosity. Three possible exceptions should be singled out, however: *La Duchesse de Langeais* (1833), with its beautiful pages describing the organ along with various indications bearing on the psychological powers of music; *Séraphita* (1834-5), where a preliminary interest in the physics of music leads to an acceptance of this art as an access to the mystic infinite; and finally *Le Lys dans la vallée* (1836), whose arrangement of themes—love, nature, flowers, colors, even playing cards—not to speak of the scattered references to the organ, to religious music, to musical psychology, and to Beethoven—combine to give the distribution of literary material a musical quality. These exceptions adumbrate the novelist's Euterpean mood of 1837 to 1839.

Years of Maturation [1837-1839]

References to music mount from 1837 onward. The year may be accepted arbitrarily as a turning point leading into a period of maturation. The sparse elements of music that have dotted his novels like shy endeavors dovetail when Balzac decides that the moment has come for a musical *prise de conscience*. In the background stand his long conversations with his friends Rossini and Liszt, and his perusal of the provocative articles contributed to *Le Journal des Débats* and to *Le Rénovateur* by another friend, Hector Berlioz. Then, too, there are Fétis and Erard, conductor Habeneck of the Conservatoire, and the partisan polemicists of Italian versus German music. In the foreground stands temporarily but prominently an obscure German musician whom Balzac hires to teach him the fundamentals of music theory, Jacques Strunz.[51] In the company of this imaginative, little bohemian, Balzac attempts both to investigate the technical side of composition and to explore the abstract side of sound. Strunz is a dreamer; his pupil likes this. Balzac begins to verbalize better the pleasure he experiences, and to probe the causes of the vague need which impels him. A psychological basis and a metaphysical superstructure—what he had suspected is true: as an art and a science, music reaches far beyond the domain of words. It must, then, enter into *La Comédie humaine* more significantly, especially into the *contes philosophiques*. But first he has to delve into the more scientific side of the art, into its esoteric nomenclature, its history and elements of style, composition, form. Then come theory and speculation. Everything is to be done in a relatively short span of time, because other subjects await treatment. There is something feverish about Balzac's new passion, and it is surprising to discover not how much he could actually absorb but how far his thoughts roamed to fill with imagination the large gaps which time forbade him to fill with study. His ideas during this period reflect a mixture of exposures, assimilations, and insights, and above all an enthusiasm which is not less profound for being of short duration. He will even return to a completed manuscript awaiting delivery to the printer's, *César Birotteau* (1837), and regardless of the detailed business quality of the novel, will insert panegyric allusions to Beethoven's Fifth Symphony.

Recalling journeys to Italy (visits to Venice's La Fenice and to Milan's La Scala), Balzac contracts to write for Maurice Schlesinger, editor of *La Gazette musicale*, his first work set in an entirely musical atmosphere, *Gambara* (1837). This leads to a second, *Massimilla Doni* (1839). He has admitted candidly that only six months ago he was "of a hybrid ignorance in matters of musical technique," and has also stated, albeit with facetious modesty: "A volume of music has always presented itself to my eyes as a sorcerer's conjuring-book." But the editor's prompting, coupled with the encouragement of George Sand who insists that Balzac is quite qualified to write on music, have their effect. If editor Schlesinger is perhaps acting from a desire to stimulate the collaboration of men of letters with his review, the urging of a person of such musical background and perceptiveness as George Sand represents more than flattery. He tells the editor how it was she who first advised him to write on music: "There were several of us. . . . I expressed timidly my ideas on *Mosè*. Oh! how those initial words—'You should write down what you have just said!'—will always echo in my ears!"[52] Now he is only too eager to treat a score not as a sorcerer's text but as a hymnal, and to demonstrate that being a sociological man of letters does not preclude being a literary musician.

He must still remedy his too evident lack of technical knowledge, however, and *Gambara*, which centers around an interpretation of Meyerbeer's *Robert le Diable* and contains page after page of musical theory, criticism, and history, requires the assiduous application of a half year of learning. For an author who will write *Honorine* supposedly in three days, the effort is a tribute to his teacher as well as to his own purposefulness.

But his readers must not think that he necessarily sides with the Germanophiles in the controversy between trans-Rhenish and trans-Alpine music. *Gambara* might give them this impression. *Massimilla Doni* will correct it, for the Italophiles have much indeed to boast about, especially when Rossini's *Mosè in Egitto* can be used to provide illustrations. An equally long preparation under Strunz's tutelage is necessary, and Mme Hanska hears about it through his letters time and again. Typical is the following, early in 1838: "Tomorrow, Tuesday the 23rd, I shall start bringing to a close *Massimilla Doni*, which forces me to study a very great deal of music, and to go to have Rossini's *Mosè* played and replayed for me by a good, old, German musician."[53] Perhaps because he feels he is much less competent in music than in any other field; perhaps because he is prouder of his friendships with composers than with most other people; perhaps because he thinks he is just as much an artist as a social historian; or, quite simply, perhaps because he likes music—we can only aver that the author of *La Comédie humaine* rarely exhibits such an unusual preoccupation with a single subject as he does during those brief years immediately preceding the final decade of his life.

The Final Years [1839-1850]

The melomanian excitement over, Balzac settled down to an

easier pace. Coincidentally, the peak period of Italian opera in Paris was over. Like a breath of spirituality that refreshed his travailed world, he injected references to music into his subsequent novels. The heroine of *Ursule Mirouët* (1841), who finds herself surrounded by mercenary relatives, sits at the piano to confide in it and transmit to it her most intimate yearnings. The courage she can draw from the art of sounds contrasts ironically with the incomprehension of those around her; the ignorant, Balzac could now declare, are incapable of understanding music. Three years later, he penned a concealed criticism of Franz Liszt in *Béatrix*, but also included more engaging comments on the psychological significance of music and asserted that this art stands first among all the rest. Almost simultaneously, *Modeste Mignon* appeared containing a page of actual music, a setting by Auber of one of Balzac's romances. Then in *Le Vieux musicien*, later called *Le Cousin Pons* (1847), he wrote about the lives of two old musicians, one of whom, strongly reminiscent of his good bohemian teacher, comforts his sick friend with the divine magic of notes. There are more novels which denote continued musical cognizance. In each of them, Balzac's opinions on, and reactions to, the world of sounds show greater confidence and understanding than the timid utterances of the middle 1830's.

There are no more musical *contes philosophiques* after Strunz disappears from the scene, but the effects of his instruction linger. His apprenticeship having centered mostly around opera, Balzac had said all he had to say about music in the two tales. Much prior to 1840, however, he had come across different, more complex waterways of music, areas he was not going to navigate to his satisfaction or with self-reliance. The world of symphony and chamber music, as it reached him through the concerts at the Conservatoire and in the homes of Fétis and Erard, tempted the novelist away from his easier operatic fascinations. He first mentions the Conservatoire to Mme Hanska on May 10, 1834, on the occasion of a performance of Beethoven's Fifth Symphony, but he had been there previously. Campaigners for the misunderstood composer from Bonn, Berlioz, Habeneck, and Liszt abetted Strunz's efforts to orient Balzac toward more characteristically Germanic music than Meyerbeer's. The task of modifying his natural and emotional attachment to Italian melody proved troublesome, and the ensuing dichotomy between the harmonic versus the melodic school, reflected in the opposite points of view expressed in *Gambara* and *Massimilla Doni*, found its convenient symbols in the two names of Beethoven and Rossini. The tension between mind and heart interfered with Balzac's formulation of well defined musical judgments as much as it had complicated Diderot's artistic evaluations of the paintings of Chardin and Greuze.

Balzac courted diversity. Since 1840, he had been attending

the meetings at the home of George Sand on rue Pigalle, famous because of the intellectual élite of Paris that it attracted and because of the poetic personality of Chopin that graced it.[54] His appearances at Fétis' and Erard's homes also became more frequent. He heard transcriptions, variations, adaptations of lieder, operas, and symphonies in varied styles. When Liszt sat at the piano to explain or comment his reductions of Weber overtures and of Beethoven symphonies, the language was relatively new for him and more abstract, but he sought to make it equally personal. When Berlioz praised Beethoven in his articles and conversations, it became increasingly clear to the novelist that he should attend the Conservatoire concerts more often, especially because Beethoven had figured on the programs with regularity since 1837. And the master from Bonn, after all, commanded respect. From the very first time he had mentioned his name to Mme Hanska in 1834,[55] Balzac had felt an awesome presence, a broader dimension which he could not analyze but which he respected. His casual remark about concerts, "those indigestions of harmony,"[56] did not refer to the composer of the Symphony in C minor. His interpolations in *César Birotteau* and his warm words in a letter of that same year leave no room to doubt his feelings.[57] Sometimes even a glimmer of understanding pierces the wonderment: ". . . the Beethoven performed at the Conservatoire as it will never be performed anywhere else."[58] The fact remains, however, that at a time when all nine of the master's symphonies had been performed in Paris, Balzac claimed he knew only two of them, the Fifth and the Sixth. He certainly did not pursue the muse of Beethoven the way Baudelaire will pursue that of Wagner. But time was not his most liberally disposable commodity, and only a few great works sufficed to provide him with the "transports" and the "grand dazzlements" of symphonic music.

The Société des Concerts du Conservatoire had been formed in 1828 by Habeneck, almost specifically to educate Parisian taste to the works of the master. Partisan opposition had condemned the organization to a struggle for survival, but the more the prejudices withered, the more the Société prospered, until it rivaled the Opéra in fashionableness. Although agreement with vogue played some part, Balzac's interest in the concerts should not be interpreted as sheer subservience to it. It seems that he attended them from time to time, but no longer as the Chevalier d'Entragues who sat with his "Tiger" friends to display his golden chains and test his voice. Werdet, whom Balzac once "dragged"[59] to the Conservatoire, described him this way: ". . . slipshod dress . . . short trousers, blue socks and heavy shoes . . . [he went] to the Conservatoire Royal de Musique in the middle of an élite society. . . . But mind, when its name is Balzac, is well received everywhere. He was welcomed by that elegant and perfumed crowd, belonging to the most aristocratic class in Paris, with flattering eagerness and exquisite politeness. . . .

For all of his dirty clothes, he was the point of convergence of every eye in that sparkling entourage which paid homage to our most famous novelist. De Balzac was led in triumph to his stall."[60] Paris, evidently, did not want to be outdone by Vienna, where Balzac "entered one evening into a concert hall, and the whole audience stood up en masse to greet the author of *La Comédie humaine.*"[61]

It really appeared that, for some time, the concerts took precedence over the operas. He consciously listed them first. With the happy prospect of being together for two months in Paris with his dear Eveline, he wrote to her in 1847: "married two months, in a corner, where no one knows us, happy, making little escapades to the Conservatoire, the Opéra, the Italiens. . . ." Again, this time to reassure Mme Hanska's daughter Anna that the capital would hold great interests for her traveling mother: "I must submit various considerable specialties to your enduring remembrance: firstly, the Conservatoire; secondly, the Opéra; thirdly, the Italiens; fourthly, the Exhibition. . . ."[62]

Still, whatever Balzac's acceptance of the symphonic and abstract forms of music, the descriptive and operatic fit his dramatic temperament more closely. Listening to Chopin spin a long melody in George Sand's drawing room, or to a great vocalist fill with passion a room in the home of Baron Gérard—this was for him a genuine and wonderful pleasure. "Rubini," "Tamburini," "*Puritani*," "*Otello*," "Chopin," "*Robert le Diable*," "Rossini," "Paganini" punctuate his correspondence with Mme Hanska from 1842 to 1850, flashes of Italianism that suggest that the Conservatoire and other concerts had far from dislodged the former loyalties. In 1849, he still lauded Paris to Anna in terms of the Opéra.[63] By this time, he could distinguish between performances at the Opéra and the more prosaic shows at the Variétés or Hippodrome: "Yesterday I tried to distract myself and went to the Hippodrome, where I was imperially bored."[64] Similarly, he spoke of distraction when he went to the Variétés Perdreau at Colombe to hear Les Boeufs sing; nothing serious, he implied: "I laughed a lot.[65]

It is significant, however, that no evidence exists of his having attended one of the performances organized by chamber music societies, begun in Paris as early as 1817, or of his reactions to Beethoven and Schubert quartets, to Weber's *Konzertstücke*, to Mozart sonatas, and to most of Schumann's piano works and lieder. He did not frequent the classical music concerts attempted by Valentino between 1837 and 1841 (when they were discontinued), the very concerts where the more leisurely and consciously refined Barbey d'Aurevilly listened to Haydn and Beethoven. Clara Wieck, the future Frau Schumann, had gone to Paris in 1838 to give a concert which Balzac may or may not have attended. All his correspondence with his "spiritual sister" Zulma Carraud contains no word on music except for one fleeting reference to Malibran, and most of the time he speaks to Mme Hanska of musicians as people rather than as artists. His silence on such occasions is inconsistent with his evident joy at hearing a good performance or at discovering new compositions, such as Félicien David's symphony, *Le Désert*,[66] and is all the more disturbing because even such appreciations as he did express for the Davids and Hérolds have rarely withstood the challenge of time.

Revelations of this sort would disquiet us if we sought in Balzac what he was not, and what he never claimed to be. That he always remained fond of music, however, whether through outer vogue or inner experience, is indisputable. One has to look not merely at his insistent, affectionate encouragement of his niece Sophie and of his step-daughter-to-be Anna in their desire to learn the piano, an encouragement he pursued in 1849 when he urged them to play together,[67] but also at the span of his attractions which embraced, on greater or lesser levels of ability, many categories of music variously approached: music of the soul, of the heart, of the mind. Plain chant, Rossini, Beethoven sometimes create strange juxtapositions; they are, however, not less sincere for their strangeness. Out of the various confrontations rises slowly an undefined dawn of meaning; the sounds of music, pale at first, gradually acquired more soulful hues. This particular Saul could not just accept the comfort of David's harp; he was drawn to seek its divine essence. The passage from sensation to imagination is the one real ascendancy in the "mounting musical awareness" which gives meaning to Balzac's musical biography.

Epilogue

Two incidents in the very last years of his life turn our sights back to the earliest hours of his contact with music. When in June of 1847 he busied himself with boyish excitement acquiring the furnishings not for "a real comic opera house"[68] but for a home he would proudly turn over to his future bride, he did not fail to include the instrument he had once craved, though up in a garret and at the price of knocking down some walls. Anna and Sophie could certainly use the piano now; besides, what fine home does not vaunt such a piece of furniture? Someday he might even perform "Le Songe de Rousseau" for an appreciative Eveline.[69] Two years afterward, while on a winter visit to Poland during which illness and exhaustion issued forebodings of what was to befall him eighteen months later, he could think of no better way of rewarding his solicitous physician than to present him with a gift of two violins, one possibly an authentic Stradivarius.[70] Too long ago to be remembered, he had displayed an intolerable attachment for a red kit, to him a toy of magic. Details of recurrence, perhaps, or subconscious memories that frame a career.

As we know, the novelist's long awaited marriage to Eve Hanska was interrupted after five brief months by his death. With this in mind, we read a passage from *Petites misères de la vie conjugale*: "Who has not heard an Italian opera during his life? . . . You must have noticed immediately the musical abuse of the word *felichittà* [sic] with which the poet and the choruses are lavish, at the moment when everybody pours out of his loge or leaves his box. Frightful image of life! One leaves it just when one hears *felichittà* . . ." (PMVC 1046). Still we are permitted to believe that one "felicity," that of sorting out some values in the complex world of sounds, was not denied him. Authors like Thomas Mann have understood music much more profoundly, but few have referred to it so consistently, and fewer yet have attempted to treat it so variously. For "Music is the soul,"[71] said Balzac, the universal spirit.

CHAPTER II

SHALLOW ENCHANTMENTS

Paris, Its Organizations and Salons

Chronologically and culturally, musical romanticism in France lagged several years behind that of the other arts. If, from today's vantage point, Berlioz not only invites comparison with his contemporaries Hugo and Delacroix but often indeed surpasses them in innovation, we must also note that serious music could not compete in appeal with serious poetry or art, and that French taste, about whose excellence Balzac was sometimes too facilely convinced, did not encourage lofty musical endeavors. Stendhal noted this with contempt. There were relatively few new compositions of prominence, and the public openly favored works of established repute and performances of virtuosity. The performer "with effects" aroused its interest much more than the composer of a "new page."[1] Not that great works were unavailable in performance, or that great artists did not galvanize the music they interpreted. What seemed to be lacking, as Berlioz knew only too well, was not so much the quality of the offering as the quality of the response. True, the small, humid, uncomfortable concert hall of the conservatory was usually filled; one subscriber to the *Revue musicale* in desperation wrote to Fétis to explore the possibility of obtaining tickets which had sold out three months in advance.[2] The season's opening was always a big event with shouts and accolades of appreciation. But in the overall picture, the French relished tuneful romances and entertaining operatic arias, and vocal and instrumental exhibitions of dexterity. Chamber and symphonic concerts were simply tolerated. Stendhal's comment in 1830 is worth quoting: "The French mind understands everything admirably, and in music it is attracted to the execution of difficulties. But since it lacks musical feeling absolutely, it delights in listening to 'atrocious' music. In music, a Frenchman has a knack only for quadrilles, waltzes, and military marches. In addition, his mind compels him to applaud the overcome difficulty."[3]

Highest on the popularity scale ranked the Académie Royale de Musique, known as the Opéra, so penetratingly described in *Splendeurs et misères des courtisanes*. Because an opera was as much a social as a musical event, as Stendhal had discovered also in Italy, nowhere could the disintegration of Lucien de Rubempré's love for Mme de Bargeton or his union with his mistress Coralie take place more conveniently than in the discreet atmosphere of the famous opera house (IP). In the setting of Empire conservatism, its repertory from 1800 to 1810 had abided by the classical tradition represented, for example, by Méhul's *Joseph*, Lesueur's *Les Bardes*, and Spontini's *La Vestale* on the tragic side, and on comic, by Boieldieu's *Jean de Paris*, Cimarosa's *Il Matrimonio segreto*, and Isouard's *Joconde*. An important stride toward a new mode was taken in 1829 by Rossini with *Guglielmo Tell*. Then with the stirring premières of Bellini, Donizetti, and Meyerbeer,[4] and the flowering of a great generation of singers, a Golden Age of opera drew all European attention to Paris.

The adulation high society reserved for the Opéra became delirious when this establishment promoted the new fad, grand opera. In 1831, Balzac stood up with the rest of the audience in approval of *Robert le Diable*. The Théâtre-Italien (the Bouffons or "les Italiens") ranked second to the Opéra, and was followed far behind by the less rewarding Opéra-Comique where actors acted badly with the excuse that they were singers, and sang badly with the excuse of being comedians.[5] We may credit Balzac with not displaying any enthusiasm over this company. Along with the names of the composers of *Guglielmo Tell*, *Semiramide*, *Il barbiere di Siviglia*, *Tancredi*, *Mosè*, *Otello*, *La donna del Lago*, *La gazza ladra*, *L'italiana in Algeri*, *La prova d'un'opera seria*, *La cenerentola*, of *La straniera*, *La sonnambula*, *Il pirata*, *I puritani della Scozia*, *Norma*, of *Anna Bolena*, *Marino Faliero*, *Lucia di Lammermoor*, of *Il matrimonio segreto*, of *Don Giovanni*, of *La vestale*, and of *Robert le Diable*, and names of Halévy, Boiëldieu, Hérold, Nicolò Isouard, Massé, Maillart, Adam, Ambroise Thomas, and Auber also appeared before everyone's eyes on the programs of the three theatres. The frequency with which someone like Balzac mentions the first two gives more than a clear indication of the formidable vogue of productions which are for the most part mere historical curiosities today. Compared with such institutions, the Gymnase, the Odéon, and the Nouveautés were minor enterprises.[6] It was not a coincidence, therefore, that Raphaël renewed contact with his gracious Pauline at the sound of the gentle melodies which permeated the Théâtre-Italien (PC). First and foremost, it was about operatic music that Parisians thought. Among a list of prizes whose establishment Balzac advocated in 1841 to a special Commission, the only musical entry referred to an award "for the most beautiful opera (lyrics and music)."[7]

Among the concert organizations, the Société des Concerts du Conservatoire[8] championed the cause of symphony with determination. Often, however, conductor Habeneck buckled under pressure to satisfy popular requests as a matter of preservation. The program of the first concert on March 9, 1828 would bewilder today's audience and sap its powers of attention:

        Beethoven: *Eroica Symphony*
        Rossini: Duet from *Semiramide*
        Meifred: *Horn solo*
        Rode: *Violin Concerto*
        Rossini: Air
        Cherubini: Chorus from *Blanche de Provence*
        Cherubini: Overture to *Abencérages*
        Cherubini: Kyrie and Gloria from the *Messe de Sacre*

The second concert, however, was all Beethoven,[9] and the fourth all Mozart.[10] Weber, Haydn, and Gluck[11] received frequent performances, at the expense of Bach, Méhul, Rameau, and Berlioz,[12] who were included rarely on the programs, and especially of Handel, Hummel, Lulli, Mendelssohn, Pergolesi, and Spontini, who were included only once.[13] On the whole, there was nothing uncommendable about the organization and its work. Its supporters would have been less militant if Beethoven, Mozart, and Haydn had pleased audiences more at first, and if much of the official criticism had been more restrained in its dislike for symphonic music. If Balzac ever enlisted himself as a supporter, he did so primarily out of friendship for Berlioz. But, like many others, he usually avoided open commitment.

The cultural expression of the age, the salons, did not always promote the finest in music. Even at the less formal gatherings, at the homes of Blangini, Meyerbeer, Zimmermann, and occasionally Liszt, it was most commonly Italian or Italianate music—much of it fine in itself but as a whole of uneven merit—that one heard: Donizetti, Vera, Rossini, Schira, Bellini, Mozart, Ricci, Fieravanti, Gabussi, Paër, Schubert (only his *Serenade* and *Ave Maria*). . . . Meyerbeer, needless to say, sponsored Meyerbeer. If someone like Mme Polmartin opposed the Italian orientation of Mme de Girardin by offering much Beethoven, she coupled him unflatteringly with Flotow or Monpou! Zimmermann presented Beethoven's *Septet* in 1828 and one of Bertini's difficult sextets in 1830, but felt guilty of having taxed the friendship of most of his listeners.

The more mundane gatherings in bourgeois circles, most

frequent from 1825 to 1848, attracted many men of letters and musicians as they joined the clangor of Romanticism. There they applauded Nourrit or Grisi, Liszt, Chopin, or Thalberg with enthusiasm but with less discernment than at Countess d'Agoult's, or in "higher circles," in the company of Hugo, Chateaubriand, Lamartine, Musset, Vigny, Halévy, Auber, and Berlioz.

At a time when some of the most illustrious pages of music had been written, and when fine music performances were available, the shallowness of the public's taste and the mediocre recognition it gave even to its most prominent contemporaries remains difficult to believe. That statistically a full tenth of the population of Paris had some introduction to music and yet the "incredible development"[14] of the art after the Revolution aroused unenlightened interests; that recognized composers had to rely on themselves or on an impresario, as did Rossini for his non-operatic scores, in order to have their works presented; that in 1824 Berlioz had to ask widely for financial aid, including from Chateaubriand (who refused it) to set up his *Messe*;[15] that Thalberg, Paganini, Chopin, and Liszt appeared frequently in special recitals more as virtuosos than as musicians; that chamber music concerts, generally less attended than the most uninspired piano or voice recital, found the small private homes of Préault, Panseron, and Zimmermann, all professors of the Conservatory, sufficiently large for the body of devotees; and finally that the public concerts of the Athénée Musical, the Concerts Historiques, the Concert Musard, and the Union Musicale, while enjoying a fair number of adherents, had to cater repeatedly to their less sophisticated desires in order to remain financially solvent: these are facts which characterize the musical climate in France during Balzac's lifetime.

When, then, someone commented in *La France musicale* on January 17, 1839 that "in this cataclysm of concerts, the artists, jealous of their own reputations, for the most part have sought refuge in society and salon music has become beautiful and brilliant, [and that] the union of artists and amateurs has resulted in an appreciable good for Art, [for] the amateurs have become artists and the artists have become people of the world,"[16] he engaged in optimistism, closing his eyes to the mediocrity that catered to a prevalent dilettantism. P. Duchambge, Masini, Louise Puget, Dalvimare, Labarre, Beauplan, Romagnesi, Pauline de Montet, Blangini, Queen Hortense, Panseron, H. Monpou, Grisar and scores of others constituted far too numerous a phalanx of "conservative mediocrity" (which, according to Jules Combarieu, is necessary to balance the revolutionary forces of an epoch[17]) to grant the originality of Berlioz's *Requiem* mass the prominence it deserved. Besides, a composer like Berlioz, who disliked sitting down to write a romance—"a simple and tender song [which] must be interpreted with the soul"[18]—was not contributing to the preferred musical form of his day and could hardly be regarded by the majority as great. Faguet described romances as elegies written by people who feel nothing for the pleasure of those who pretend to feel. Balzac's society liked the flat melodies on doggerel verses, rendered ecstatically as if the lyrics were by Hugo or Lamartine and the music by Liszt or Chopin. It was not disturbed by affected treatments of love, forced refinement in search of effects, platitudinous themes and stilted accompaniments.[19] On the contrary, it sought avidly the 150,000 that appeared yearly, inserted them commonly between two arias of serious repertoire, and paid inflationary prices for a compilation of the ditties.[20] After 1840, the fad fortunately began to dwindle, yielding gracefully to the more refined *Lieder* of Schubert. But throughout the 20's and 30's, society indulged in romances. Paris as a city may have claimed stardom among European capitals, but its indigenous musical taste remained limited. A Balzac, whose melomanian years coincided with this period in French cultural history, necessarily reflected some of its superficial attachments and enthusiasms. But he also achieved some remarkable breakthroughs.

Balzac, Romances, and Folksongs

Balzac's favorite Cramer romance appears in *Ursule Mirouët*: "'Le Songe de Rousseau,' the number chosen by Ursule . . . is really not lacking in a certain depth which a good execution can bring out" (UM 384). Before that, she had chosen variations on the "Dernière pensée de Weber" to play for her godfather. Césarine Birotteau, for whose musical education her father has paid liberally, recompenses him adequately when he hears her play a sonata by Steibelt or sing a ballad (CB). She too thinks highly of the "Songe," because she uses it to soothe her troubled parent. Another novel, *Le Père Goriot*, abounds in romances, sung at different times by various characters and reflecting, here also, the popularity of the form: "Dormez, dormez, mes chères amours" (by Amédée de Beauplan); "Soleil, soleil, divin soleil"; "Ma Franchette est charmante dans sa simplicité". . . . Again, Sister Thérèse expresses the sorrow of an exile with "Fleuve du Tage" which she blends into a "Te Deum" at the organ (DL). The heroine of *Modeste Mignon*, elated over a favorable swing of fortune which would permit her to marry the handsome poet Canalis, hums Balzac's own "Chant d'une jeune fille," whose first stanza reads:

> *Mon coeur, lève-toi! Déjà l'alouette*
> *Secoue en chantant son aile au soleil.*
> *Ne dors plus, mon coeur, car la violette*
> *Elève à Dieu l'encens de son réveil.* [MM 449]

> *(My heart, awake! For now the lark*
> *Singing shakes its wings to the sun.*
> *Sleep no more, my heart, the violet too*
> *Lifts its wakened incense up to God.)*

Auber set it to music, after several consultations with the author.[21] While typographical difficulty prevented publication of the score in the original edition of the work, subsequent editions—much to the joy of Balzac and his contemporaries—printed the music and text in their entirety as an integral part of the novel. The vogue was such that several other composers vied for permission to set the romance to music even before Auber had finished the score. To one of them, H. Chélard, Balzac replied with obvious pride that Auber had already done so; he added that he, Balzac, had heard of him (Chélard was living in Weimar) as he had of Lipinski and Mendelssohn, and that he knew personally Berlioz, Liszt, Rossini for a long time, Auber, "and all those who are at the head of the art."[22]

The Balzac-Auber romance is typically static: little concern for harmonic progression and a melody which reflects accurately the lack of inspiration in the lyrics. To us it seems made to order for that unattractive Monsieur du Châtelet, a former Imperial Secretary "with all the inabilities required by his station," a singer of romances . . . ignorant of music" who wrote "flat" lyrics "in which rhyme replaced idea" (IP 500). Yet the "irrecusable testimony of that melody" (MM 454) proved to Modeste's mother that her daughter was in love!

There was, however, a keener side to Balzac's interest in the more popular forms of musical expression: the folk music which appears in many of his novels, the village feasts and dances of which George Sand was to make expert use. The Romantics believed strongly in a "poetic primitivism," a desire to dip into the lastingly fresh wells of ancient rhymes and airs, of early melodies that were not diluted with artifice like the romances. "Song," explained Balzac, is "the first desire of any creature."[23] Spontaneity, naturalness, primordiality—the secret to folkloric distinctiveness and purity lay there. "In primitive races they sought above all a little of their own sensitive and moving vehemence, present in popular poetry which was forever asked to reveal its secret."[24] Accordingly, to cite but two authors, Mme de Staël made use, in *Delphine*, of an air sung by Languedoc harvesters, and in *Les Aventures du dernier Abencérage* Chateaubriand followed suit. But because neither of them distinguished between *romance* and *chanson populaire*, Julien Tiersot may be justified in stating that Balzac was perhaps the first to use folk songs *qua* folk songs in his novels.[25] Before the great folklore exponents Gérard de Nerval (who used songs from the Ile-de-France in his *Les Filles du feu* and *La*

Bohème galante) and George Sand (who adopted popular songs from Berri in her rustic novels), and also before Henri Mürger (who incorporated "Je me suis engagé—pour l'amour d'une brune" into *Les Vacances de Camille*),[26] the author of *Les Chouans*, *Pierrette*, and *Les Paysans* was borrowing melodies which have been rediscovered since and collected in the various French provinces. "L'air de la ballade du capitaine" in *Les Chouans*,

> *Allons, partons, belle,*
> *Partons pour la guerre,*
> *Partons, il est temps,* [C 1036]
>
> (*Come, let's leave, my love,*
> *Let's leave for the war,*
> *It is time, let's leave,*)

not only attained popularity in Western France, as Balzac indicates, but in the country at large.[27] At the very beginning of *Pierrette* is heard "La Chanson de la mariée:

> *Nous v'nons vous souhaiter bonheur en mariage,*
> *A m'sieur votre époux*
> *Aussi ben comm' à vous. . . ,* [P 652]
>
> (*We come to wish you married happiness,*
> *To sir your husband*
> *As well as to you. . . ,*)

to which the novelist gives relief with his own analysis: "This national music . . . for a young lady of Brittany was to be the subject of compelling remembrances. . . . It is dominated by a kind of melancholy caused by that aspect of real life which affects us deeply. This power to awaken a world of serious, sweet, and sad things through a familiar and often happy rhythm, is it not the characteristic of those folk songs which constitute the superstitions [vestiges] of music, if we are willing to accept the word superstition as meaning all that is left after the decay of societies, and all that survives their revolutions?" And again in *Modeste Mignon*: "Melody is to music what image and feeling are to poetry, a flower that can open and expand spontaneously. For this reason societies had their national melodies before the invention of harmony. Botany came after flowers" (MM 388).

Always a favorite of Balzac's, the theory was inspired to a large extent by his instinctive preference for melody over harmony, for the former, he held, represents the timeless element in music. Less than a century earlier, Jean-Jacques Rousseau had voiced a similar preference. When Balzac finds the opportunity to place his theory in a broader, historical dimension, he reminds us of certain passages in Michelet's *Tableau de la France*, where the historian espouses the idea that folk airs are in many respects scrolls of the past and at once the preservers and transmitters of customs. Some latter-day Darwinism is foreshadowed by Balzac when he seeks part of the importance of music in its origins, in its survival value, in the vestige of some formerly characteristic instinct it preserves. As the social historian he wanted to be, Balzac could not remain unaware of the value of such a heritage, for which he found an appropriate poetic idiom. He thanked Beaumarchais for having written fittingly poetic words to "Malbrough s'en va-t'en guerre" (MC). Conviction matched interest when he wrote: "It is melody and not harmony which has the power to cross the ages. . . . From antiquity to our days, societies have safeguarded certain songs like precious treasures, songs that summarize their manners and their habits, I should almost say their history. . . . Listen to one of those national songs, and you will find yourself plunged in profound dreams; before your soul unfold unprecedented, wonderful things, immense things, despite the simplicity of those rudiments, of those musical ruins" (MD 378, 377).[28] What Bonald had claimed about languages, that they stand as the "archives of peoples," Balzac would apply willingly to folksongs. Their music has powerfully evocative features; it proclaims a race. Therefore, he thought, one saw the French people adopting the most poetic and the most modulated airs, adhering to the simplest ideas, loving incisive motives that contain the most thought. The implication is clear: a composer need only draw inspiration from the "ruins" or from the "superstitions" of music in order to produce precious, enduring, ethnic documents of high artistic caliber. The author of *Massimilla Doni* would have welcomed heartily the works of Dvořák, Smetana, Grieg, Albeniz, Villa-Lobos, Copeland, and others who have put to such effective use the raw material of their civilizations.

That the whole matter of folk music held Balzac's attention as much as it held that of his century can be demonstrated by the number of novels in which reference to such music is made. From the Burgundian background of *Les Paysans*, for example, comes the Christmas melody "Ein bel endroj de sainé," closer to a drinking than to a religious song and authentically accompanied by accurately described period instruments.[29] A Polish song leaves the hero of *L'Envers de l'histoire contemporaine* "stupefied with admiration and overcome with sadness," because "that melody, somewhat similar to the languid and melancholy airs of Brittany, is one of those poems that vibrate in the heart long after one has heard them" (EHC 385) Vautrin bellows forth "O Richard, ô mon roi!"[30] and "J'ai longtemps parcouru le monde" in *Le Père Goriot*, and so numerous are the references to folk music in *Le Médecin de campagne* that one critic has surmised that they resulted from Balzac's repeated requests of

Berlioz for information about the Dauphinois.[31] The novelist did not overlook Béranger, to be sure, and endorsed the balladist's merit when he used "C'est la faute à Voltaire, c'est la faute à Rousseau" in *Un Début dans la vie*, or when he asked him to supply a song for *Un grand Homme de province à Paris* (IP).[32]

The Great Singers

It was natural for the period's interest in folksongs, which emphasize melody, to coexist with the widespread admiration for the style of *bel canto*, which stressed tonal lyricism and technical facility. As Berlioz recorded,[33] these qualities shaped an Italian domination of the operatic stage. Some of the melodic inventions became veritable concertos for the voice, and Balzac as well as Stendhal and Musset noted the beauty of the training that made them possible. Their century enjoyed an incomparable wealth of vocal artists. The remarkable soprano voice, beauty, and acting ability of Pasta, the fine contralto of Pisaroni, the undisputed queenliness of Giulia Grisi who reigned over the Opéra for a decade and a half, the nostalgic memories left by her sister Giuditta's brief appearance in France, the brilliant *vocalises* and arabesques of Persiani, the communicative powers of Cinti, Faustina, Cuzzoni, Dotti, Grassini, Vigano, Coradori, and Blasio, made the art of singing synonymous with the name of their country, despite the stirring performances of their Latin and Germanic sisters Malibran, Pauline Viardot, Marie-Cornélia Falcon, Fodor, Florine, Henriette Sontag,[34] Rosine Stolz, Wilhelmina Schroeder, and Jenny Lind. Among the men who hailed from the peninsula, tenor Giovanni Battista Rubini ruled Paris with his magic brilliance for an unbelievable twenty-nine years, but shared his laurels with the powerful basso Antonio Tamburini, baritone Galli, Mario (Count of Candia), Senesino, Baldi, Boschi, Palmerini, Barrilli, Begnio, Graziani, Pellegrini, and Bordogni. Even the vigorous and genial Lablache, along with other favorites like Nourrit, Duprez, Roger, Levasseur, Michaut, and Cazaux, could not dislodge the Italians from their pre-eminence.

Balzac submitted most willingly to "the languorous originalities of those ably wedded Italian voices" (Sa 95). Like others, he thrilled to the singing of Vigano and Coradori during Gérard's Wednesday soirées, or praised the "demonic voice" of Lablache and the "seraphic throat" of Malibran. Indeed, he often took pleasure in imagining his influence over these artists. Once, at Gérard's, Vigano had refused to sit at the piano; said Balzac: "I arrive, I ask her for an aria, she starts to sing. . . . I am a Kreisler for her."[35] But among the sopranos, his idol was Pasta, while among the tenors, no one could excel "the divine" Rubini, whose name figures conspicuously in the author's novels and correspondence. And his appreciation of this master of florid execution as well as of unadorned, direct projection was not misplaced. We can understand the author's implication to l'Etrangère that he had sensed a lack of enthusiasm over a performance of Bellini's *Norma* simply because Rubini had had to be replaced.[36] Again, he praised the management of the Italiens "which has arranged an unparalleled cast: Lablache, Tamburini, Rubini."[37] But never was his eulogy more soaring than when he wrote to Mme Hanska: "What a joy I feel in your delight in listening to Rubini. Rubini, you see, is perfection, heart-rending perfection. Oh, if you could ever hear him sing the great aria of suspicion, when Iago rankles him, during the second act of *Otello*! There's his triumph. But such perfection must also be seconded by that of Tamburini, who, believe me, is no less great an artist than Rubini for not enjoying as high a reputation. But Rubini is the tenor. The tenor is love; he's the heart's emotion. Therein lies his success." Balzac's personal taste for transalpine voices sometimes made him ungenerous to the fine qualities of Nourrit, although later in the same letter he manifests more than usually a complimentary attitude: "What beautiful evenings I spent at the Italiens when Lablache, Rubini, Tamburini, La Grisi sang together! . . . But some rather great things came out of that poor Nourrit too. To listen to *Guglielmo Tell* at our Opéra, or to *Robert le Diable*, is, you know, as grand as thought itself, as grand as fantasy! In "Ce rameau qui donne la puissance et l'immortalité" of *Robert le Diable*, Nourrit made our flesh creep. It evoked our vision of the happy life, with all of its dreams fulfilled."[38]

It was the Italian artist who almost always earned Balzac's praise, as a quick glance at *La Comédie humaine* will illustrate. Before the narrator of *Facino Cane* learns the name of the awesome clarinettist, he says, inspired by the musical features of his face: "I wanted him to be an Italian, and he was Italian" (FC 69). Instrumentalists, however, generally become associated in his mind with Germany. But the epic's great singers are Gennaro Conti (B), Luigia (DA), Clarina Tinti and Genovese (MD, AS), Marianina and Zambinella (Sa), Carthagenova (MD), and if there exists a Josépha Mirah (CBe), an Israelite, it is quite evident that the author's interest in her centers more around her role as a mistress than as a vocalist. Furthermore, he will admit in passing the triumphs of Malibran, Florine, and others (MM 394), but diminishes their glory in comparison with his own fictional, Italic Marianina, who sounds very much like his favorite signora Pasta: "Her voice paled the incomplete talents of the Malibrans, the Sontags, the Fodors, where a certain dominant trait has always excluded perfection from the whole; whereas Marianina knew how to blend evenly purity of sound, sensitivity, correctness of movement and of intonation, soul and knowledge, precision and feeling" (Sa 81). Stendhal and Blaze de

Bury would have agreed that Pasta matched Marianina's artistic specifications.

It must be noted that Balzac's opinion of "the Malibrans" differed considerably from that of his contemporary aficionados. While the public had excellent reason to extoll the divas he mentions, we must not overlook the importance of Balzac's slight reservation. Here his judgment showed insight. Any statement, around 1831, the time of *Sarrasine*, implying that the talents of Malibran, Sontag, and Fodor were "incomplete" rubbed against the grain of common opinion. For the unusual range of Malibran's voice, coupled with her command of dramatic singing; the unsurpassed execution and tonal control of Sontag, at which Weber had marveled and which covered both German and Italian opera; and the exquisite style of Fodor, which served as a model for Sontag and which earned her the acclaim of Mendelssohn, elicited a widespread adulation that frequently amounted to frenzy. Yet the fact remains that each had her "dominant traits" of weakness: the first, a questionable taste in her choice of improvised ornamentation and an interval of concealed but present dead notes between her normal contralto voice and a superadded soprano register; the second, a clear deficiency in dramatic power, passion, and emotion, which made her appear at highest advantage only in works of easy and placid style; and the third, a lack of charm, despite her gentility, and an insecurity which had caused a voice failure in 1825 and an extended period of hoarseness—while Pasta, whatever her own faults in vocal production, possessed rich laryngeal resonance and overall dignity, splendid individuality of impersonation, and a penetrating fire of expression, which, in the final analysis, may well have made her more distinguished than her famed counterparts and the most exciting singer on the stage.[39]

Balzac evidenced far less sagacity when he dismissed the "Swedish nightingale" Jenny Lind in 1847, for reasons other than artistic, with a scoffing epigram: ". . . Jenny Lind, that big German puff in petticoats. She has refused to come to Paris."[40] He made no comment about her artistry. At the time, he seemed more annoyed at the month-long stories of broken contracts, long diplomatic *pourparlers*, maneuvers, and vacillations that surrounded frøken Lind's attempts to excite the operatic public's interest.

Styles of Singing

The vocal demands made by Rossini and Meyerbeer on their interpreters were such that, when successfully met, any Romantic audience would express its approval exultingly. Acting ability had to complement singing dexterity to communicate fully the sensual experience. Society could not resist the *bel canto* appeal to the senses, nor did it realize how this very refined artistic method can cheapen expressiveness at the slightest exaggeration or misapplication. When the cult of the human vice became a fetish, egoisms lorded more than ever in the theatre, and when melody alone satisfied demand, instrumental and harmonic developments lost their value of necessity. Dramatic integrity quickly drowned under waves of misused vocal flourishes. Having once sensed the oddity of "Se il padre m'abbandona" in *Otello*, which overflows with roulades, Alfred de Musset still did not choose to criticize it on grounds of good taste; on the contrary, he saw in the swarm of its *fioriture* the best gauge of the singer's competence.[41] George Sand's implied criticism of this practice through the incomplete talent of Anzoletto in *Consuelo* would not have found many assenters. Audiences swooned before the long and well executed roulade or cadenza and the high C or F it invariably contained, the *difficulté vaincue* which seemed to define aesthetics. Musset's "this voice of the heart which alone reaches the heart"[42] found corroboration in Gautier's remarks: "The voice comes from the soul, one says; as for me, I believe simply that it is part of it. This is why, perhaps, its disappearance from a world where everybody leaves his dust behind is so complete. The voice is the incarnation of the soul, its evident, sensual manifestation. Listening to a voice, I know a soul, and the words it speaks do not deceive me about it."[43]

Vocal music excited Balzac more than any other kind. He enjoyed it equally well in the Neo-classical *Il matrimonio segreto* and the Romantic *Lucia di Lammermoor*. His ideal finds expression in *Sarrasine*, at the moment of the hero's enchantment with Zambinella: ". . . that agile voice, fresh and silver-like, supple like a thread which assumes the shape of the slightest breeze, rolling and unrolling, developing and dispersing it: that voice affected him so violently that he emitted more than once some of those loud gasps which are the involuntary result of convulsive delights, and are too rarely provided by human passions" (Sa 97). How far from the author's mind was a memory of Persiani in this instance? It was the tenor voice, however, that lured him instinctively. Most likely the great Rubini, whose sovereign tenure in opera amassed him a fortune, prompted the comment in 1846: "There is no more poem possible, no more music, no more performance, without a famous tenor whose voice can reach a certain note. The tenor is love; he is the voice which touches the heart, vibrates in the soul, and this adds up to a more considerable salary than that of a statesman" (CSS 19).

For Balzac too, the roulade, which offers the voice the possibility of full deployment, constituted a climactic height of artistic expression. Sainte-Beuve would have frowned and would have been applauded by Berlioz, whose unequivocal dislike for prevailing practices spurred him to personal insult and to the threat of blowing up all theatres that performed Rossini's music. But regardless of his friendship for him, Balzac adhered to his own ingenious theory of the roulade, verbalized by Capraja in *Massimilla Doni*, though his ultimate preference is for the ethereal union of two sounds, as stated by Cataneo. If his starting point reflected a fad, his conclusion left behind the more pedestrian explanations of that vocal device. In the first place, like E. T. A. Hoffmann, he shows awareness of the inherent danger of a practice that could lead to chaos if used gratuitously and if not generically bound to the expression of an emotion. In the second place, he adumbrates the theory of synaesthetic correspondences which will become a creed later in the century. And finally, he even suggests a preference for pure over descriptive music. For there is a sense to the whole roulade experience that allows the exterior sensation to penetrate beneath the structure of conscious sensitivity into the subconscious. Hence Capraja's statement about the roulades "performed as I have often heard them in certain dreams awakening from which I seemed to see the sounds flutter in the air," to which he adds:

> The roulade is the highest expression of art, the arabesque that adorns the most beautiful suite in the house: a little less and there's nothing at all, a little more and all is confused. Entrusted with awakening a thousand slumbering ideas in your soul, it soars, traverses space while sowing the air with seeds which, gathered by the ear, proceed to germinate in the depths of the heart. Believe me, Raphael gave a higher priority to music than to poetry in painting his St. Cecilia. And he was right: music addresses itself to the heart, whereas the written word addresses itself only to the mind; the former communicates immediately its ideas like perfumes. The singer's voice strikes not our thought nor the memory of our happiness, but the very elements of thought, and it sets into motion the very principles of our sensations. It is deplorable that the common herd has forced musicians to adapt their notes to words, to factitious interests; but it is also true that if they did not, they would no longer be understood by the masses. The roulade is, therefore, the only thing left to the friends of pure music, to the lovers of undisguised art, to cling to. [MD 349-350]

The contradiction between Balzac's love of singing and his respect for an art of wordless expression is only superficial. The latter does not preclude the former. A roulade may not be all he says it is, but some truth lies behind the theory. The roulade has its reason, and through it, a unique expressive power. If ornamental scales, trills, and cadences were deleted from the piano compositions of Mozart, Beethoven, and Weber, the blandness of directness, without the enhancement of fantasy, would set in. Bach recognized this in his *English Suites* without and with *agréments*. And in the matter of singing itself, Balzac would claim, did not Gregorian chant bestow eminent dignity on the *vocalise*, calling it "jubilation," the exaltation of the soul, according to St. Augustine, which music alone can render and not words? While Balzac was not comparing vocal practice in a *Lucia di Lammermoor* or a *Matrimonio segreto* with that of *cantus firmus*, he was talking about an aesthetic principle that has universal validity and that he was to apply more appositely when he condemned the ostentatious flourishes marring the purity of liturgical plainsong. In opera the roulade has its place; it can express jubilation as well as grief, as Rossini had experimented in *Otello*. It is unfortunate that the century of bravura should have misused so poignant a device, to the extent of annoying not only Balzac, but also Rossini (who frequently wrote his own roulades lest singers improvise worse ones), Sand, Stendhal, Berlioz, and before them, Grétry.

Where Capraja contradicts himself, however, is on the levels expressed in his discussion. While on the one hand he refers perceptively to the "elements of thought," on the other he alludes too pointedly to the senses: sight, smell, and touch as well as hearing. The dichotomy needs a higher synthesis. As "the highest expression of art," he might have done better to consider the roulade on the level of a single, autonomous and homogeneous expression. Duke Cataneo, on the other hand, is more consistent when he opposes Capraja's emphasis on sensation with a synthesizing pureness of experience. To the roulade he prefers

> . . . the concurrence of two voices or of one voice with a violin, the instrument whose effect most closely resembles the human voice. . . . This perfect accord leads us farther ahead toward the very center of life on the stream of elemental principles, which revives the senses and which bears man into the midst of the luminous sphere where his thought can convoke the whole world. You still need a theme, Capraja, but the pure essence alone suffices me. You want the water to pass through the thousand canals of the millwright, thence

> to fall back in dazzling cascades, whereas I am
> happy with a calm and pure sheet of water: my
> eye scans an unwrinkled sea. I can embrace the
> infinite.[44] [MD 350]

Here is a poetic and singularly stimulating utterance which, if carried logically forward, would place Cataneo today on the side of the formalists as opposed to the descriptives. The opposition raged just as fiercely in Balzac's day as perhaps it always will, and while in the light of vogue and tradition he may not have been willing to declare a preference explicitly, he nonetheless suggested one implicitly. The man who preferred opera to symphony also preferred, on another level, pure tone to sound with words, or to flowing sounds related to a descriptive context. If only because *Massimilla Doni* was dedicated to him, Strunz's ideas are not to be discounted in such instances. But we should not discard Balzac's share in them any more than we discard Plato's in favor of Socrates, and while the German teacher deserves no small credit for amplifying Balzac's meager musical visions, it was the pupil who expanded them with poetic breadth. He hinted at the very essence of music, whether by accident or by design, the essence that exists even beyond the perfect blend of a voice and a violin, in the sphere of tone and sound after their final filtering.

Instrumental Virtuosity

Dexterity and bravura shaped much of the musical aesthetics of the time. If the voice is an instrument, the instrumentalist had to match the vocalist in virtuosity. A sparkling execution of a page laden with chromatic and dynamic difficulties always arouses one's sensitivity to awe, and the era of Paganini and Liszt, performers acclaimed more for their prowess than for their musicianship, carried this natural inclination to the point of mythology. Fascinating legends abetted the public's mood. Paganini, for instance, was advertised through magic and mystery (according to Vigny's testimony[45]) to Paris audiences in advance of his arrival. The violinist, who was supposed to have locked the soul of his mistress inside the sonorous coffin of his instrument, started a furore in the capital in 1831 with his legerdemainist's variations (on the "Prayer" from *Mosè in Egitto*) on the E string alone. Liszt, who arrived in Paris as a child prodigy of twelve in 1823, also inspired otherworldly and legendary associations, fighting the demonic keyboard "as Achilles fought the Trojan battalions and redoubts."[46] The *Gallop chromatique* is the type of selection which adduced Gautier's declaration that Briareos' one hundred arms could still not match Liszt's ten fingers, as they sounded every last key and disappeared from view by virtue of their own velocity.[47]

To astound, however, was not what these artists considered their goal. Both were acquainted with the pedestals and quicksands of Romantic popularity, and both harbored a profound reverence for the old masters: Paganini for the Italian classical school, Liszt for Beethoven and Bach. But their influence on contemporary expression seemed to restrict itself to the charlatanism of bravura. One possible exception was Thalberg, Heine's Austrian *gentleman musical*, who vied unsuccessfully with the Hungarian for the crown of virtuosity,[48] but whose quiet and serious demeanor at the piano produced a gradation of singing tones and unrivaled *legati sostenuti* that impressed even Schumann. Another was the Belgian violinist and composer Vieuxtemps, just launching his career around Balzac's time, whose bow command and amazing staccato never diverted attention from a solid interpretation. Others, however accomplished, bowed too subserviently before the idol of skill to do justice to their talents. Kalkbrenner delighted in being labeled by Fétis the most technically astounding pianist of his day; Herz defended his German method on the basis of his ability to execute rapid leaps from one end of the keyboard to the other; much to Fétis' dislike, Field, a Dubliner, composed and performed showy medleys and variations of operatic arias in the manner of Steibelt; Rodolphe Kreutzer camouflaged his faulty musicianship with violin executions of technical ingenuity. Marie Pleyel on the piano, Baillot, Bériot, and Rode on the violin, Franchomme on the violoncello, Tulou and Dorus on the flute, Gallay on the horn, and Vogt and Brod on the oboe, were swept aloft by the same fancies that gave prominence to Paganini and Liszt.[49]

In this picturesque whirl of sounds, Chopin placed himself unassumingly in a category apart. He did not seek the regalia of a concert hall, and if he could not avoid appearing at a gilded salon, he played only late at night, when the regulars had left, and when an intimate few cared enough to stay behind to listen to him.

Balzac's praise of the virtuosos showed some discrimination. Whether aided by Berlioz or not, he gauged them adequately on his own scale of merits. Only Chopin, Liszt, Paganini, and Alexandre Batta[50] he admitted to his restricted ranks; "all the other performers do not exist. Thalberg is an expressionless bird-organ."[51] Furthermore, it is noteworthy that he chose the first in preference to the second: Chopin's Ruggiero-like perfection gained a qualitative advantage over Liszt's Orlando-like impetuosity. "[Liszt] is the Paganini of the piano; but Chopin is far superior to him."[52] On another occasion, he paraphrased the comment: "He [Liszt] has an executorial talent that finds analogy only in Paganini; but he has no genius for composition. In order to deserve all that is being done for him, he should be simultaneously Rossini and Liszt. You will be able to judge Liszt only after you have had the chance to hear Chopin. The Hungarian is a demon; the Pole is an angel."[53] Though vexed with Liszt at the time, the comment stands.

Given the fact that by this year (1843) Beethoven had all but been completely accepted in France, Balzac's choice of Rossini leaves something to be desired. But on the other hand, the author's friendship-bound admiration for the composer of *Guglielmo Tell*—an opera, as we have come to realize today, of more depth than we have normally attributed to it in the past—cannot be held against him too severely. The spirit of his remark remains clear: that virtuosity, considered strictly from a musical point of view, has its importance, but that, reduced solely to its sensational dimensions, it appears as nothing more than athletic exhibitionism, a soap bubble which a more vivifying artistic reality will burst. Paganini revealed to the gaping world many hitherto unfathomed nuances and beauties of the violin, whose sonorous range he decupled by the use of harmonics; but he was also capable of communicating all the shades of expression required of an accomplished interpretation. Liszt, too, availed himself of the piano's harmonic, modulatory, and color potential, extending its limits to the very threshold of the orchestra. But less magically, deemed Balzac. Was it not, then, more moving to stand in the presence of a subtler and more creative virtuosity, which includes both technical proficiency and an ability to transmute the performer from instrumentalist to poet, like Schmucke when he sat at the keyboard to console his sick comrade Pons? "He hit upon sublime themes, over which he embroidered certain caprices executed at times with the sadness and Raphaelesque perfection of Chopin, at times with the fury and Dantesque grandeur of Liszt, the musical combination which comes closest to Paganini. Execution, once it has reached this degree of perfection, seems to place the performer on the same high level as the poet; he is to the composer what the actor is to the playwright, a divine translator of divine things."[54] The spirit of the interpreter, to illustrate the meaning and illuminate the poetry of the composition: this was one of Balzac's favored notions. "The violin only knows what Paganini makes it say" (MD 380). Indeed, such interpreters are less musicians than "souls" that become visible through sounds. If Balzac as the Napoleon of letters saluted Paganini—"He is the generalissimo of the virtuosos who have appeared since the Deluge; he is the Napoleon of violins"—he also commended him more simply and more sincerely when he remarked: "[he] changes all the conditions of music by converting them into a poetry that exists beyond musical creations."[55] Félicité Destouches, in speaking of Gennaro Conti, says: "It's no longer a voice you hear, my friend, it's a soul" (B 398). *Ursule Mirouët* contains the best example of Balzac's views on musical interpreters: "In any kind of music, apart from the thought of the composer exists the soul of the performer, which, according to a privilege granted only to that art, can give meaning and poetry to phrases of no particular value. Chopin proves today for the thankless piano the truth of this fact already demonstrated by Paganini for the violin. That wonderful genius is less a musician than a soul that becomes perceptible and that would communicate through all kinds of music, even through simple chords" (UM 384).

Despite a passing enthusiasm in *Massimilla Doni*, Balzac, of course, did not confuse the roles of interpreter and creator. On the ladder of merits, the latter occupies expectedly the highest rung; a fine singer in *Fidelio* will never rank equally with its composer. Gennaro Conti suffers at being only a remarkable vocalist and modest composer: "he prefers to be a man of genius like Rossini rather than a forceful performer like Rubini" (B 400). When, in the *Théorie de la démarche*, Balzac appears to place Paganini, Huerta the guitarist, Taglioni the ballerina, and Liszt on the same level as creators like Raphael and Michelangelo, he does so only within the framework of "the marvels of touch," in which case those who use motion, brushes, and instruments are "all artists who transfuse their souls by movements whose secret they alone possess" (ThD 594). Skill and creativity, he argued, are not synonymous. At best, a performance by the fabulous Italian violinist would only "seem" to match the creator's greatness; he remains a "translator." The same applies to other consummate artists like Moschelès and Farinelli: "Moschelès at the piano, Paganini on the violin, . . . Farinelli with his larynx! people who developed tremendous abilities, but who did not create any music. Between Beethoven and La Catalani, permit me to grant the immortal crown of genius and martyrdom to the first, and many one hundred sou pieces to the second. From the latter we have good riddance, whereas the world will always be indebted to the former" (MM 528).[56] The interpreter's task, that of keeping pace at once with the most delicate and the most arduous demands of the work, draws only brief attention from Balzac at first: "Constant work is the law of art as it is that of life; for art is idealized creation." On the same page, however, he shows a more specific understanding of the nature of the preparation exacted by musical performance: "If Paganini, who made the strings of his violin describe his soul, had spent three days without practicing, he would have lost, in his own word, the 'register' of his instrument; by this he referred to the marriage that exists between the wood, the bow, the strings, and himself. If this union had been dissolved, he would have quickly become an ordinary fiddler" (CBe 322). For this reason Chopin and Liszt are admirable: they come closest to Paganini. Under the great performer's fingers, the idea and feeling locked in the composition are liberated, but this only occurs and perpetuates itself, as Balzac sees it, when he has become a prisoner of his art through hours and hours of practice. The same applies to creators. Lethargy disintegrates talent. Balzac commented on the "prodigious laziness"[57] of Rossini, whose production ceased long before he died. Wenceslas Steinbock (CBe) and Lousteau (MuD) both do not attain their goals because of a reluctance to act.

In some respects, therefore, Balzac recognized the asset of virtuosity as a means to an exciting end, and its liability as a stimulant for pathos or triviality. He mocked Liszt when he became excessive, for example, in his article in *La Caricature* of July 28, 1831, "Rondo brillant mais facile." We detect a desire to see through the simpler infatuations of his day, and discern an effort to plumb the associations between interpretation and creation, communication and beauty.

Favored Instruments

Using the human voice as the standard of excellence in tone production, the century favored the string instruments, particularly the violin, because it appeared to reproduce the pure resonances of the human organ. Through Cataneo, Balzac agreed; it was also Paganini's instrument, and, we might add, the first musical toy of his childhood. The febrile excitements also aroused around him by the piano elicited a more modest response. To the man who never mastered "Le Songe de Rousseau" as he had wished, the piano appeared "thankless," less rewarding than the violin, except, of course, under the fingers of Liszt and especially of Chopin.

Most of the other instruments Balzac treated literarily—rhetorically or metaphorically, at times clumsily. A gracious "oui" is likened to "the sweetest note ever sighed by Tulou's flute" (SPC 47); an ethereal essence is evoked through a "concert of harmonious harps" (S 473); a shocking, succinct remark resembles "a tam-tam beat struck in the middle of a passage of music"; a sudden realization of not being loved produces inwardly the effect of "the peal of a trumpet" (C 775, 937)! He speaks in commonplaces of the rustic or sylvan moods of woodwinds, of the warrior impetuosity of brasses, or of the flowing sensations of strings as they affect "the most delicate fibers of our organism" (MD 376). Nor does he avoid perfunctory allusions to the "music of the aeolian harp" with which poets animate forests and mountains (S 475).[58]

Analogies with painting abound in a manner suggesting that Balzac groped toward an understanding of music through similarities with pictorial art. Capraja does not refer simply to St. Cecelia, the patron saint of music, but to Raphael's St. Cecelia. So Balzac makes Chopin the Raphael of the piano, Marcello the Giotto of music, and Beethoven akin in power to Michelangelo. By extension, the sounds of instruments, too, relate synaesthetically to colors, enjoying a primacy not shared with the other arts: "In music, instruments perform the function of colors in painting. . . . Each instrument, having duration, breath, or the hand of man for expression, is superior as a language to color, which is fixed, and to the word, which has limitations. The musical language is infinite, it contains all; it can express everything" (MD 377).[59] With its particular timbre and in multiple combination, each enriches the orchestral palette by virtue of an infinite play of shades.

The "lure of the infinite" drew many a Romantic imagination to appreciate religious faith. Whether out of a nostalgia for belief or out of an attraction to vagueness, the French public—and Balzac was no exception—approached music on the basis of such sentimental criteria; its reluctant acceptance of Beethoven owed no little thanks to the abstract and poetic language Berlioz could fashion in his articles in praise of the composer's "infinite" attributes. For Hugo, Number reveals itself to art through rhythm, which is "the beating of the infinite,"[60] and in his poem "Que la musique date du VXIe siècle," the Romantic sense of limitlessness finds an apposite symbol in the music of the spheres. Not unexpectedly, the instrument considered to be the most capable of transcribing the vast, accumulative movements of nature and most fittingly designed for the cathedral, was the organ.[61]

Balzac availed himself regularly of metaphors relating music to infinity and light. A singing voice is like "a column that rises from the lips of certain saints in the pious legends," and an orchestra so composed he compares to a "clavier of lights that one irradiates at will, at times to charm our sight, at times to fire it with lightnings"—an obvious allusion to Father Castel's invention, the "clavecin eculaire," which receives more specific mention in *Le Lys dans la vallée*.[62] He paid special tribute to the organ when a seraphic voice "unfurled the divine expanses, like an organ which, when played, fills a church with its soughing and reveals the musical universe by moistening the most inaccessible vaults with its solemn tones, and by sporting, in the manner of light, with the airiest flowers of the capitals" (S 560). Again it was an organ in a cathedral that sets architectural details, "bizarrely lighted," into motion: a trembling, dancing, laughing, jumping movement through which the instrument "spoke," conveyed "a divine harmony" and a "nervous pleasure" (JCF 262). But his most emotional page on any instrument was written at the beginning of *La Duchesse de Langeais* where his love for the organ infiltrates tacitly Louis Lambert's desire for the harmony of universal unity:

> The organ is certainly the most grand, the most audacious, the most magnificent of all the instruments created by human genius. It is a

whole orchestra, of which an able hand can ask anything; it can express everything. Is it not some sort of pedestal on which the soul readies itself for a flight into space, where, in course, it tries to trace an endless series of patterns, depict life, survey the infinite that separates heaven from earth? The more a poet listens to its gigantic harmonies, the better he realizes that nothing save the hundred voices of this terrestrial chorus can fill the space between the genuflecting people and the God concealed by the dazzling rays of the Sanctuary. Music is the sole interpreter powerful enough to transmit human prayers to the heavens, prayers in their omnipotent ways, in a diversity of melancholies, with the hues of meditative ecstasy, with the impetuous surge of repentance, and through the myriad fancies of their creeds. [DL 132]

At the end of the novel, as the hero is leaving forever the Carmelite site which will seclude his beloved lady, the "faint chords" of the organ sound in the distance (DL 252), as though the wind that rushed through the pipes had blown in from unknown regions, similar, continues the novelist, to the aeolian lyre which seems to sound at the touch of God's unseen finger. The second tale of the *Histoire des Treize* concludes the way an Amen terminates a prayer.

* * *

French writers reacted variously to the tyrannical standards of vogue. Some exhibited sensitivity and perspicaciousness, most notably George Sand.[63] Some sought intellectual content, like Deschamps, while others, like Mérimée, revealed more philistine dispositions. Still others intellectualized, or attempted to do so, their musical awareness, like Hugo and Vigny, and there were those, like Musset and Stendhal, who experienced the full sensual impact of what they heard and proclaimed it. Balzac followed all the events, noted all the reactions. He would read about the jousting contests of roulades between Bordogni and Rubini[64] or about the keyboard athletics pitting Thalberg against Liszt, marvel at Mme de Girardin's generous support of mediocre romances while she penned concurrently the most sensitive appreciations of Chopin ballades and Mozart sonatas, and listen to the praise of Weber and Beethoven by Berlioz or Habeneck, all within the space of one day. Superficial enthusiasms, idle victories, and ephemeral experiences—a discriminating judgment was something rare. Critic H. Blaze de

Bury's attitude was typical: "Music, as I see it, is La Malibran in ecstasy, singing 'Le Saule' during a nice evening at the Italiens."[65] Music to quench a soul's thirst for the infinite, to provide a refreshing balm or a tranquilizing drug for exasperated nerves, to express love or to identify it with remembrances and dreams: one must agree with a modern musicologist, J.-G. Prod'homme, who condemns all opinions on music expressed by Romantic writers. But this same critic makes an exception of Balzac,[66] who responded to every category and marked each with a brand of vision which was not less personal for being eclectic.

CHAPTER III

CELEBRATED MUSICIAN FRIENDS

The man who boasted of knowing "all those who are at the head of the art" did indeed include among his friends some of the most prominent personalities of his day: Rossini, Liszt, Berlioz, and to a modest extent, Chopin. Something he learned from them, if only through their presence, and also every now and then in conversation. But Balzac did not crave to discuss music with them; to his equals he disliked to admit ignorance in any field. Surely their genius influenced his own musical interests.[1] While he looked upon them, often with puerile pride, as he did upon Hugo or Mme de Castries, essentially as friends, he still identified them as eminent practitioners of the art of music who gained from their association with him as much as he gained from theirs. Influences of this sort can be traced only tenuously, without linear comparisons and through a fluid mass of indications. And inside this mass we detect that Balzac's musician friends were far more important to him for what they represented than for the occasional gestures of friendship that knit together their lives.

Gioacchino Rossini

Rossini, who conquered Paris in 1823[2] by liberating it from the pompous dullness of Neo-classical productions, formed an enduring friendship with Balzac from the earliest days when each discovered in the other similar qualities: youthfulness and exuberance, and similar likes: melody and coffee.[3] Balzac had met him around 1831, either in Olympe Pélissier's loge or at her home, along with Auber and Berlioz. At a time when Balzac had only the vaguest technical notion of what was meant by harmony and counterpoint, and when he could do little more than hear musical surfaces, the Italian composer helped him to conceptualize a few of his more undefined bents, especially his Stendhalian love of melody.

More than any other visible contemporary, one expects Balzac to "go to listen to his little Rossini opera," as the expression went, as if perpetually engaged in one of those "little escapades" to the Opéra or Italiens with which he tried to lure Mme Hanska to Paris. A Rossini opera he thought of as an orgy of pleasure, and the commanding yet supple composer earned in his eyes the title that Musset, Gautier, and Lamartine would also have given him, that of "the King of music."[4] In the royal presence, Balzac felt flattered and regaled, above all when the seductive and still single Olympe Pélissier invited the two men to a private dinner. Sometimes his pride sounded embarrassingly naïve, as it did once during the performance of a Galuppi opera when Olympe, now Rossini's wife, extolled her husband's "beautiful and sublime soul," to which Balzac responded by tenderly seizing the maestro's hand and saying: "We understand each other."[5]

If the duration of their friendship is any indication, Balzac's remark contained some truth. He certainly cheered his friend's works. In 1830, he applauded wildly *Guglielmo Tell*, in 1833 *La gazza ladra*, and in 1834 he declared *Mosè in Egitto* and *Semiramide* to be his "only pleasures."[6] By the time he began corresponding with Mme Hanska, Balzac had exchanged many invitations with Rossini, who often entertained his host with talk and music.[7] The composer gave him an opportunity to impress the distant Etrangère with his contacts, and the novelist made great show of obtaining a note signed by Rossini for the Hanski autograph collection.[8] On another occasion, he asked to become Rossini's poet for a romance in honor of his Polish lady,[9] and submitted to him verses that deserve no comment:

> *Rive chérie*
> *Où sont nées mes amours,*
> *Sois ma patrie!*
>
> *Là mon amie,*
> *Des cieux la fleur,*
> *S'est attendrie*
> *De mon malheur!*
>
> *Rive chérie* etc.
>
> *Là de ma vie*
> *Commenca l'heur* (sic);
> *Mélancolie*
> *N'est pas douleur.*
>
> *Rive chérie* etc.

(Riverbank dear
Where my love was born,
Be my country!

There my friend
The blossom of heaven,
Felt compassionate
At my sorrow!

Riverbank dear etc.

There began
The hour of my life;
Melancholy
Is not pain.

Riverbank dear etc.)

Always very "obliging,"[10] Rossini impressed his friend with his modesty, and above all with his joviality and humor. The wittiest man in Europe, as Mérimée also believed, was "the humble igniter who, during a display of fireworks, will set fire to each sun."[11] Balzac was happy not to disregard Rossini's compliments, such as those in a letter of 1833: "My dear Balzac, You ask me for an autograph; well, here it is. What shall I talk to you about? About you, perhaps, who mark this century with your masterpieces? You are, my friend, too great a colossus for me to banter about; and besides, what would the vote of a naïve foreigner mean to you? I shall limit myself, therefore, to telling you that I am very fond of you and that, in turn, you must not disdain having bewitched the 'Pesarote.'"[12] Balzac responded to the cordiality. One year later, he gave a banquet in his honor in the rue Cassini, to which he invited Latour-Mézeray, Nodier, Sandeau, Bohain, Werdet, Olympe Pélissier, and all the "Tigers" of the Infernal Loge of the Opéra. In order to "distinguish" himself, he ordered "the most exquisite wines of Europe, the rarest flowers, the finest meat." Perhaps primarily intended to dazzle l'Etrangère, to whom he gave a full account, the dinner of 4000 francs in an apartment decorated by Moreau, Teissier, and Tournier did not fail to stun the guest of honor himself, an indisputed gourmet, whose comment, "I have never seen, eaten, or drunk anything better in the homes of sovereigns,"[13] was a compliment indeed.

Rossini's name appears frequently in Balzac's works from before *Le Père Goriot* (even in *Code des gens honnêtes*!) to after *Honorine*, and in his correspondence,[14] especially in that to *la cara donna assoluta*, as the composer had dubbed Mme Hanska.[15] Because of what he considered their parallel experiences, Balzac found in him appreciation and understanding of his own hardships as an artist, and concurrence in the desire for easy and lavish living. Both, to be sure, considered financial independence a legitimate reward for their creative ability. Balzac, therefore, was moved by Rossini's preoccupation with affluence and echoed him time and again: "Oh! independence! Rossini was quite right: the only kind is that of money!," or "I am in a vise, the vise that made Rossini write his operas," or "Oh! necessity! what started Rossini on so many operas!"[16] These commonly held attitudes strengthened the bond through which each—Balzac perhaps more than Rossini—derived pride in associating with one of the great men of the century. A disgruntled airing of the pecuniary concern came in 1846: "Pretentions of genius! . . . Bah! . . . Does one think of all that when one has one's fortune to make and one's bread to earn? Did Rossini think of glory while he wrote *Il barbiere* for a hundred écus? He did as I did when I wrote *La Physiologie du mariage*: he thought about his bread and butter. We admitted this to each other."[17] It is no coincidence that Balzac chose to comment on the "Calunnia" aria from *Il barbiere di Siviglia* in that financially travailed novel *La Maison Nucingen*. Behind his attitude lay the belief that money and artistic creation are in no way incompatible. "No, the best works have been the children of opulence. . . . Therefore, stop holding misery up to us as the mother of genius."[18]

Yet Rossini was at the same time the man who came to symbolize for Balzac the magic of melody and who made him a more imaginative listener. The composer's style ranged from lyrical sweeps to tonal piquancies of coloratura, from dynamic harmonies to rhythmic contrasts. These constituted virtues even the untutored Balzac could appreciate. He found irresistible his melodic sinuosity because it was evocative; it conjured sensations and psychological associations with which other advocates of melody like Musset, Lamartine, Stendhal, and Nerval, were not unfamiliar. Balzac wrote that some themes of Rossini are among the very few things that "have been able to transport me to the divine regions of my first love" (PC 107). He deserves all of our concentration, "for one must be at once a poet and a musician to understand the import of such music" (MD 355). Without this early and enduring contact, Balzac's interest in music may well have developed differently. Whether or not he was conscious of the impact the convivial composer made on him, the fact remains clear that the mere presence of Rossini in the immediate sphere of Balzac's friendships was significant in that it convinced him of the importance of melody. In 1842, he changed the title of *Fleur des pois* to *Le Contrat de mariage*, a work dedicated to his friend. Was it a recollection of the maestro's *La Cambiale di matrimonio*?

Franz Liszt

The relationship between Balzac and Franz Liszt[19] was more uneven and complex. They could have met originally at a concert, at Baron Gérard's, at Mme Merlin's, at Duchess de Rauzan's, at Mme de Girardin's, or at the Austrian Embassy, sometime during the early 1830s. Before meeting the child prodigy, Balzac had spoken flippantly of him: "We like green fruit. . . . Literature has its Litz [sic], its Jules Regondis, its Léontine Fays, who are supposed to have left Punchinello to create masterpieces"[20]; and again, in mocking excessive virtuosity in improvisation, he referred to "the old-young Lintz [sic]."[21] But the sarcasms ended quickly. At one of Erard's soirées, Liszt gave a recital of Bach, Beethoven, and Weber in the presence of Berlioz, Balzac, Fétis, Préault, and one Augustin Challamel who left an account of the evening. Berlioz's pleasure over the pianist's interpretations vanished under the din of Balzac's histrionics: "Bravo! Sublime!" he shouted, rolling on the floor; "he is the God of the piano!"[22] Liszt, who from one end of his life to the other complained about the public's deafness to his art, remembered this athletic tribute in 1833 when he invited him to another recital: "Try, dear Balzac, not to fail me Saturday morning. 'Eloquence,' Ballanche has said, I think, 'is found as much in those who listen as in him who speaks.' The same holds true for music. I need listeners like you, and, lacking 'listeners' in the plural, I need 'you' in the singular."[23] Liszt sought those who could both understand and listen. Balzac's may have appeared an overreaction, but the pianist nonetheless recognized in it an outburst of sincerity which pleased him and which prompted him to add the author's name to the copious list of writers, historians, poets, and philosophers he liked to consider his friends.[24]

The invitation augured a cordial friendship, for each discerned in the other indications of his own excessiveness, power, and energy. In retrospect, we note that the styles of both men, easily open to criticism but richly diverse, betrayed similarities: faults that became useful dissonances in their personalities, mistakes so passionately committed as to become lyrical, lengthiness of expression that reminds us of Wagnerian sagas, and a definite courting of virtuosity.[25] They agreed on the superiority of talent over the accident of birth and on the artist's prophetic mission in society, and they demonstrated the same assiduity in pursuing all the intellectual manifestations of the human spirit. Understandably, then, Liszt's correspondence of 1833 and 1834 overflowed with references to his recent friend, and Balzac spoke often of the man he will dub later "the Paganini of the piano."[26] Sometimes he sent him one of his novels as a gift. In turn, Liszt urged Countess d'Agoult in 1833 to read *Séraphita*, referred her to *La Peau de chagrin*, and in 1837 sent her a copy of *César Birotteau*. Often the two men sat down together for hours of chitchat ranging from the seven types of women necessary for man to Swedenborg's theory of angels.[27] Or Balzac listened to Liszt execute at the piano variations on themes by Rossini, transcriptions of Lieder by Schubert (very often "Der Erlkönig"), selections from Weber, and his specialty, sonatas by Beethoven. It was perhaps in Liszt's presence more than in that of anyone else around 1833 or 1834 that the name of Beethoven sounded most frequently in his ears, and although the Rossinian supremacy of melodic over harmonic music held firm, Balzac found it difficult not to respond positively to the stately discipline of sounds that Beethoven offered him through Liszt's pianistic skill.

When his friend eloped to Switzerland with Countess d'Agoult, an escapade which scandalized his very admirers, Balzac at first appeared to remain faithful to him, but innuendos soon crept into his comments. "Mme d'Agoult who is running all over the place with Liszt,"[28] he wrote sarcastically from Milan in 1838, jealous of the latter's greater economic freedom. When George Sand entered the picture, we witness a nineteenth century game of literary charade mixed with hide-and-seek, in which Balzac seems to have participated fully while posing as an outsider. Sand liked Liszt and was offended at his flight with the countess (a close friend of hers to whom she had originally introduced him), but also felt concern over the tensions that had sprouted between the lovers and sought to bring about a graceful separation.[29] Rankled at the course of their liaison, she invited Balzac, with whom she shared a deep dislike for Jules Sandeau, to Nohant, and there urged him to write two stories based on the material she would furnish him regarding the pianist and his mistress. Making no reference to Sandeau, Balzac explained to Mme Hanska: "It's about Liszt and Mme d'Agoult that she spoke when she gave me the subject of the *Galériens* or of the *Amours forcés* which I shall write, for in her situation, she cannot do it."[30]

Having deemed the first title "too insulting," the author changed it to *Béatrix*, the first two parts of which, causing a considerable stir, began appearing in *Le Siècle* on the 13th of April, 1839. Now it was Balzac's turn, whether *in veritate* or *pro forma*, to arouse George Sand's displeasure for having "blackened terribly, in this book, a candid acquaintance of mine."[31] The novel appeared to portray Marie d'Agoult in Marquise Béatrix de Rochefide, Gustave Planche in Claude Vignon, Liszt in Gennaro Conti, and George Sand (Aurore Dupin) herself in Camille Maupin. Although Spoelberche de Lovenjoul disagrees with these equations, Camille, the brilliant authoress who had changed her name (From Félicité des Touches), her masculine clothes, her hookah, and her fine musical sensitivity, as well as Vignon, the keen critic and disaffected psychologist, point unmistakably to their suspected models. One of Balzac's several admissions may be found in a letter in which he claimed never to have portrayed anyone, such as G. Planche and G. Sand, without his or her consent.[32] As for the two remaining literary transpositions, he would have admitted them only with grave reluctance. For the slender, blond Béatrix is a vain, heartless and not overly intelligent coquette who has abandoned her husband by eloping to Italy with her suitor, the musician Conti, after having turned him away from Mlle des Touches. And Conti detracts from his stature as a composer and accomplished singer by acting like a petty and selfish scoundrel. Charges of libelous depiction were not late in coming, and Balzac could only defend himself on the grounds that he had "never yet seen" Countess d'Agoult, that he "adored in Liszt the talent and the man, and [that] to claim that Gennaro can resemble him is a double insult to both him and me."[33] But why then did he confide to Mme Hanska in 1840?: "No, I wasn't happy writing *Béatrix*—as you might have guessed. Yes, Sarah is Madame de Visconti; yes, Mademoiselle des Touches is George Sand; yes, Béatrix is Madame d'Agoult only too well. George Sand could not be happier; she is taking here a little revenge on her friend. Except for a few variables, the story is true."[34] Actually, Balzac had met the countess shortly before 1840, before publishing *Béatrix*. And in what concerned Liszt, Balzac did regard him artistically supreme but by this time personally somewhat unsavory, a man "of little ridicules and of great qualities," as he said later.[35]

Exact portraiture was not Balzac's end; the man's mannerisms and foibles were. He had no particular personal grievance against Liszt during these years, and in the light of his statement: "Alas! I have never been able to tell him that Conti is Sandeau in musician's garb,"[36] we should more plausibly turn to the disliked Sandeau. Moreover, as Thérèse Marix points out, Conti's inflated egoism, calculated falseness, and narrowmindedness, not to mention his physical traits, are not consistent with the Lisztian personality as we know it, a personality distinguished by altruism, sincerity, and disinterestedness. This explains Liszt's lack of concern over the gossip when he wrote to his distressed Marie: "People have wanted to set us at variance. . . , they wanted to insinuate that Balzac had draped me in unflattering robes under the name of Conti, but as I did not recognize myself in him, I have not accepted the portrait."[37] Indeed he could not. We read of Conti: "His nature is charming on the surface, and detestable basically. In matters of the heart, he is a charlatan. . . . Such men deceive themselves. Mounted on stilts, they think they are standing on their feet and perform their hocus-pocus with a kind of innocence; their vanity is in their blood; they are born comedians, braggarts, and as extravagant of form as a Chinese urn" (B 399).

In a sense, Marie could have said the same, given the character development of Béatrix which makes her a very different person at the end of the novel. She had benefitted Balzac as a study in aristocratic beauty, pride, and breeding; he made her the dupe of an artist who, for all his profession of religious idealism, is in the end unfulfilled in matters of art and a trickster in matters of life. But beyond this point, Balzac engaged in a web of his own spinning, working out a complicated set of psychological circumstances in which the characters obeyed no law except that of their own desires. *Béatrix* is a vaudeville of love in which the novelist observes all the possible love situations that individuals get into. This purpose was clear to Liszt, who always considered his friend "the observer of observation."[38] Balzac's hedging, therefore, on the matter of identifications is understandable, and when he said "the story is true," he referred to the skeletal outline of a plot that bore superficial resemblances with living persons, while telling particulars, barring a few idiosyncracies, were omitted.

The ties of friendship between Balzac and Liszt, in fact, grew stronger when they discovered a common adversary in Sainte-Beuve, the relentless critic of the author of *La Comédie humaine*, who began to court the lovely countess around this time. Moreover, when Balzac's *Revue* ceased to exist for lack of funds after three issues, it was the ever generous pianist who tried secretly to solicit money to assist him. The dedication of *La Duchesse de Langeais* to Liszt had constituted a still valid and truthful tribute.

Suddenly the picture changed. His constant need to present himself in the best light led him with pride to arrange for the celebrated Liszt to visit Mme Hanska in Poland. Having provided the Hanskis with his autograph for their collection was not enough; now Balzac urged the traveling artist to stop at Wierzchownia to play for Eve and her daughter. He soon regretted his imprudence; Mme Hanska changed her lover's bragging to jealousy. The letters Balzac wrote from 1843 to 1845 began with suspicious insinuations, then modulated to aggressive remarks and finally to insulting criticisms. At first, some innocuous comments: "Ridiculous man, sublime talent,"[39] followed by a tactfully controlled assessment: "Between you and me, the Hungarian is a bit of a comedian, but a well-intentioned comedian—at least, so I think. He has a sublime talent of execution, whose only analogue is Paganini, but he does not possess the genius of composition."[40] Then, fewer innuendos and more straightforward warnings about the discredit into which Marie d'Agoult's wooer had fallen: "Be prudent . . . I'm ashamed of my dedication." He entreated her to dismiss him, not to write to him, though he caught himself, temporarily, in a moment of selflessness: "Listen, I was wrong. Write to L[iszt]. How could I ever think that anything you do would not be done well. . . . From the point of view of love, this jealousy is charming and flattering, but from the point of view of a celestially conjugal affection, it's a suspicion for which I scold myself."[41]

Eve Hanska, whose treatment of Balzac can be censured, could have dismissed the matter on the spot, had she but expressed herself. But her silence about Liszt in 1844 exploded her admirer's self-control and occasioned a succession of thorny, epigrammatic invectives: Liszt was an actor "bordering on folly," a "monkey," a "real Bohemian" and a "mountebank" with "the hatred of a public prosecutor," a spoiled "piccaninny," a "Lara" who "has only fingers" and "ignores everything outside of musical execution."[42] He complained that Lara was deriding him ("remember me to her if, of course, you see her before I do") and reported Princess Belgiojoso as saying with a smile that at a farewell dinner in Lyon "every guest found in his plate a chocolate medal representing Liszt the Great."[43] And in 1845, upon learning that his distant lady had again seen Liszt, he wrote that the Hungarian this time was mocking her, and six months later exclaimed with exhaustion: "Liszt! . . . That's inconceivable! . . ."[44]

Balzac had more than smelled the dangerous situation of a rich widow and music lover in the presence of a celebrated young artist, whose discoursing on music, morals, art, and religious mysticism, as her letters to her daughter reveal, captivated her.[45] Eve Hanska herself was aware of her "taste . . . for dangerous relationships."[46] After Liszt had visited her daily during the summer of 1843, and when the familiarity cultivated over nearly two years looked indeed risky, she put a gradual end the affair. Upon Liszt's brief return to Paris in 1845, a reconciliation between her two friends did not take place only because there had never been an avowed break. And it would be difficult to blame Liszt, in any event; just how well he knew of the Polish lady's tie with Balzac is not certain. What is is his admiration for a man whose novels he never ceased to read. As late as 1881, he still spoke of "the fine brush of Balzac," or "the exquisite charm of Balzac," and retained a special fondness for *Le Lys dans la vallée*.[47]

Liszt's constancy contrasted with Balzac's fits of jealousy. Korwin-Piotrowska suggests that during one of them, Liszt may well have become the prototype of a repulsive poseur, the poet Canalis in *Modeste Mignon*.[48] Although other candidates for the dubious honor exist—men who more successfully than Balzac attempted to combine art with politics, or who used the former as an avenue to a career in the latter (Chateaubriand, Lamartine, Hugo, Sue, Adolphe Thiers, and even Vigny come to mind)—the following genesis of the novel of 1844, a strained year in the Balzac-Liszt relationship, is entirely possible: (a) in Berlin, in 1842, Liszt meets Bettina von Arnim, whose epistolary *Bettina* revealed the love of a girl of twenty for the venerable sexagenarian Goethe, a situation Balzac found ludicrous; (b) in Poland, one year later, Liszt speaks to Mme Hanska of the letters, something Balzac too had done recently in order to point out the differences between their own case and that of Goethe and Bettina; (c) later that year Mme Hanska attempts a short story about that relationship and, after abandoning the project, sends a sketch of it to Balzac for his own use; (d) discarding the original protagonists, Balzac impatiently expands it during a period of anger into a novel about the romantic love of a girl for a genial poet who is also an ostentatious, vain charlatan, a seeker of glory and luxury, a declamatory and emphatic cad, in short, an insufferable boor. The work could also have served to teach Mme Hanska a gentle lesson, that of the danger for a naively sincere soul to attach herself too incautiously to a great reputation, for reputations of any kind are often spurious and undependable. If the Liszt-Canalis parallel, then, is even moderately correct, Balzac thereby quenched his thirst for a revenge to which he felt entitled.

We cannot place too much weight, however, on what amounts to the whims of overcharged emotions and conclude erroneously against his like for Liszt and above all against his respect for him as a musician. Even at the height of his rage, he never cast aspersions on his rival as a pianist. He loved a "soulful discharge in the Lisztian manner" (G 460). During the storm of 1844, and after it had subsided, Liszt remained for him what he had always been, a magnificent performer attaining "the heights of a poet" and a "divine translator" of divinity. In the "Lettre sur Kiew" of 1847, published in the *Revue de Paris*, he coupled him with Berlioz as one of "the last voyagers of the great family of artists" (LK 547), and less than a year before his death continued to praise the man with the "iron fingers."[49] Deep inside him, Liszt had always remained "the Paganini of the piano."

Byron, Chateaubriand, Senancour, Sand, and Lammenais influenced Liszt much more than did Balzac who, on the other hand, gained much from the association. The mission of Art, the social universality of Genius—these were common concerns of theirs, concerns related, for Liszt, to an acceptance of the newer, more abstract (for Balzac) art of Weber, Schubert, and Beethoven. Through the example of Liszt's art came an intensification of spiritual attitudes toward the art of music, its more effusive as well as its more incisive moods. It would be difficult to conceive of Balzac's response to the religious, the idyllic, and the heroic in Beethoven in the absence of the Lisztian dimension in his life, and it will always remain interesting to speculate what adjectives he might have found to welcome the *Faust Symphony*, or even more so, the *Dante Symphony*.

Hector Berlioz

While Balzac listened to Liszt's Beethoven, he read about him in the panegyric writings of Hector Berlioz. Balzac knew Berlioz before 1833, the year he dedicated *Ferragus* to him, and was on sufficiently intimate terms with him toward the end of his life to lend him his pelisse for a trip to Eastern Europe. By then an expert on the cold winters of Russia, Balzac delighted in being of such practical service. Perhaps the strongest written testimony of the friendship came in a letter of June 12, 1850 when the novelist, now married and back from a second Russian journey, received from the composer these reverential words, through whose obfuscation glowed much sincerity: "Dear and admired master, I learn simultaneously of your marriage and of your return. I haven't seen you since the eve of my departure for Russia three enormous years ago. Have you ever thought of the torment that certain impassioned souls experienced in seeing the features of their idols only in the reflection of the reflection of a mirror placed next to them, when by a simple movement of conversion the living idol could appear in reality? . . . This torment I experience about you; so let the mirror pivot and let yourself be seen in person. In less nonsensical terms, tell me when I shall be able to come to clasp your hand, and to beg you to introduce to Mme de Balzac one of her most humble servants."[50]

At the source of Berlioz's esteem lay his fondness of Balzac's novels and, irregular though their encounters were, his pleasure in their chats. In like fashion, Balzac did not conceal his interest in the unrewarded composer, following at close range the peripeteia of his career, applauding his concerts, and encouraging him on occasion with well intentioned flattery. A remark like "Your concert hall was *a brain*" elated Berlioz in 1839.[51] After the failure of *La Damnation de Faust* in 1846, Balzac wisely induced him to go to Russia where his baton alone would assure him a minimum of 150,000 francs. He even saw him to the stagecoach on the day of his departure.

Yet, besides the single dedication of a short work and a passing mention in *La Muse du département*, the name of Berlioz is as strange to *La Comédie humaine* as it is to the works of Hugo. No mention is made also in the correspondence. One might expect that *Benvenuto Cellini*, which caused so much grumbling in Paris in September of 1838, and so many hostile rumblings in the press, would have loosened Balzac's clamp of silence, especially since he was at that time at the height of his melomania. One might also expect that the *Roméo et Juliette* symphony of 1839, with its many startling innovations, would have done the same. Instead, all we find is a passing reference in a piece he did in 1842 for *La Revue Parisienne* called "Les Amours de deux bêtes" to the symphony's Queen Mab scherzo. It is, to be sure, in praise of the composer "who extended the limits of the instrument maker's art" and whose music is "divine." The scherzo is "delicate and delightful" (ADB 326). But the praise says little, and is not woven into more substantial works. The most plausible reason for the silence must be found in the unconventionality, even oddity, of Berlioz's innovative aesthetics in comparison with the accessibility of Rossini's compositions and of Liszt's executions; Balzac did not possess the musical sophistication to grasp Berlioz's endeavors, and he did not care to strain a friendship over such matters. The extravagance and the bombast bewildered him; it was enough to limit his remarks, as he did in the "Lettre sur Kiew," and couple him with Liszt as one of "the last voyagers of the great family of artists," followed by a bit of questionable history:

> [They] didn't mention a word to me about their travels in that great empire where they made considerable money with their knouts as orchestral conductors. Berlioz, probably impressed by that perfect accord between the people and the tsar, saw quite well he had nothing to do in a country full of harmony. What a magnificent organ point hovers between Archangel and Warsaw, from Kiachta to the Black Sea, from the Gulf of Kamchatka to the Gulf of Finland. Those two musicians, attracted by the rumor of the tsar's passion for music, recognized that he was the author of a score quite superior to all their symphonies and fantasies. Speak to me more convincingly, if you can, of a single voice that vibrates from Lake Baikal to Lake Poipous, and from America to Asia, with the accompaniment of the hunter's cornets. . . . [LK 547-548]

In turn, Berlioz hardly mentions Balzac in his various writings, including the *Mémoires*, and when he does, generally after the latter's death, his judgments are as barbed. So are his judgments of Stendhal, Gustave Planche, and other persons, especially men of letters whose musical opinions he regarded with open scorn, for "the majority of great poets do not feel music or they only have a taste for trivial and childish melodies."[52] Balzac may have been one of those who in *A Travers chants* "are constituted for this beautiful art like the grisettes of rue Vivienne or the singers at the Vaudeville."[53] He is definitely relegated to the ugly category of the Grotesques, defined as "letterati who write . . . on matters of musical theory which they do not understand even in the most elementary way, using words whose meanings they do not know, men who become enamoured in cold blood of old masters never having heard a note of theirs, who attribute generously to them melodic and expressive ideas which these masters never had . . ., who admire with the same effusive heart two pieces they have lumped together, signed with the same name, one of which is truly beautiful, the other absurd; men, finally, who speak and write astounding buffooneries that no musician can hear without laughing."[54] The indictment is complete. Concerning Rossini and Italian music, the differences of opinion between Balzac and Berlioz were strong and would have infuriated both if debated *viva voce*. For Berlioz, no middle of the way existed, no compromise between the melodic and harmonic schools; his idols were born across the Rhine, not across the Alps. Balzac prudently avoided antagonizing the moody genius, and we note that while he may have been one of those whose "brain" was "deranged" by music, as Berlioz viewed the Grotesques, the composer-critic aimed his shafts more at the various Gustave Planches who posed as music critics than at his friend Balzac. "Balzac's folly was touching," he wrote; "he admired without either understanding or feeling and thought he was flushed with enthusiasm." But as for Planche, his insanity was, "on the contrary, irritating and stupid; he didn't understand, didn't feel, didn't know. . ."[55] Berlioz could not spank his "crazy" friend too heavily because, as it happened, a number of the musical ideas expressed by the novelist echo Berlioz's own opinions published in *Le Rénovateur*.

Again in this relationship, Balzac benefitted considerably. Three items—one biographical, one technical, and one intellectual—in three novels illustrate this. It has been acknowledged that the historical counterpart of Dr. Bénassis in *Le Médecin de campagne* was Dr. Amable Rome, whom Balzac had met in the Dauphiné in 1832. But we should not overlook the likelihood of Berlioz's own father, also a medical doctor and a ubiquitously beloved benefactor, described by Berlioz when he answered Balzac's probing questions about the Dauphiné. Many personal traits and social outlooks of the physician who transformed a languid institution for cretins into an active and prosperous cantonal organization coincided with those of Berlioz *père* as well as with those of Rome.

A second and more significant influence may be detected in the mortuary mass for Mme Jules at the end of *Ferragus*. The choir singers are stationed in the six lateral chapels of Saint-Roch in Paris, a disposition of voices that recalls a similar arrangement in Berlioz's *Requiem: messe des morts*, whose Romantic evocation of the terrors of Judgment Day requires a huge chorus and five orchestras with groups of trumpets placed to the north, south, east, and west, destined to sound forth the fearful music that is to raise the dead from their tombs. The spirit and effect of this setting are captured by Balzac in his description of a majestically macabre "Dies Irae" in Saint-Roch emanating from the voices in the lateral chapels when they join those on the altar and in the choir loft. Surrounded by the shrill, young sonorities of the choir boys and the deep tones of the older males, the listener trembles together with the vaults of the church in the presence of the "strident harmonies" (F 111) that recreate the thundering utterance of God the avenger. Berlioz's *Requiem* was first performed for General Danrémont's funeral in 1837, that is, several years after *Ferragus*. But in 1825 (July 10) and in the same church of Saint-Roch, Valentino had presented the composer's *Messe solennelle* for large orchestra, a work principally impressive through its "Judgment" theme, the *Credo* section entitled "Interum venturus est." If Balzac had not attended this performance, he would have heard about it, and he probably heard it two years later, in Saint-Eustache, when Berlioz himself conducted it.[56] Balzac knew that Berlioz inserted the "Dies Irae" into his *Symphonie fantastique* which was performed with clamorous aftermath in 1830 and again in 1832, when the music critic of *L'Artiste* exclaimed in wonder that "the infernal *Dies Irae* . . . is sung to the din of shouts, laughter, [and] the dances of sorceresses and monsters," and that it "freezes us in astonishment and fright."[57] Musical allusions in *La Duchesse de Langeais*, which also antedates the *Requiem* but postdates the *Messe solennelle*, reflect the forbidding effect of the composition. In *Ferragus*, the torrent of Balzac's images easily flattered the composer of the *Symphonie fantastique*. He recalls the music in *Melmoth réconcilié* as well. Berlioz's fantasies of sound turned back Balzac's memory to the mysterious sensations he had experienced as a child engulfed by the harmonies of the "Dies Irae" in the cathedral of his native Tours. So while Balzac may not have understood his friend's aesthetics, he certainly felt some of its emotional thrusts.

Finally, the impact of Berlioz can be found in the intellectual dimension of *Gambara*, which was published while the ink was still wet on the last pages of the *Messe des morts*. Balzac's tale could not carry so much musical freight in the absence of some of Berlioz's opinions. One of the first references to music in it alludes to "that fulminating mass of the dead" (G 429). And further on, much of the advanced concepts presented by Count Andrea in his harangue in favor of Beethoven at the expense of Italian music condenses some of Berlioz's favorite arguments. Given the partly satirical nature of the story, one critic believes that the program of *Mahomet*, Gambara's imaginary opera, was worked out by Balzac with the help of his friend in the spirit of a comic hoax, despite the fact that Berlioz held religious fanaticism and politics to be unsuited to musical treatment.[58]

The plausible collaboration would suggest a tie between

Berlioz's use of the *idée fixe* in his *Symphonie fantastique* and *Harold en Italie* and a similar idea developed even further by Gambara who talks about the leitmotiv years before Wagner. Gambara also speaks of a new flexible melody patterned on the voices of nature, of a philosophy of tonal color, and of a blending of symphonic and vocal resources in musical drama, uncommon ideas at that time that Balzac valued enough to adopt, as he adopted, in relation to Meyerbeer's *Robert le Diable*, Berlioz's views on eclecticism which others did not share.

It would seem, then, that the friendship helped Balzac to realize the possibility of new developments in music. But not much more than this. He was at a loss to evaluate him as a musician. Berlioz had been labeled a composer of fragmentary melodies and forced harmonies, a person with a convulsive imagination that interfered too often with his technical achievement, and an artist who, as Grillparzer said, was a genius without talent. Regardless of the warm words of Gautier and Deschamps, the fact that he never achieved popularity in Paris either in the eyes of the general public with all of its acclaim of the *Symphonie fantastique* or in those of the critics Fétis and Paul Scudo, must have encouraged Balzac's reticence. But, as *Gambara* suggests, he stood ready to power his vision with Berlioz's eccentric views.

Frédéric Chopin

Unlike the gregarious Liszt and Berlioz, Frédéric Chopin chose his friends with circumspection, anxious to avoid the more boisterous practices of Romanticism. While others fought musical prejudices openly, he fought them unobtrusively by introducing new harmonies and a new melodic spirit into his compositions. Apart from George Sand, no one knew him better than his concert partner Liszt, who wrote a sympathetic book on him, and no one appreciated him more than Delacroix and Franchomme. Balzac was drawn to him at the height of his Parisian popularity and when he heard that Clara Wieck had performed some of his works in 1832. But however heartfelt his homage to the concertizer from the land of Mickiewicz, Balzac could not count him more than an acquaintance. They saw each other frequently at Sand's reunions on rue Pigalle in 1840 and at her home in Nohant in 1842, but not once do we find Balzac's name mentioned in Chopin's letters. Due to temperamental differences, Balzac's respect for Chopin's abilities was not returned. The pianist felt like Delacroix who, referring to his comfortable ennui at Nohant, wrote: "I lead a convent life here, one that resembles her [Sand] the most. No event varies its course. We expected Balzac who didn't arrive, and I'm not unhappy over it. He's a prater who would have disrupted that harmony of nonchalance in which I lull myself with great pleasure."⁵⁹

The occasions were many when the novelist delighted in what Bixiou describes as "the talent that the pianist Chopin possesses to such a high degree to mimic people" (HA 807). But many more were the occasions when he sat in rapture listening to him play the instrument which, it has been said, never existed except under his fingers, the instrument on which he could articulate the most subtle shades of feeling. In addition, their musical tastes coincided in a variety of ways: in their like for Bach and Mozart, in their immense admiration for Rossini and for the delicacy of Bellini's melodic line, in their appreciation of the roulade, and in their wonderment at Meyerbeer's *Robert de Diable*. Both, too, knew less of Weber than of other composers, and knew little of Mendelssohn, even less of Schumann, and both had nothing particular to say about the music of Berlioz, Halévy, and Auber. Balzac's reservations at the end of *Gambara* about Meyerbeer's melodramatic and blatant opera find concurrence in Chopin's later disenchantment with the composer's works generally. In what concerns Beethoven, however, the coincidences weaken. While Chopin, despite his reductionist declaration that for him there existed only the German school, accepted the "athletic" and "roaring" genius with diffidence on grounds that he really never possessed a Germanic spirit for music,⁶⁰ Balzac felt much too awed before the Fifth Symphony to harbor such disquietude.

Chopin was the first in Balzac's musical circle to believe exclusively in the preeminence of non-descriptive music. The matter is of little relevance, however, since Balzac regarded him as a pianist and not at all as a composer. Informed as he was by both the sensual and mystical elements of the art, he saw in the Pole essentially a performer of Raphaelesque perfection, a poet of the infinite, with the winsomely communicative power of a love song. The captious opinion that Balzac was wont to extoll the abilities of anyone who regaled him with friendship is belied in this case. For although he new Liszt much better, and although Chopin retained a dreamer's aloofness from the world around him, Balzac nonetheless placed him a notch above the Hungarian. As a "demon," Liszt was fascinating; as an "angel," Chopin was preferable. Rhetorical verve took second place to eloquent intimacy. Chopin created an illusion of friendly communication through a constant softening of the blunt edges of form. The descriptive, pictorial approach to music remained foreign to him. He rendered moods of melancholy and depression with lyrical sensitivity, never with trite sentimentality. This Balzac admired more than the energy of Liszt. "Chopin is well superior to him." Of the Polish pianist he wrote one of his finest appraisals, alluding less to the musician than to the soul that makes itself perceptible. He may have been thinking of the "Berceuse," suggests

Hucher,[61] as he may have been recalling the "Fantaisie-imprompu" of 1834 when he said that beyond the composer's thought exists the performer's soul. And when Balzac sought a genuinely poetic thought, he hoped his imagination would encounter something radiant, "as if a Chopin were striking a note on the piano; the hammer is awakened by the sounds which vibrate in his soul, and a vast poem then comes to life."[62]

* * *

Balzac knew his celebrated musician friends less as musicians than as people who experienced material and social difficulties and who supplied him with anecdotes. The agony of genius he could imagine by looking into himself and by giving literary vicissitudes a musical cast. Still, Rossini, Liszt, Berlioz, and Chopin constituted significant presences in his life. Other composers and connoisseurs pale by comparison: Auber and his modest, albeit flattering, collaboration in *Modeste Mignon*; Sauvageot, formerly concert-master of the Opéra, and his role in procuring a violin for Balzac; Giuseppe Mercadante and the autograph he gave Balzac for the Hanski collection;[63] his physician Dr. Knothe and the occasional musical advice he supposedly gave Balzac, in recognition of which he may have been the intended recipient of the Stradivarius in 1849; Habeneck and his "magic baton"[64] which opened so many avenues of appreciation onto Beethoven; Marquis de Belloy and his central role in the conception of *Gambara*; Cherubini, Ambroise Thomas, Halévy, Adam, Hérold, even Paganini and Meyerbeer. There is no evidence that he formed earnest personal ties with all of them, but the composite picture suggests more than a casual contact with the world of music, a world he tried to put into studied perspective as a zealous pupil of Jacques Strunz.

CHAPTER IV

AN OTHERWISE FORGOTTEN TEACHER

The Life of Jacques Strunz

Balzac tended to categorize musicians with epithets of convenience; Rossini represented melody, Liszt harmony, Berlioz descriptive music, Chopin pure music, Meyerbeer grand opera, and Paganini creative virtuosity. Each category furnished insights. But he needed to develop another area of knowledge to buttress those insights: the science of composition. Such technical background he could not have acquired in conversation with his musician friends. Therefore, he looked for an instructor to give him the authority to approach with confidence the musical dimension of *La Comédie humaine* and in the process to sound reasonably knowledgeable with his friends.

The responsibility fell upon Jacques Strunz. His existence and achievements have been obscured beyond memory in the annals of music, but he was well enough known during his lifetime for Balzac to entrust him with his formal musical education. His origin remains unclear, although Fétis believed that he was born in the small Bavarian village of Pappenheim in 1783,[1] into a modest middle class family that laid great stress on the study of music. A respectable violinist at fourteen, or possibly a flutist, he was sent to study composition in Munich, where his talents gained him entry to the Prince's chapel. As a youth, he was rather waggish, delighting in the little malices that charmed the gallant court remembered in Musset's *Fantasio*. The fad of virtuosity oriented his performances toward variations on known melodies which he embroidered with arpeggios, pizzicati, and trills. The jealousy of others and his own aggressive disposition coupled with a few questionable escapades made him leave the court and travel through Germany, Holland, England, and France, everywhere to the accompaniment of applause. But this type of plaudit did not satisfy his aspirations. More and more he veered away from easy displays of bravura and assumed instead the role of musical philosopher, envisioning glorious adventures in grandiloquent scores—virtuosity of another sort, but, to his way of thinking, more sophisticated and significant.

Paradoxically, he is next seen in Paris at seventeen as a band leader for an infantry regiment which he followed to the very battlefield of Marengo in 1800, and afterward to a garrison in Antwerp. It was here, during a lively scene, that he is supposed to have grandly slapped a colonel across the face for insisting that he play a number he considered mediocre. Thanks to the propitious intervention of friends, he left the military and began composing. A Violin Concerto received favorable attention, a *Messe solennelle* was performed in a cathedral, and a comic opera, *Bouffarelli ou le Prévôt de Milan*, gained acceptance at the Brussels opera theatre. Years later, in 1818, the Théâtre Feydeau performed another comic opera of his, *Les Courses de New-Market*, which met with no success. Flute, horn, and cello concertos also appeared bearing his name.

Throughout his visionary speculations persisted, focussed on the aesthetic value of gigantic musical effects, of enlarged sonorities, and of cantatas or operas portraying whole nations. Once he put some of his theories into practice when he improvised, within a few days, a heroic cantata in honor of Napoleon's visit to Antwerp. Encouraged by its notable success, he returned to Paris in 1808, but owing to his inability to apply himself and to his incorrigibly endless talk, he accomplished next to nothing, squandering most of his time inveighing against human folly. Soon he was again forced to accept a position with the military, this time as an inspector, in which capacity he journeyed, during the Restoration, to Africa, Asia, and those sections of Europe blighted by the Spanish War. With an ineptness comparable to that of Balzac, years before they met, he ruined himself financially in naïve investments so that when he next appears in Paris, in 1831, he is a penniless composer and part-time conductor. One of his favorite topics of conversation related to his great dream: a grand opera with extraordinary melodies and harmonies, supported by a massive orchestration. As author of "La Dernière pensée de Weber" and a confirmed Weberian, he spoke often of his idol and of *Der Freischütz*. As a composer for wind instruments, he emphasized woodwinds and brasses and discussed their uses.

Then in 1834, the Théâtre Nautique of the Salle Ventadour organized pantomime ballets "accompanied by water effects" and it was Strunz who was commended in *La Revue musicale* as the composer-arranger of the first show. Music from *Guglielmo Tell* and *Les Ondines* was "partly composed and partly arranged by M. J. Strunz, a distinguished composer to whom we are indebted for a rather large number of quartets and quintets for wind instruments. . . . The numbers borrowed from other composers are chosen with discernment and well arranged; those composed by M. Strunz himself are nicely effective and orchestrated with as much elegance as purity. There is a particular merit in the composition of scores like these, and in this endeavor M. Strunz has shown great ability."[2]

Later that year, the same theatre embarked on an abortive plan to install a German opera company, and it relied on Strunz's aid to reveal *Fidelio* and *Euryanthe* to the Parisian public. *La Gazette musicale* contributed simultaneously the opinion that "M. Strunz's talent, his respect for true music and his quality as a German make him in all respects the special person whose collaboration is necessary."[3] As artistic director, he was to recruit in Germany singers, a chorus, and the necessary brass instrumentalists for the undertaking. Again one read in *La Revue musicale* about Jacques Strunz, his qualifications as a composer of "a large number of excellent pieces for wind instruments,"[4] his mission across the Rhine, and the disappointing decision of the board of directors to renounce the idea after their envoy had hired most of the personnel needed. The Théâtre Nautique enjoyed as brief an existence as the Théâtre de la Renaissance, where Strunz had also become musical director, and for whose performance of *Ruy Blas* he had written an overture and intermission music. In 1835, both before and after his tenure at the Renaissance, he received a tribute in *La Gazette musicale* over his appointment as singing master of the Opéra Comique: "This is an excellent selection about which we can only congratulate the able administrators of this theatre."[5]

Balzac had met the "talented composer"[6] about this time at the home of Maurice Schlesinger. It is a simple matter to imagine the ease with which the collaboration between the novelist and the wandering musician began, Balzac out to learn the mechanics of music, Strunz hoping to defy his misfortunes by inviting celebrity through an association with a great literary figure. Balzac delighted in absorbing all he could about the mysteries of tonality, modulation, movement, form, interval, plagal cadence, rondo, recitative, triplet, allegro, andante, stretta, cavatina, contralto, diminished seventh, augmented fourth, tonic, subdominant, baritone, tutti . . ., all terms he displayed with the boast of a parvenu in *Gambara* and *Massimilla Doni*. The collaboration prospered also because of a similarity of views such as an admiration of Rossini, of desires such as a dream of writing an opera, and of qualities such as a bold intuition. Both were visionaries, but Strunz lacked the energy for creation that Balzac possessed to an astounding degree. It was the tutor, then, who turned over a number of seemingly eccentric ideas to his pupil, that he might in turn bestow upon them some kind of literary permanence. Vast conceptions and successive failures—the subject matter of much that is romanced in *Gambara* was inspired by "the good old German musician," twenty years the novelist's senior.

The tutorial period lasted but a few years and was over before 1840. Strunz left Balzac with a usable understanding of the science of music, not necessarily in its subtle technicalities and intricacies but in the nature of the difficulties inherent in the broad aspects of composition. Strunz was still believed in Paris in 1846, and Fétis located him back in Munich in 1849, enjoying a late inheritance. He disappeared from Balzac's life as unobtrusively as he had entered it, an important contributor to the segment of his pupil's human epic concerned with music. Balzac's most effective musical friend was also his most humble, and not without gratitude was *Massimilla Doni* dedicated to him, thereby guaranteeing him the immortality he would never have achieved by cultivating his own artistic resources:

> My dear Strunz, it would be ungrateful of me not to affix your name to one of the two works I never would have been able to write without your patient complaisance and your kind attentions. May you find here, therefore, a testimony of my grateful friendship, for the courage with which you have tried, perhaps unsuccessfully, to initiate me to the depths of musical science. Whatever the case, you definitely will have taught me what difficulties and labors lie concealed in the genius who pens those poems that for us are sources of divine pleasure. In addition, you have provided me more than once with the little amusement of laughing at the expense of more than one supposed connoisseur. Some accuse me of ignorance, suspecting neither the counsels I owe to one of the best authors of feuilletons on musical works, nor your own conscientious assistance. Have I perhaps been the most unfaithful of secretaries? If this is so, then unwittingly I am certainly a traitorous translator, but I want nevertheless to be able to call myself always one of your friends. [MD 415]

The length of the dedication is a lasting inscription honoring the grave of an otherwise forgotten musician.

The Panharmonicon

The "Panharmonicon" is an example of the ideas that Strunz imparted to Balzac. It was like an echo out of Hoffmann's *Die Automate*. In order to satisfy the multiple exigencies of his genius and the fantastic demands of the music he envisioned, Gambara had invented a stupefying "strange machine" (G 452) capable of replacing a whole orchestra. When he played it, "orchestral effects could not have been as grandiose as were the sounds of the wind instruments which recalled the organ and which blended marvelously with the harmonic richness of string instruments" (G 452).[7]

Such an instrument along with its sonorities might well sound apocalyptic, except for the fact that something similar and called by the identical name had been constructed in Vienna in 1804 by Johann Nepomuk Maelzel, the inventor of the metronome and a friend of Beethoven. Maelzel had brought it to Paris, and Beethoven wrote the *Battle Symphony* ("Wellingtons Sieg," op. 91) for it in 1813. It was a colossal barrel organ provided with forty-two instrument-bearing automatons,[8] and when the inventor enlarged it in 1812, it reproduced the sounds of violins, cellos, flutes, clarinets, trumpets, drums, cymbals, and the triangle. Weights acted upon cylinders, hammers struck strings.

Strunz knew Maelzel and, familiar with Balzac's interest in oddities, especially in those bordering on the grotesque, undoubtedly mentioned it to him. We should note also that *La Gazette musicale* of July 19, 1837, four days before *Gambara* was scheduled to appear, contained an article on a "Harmoniphon," a claviered hautboy, regarding which the writer mentioned bowed pianos like the "polyplectron," the "plectro-euphone," the "violicembalo," the "orchestino," the "aelodion," the "harmonichord," the "apollonicon," the "terpodion," and many more.[9] Through several of them, Balzac implemented his fancy. His panharmonicon clearly expands Maelzel's technically, and transcends it in effect. The idea of the extra manuals is built into the apollonicon, a large chamber organ with two keyboards and barrels, forty-five stops, and six manuals. The pedal work and dynamic compass of Gambara's instrument suggest the harmonichord, basically a revolving cylinder set in motion by a pedal worked by the foot, with finger pressure producing all gradations of tone, including the power of swelling or diminishing the sound of a sustained note. We should note, too, the friction instrument, the terpodion, for its shape: a square-like piano spanning six octaves, as well as the physharmonica, a mechanism placed under the piano's keyboard in order to sustain the melody. The long vibrating tones implied in Balzac's description of the panharmonicon remind us of it. No object could have better functioned as an objective correlative of the high-flown personality of Gambara than his "bizarre instrument" which was "as large as a grand piano, but with an additional organ case, . . . the bells of some wind instruments and the sharp mouthpieces of some reeds" (G 452).

More than a development of Father Castel's eighteenth-century ocular harpsichord that had interested Voltaire, the panharmonicon, without color structures, produced the sounds of strings, brasses, and woodwinds in Dionysian combination. More than a coarse anticipator of the pianola and the gramophone, it reproduced a dream that lies beyond them: the sighing and disorder, sweep and magic, oceanic froth and fury of the orchestra of the future. The concept leaves behind even the instrumental innovations of Debussy, Richard Strauss, Respighi, and Stravinski, and adumbrates the yet unexplored peripheries of electronic combinations.[10]

The Social Mission of Music

Any number of ideas concerning the social mission of music passed between the "philosopher" Strunz and Balzac. What Liszt called the great religious and philosophical synthesis in his six articles *Zur Stellung der Künstler* of 1835, the models for which could be found in the writings of Claude-Henri Saint-Simon as well as in those of Ballanche, enticed the maladjusted bohemian whose artistic life had been spotted with adversities. The Saint-Simonians recognized that an art that appeals directly to the heart is capable of moving the masses by contagion. Fourier in particular located music centrally in his plan for a new industrial world. If the symbolism of Gambara's *Mahomet* is any indication, Strunz combined his reveries about new music with visions of an artist-priest, a vatic figure, entrusted with the moral upbringing of mankind. Lifted out of his old and unsanctified social context, the artist was to be privileged in freedom above the masses. Emile Barrault's manifesto of 1830, *Aux Artistes: du présent et de l'avenir des beaux-arts*, formulated for the artist generically what Victor Hugo formulated for the poet and Liszt and Berlioz for the musician. Berlioz crusaded for higher standards through his cult of Beethoven, using all forms of ridicule, irony, and despair in his criticisms of the musical situation in Paris, and Liszt through his attempts at reorganizing concert life, at instigating the establishment of new schools and libraries, at proposing to stimulate creative activity by conventions of musicians and prizes for exceptional works, and at adopting a firm stand against the inferior quality of public appreciation and the ravages of poor instruction. The new utopian state that would erect a temple to Art would obviate Strunz's need to deprecate human folly. Enlightened by Strunz and the others, Balzac eagerly expressed his own views in *Des Artistes*.

The artist's ruling social role determines his mission. "Kings command nations during a given period of time," he wrote; "the artist commands entire centuries" (Art 221). Even when he shed his Saint-Simonian convictions (a few years before he met Strunz), he reiterated the notion of the artist-priest.

Balzac's sympathy with his Strunz's social fancies stopped short of a demand for total freedom which would isolate the artist from his milieu. Even if social involvement were not art's essential function, Balzac would not deny the fundamental interdependence of the human species he was portraying in *La Comédie humaine*. If Strunz held to views of absolute freedom, Balzac's tentative comment is implicit in the social implications of *Gambara*, whose protagonist suffers the pain of isolation and the liberation of superiority. He walks in the shadow of Strunz. Is not Gambara, who claims that "every great talent is absolutistic" (G 425), caught between his desire to find "an immense framework which could contain effects and causes, for [his] music sets for itself the goal of painting a portrait of the life of nations from its loftiest viewpoint" (G 443), and his inability to communicate it to the society around him? But at the same time, if Gambara is the victim of his own transcendence, was not Strunz's dream of the musician's mission implied in the work dedicated to him, when Massimilla Doni, inflamed with the faith of a nineteenth-century Italian patriot, declares during a performance of *Mosè in Egitto*: "Moses is the liberator of an enslaved people! Remember this, and you will see with what religious hope the whole of La Fenice will listen to the prayer of the delivered Hebrews, and with what applauding thunder it will respond" (MD 556)?[11]

It was about this time that Giuseppe Mazzini wrote *Filosofia della Musica*, one of the most significant Romantic works relating to the sociology and future of music. Its tenets reached Balzac who, while unwilling to "give utility precedence over art" because "Beauty lies only in what seems useless," echoed the Mazzinian views later: "Every work of art, be it literature, music, painting, sculpture, or architecture, implies a positive social utility," and "All works of genius are the *summa* of a civilization and presuppose an immense utility" (MM 529, 531, 532). Yet society's pragmatic point of view may differ from that of the liberated artist, whom Balzac nobly urged, in *Des Artistes*, "never to forget to *cultivate art for its own sake*, [and] not to ask it for pleasures other than those it gives. . ." (Art 323).

When developed logically, these views embrace Lamennais's hope for a social regeneration based on the rehabilitation of the arts through a direct collaboration with the Christian religion. Although Balzac did not go so far, along with Vigny and George Sand he entertained the opinion that Art, as a cultural vehicle and religious expression, could contribute toward the solution of some of the gravest questions which torment mankind. Without overstressing the intellectual role of Strunz, we may conclude that without the old musician music may well have remained an isolated phenomenon for Balzac instead of becoming an integral part of the social structure.

Musicians and Society

The social organization of *La Comédie humaine* includes a variety of examples of nineteenth-century musical lives, ranging from composers and interpreters to amateurs and simple listeners. Gambara is but a piece in a mosaic as broad as that illustrating literature or painting. There are the bohemians, the bourgeois and the aristocrats, the genial and the competent, the mediocre and the gifted, the ambitious and the *ratés*, the young and the old.

The most endearing and artistically realized mirror many of the traits of Jacques Strunz. But the less savory characters also exist. In the creation of one of the latter, the uncompromising aversions of Strunz coincided with passing irritations of Balzac to shape, in one case, the portrait of the artistically accomplished but personally vain and dissembling Neapolitan singer and composer from Marseille. An epicurean socialite for Strunz, a Sandeau-Liszt hybrid for Balzac, Gennaro Conti is presented unsympathetically:

> [Conti's] art reflects that famous Italian jealousy that induced Carlone to murder Piola and that got Paesiello a stiletto stab. This terrible envy lies hidden under the most gracious fellowship. Conti does not have the courage of his vice; he smiles at Meyerbeer and congratulates him when he would rather tear him apart. He feels his own weakness and assumes a pose of strength; for he possesses the vanity to display feelings which could not be farther removed from his heart. He pretends to be an artist who receives his inspiration directly from heaven. Art for him is something saintly and sacred. . . . He is a visionary, a demon, a god, an angel. . . . Just listen to him: the artist is a missionary, art is a religion that has its priests and must have its martyrs. . . . You admire his convictions, but he himself believes in nothing. . . . Finally, he has an insatiable thirst for applause; he

apes everything and mocks everything. . .; he prefers to be a man of genius like Rossini rather than a performer with the forcefulness of Rubini. . . . Conti, like many artists, is dainty; he likes his comfort, his pleasures; he is natty, elegant, well-dressed . . .; he loves no one but himself. That he possesses a fine talent, enough to overwhelm even the diffident Calyste, means little to this characterization. Camille may well say that more than a voice he is a soul, but his vanity and ambition subtract a telling score from his moral worth. [B 399ff]

Conti's personality is akin to that of the far less talented M. de Bartas, a self-centered musician whom Balzac describes with Theophrastian conciseness as a singer with "enormous pretentions" who "paraded himself, . . . feigned modesty," and "went from group to group [during a party] to receive compliments" (IP 533).

Without the background of personal annoyances, Balzac's other musical characters fare far better as individuals than Conti. His most striking portraits relate to a different class, socially undistinguished and often anomalous, but for that not less touching and amiable. Despite his success, a "strolling player" like Conti disassociates himself quickly from professionals of higher integrity like Bricheteau, Gambara, Schmucke, or Pons. By being more acceptable as human beings, they are to that extent more complete.

Observations about the conditions of music and musicians fill some of the most rewarding pages of *Le Cousin Pons*, whose protagonist reminds us immediately of Strunz. The original title of the novel, *Le Vieux Musicien*, subsequently called *Les Deux Musiciens*[12] to take into account his German friend Schmucke, points to Balzac's good German musician, "one of those men born old" (FE 65). There is some evidence that Sauvageot, the venerable violinist and "one of the most celebrated connoisseurs of bric-a-brac" who owned "the most beautiful collection in Paris,"[13] served as Sylvain Pons's historical counterpart, except for the fact that he was not, like Pons, like Strunz, a composer. Both the grotesque Pons and the bohemian Strunz remained composers of the third order, despite the former's Prix de Rome and the latter's great heroic cantata for Napoleon. Both had a certain melodic gift that they put to use in composing romances—Strunz for the *Chansonnier des Grâces* of 1815, Pons for those who appreciated the kind of tune "cooed by our mothers"—as well as more serious scores. Both were connected with the Théâtre Feydeau, and both were conductors for an enterprise that attempted to realize an opera for the people.

Had the proper persons given Pons reasonable support, he could have become, by implication, not a first rank artist like Rossini, but a respectable composer like Hérold. Without the support, publishers ignore him, the several operas and operettas to his name notwithstanding. He finds himself "soon drowned in the tide of German harmony and in the Rossinian productions," and suffers an "exorbitant" lack of recognition (CP 530, 531). Ironically, though not unusually in Balzac's Darwinian world, the capable Pons is replaced as conductor of a small theatre orchestra by a talentless violinist and incidental composer, Grangeot, who has taken advantage of an actress' protection. Resigned, Pons consoles himself in his gourmandise and in his Italian-acquired hobby, knick-knacks and art objects, that devour the greater portion of his savings. Unlike Sauvageot, who willed his collection to the State to be housed in the Louvre, Pons remains ignorant of the value of his innocently assembled museum, and his ingenuousness quickly lures a covetous society made up of Madeleine Vivet, Amélie Camusot, the janitress Mme Cibot, Fraisier, Poulain, Remonencq, and the sly art dealer Elie Magus. The same ingenuousness that had thwarted his success as a musician causes his death by hepatitis in 1845.

By arousing our compassion, isolating the modest conductor's two human passions and making an artist of him, Balzac underscores the injustice of Pons's lot. "A beautiful performance of some choice pieces used to make him cry," because "his soul lived in tireless admiration of the magnificence of human labor, that beautiful combat against the workings of nature" (CP 531, 533). The novelist summarizes respectfully: "The genius of admiration, of understanding, the sole faculty by which an ordinary man becomes the brother of a great poet, is so rare in Paris, where all ideas resemble travelers passing through a hostelry, that we must grant Pons our respectful esteem" (CP 531). A sensitive individual, he always finds the things of life discordant with the ideal that he has created for himself, and his unassuming nature compels him to accept reluctantly the disagreements that exist between reality and the harmony of his spiritual being.

Oddly enough, the winner of the Prix de Rome knows nothing about harmony, counterpoint, and orchestration, subjects in which, needless to say, Strunz was quite proficient. How the coveted prize was ever granted to a musician with such technical deficiencies remains unclear, unless the anomaly was Balzac's way of stressing the importance of melody and of creating an ironic juxtaposition with another recipient of the Prix, Berlioz, whose qualities stood opposite to those of Pons. Whatever the explanation, here Balzac is guilty of an irregularity.

Pons finds solace in his alter ego, Wilhelm Schmucke, an

incomparable teacher but a naïve and distracted individual. Good, simple, and candid, he too becomes the prey of the material greed of others. Before meeting Pons in 1834, he had served as chapel master of the margrave of Anspach, and as harmony teacher of the two Granville daughters, Mmes de Vandenesse and du Tillet (FE), of Lydie Peyrade (SMC), and of his favorite among these, the heroine of *Ursule Mirouët*. Inasmuch as Germans, imagines Balzac, "know how to play all musical instruments naturally" (CP 543), theatre director Gaudissart hires him to play in Pons's orchestra and as *entrepreneur de copies*, a position of some responsibility. Schmucke's knowledge of harmony, counterpoint, and orchestration complemented Pons's melodic gifts and readiness to work, an artistic partnership that parallels that of Balzac-Strunz. But the historical combination achieved more than the fictional. Constantly denied recognition, Pons and Schmucke see their novel compositions described with the word "progress" by connoisseurs who never inquire about the composers. As Strunz implied many times, an artist's life is an endless struggle against a society attracted only by the schemes of a Gennaro Conti. "In Paris, especially since 1830, no one succeeds without shoving *quibuscumque viis*, hard, a fearsome mass of competitors; then you need much too much strength in your loins, and the two friends had this gravel in their hearts, which impedes any ambitious movement" (CP 542). Schmucke in particular cannot cope with the demands of such an existence: "Though a great composer, Schmucke could only be a demonstrator, so much did his character refuse to assume the boldness required of a man of genius to make himself be known in the field of music" (CP 538). If with Pons music yields little by little to his love of art objects and gastronomic creations, with Schmucke it dies in dream and lack of ambition. The former is an artist by taste, spirit, and pleasure, and the latter by youthful imagination, purity of heart, and goodness of soul. In either case, as well as in that of Strunz, inadaptability to the established rhythm of society spells final failure.

More pragmatic are those musicians in Balzac's novels who can do what Strunz could not: cast aside their instruments in order to avail themselves of the material advantages of the business world, like the flutist in Pons's orchestra "who throws his flute to the dogs to become a banker" (CP 584). There are those, too, like Sauvageot (he appears in *Le Cousin Pons* under his real name) who supplement their modest income as instrumentalists with profitable sidelines. And finally, there are those who increase their annual revenues by moonlighting, like the sub-head of the Ministry of Finance who plays the clarinet for the Opéra-Comique (PB).

The mediocre members of any profession are numerous, and Balzac could not overlook even this reality. Besides the uninspired violinist Grangeot (CP), we might mention Fourchon, the windy clarinettist in Blangy in 1823, and Vernichel, the scratchy violinist for public dances, both uninhibited drunkards (Pa), as well as Facino Cane's two vulgar blind companions, a violinist and a flageoletist (FC). There are, too, the stumbling dilettantes like du Châtelet and de Bartas (IP). These and others, ranging from respectable professionals to street players, compare unfavorably with competent musicians like Collinet, who conducted at Birotteau's famous ball (CB), Steibelt (B), Schwabe (CP), and Gigelmi (G). A superb basso like Carthagenova (MD) stands out saliently, despite his brief appearance, in the society Balzac portrays, as does a genuinely great figure like Jacques Bricheteau, the organist of Saint-Louis en l'Ile, whose life represents a long and sincere devotion to his art, and who died in Rome as the organist of San Giovanni in Laterano (DA). But these artists—the Fourchons, Collinets, and Carthagenovas—are not developed sufficiently in the novels to contribute substantively to the overall movement of *La Comédie humaine*.

More frequently portrayed are those amateurs who reveal their love for the art through an occasional performance. Princess Gandolphini sings with an exiled Italian prince, Genovese, and his mistress, the famous quartet "Mi manca la voce" (AS). In this category, the most striking characters are those sensitive heroines who imbue music with psychological significance: Ursule Mirouët (UM), Modeste Mignon (MM), and Félicité des Touches (B). Indeed, so evolved are the feelings of Ursule and Modeste, and the ability of Félicité, that they deserve the classification of musicians in *La Comédie humaine*. Ursule, Schmucke's best pupil, traces her musical heritage back several generations, being the orphan of an army *capitain de musique*, Joseph, whose earlier wandering life in Germany resembles Strunz's, and being in addition the granddaughter of a renowned harpsichordist, organist, and instrument maker, Valentin. Her father brings to the reader's mind the oldest of the three Miroir brothers, all organists as well as harpsichordists in Paris toward the end of the eighteenth century, whom people came from great distances to hear in Saint-Germain-des Prés. In Ursule's life, music is a process of thought without words, a tacit transmitter of her intimate emotions to the man she loved.

Modeste appears even more gifted. She composes naturally, "as one can compose purely melodic ballads without knowing harmony," and sings when she wants to express her love, accompanying herself on the piano, "the confidant of so many young ladies" (MM 388, 448). Her quiet dedication contrasts with Félicité's questionable early motivation to learn music. The latter had become a "consummate musician" because she could not bear to see herself as the interior of "dolls who played the piano and acted pleasant while singing romances" (B 372). But later her interest becomes real to the point of learning harmony, counterpoint, and of composing two successful operas. She too confides in her piano, and not infrequently she has to stop playing when her eyes swell with tears. The list of such heroines could include others—for example, Pauline (LL and PC) and Luigia (DA)—who match their sisters in sensitivity and intelligence and to that extent appear as assets in the social structure, contributing to it the warmth they draw from their art. Any regeneration of society through Art would involve them. Except for her mental illness, Lydie Peyrade, "a musician capable of composing" (SMC 760), would be included in this group. Marianina (Sa), with her vocal gift and graceful modesty, already belongs to it.

Not all of Balzac's *musiciennes* enjoy favorable reputations; Gennaro Conti has counterparts. Josépha Mirah, Prima Donna of the Académie Royale de Musique though she is, and brilliant though her performances in *Guglielmo Tell* and *Robert le Diable* are (CBe, CP), leaves much to be desired on a personal level. So does Clarina Tinti, equally beautiful physically and vocally, but tainted with the volatile mores of the most capricious of mistresses (MD, AS). This operatic soprano embodies the ultimate in seductiveness, Balzac declares. He describes voluptuously the Sicilian Clarina who, "unfastening the cuffs of her dress, began to sing not in a voice destined for applause at the Fenice but in a voice troubled with desire" (MD 326). All open seductresses bear the mark of some cruelty.[14] Foedora, of course, surpasses all in heartlessness, epitomizing the loveliest and the ugliest in a courtesan, but she joins the ranks of Balzac's musicians more unprofessionally than professionally. Her cruel behavior outweighs her beautiful voice. In the light of Balzac's friendship with Rossini, the possibility that she resembles Olympe Pélissier is intriguing, but to support the parallel there is only the evidence of a brief description of her to Mme Hanska as an evil courtesan famous for her beauty. None of Balzac's *musiciennes* is as cold and tarnished as Foedora, from the early heroine harpist in *Jane la Pâle* to the late and splendidly talented Luigia in *Le Député d'Arcis*.

The final category that completes Balzac's musical scenario reveals aficionados like Duke Cataneo, Andrea Marcosini, Prince Emilio Varese, Massimilla Doni, Capraja, and Vendramini, who make conversation about music their principal pastime. Somewhere in this group should also be included the notorious criminal Vautrin, alias Jacques Collin, who appears in various novels in many incarnations and with as many names as well as in as many roles, among them as Halpertius (DA), a Swedish philanthropist and music lover, Luigia's protector (DA). With them, a tableau of many facets and shades is complete. Not even the musical philistine Gambini (G) and the *castrato* Zambinella (Sa) are forgotten. They create an atmosphere in *La Comédie humaine*, one made tangible by the corresponding presence of great historical names—Malibran, Pasta, Paganini, Sontag, Rossini, Farinelli, Beethoven, Fodor, Moschelès, Mozart, Rubini, Chopin, Gluck, Liszt—and destined to secure for the field of music a palpable role in the vicissitudes and dreams of Balzac's restless society.

The true musician's vicissitudes and dreams differ from those of his fellow man the non artist, or the lesser artist, and create variances in reader reaction. Because of the purity of her devotion, Modeste Mignon's plight moves us more than Ester Gobseck's or Josépha Mirah's. If art enjoys a sacred mission, then at least theoretically the musician's place in society is central. But as society is constituted, this place remains minor because his endeavors appear pragmatically useless. Without Maecenases, he lacks leadership and awesomeness. Materially rather than spiritually motivated, his impact on those around him does not submit to immediate measurement; the merchant, the soldier, the usurer, the politician, the lawyer, and the criminal have a more immediate impact on society, and they are the ones, then, who stand out in Balzac's social history. The true musician's values do not function on expediency.

Balzac is concerned less with the competent or even brilliant professional à la Collinet or Tinti or Conti or Steibelt—people who find their places in society by posing no great challenge to it—than the genuinely creative talent, the hard-pressed, suffering artist. This person looms as a social misfit, belonging "to the amiable class of forgetters who give their time and their soul to others, just as they leave behind their gloves on all tables and their umbrellas by all doors" (FE 65). Pons, Schmucke, and Gambara, like Strunz, aroused poignantly Balzac's sense of justice because their human and artistic dignity remained unrecognized, and with it the potential of their contribution to mankind. Especially distressing is the fact that, like the poet, the musician knows immediately where he stands; without the benefit of illusion, he recognizes "like a plant" if he is in a "friendly or inimical atmosphere" (IP 538-539)—and Balzac's bohemians always "wither" in the latter. Strunz revealed to the moral historian the fictional possibilities of much unobtrusive lives, doubly harassed by magnificent visions and economic squalor. Plebeian origins often, weak temperaments (Schmucke), with original ideas that lie misunderstood (Gambara), inspiring jealousies (Pons)—these are the reasons for their lack of recognition and for their isolation in a century of bourgeois materialism. In *Des Artistes*, Balzac brings together his views of art and the artist:

> First of all, an artist . . . does not possess
> that understandable avidity for wealth that

animates all the thoughts of a merchant. If he runs after money, it's for a momentary need; for avarice is the death of genius. A creator's soul has too much generosity to make room for such a petty feeling. His genius is a perpetual gift . . . A work of art is a [powerful] idea . . . Yet in a sense thought is something against nature . . .; the arts are a misuse of thought. We don't . . . suspect the pains [that brought them to us] because we have amassed the legacy of twenty centuries. But we must not lose sight of the fact—if we want to understand the artist fully, his misfortunes, and the oddities of his terrestrial cohabitation—that there is something supernatural about the arts. The most beautiful work can never be understood . . . The artist, whose mission is to grasp the most remote relationships, to achieve prodigious effects by bringing two common things together, must often seem nonsensical. Where the whole public sees red, he sees blue. He is in such close touch with secret causes that he hails a misfortune, curses something beautiful, praises a fault, and defends a crime. He has all the symptoms of madness, because the means he uses always seem as far from their end as they are close to it . . . He becomes quickly his own obstacle to his social ties. Everything repels a man whose rapid movement through society ruffles people, things, and ideas . . . *A great man must be unhappy* . . . Now, the history of humanity is unanimous about the live repulsion and revolt that new discoveries excite . . . Then all manner of impassioned wrath falls on the artist . . ., so his apostleship and intimate conviction result in a serious accusation that all thoughtless people level against talented individuals . . . But an artist is a religion . . . [and] how do you make an ignorant mass understand that there exists a poetry independent of an idea . . ., then that there also exists a poetry of ideas. . .? [Art 225-230 passim]

Gambara is this kind of artist, a man who freed himself more and more from the pressures of an antagonized society, a creator who became increasingly isolated when he did not succeed in conquering it, a would-be high-priest who authored an ambitious and ill-starred work that slumbers in his memory as an unfulfilled appeal to the future. With all of his Strunzian overtones, the name of Gambara is synonymous with music in the social epic.

Near the beginning of his association with Strunz, Balzac had engaged in a brief physiognomical idealization of the Gambara-Strunzian type musician: Facino Cane's countenance becomes a dramatic symbol. The clarinettist, blind like his two companions, looms as "one of those phenomena that stop short the artist and the philosopher" (FC 69). His hallucinations of wealth constitute the principal concern of the story, but his image towers above them in what amounts to a fusion of integrity, nobility, intellect, and suffering. Elsewhere, Balzac provides us with a glimpse of the artist generically: "Few of those faces, originally so magnificent, remain lovely. Besides, the flamboyant beauty of their heads remains misunderstood. An artist's face is always exorbitant; its lines always fall beyond, or short of, the conventional that imbeciles call ideal beauty" (FYO 265). With Facino Cane, Balzac focuses on a particular artist, the musician: "Imagine the plaster death mask of Dante, lighted by the red glow of an argand lamp and surmounted by a forest of silvery white hair. The bitter and sorrowful expression of that magnificent head was intensified by his blindness, for his deadened eyes relived through his thought. It was as if a fiery glimmer emanated from them, a glimmer produced by a single, insatiable desire, inscribed in large, vigorous characters on an arching brow, scored across with as many lines as run through an old stone wall" (FC 69). Such a face could be chiseled above the words LE VRAI MUSICIEN in *La Comédie humaine*.

PART TWO

DEBATES, PREMISES, AND COMMENTS

CHAPTER V

FROM BEYOND THE ALPS AND RHINE

Melody Versus Harmony

Noting the rivalry between the proponents of Italian and German music, otherwise identified as the defenders of melody and the advocates of harmony, Stendhal pictured a full-scale war,[1] and in siding with the former he reflected dominant current opinion. Among the men of letters, however, the battle lines were blurred with mixed or eclectic views. In the first group, Musset, Deschamps, Senancour, Mérimée, Stendhal, and Gautier had no intention of crossing swords with Vigny, George Sand, Lamennais, Planche, Borel, and Hugo, who listed themselves in the second, for, with the exception of the critic Berlioz, the admirers of the German style sought less to replace Italian expression than to supplement its merits. The studied forms of Weber and Beethoven did not preclude the spontaneous beauties of Cimarosa and Rossini.

The outcries from both camps sounded militant, and Balzac saw fit to debate the rival viewpoints in *Gambara* and *Massimilla Doni*. Under Strunz's tutelage in particular, he had surveyed the history of the opposition that dated back to the seventeenth century. He learned of how the school of Louis XIV's great Florentine composer Lulli, based on objective expression, had yielded to the Neapolitan school of Scarlatti and Pergolesi with its wide range of innovations (including vocal *fioriture*, bel canto, and *castrati*); of how Rameau, after adhering to polyphonic structure, had declared in the late 1740's: "If I were thirty years younger, I should go to Italy: Pergolesi would become my model, and I should subject my harmony to that truthful declamation which must be a musician's sole guide";[2] of how the squabbling "Ramistes et Lullistes" had joined ranks in opposing the upholders of the Italian dispensation Grimm, Diderot, d'Holbach, Rousseau—during the "Guerre des Bouffons"; of how, after Benedetto Marcello's condemnation of the submission of many Italian composers to the whimsical tyranny of singers, Gluck's attachment to plain dramatic truth had been challenged unsuccessfully by his rival Piccini in a match during which the agitated partisans and not the composers had created all the furore; and of how opera in France, not long in the trough of any one tradition, had drifted toward fresh adventures, from Gluck by way of Méhul, Salieri, Lesueur, Spontini, and Berlioz, and from Piccini by way of Sacchini, Martini, Paesiello, and Rossini. Balzac was aware of these historical developments, though he may not have put them into a viable aesthetic perspective.

Mazzini published his treatise, *Filosofia della Musica*, in Paris in 1836, one and three years before *Gambara* and *Massimilla Doni* respectively. Balzac does not allude to it, but many of its ideas relating to the future of musical drama in terms of a balanced fusion of the melodic and harmonic schools parallel those of the novelist. Mazzini felt that music as an art accompanies the movement of civilization and that it is subject to the laws of progress.[3] The crepuscular melancholy of Romanticism, barring the isolated endeavors of various individuals, was not awake to its potential. In fact, it had more than estranged music from civic life, using it for sheer sensuous distraction and stripping it of any unity of purpose. A necessary reform—the "new music"—should blend melody, or individualism (symbolized by Rossini), with harmony, or collectivism in the sense of social unity. Such music would be rendered spiritual through the sanctity of faith or the religious infinite inherent in the German concept, and would be dynamically charged with the power of action inherent in the Italian. He advocated the adoption of local time and color to enhance musical drama's immediate meaning, the development of the choruses to create the atmosphere of collective individuality found in Mozart's *Don Giovanni* and Meyerbeer's *Robert le Diable*, the enlarged use of the recitative to free it from the slavery of cadenzas and arias, and the recognition of poetry as the sister and not the servant of music.

Mazzini's views form a synthesis of Balzac's ultimate resolution of the rivalry between Italianism and Germanism. On the surface, his stand seems as confused as Gautier's: fine insights laboring against indecisions. The gaps of a too quickly acquired knowledge and an insecure familiarity with the subject matter compelled him to bow in both directions simultaneously, for *Gambara* reveals his congeniality with the harmonic school and *Massimilla Doni* betrays the reverse in its averment of the primacy of the melodic. Yet Balzac's synthetic instinct sensed the value of varying styles of music without allowing them to become mutually exclusive. He pleaded for and against both schools with equal fervor, favoring what he deemed their assets and condemning their liabilities. Not by juxtaposing the two musical tales but by integrating them are we permitted to infer his sensible conclusion of a *juste milieu*, Mazzini's fusion of art and science, which became in his words "the noble alliance which allows us to blend in a single whole the beauty of melody and the power of harmony" (G 435).

Italian and French Music

With reservations, Balzac placed himself in the lineage of those like Rousseau and Stendhal who denied or distrusted French ability to produce great music. He criticized the "*pont-neufs*" (the popular street songs of merchants) of French music, and when he censured the low aesthetic standard of some Italian operas, his mouthpiece character Marcosini adds sarcastically: "I even prefer French music, and that's going a long way" (G 431). Elsewhere, Balzac showed a Stendhalian displeasure at that aspect of his compatriots' character that cloaked in frivolity an intense experience. To Massimilla's ecstatic comments about Rossini's interpretation of the drama of Moses, the French doctor adds: "Yes, that would make a charming air for a quadrille!" The Italian lady reacts severely: "Frenchmen! Frenchmen! always Frenchmen! . . . Yes, you are capable of using this sublime elan, this noble and elegant rejoicing, for your rigadoons. A sublime poem never receives open welcome in your eyes. The loftiest genius, saints, kings, the unfortunate—all that is sacred must undergo the shaft of your caricature. The vulgarization of great ideas with your quadrilles is caricature in music. With you, wit kills the soul, as analysis kills reason" (MD 362). Massimilla's criticism echoes Balzac's own of nine years before: "In France, mind stifles feeling"; this is a "national vice" (Art 220).

Just as we may understand the spirit of Rousseau's sallies which came at a time when the "French" school of dramatic music was represented by Lulli, Gluck, and Rameau, that is, by two foreigners and by a Frenchman who had admitted the superiority of the Neapolitan composers, so we may forgive Balzac who wrote at a time when French music meant Boieldieu, Auber, Adam, Halévy, Hérold, along with Berlioz who, greatness notwithstanding, was guilty of gross eccentricities. Balzac respected the French representatives, but he esteemed Rossini and Beethoven.

Yet, while Rousseau and Stendhal denied the French any future in the art, Balzac expressed more confidence. If he echoed the Genevan when he had Massimilla say to the doctor: "You belong to a nation whose language and genius are too positivistic for it to embrace music effortlessly," he had her add: "But France is also too understanding not to end by loving it, by cultivating it, and you will succeed here as you have succeeded in everything else" (MD 355). He thought more of French than of German as a language for opera; in Berlin in 1843 he found nothing particularly wrong with seeing plays like *Medea* and *A Midsummer Night's Dream* translated into German, but described a German version of Auber's *Fra Diavolo* as "an excellent preparation for sleeping."[4]

One reason for the poverty of French music, Balzac believed, stemmed from the lack of what Mazzini would have regarded as the idealistic stimulus provided by tense political conditions. *Gambara*, *Les Proscrits*, *Massimilla Doni* and other works endeared themselves to many an Italian patriot of the Risorgimento. Mazzini's confidence in Italian musical genius rested in part on immanent historical realities. After the Overture of *Mosè in Egitto*, Massimilla declares: "You Frenchmen, who not long ago occasioned the bloodiest of revolutions, in whose land the aristocracy was crushed under the paw of the popular lion, the day this oratorio will be performed in your theatres you will understand this magnificent lament of the victims of a God who avenges his people. Only an Italian could write such a fecund, inexhaustible, and completely Dantesque theme. Do you think it meaningless to dream of vengeance for just a moment?" At this point she utters her famous hyperbole, so abused by critics bent on proving the novelist's incorrigible Italianism: "Old German masters, Handel, Sebastian Bach, and you too, Beethoven—on your knees! here is the queen of the arts, here is Italy triumphant" (MD 357). Lifted out of their emotional setting, her words sound overstated; but placed within their patriotic context, they burst forth from the fervor of a citizen fired by the ideal of a united homeland. Balzac's characters reflect his thoughts on music, except when an overriding dramatic concern intervenes. In the case of Massimilla's exclamation, psychological truth becomes a determinant.

Camille Bellaigue exaggerates when he claims that Balzac accepted and professed all principles of Italian taste, and that he loved Italian music down to its very weaknesses which he transformed into beauty.[5] Balzac's criticism of Italian bad taste indicates an awareness that sensuous music appeals more facilely than intellectual music and that the transalpine composers had often sinned against art by catering to the uneducated wishes of the public. He respected Marcello's injunctions. Count Marcosini's invective, though designed to provoke Gambara into a discussion rather than to expostulate a creed, is too complete and too largely justified to reflect a simple exercise in debate:

> Compare the sublime productions of the author [Beethoven] about whom I have just spoken with what one generally calls Italian music: what inertial thoughts! what a dastardly style!

> Those uniform figures; those banal cadences; those eternal flourishes hurled about haphazardly whatever the situation; that monotonous "crescendo" made into a vogue by Rossini which today forms an integral part of every composition; finally, those nightingale imitations, create a kind of chattering, gossipy, sweetish music whose only merit depends on the singer's greater or lesser ability and on the nimbleness of the vocalizing. The Italian school has lost sight of the high mission of art. Instead of raising the crowd to its level, it has descended to that of the crowd; it has become popular only because it has accepted anybody's and everybody's liking by addressing itself to ordinary intelligences, those that form the majority. This fad resembles a prigging on a public street. And finally, the compositions of Rossini, who personifies this kind of music, as well as those of the masters who derive from him more or less, seem to me at best worthy of gathering people in the streets around a barrel-organ, and of accompanying the capers of Punchinello. [G 430-431]

Later, the Count persists, referring to "the tinsel of Italian music" (G 463). That this diatribe is not just a forensic play is suggested not only by Balzac's remarks on German music and Beethoven but also by his disapproval of certain standard practices: the vexing necessity of satisfying the egos of prima donnas with "those bravura and contrived arias to which [Italian] composers are condemned and which harm the general design of the poem" (MD 371), or Rossini's unfortunate lapses when he catered to public taste rather than to the organic demands of the musical situation. If Balzac loved Italian music passionately, he loved even more passionately his theory that music that denies itself a mission by considering its goal the sensuous display of song may not be honored as an art. He modified Musset's and Mérimée's fondness for vocal compositions when he insisted that "the composer who sings for the sake of singing is an artisan and not an artist." His song becomes "something of a melodic poverty" (G 433, 431).

The Unity of Melody and Harmony

When through Count Marcosini Balzac avers that Beethoven could not be understood in Italy because of the harmonic resolution of his climaxes, he did not imply, as did a number of his contemporaries simplistically, that Italian music was devoid of harmonic concepts. On the contrary, he associated Rossini with Haydn, Mozart, and Beethoven, praising him—despite the limitations implied by the Count's words—as a composer who made fine use of harmony, and in his scores he prefers indeed those sections that draw their effect from the emotional power of chords, such as the three-chord opening of *Mosè in Egitto* and the famous prayer in the second act. About *Mosè*, Massimilla says: "Dear Rossini, you did well to throw this bone to the *tedeschi* to chew on, those Germans who would deny we possess the gifts of harmony and erudition!" (MD 357), and she discourses on the "sinister melody which the master extracted from that profound harmonic composition, comparable to what is most complicated in German music, but resulting in something with which our souls get neither weary nor bored" (MD 357). Even more eulogistically, she refers to Rossini's harmonic "secret" that is found only in a rare number of works by human beings, for it "hurls" us for a while into "the infinite" where "endless melodies" are "chanted around God's throne." (MD 375).

Massimilla is still agitated by political fervor, and we are not prepared to accept all of her rhetoric literally. We must shrug when we read about the Tempo di Marcia: "Their Beethoven has not written anything which is more magnificent" (MD 372-373). But through this *boutade* peers Balzac's affinity for harmony. Emotionally drawn to melody, he was also intellectually conscious of harmonic expression. The March is an imposing and gladdening score, energized by forceful harmonies; the opera as a whole, uncharacteristic of Rossini, demands austerity of treatment because of its sacred subject (as Balzac noted in *La Duchesse de Langeais*), of its denouement permeated with a sense of divinity, and of its inspiration that unfolds along the harmonic lines of an oratorio. The roulades themselves, while abundant, are treated with consistent expressiveness. They differ in use from other compositions where "[they] and the soul of the singer are all there is," and where a mediocre performance renders everything meaningless (MD 373). Balzac appreciated the harmonic qualities of the score of *Mosè in Egitto*, and it is significant that he chose this opera in the composer's second manner as his novel's centerpiece, the kind of opera for which Stendhal accused Rossini of becoming German and of plunging into the "somber regions of the North," into "the night of harmony."[6]

Balzac's attachment to Italian music, however, centered around his love of melody. He always showed a special interest in experiencing its meaning, its power of permanence which survives time as in folksongs, and its faculty of psychological penetration which, Mazzini would concur, can succeed where Germanic greatness fails. "It is melody and not harmony that has the power to traverse the ages" (MD 377). It motivates the listener to sense a universality, a truth. Melody is for everybody, as his friend Zulma Carraud had written to him in 1833; harmony, counterpoint, chromaticism, and the like are for musicians.[7] Gambara, for instance, feels the weakness of Meyerbeer's Germanic structure that purports to depict the triumph of spirit over matter and of good over evil in *Robert le Diable*. The liberation from "the weight of Hell's enchantments" does not possess the sublimity deriving from the universal emotions demanded by the situation. Says the composer: "I needed another prayer from *Mosè*; I wanted to know how Germany would have fared against Italy, what Meyerbeer would have done to oppose Rossini" (G 466). The underlying principle, vindicated later by Verdi in the "Pace, mio Dio" aria from *La Forza del Destino* and in the "Ave Maria" from *Otello*, is an inspired melodic concept that endows the prayers with a blending of longing and confidence, hope and serenity. It springs for Balzac from an inner reserve of spirituality that shrouds its material origin, sublimating its humanity.[8]

Like Mazzini, Balzac urged composers to combine the Italian and German aesthetics. The human qualities of melody and the celestial qualities of harmony must complement each other's virtues. His tenet is best summarized by Gambara, sitting at the table of restaurateur Giardini and tempering the Count's invective with a warning: "There are many things that sound sensible to me in everything you have just said; but beware! Your pleading, by blighting Italian sensualism seems to incline toward German idealism, which is no less fatal a heresy. If men of imagination, of common sense, such as you, merely abandon one camp in order to cross over to the other, if they do not know how to remain neutral between the two excesses, we shall undergo eternally the irony of those sophists who deny progress, and who compare man's genius to this tablecloth, which, being too short to cover entirely signor Giardini's table, can only deck one end at the expense of the other" (G 432). Mozart's *Don Giovanni*, therefore, is for Balzac the finest opera written; it is perfection itself, "the only musical work in which harmony and melody are in balanced proportion" (G 459). All depends on an intuition of the correspondences between sound and thought, along with their disciplined utilization. An ability to set forth long lyrical lines over a full orchestra which delineates character in its texture would be the logical result of Balzac's advocacies in his search for perfect coordination. Several statements confirm the combination of melody and harmony: "The golden thread of melody always runs alongside the powerful harmony like a celestial hope; it embroiders it, and with what penetrating ability!" (G 463); "The flowers of melody lean on harmony as on a rich terrain" (MD 355). Balzac never consented to the extremes of theoreticians and grammarians of music, whom he compared to critics incapable of creation. Hence he maintained that the supposed dualism of harmony and melody must be regarded rather as a unity, with the "golden thread" of the latter subtending and fixing the former's fabric. Meyerbeer's finale was weak because it lacked melodic resources; Pons's music was weak because of the clumsiness of the harmonic texture which gave defective support to competent, overlying melodies.

"Italian sensualism" and "German idealism," then, or emotionalism and intellectualism, meant little ultimately to Balzac as abstract and isolated concepts. Both were valid if their values were accepted eclectically: neither volatile washes of unsupported melody nor floods of overbearing harmony. Melody should dominate, over a strong harmonic understructure to give it meaning. "Melody . . . must never break" in a vast composition, and harmony must provide "the background from which the groupings of the musical picture must stand out conspicuously" (G 457). For "music is both a science and an art" (G 434). If it is true that it speaks primarily to the heart whereas literature speaks primarily to the mind (G), it must not be forgotten that art proceeds from the mind and not from the heart (MD). At its origin lies inspiration, at its creation a disciplined labor. Melodic sequences, after all, do correspond to the movements of feeling and thought. For the more sensitive individual, they are, through various tonalities and rhythms, a direct expression of them. The harmonic ensemble, on the other hand, being a studied assessment of relationships where each chord is a structure in itself, corresponds less to movement than to a determined effect the composer wishes to create. Balzac's point of view is quite reasonable. Aided by these theses, he distinguished between excessive and insufficient harmony, and between two kinds of melodic expression: one exterior, without any intrinsic qualities, meaningful only if sung well, and subject to the mutations of time and custom, "small and paltry, second rate, everywhere the same, which relies on a hundred or so phrases that every musician appropriates, and which constitutes a more or less pleasant prattling that most composers live with"; and the other interior, personal, permanent, and fundamentally musical, "a type of purely human value" like folksongs, plainchants, or the symphonic and operatic productions of "the Homers of music" (MD 377).

A pedantic vertical concept of musical composition elicited in Balzac as much revulsion as an ingenuous horizontal concept. In practice he often belied his beliefs. But in theory he held to them. In order to understand his final thoughts on the matter, we must underscore Count Marcosini's exclamation and afterthought: "Long live German music! . . . when it knows how to sing" (G 431)—in other words, when it knows how to be Italian. Not surprisingly, almost all of Balzac's singers in *La Comédie humaine* are Italian (Conti, Tinti, Marianina, Genovese, Cartagenova), and many of his gifted musicians in other categories are German or of Germanic background (Schmucke, Schwabe, Steibelt; Ursule, whose father had married a Hamburg German girl "mad about music" [UM 307], and Modeste, whose mother, Bettina Wallenrod, was not only from Frankfurt-am-Mein but was also an "ideal figure of Germany" [MM 373]). His one musical genius, Gambara, represents, appropriately, a cultural mixture: an Italian who studied in Italy and went to Germany to absorb Germanic principles.

Balzac's approach to the question of melody and harmony is perhaps not subtle, but we may credit it with being basic and direct. Always an observer, he liked clarity too much not to appreciate the distinctiveness or luminosity of melodic contours; always a writer, he liked fullness too much not to be gratified by the richness or firmness of harmonic textures. He surmounted the old rivalry in 1839 when he voiced his credo of unity: "Melody, Harmony, Composition, these three daughters of Heaven" (FE 66).

CHAPTER VI

CRITICAL ESTIMATES

Startling Conjunctions

To a musicologist, Balzac's documentation seems elementary. He throws data together with childish exuberance and with a versatility that pays little heed to historical sequence. His ritualistic enumerations of the great names in music strike more a note of virtuosity than of knowledge. As Baldensperger remarked: "It's the perfect disarray of the impoverished melophile."[1] Yet there is something appealing about the way Balzac ventures forth to validate his views. Fearlessly he will couple names that seem to bear little artistic resemblance with each other: Beethoven and Scott, Marcello and Giotto, Mozart and Homer, Meyerbeer and Byron, Gluck and Mesmer, Mozart and Molière, Grétry and Racine. If they cannot be justified, some of the analogies may be explained by the manner of thinking of Balzac's contemporaries, as well as by his personal approach to music history.

To compare Beethoven's use of a theme in a symphonic "order of battle" (G 430) to Sir Walter Scott's integration of a novel's last minor character into the plot's main action is not an ineffective way of placing an abstraction into the more immediate perspective of a public generally unenlightened in the symphonic process. There is no wastage in a Beethoven score; every last musical figure has its place. Balzac paid great homage to the composer in 1837 when Gambara associates him with a novelist who was receiving among the most enthusiastic tributes Europe had ever accorded any literary mortal.

Laubriet is one of several[2] who frown at the equation "Marcello is to music what Giotto is to painting" (MD 375). Still, some validity exists in coupling a composer-theorist, who has left us in the *Psalms* one of the finest musical compositions of their kind and in his writings many appeals to reform an abused aesthetics, with a great painter-reformer, who has left us in the Arena chapel one of the finest examples of sequential frescoes and who reformed the dimensions and emotionlessness of a severe art.

As for joining Mozart and Homer—"I admire them both on an equal plain" (G 467)—Balzac's criteria were those of balance and perfection, characteristics (also of Marcello and Giotto) that associate the Austrian with the Greek. In an ill-advised comparison between *Don Giovanni* and *Robert le Diable*, the former nonetheless receives higher praise: "*Don Giovanni* stands higher because of its perfection, I agree; *Robert le Diable* represents ideas, *Don Giovanni* excites sensations. *Don Giovanni* is, besides, the only musical work in which harmony and melody are in balanced proportion; here and only here is the secret of its superiority over *Robert*, for *Robert* is more abundant" (G 459). Balzac prizes the quality of feeling in Homer or Mozart over the quantity of intellect in Meyerbeer. Indeed, *Gambara* eventually renders an unfavorable verdict on Meyerbeer's opera while heaping praise on *Don Giovanni*. Perfection is again the secret of our admiration of *Don Giovanni*'s Finale, "one of those classical forms invented once and for all" (G 465); it makes for unparalleled dramatic effectiveness. With *Don Juan* in mind, the analogy with Molière comes easily: "If anything can prove the immense power of music, isn't it the sublime way it has of translating the disorder and embarrassment that stem from an exclusively voluptuous life, the frightening description of the choice to become overwhelmed with debts, duels, unfaithfulness, and bad gambles? In this work, Mozart is the felicitous rival of Molière. That terrible finale—fiery, vigorous, despairing, joyous, full of horrible specters and wanton women, marked by the final attempt excited by dinner wines and by an enraged self-defense" (CA 402). The paragraph appreciates the musical intensity and the dramatic amplitude of Mozart's masterpiece, a perfectly coordinated opera. The *Iliad* or the *Odyssey* is not an impossible match for it.

The analogy between Meyerbeer and Byron rests on superficial grounds that Balzac himself hesitates to elucidate: "judged just by bringing them together in this way" (G 467). Balzac saw *Manfred*, *Don Juan*, and *Robert le Diable* in Faustian terms through the presence of evil spirits, prophesies, and obsessive wants, but his statement ends abruptly, its meaning out of the reader's reach. The same happens with his bewildering association of the rationalist Gluck and the spiritualist Mesmer, which he rationalizes on the basis of innovation: "Toward the end of the eighteenth century, science was as divided by the appearance of Mesmer as art was by that of Gluck" (UM 316). Grétry and Racine are coupled in an early letter when Balzac alludes to the composer-theorist who rivaled in popularity the loftier reputation of the tragedian. But rather than establishing an equation, here the conjunction points to attributes craved by Balzac. "The devil with mediocrity! . . . One must be Grétry and Racine,"[3] that is, popular *and* great. All in all, then, Balzac's pairings, albeit startling at times, do retain more than a semblance of plausibility.

Historical Lacunae

Numerous lacunae make Balzac's historical background uneven. Gambara reveals them in his survey of the development of music. He says nothing, for instance, of the Franco-Belgian school of which Palestrina (mentioned only once in *Gambara*), extolled by other Romantics, notably Hugo, was the Italian apogee. Balzac shared Vigny's awareness of the classical school of Carissimi, Cavalli, Scarlatti, and Rossi, but did not allow his eye to roam beyond Italy, "that classical land from which Germany and France drew their first lessons" (G, 431). He was resigned to consider his own country as the land where "the violinists at the Paris Opéra had the singular privilege of playing the violin with gloves" (G 431). Monsigny and Grétry enter timidly the ranks of his composers. While it is true that many of the Italian composers were in advance of their French and German colleagues of the seventeenth and eighteenth centuries, it is inaccurate to say that "during that time, Germany, with the exception of Sebastian Bach, ignored music" (G, 432). How wrong he was in excluding Keiser, Reinken, Buxtehude, Kuhnau, and Telemann needs no explanation. Balzac interpreted wrongly the fact that Germany remained longer than other nations in the traditions of the Middle Ages, and reflects, despite Fétis, how commonly neglected was the history of music in his day.

Errors, too, mar his background. Lulli becomes a contemporary of Bach, when actually around a half century separated their births. Lulli also becomes erroneously the man "who expanded the domain of harmony and classified dissonances for the first time" (G 432). Again we read Gambara's sweeping opinion: "All that is left to us of the musical world before the seventeenth century has proved to me that the old composers knew only melody; they ignored harmony and its immense resources" (G 434). In this case it was Balzac who, perhaps with the monody or homophony of Gregorian chant in mind, ignored the subtle, harmonizing logic of Renaissance polyphonists like Orlando di Lasso, Vittoria, and Josquin des Prés. But by itself this fact is not startling when we consider that musicologists like Alexandre Choron in his *Dictionnaire historique des musiciens* of 1810 had also ignored these polyphonists.

Bertault reveals Balzac's mistakes even in one of his favorite styles, plainchant. According to the novelist, its origin lies lost in the remoteness of time. In *Jésus-Christ en Flandre*, a story which takes place during the fifteenth century, a young mother cradles her child to sleep with an old church hymn, and in *L'Enfant maudit*, a study of upper-class morality under Henry IV, a pious young lady catches a glimpse of love through liturgical songs. It would seem, then, that plainchant borrowed from popular repertory and vice versa, an incorrect idea for which Chateaubriand's chapter on Gregorian chant in *Le Génie du Christianisme* is to blame. More often, Balzac mentions the "O Filii, O Filiae" of Easter and the "Dies Irae" of funeral services in their thirteenth-century sequences, without referring (as he should have done if he was going to indulge in musicology) to the twelfth-century collections and anthologies of chants that contained both new materials and modifications of the previous century's usages, the *Antiphonaire* and the *Gradual* issued by the Church's great mystic St. Bernard de Clairvaux. These chants are definitely not derived from anterior popular songs or national airs. They are, rather, the outcome of the constant and sacred meditation of those monks who concerned themselves with music. This bit of history was known in Balzac's time: Lamennais, for one, indicates as much with his references to St. Ambrose and St. Gregory in his *Esquisse d'une philosophie*. Furthermore, it is not clear, even if Balzac's point of departure was the thirteenth century, why in *Ferragus* he attributed the "Dies Irae" to Spanish genius when Tommaso di Calano, an Italian Franciscan monk of that century, was usually associated with the composition.

A still clearer fallacy occurs in *La Duchesse de Langeais* when General Montriveau is overcome with emotion at hearing the voice of Sister Thérèse "which cuts through the mass of the chanting like that of a *prima donna* in the concordance of a finale; . . . that voice so rich continued to broadcast its charm: it came like a balm . . ., vibrating beneath the arches" (DL 134-135). The fact is that the Carmelites were not allowed such singing. They had to render the psalms of the office *recto tono*, and only in 1903, with the approbation of Pope Pius X, did the rendering *motu proprio* reform plainchant and Church music in general.

In what concerned more prominent names, Balzac's references are sparse. Gluck, Handel, Pergolesi, Haydn, Mozart, and Weber are briefly evoked. He leaves it to us to determine which is "the great symphony of Haydn" (CD 603), what are the "new inventions" of Pergolesi (BS 110) or what characterizes "Handel's manner" (G 466), just as he merely mentions the names of Crescentini and Veluti to describe Genovese's sober (*sage*) singing method (MD 364), and even so, Veluti was known for his ornamental exuberances! Weber, who made an impression on Nerval and other Romantic writers, is remembered cursorily in *Lettre aux écrivains français du XIXe siècle* and in

Les Illusions perdues, and in *Voyage de Paris à Java* "certain phrases of his contain a poem of melancholy" (VPJ 196).[4] We know that Balzac admired Mozart, even if we only read about *Le Nozze di Figaro* (EG) and *Don Giovanni*, to which he alludes in eight novels (CA, MM, FM, I, MN, MD, G, DBM) and in a preface (*Etudes philosophiques*). He may not have appreciated Gluck with the warmth of Victor Hugo, but he understood his role, including his style of recitative (P). In accusing Meyerbeer of lacking inspiration and of borrowing freely thematic material from other operas, he praised Gluck: "Before writing, Gluck thought for a long time. He calculated all the possibilities and devised a plan that could be modified later by the use of inspired details which, however, never made him stray off the road. Hence that energetic accentuation, that declamation throbbing with truth" (G, 457). Balzac considered Gluck, along with "Lulli, Rameau, Haydn, Mozart, Beethoven, Cimarosa, Paesiello, [and] Rossini" as composers who worked with a relatively new art, unknown to the older generations "which did not possess as many instruments as we possess now," and which had not witnessed the revolutionary consequences of the recently developed notions of harmony. "Such a new art demands that the masses study, so that they will cultivate the feeling that music addresses" (MD 355). Balzac correctly directed his contemporaries' attention to the different mode of sensitivity required by contemporary music. He mocked certain abuses like bravado singing (SMC) and refrained from disparaging older forms ("Rondo brillant"), but he felt strongly his century's progress in broadening the scope of the art, in reconciling the demands of harmony and melody, and in bettering the actual tools of the trade, instruments. A passage from *Béatrix* summarizes his attitude: "Calyste listened to the poetic tones of the most beautiful and surprising music of the nineteenth century, in which melody and harmony wrestle with equal force, where singing and orchestration have reached unprecedented perfection" (B 388).

Judgments of uneven merit characterize Balzac's attempts at musical criticism. If he sensed the weakness of *Fra Diavolo* ("The music was unfelicitous: *Fra Diavolo* is a long street song, except for the *Parisienne* which, to use Rossini's words, is the best cavatina of the century—but everything else belied the promises of the past")[5] on the one hand, on the other he experienced great pleasure at *La Muette de Portici*, because he thought he heard in the music "a voice of the future, a religious expression that the other fine arts could no longer afford me."[6] If he liked *Il barbiere di Siviglia* and the Fifth Symphony, he also liked "Le Songe de Rousseau" and *Le Désert*. If he correctly censured Castil-Blaze's and Meyerbeer's potpourris, a style in vogue during the previous century even attempted by Gluck, he still granted the composer of *Robert le Diable*, at least on the surface, too much importance by devoting lengthy attention to him in *Gambara*. He enjoyed Boieldieu's *Le*

Calife de Bagdad and *La Dame blanche*, but wisely did not grant them prominence. He was right in keeping quiet about *Ernani* by Gabussi (he had seen the première in Rossini's company in 1834),[7] a young composer much applauded in the fashionable salons. But unfortunately he did not exercise the same discretion in speaking of Hérold, Cramer, and David, and in inviting Auber to compose the romance for *Modeste Mignon*. Perhaps his most unfortunate silence came with reference to his friend Berlioz, about whose compositions he remained undecided. On the other hand, he extolled whole passages from the operas of lesser composers like Cimarosa and Zingarelli with as much fervor as he showed for Beethoven and Rossini. Again, some justification exists for his choices. An allusion in one novel to the "divine pages of Rossini, Cimarosa, and Zingarelli" (PC 128) is substantiated on three occasions in another. Besides Rossini's "Il mio cor si divide" from *Otello*, he referred to the duet "Dunque il mio bene tu mia sarai" from Zingarelli's *Romeo e Giulietta* as "one of the most moving pages of modern music, . . . a poem of divine melancholy" (B 427), and to "Pria che spuuti l'aurora" from Cimarosa's *Il matrimonio segreto* as "the greatest masterpiece there is for performers" (B 506). These are excellent numbers, well worth singling out from their broader contexts.

While he hailed Paganini, Liszt, and Chopin as performers as enthusiastically as Rubini, Pasta, and Persiani, he neglected them completely, as we have noted, as composers. Paganini did attain more fame as a violinist, and Liszt, whom Balzac thought lacked "the genius of composition," was also more recognized as a pianist than as a composer in the 1830s and 1840s. Yet, although his productive period of preludes, symphonic poems, and concertos came later, his importance as a creator of a new and expanded musical idiom had already been recognized by contemporaries like Nerval and Deschamps. And as for Chopin, again more visibly a performer, Balzac, unlike George Sand, missed discerning his role in liberating harmony from the tyranny of rules.

We have also noted other inconsistencies. Gambara's knowledge of the importance of harmony, the role of counterpoint, and the employment of instruments, runs counter, ten years later in *La Comédie humaine*, to Pons's award of the Prix de Rome (mentioned as proof of his merit), when he barely knew harmony, counterpoint, and orchestration. Elsewhere in *Le Cousin Pons*, however, the protagonist's and Schmucke's attitude toward ballets in opera, strongly reminiscent of Gambara's and Massimilla's aversion to the unnatural intrusions, makes better sense: "They had placed patches on their eyes in order not to see the evils that befall a company when a corps de ballet commingles with actors and actresses—one of the most atrocious combinations that the necessities of gate receipts has created to torment directors, authors, and musicians"

(CP 543).

When it came to the technique of constructing a symphony, Balzac would have liked to demonstrate greater knowledge but could not, a lacuna he camouflaged under an awareness of the technical complexity of putting together a coda, "the most difficult section with which to wrestle successfully."[8] He had heard about the brilliant conclusion of Mozart's "Jupiter" Symphony, as well as about the part played by Beethoven in expanding the final segments so as to make them often the more challenging moments of his symphonies.

When we gather the fragments of Balzac's musicological and critical knowledge (outside of his two musical tales which reflect Strunzian inspiration), we are left with the same sense of disorder that characterized his musical education. But one point emerges consistently through the disarray, a point that distinguishes him from many of his contemporaries: overtly or by implication, he sets aside the lay music of the sixteenth, seventeenth, and eighteenth centuries in favor of that of the nineteenth. He is definitely modern.

Balzac, Meyerbeer, and Diplomacy

It has long been assumed that the author of *Gambara* extolled Meyerbeer and *Robert le Diable*.[9] The assumption seems logical in the light of statements like "that great symphony of song," "What art!," "the sublime fantasy," "Never has there been such passionate and dramatic music," or "that great musical drama" (G 461, 463, 465, and 456). Yet a case may be made for the opposite, namely, that Balzac purposely said one thing while meaning another. We know of the enormous acclaim the opera received, and that Balzac was not immune to the directives of popularity. We know that he wrote *Gambara* and chose *Robert le Diable* in part to present the German side of the dispute for which he created an Italian counterpart with *Massimilla Doni*. We know, in addition, of his weakness for descriptive music and melodramatic situations. But we also know that he had promised Meyerbeer a role in one of his works and that the use of an opera which was the talk of Paris presented itself as a logical opportunity to keep his word. Yet we should recognize, too, that Gambara more than Meyerbeer represents the German point of view; that the composer ends by debunking the opera;[10] that Count Marcosini opens the discussion with an attack against it; and that the whole of Gambara's apology in between is delivered while "plunged in one of those half-sleeps with which drinkers are familiar" (G 456). Balzac had asked Schlesinger to send him from the files of the *Gazette musicale* the best articles in praise and in dispraise of

Robert le Diable, not merely to give his words an authoritative ring in presenting the contrasting views of Gambara and Marcosini, but also, we believe, to give him tools with which to carve his way out of an embarrassing situation: that of having to fulfill a promise and extoll a composer whom he did not prize as highly as he did Beethoven and Rossini. A close look at the text reveals the novelist as a critic whose subtlety matched his diplomacy.[11]

As in the case of Marcosini's invective against the foibles of Italian music, his foray against Meyerbeer's opera only ostensibly serves the function of inducing Gambara to react. He claimed appropriately that the French librettists, though dealing with an interesting subject, made little more than a fable out of it, structured an improbable story, "a veritable dramatic nightmare which oppresses the spectators without giving rise to strong emotions" (G 456). Musically speaking, melody and voice disappear frequently under the weight of orchestral harmony, indicating that the composer sought to be bizarre and fantastic, alienating musical truth and unity in the process. Although the Count sees Meyerbeer as a sensitive musician, he decries the fact that he nourished his inspiration with countless themes from other operas, that he failed to control the use of enharmonic transitions and plagal cadences, and that he did not vary sufficiently his rhythms.

If when drunk Gambara composes music to the liking of all the people to whose level he has descended, it is logical that in a pronounced alcoholic state he should often interpret music on that same level. The masses adored the opera; the drunken composer praises it. His views alternate sagacity with wine-swelled exaggerations which at one point would have *Robert le Diable* compete with Mozart's *Don Giovanni*, a rodomontade even in Balzac's language. Furthermore, Balzac proffers two elusive comments. The first sounds better than what it says: Meyerbeer's music is not written for incredulous listeners (presumably referring to the sacred subject) or for listeners incapable of love (presumably referring to Robert's final decision). The second is of voluntary and piquant ambiguity: "This music is *chosen* with love, but from the *treasures* of a rich and fecund imagination in which science has *pressed* the ideas in order to *extract* from them their musical essence" (G 458: stresses added). In other words, Meyerbeer *borrows* well; the ambiguity is preserved in his favor by keeping "imagination" in the singular. The same suggestion is made even stronger in the epithets "an able harvester of notes" and "a setter of precious stones" (G 458). Having laid the groundwork, Balzac embarks upon an act by act and scene by scene analysis of the opera, some of whose sections are in fact rewarding. Given the Count's opening invective and Gambara's critical closing remarks as well as his condition in between (drunkenness becomes Balzac's device of diplomacy), Balzac now need not fear overstating his "tribute."

The Overture's Andante in C minor makes Gambara shiver; he compares it with Mozart—quite correctly if we recall his piano *Fantasia XVIII* which resembles it down to the detail of tonality. He then describes the opening bacchanal, the frenzy that seizes men when dancing over an abyss, and the wonderful movement of the introduction. Indeed there are correspondences between thematic variations and stage actions, and between orchestra and singing voices, which propel this section forward. Gambara then admires the "marvelous" song of the troubadour Raimbaut, which for us has simple charm but little more. The same may be said of the passage portraying Robert's anger over his banishment and Alice's soothing words. Gambara lauds highly Alice's romance in E major and the religious feeling which animates it. Here he is right. The romance is a well crafted piece whose flowing phrases spring from a common source and gradually assume the likeness of a prayer.

If the musical accounts of the opera that Schlesinger had lent Balzac represented popular opinion, they made much of Robert's "Je lui dus la victoire et perdis le bonheur." Actually a somewhat banal passage, Gambara glosses over it. Instead he extols the thematic linking of Bertram's entrance with Raimbaut's ballad which had mentioned him as Berthe's seducer, together with the dramatic opposition that arises between Bertram and Robert and that adopts the style of a Gluckian recitative. Accordingly, Gambara likes the eight-measure, tender and distressing line of Bertram, "Tu ne sauras à quel excès je t'aime!" The Finale's mixture of wrath, gaiety, liveliness, and barcarole restfulness may be considered a conclusion consistent with an act that had begun with a drinking orgy.

If the first act elicits some interest, the second is unquestionably sterile, despite the judgments of reviewers in the *Gazette*. Gambara continues his enthusiastic account, alluding to Isabelle's "fine, fresh, and slightly melancholy phrases," the "charming" duet with Robert, the ensuing love scene, and Bertram's "Si je le permets" (G 461, 462). In reality, these are dull sections, in part frilled with vocal acrobatics and often contributing to a music hall atmosphere rather than to a grand opera setting. On closer reading, we note that Gambara says much less about this act than about the first, and in more literary language, obviously finding it unproductive to insist on purely musical details. About its prolixity he says nothing, but begins by injecting a prolix (and purposely bewildering?) comment of his own: the beginning is "overpowering for those who develop the themes in the bottom of their hearts by giving them the expansiveness that the music has ordered them to communicate" (G 461)! Then at the end, after having talked about an act comprising dances, choruses, march tempos, knights preparing for tournament, fanfares, and Isabelle singing scales above the whole, he says that "everything is homogeneous . . . You have seen human life in its sole and unique expression. . ." (G 462)!

The opera gains in interest in the third act, largely through the development of Bertram's character. From the comic duet in which he attempts to win over Raimbaut—"pleasantry alongside horror . . . sublime fantasy" (G 463), exclaims Gambara, underlining the basic tragedy of the situation—to the *Valse Infernale* and the Devil's "paternity mingled with those demonic songs through frightful despair," Meyerbeer expresses his idea musically with considerable effectiveness, raising it by degrees from the key of B to that of G, where it establishes itself and expands in the process. Alice's much hailed "Quand j'ai quitté la Normandie" draws a "marvelous" from Gambara, although to us the aria seems awkward and static. In his condition, Gambara is more apt to judge drama than music. For this reason, a recitative, the verbal duel between Bertram and Alice (symbolically between Hell and Heaven), constitutes the climax of the opera's musical interest, "comparable to the most grandiose inventions of the great masters" (G 463). But for us it is difficult to see how a section in which Meyerbeer drags together disparate styles—the Devil's Germanic, symphonic questioning and the maiden's Italian comedy replies—can be so "violently moving." Its ferocious joy cannot conceal its artistic weakness. However, though brief, the subsequent, unaccompanied trio is successful. Gambara correctly points to it because it enhances the opera's impression of mystery and represents a genuine climax; the "avalanche of music" has led to "this battle of three voices" (G 464).

Gambara properly wastes no words on the duet "Des chevaliers de ma patrie" which brought applause to many a tenor, but which imitates poorly the Finale of Beethoven's Fifth Symphony. Balzac, who knew this Finale well, could not flatter Meyerbeer on this point. Bertram's exhortation to Robert to procure the magic branch from a nearby cloister sounds incongruous, given its dance-like 6/8 tempo. Gambara, again appropriately, does not discuss it; again the littérateur, he situates it in the plot. The Evocation scene which follows, a well wrought section with a strident orchestration that salutes Bertram's infernal royalty, evokes Gambara's warmest praise, especially the phrase "Nonnes, qui reposez sous cette froide pierre, M'entendez-vous?." "Here is truly the triumph of Hell . . . Roll on, music, . . . Roll on and seduce!" (G 464). But if the music "rolls," it rolls unevenly; if the symphonic interlude is good enough to have won the approval of Berlioz himself, a gesticulative Procession of Nuns and three intermittent, dreary ballets outweigh the approval sufficiently for Gambara not to utter a word about any of them. Instead, as if Meyerbeer's handling of the final bacchanal were insufficient, Gambara improvises his own development in the form of variations.

The fourth act does not roll along either. Instead of expressing the Overture's Heaven-bent lamentations of human beings, it puts forth the wail of a weak woman struck with love and fear, Robert's betrothed, Princess Isabelle of Sicily. Again Gambara can only talk plot. In one instance, however, he commits himself strongly in favor of her "adorable melody in the cavatina 'Grâce pour toi,'" an exquisite aria that has remained in the repertoire to this day; "this piece alone would make the opera's fortune" (G 465). But nothing else in the act deserves Gambara's comment, not even the Finale, too reminiscent, he implies, of the end of *Don Giovanni*.

The last act drew almost unanimous praise in the *Gazette* accounts. Today we find nothing in it except the Prayer. In the light of this, we follow easily Gambara's eclecticism which limits its homage to the "capital number . . . 'Gloire à la Providence.'" Everything else he touches upon mainly in terms of the drama. The Prayer "rises brilliant with light" (G 466), an achievement for Meyerbeer whose style is usually heavy and dry. Gambara places the number in the best musical tradition. What follows—the "grand trio toward which the opera has moved: the triumph of the soul over matter, of the spirit of good over the spirit of evil"—misses the mark. The music fails in its opportunity to expose the hero's conflicting passions, and makes him a lamenting, confused man without the will-power to seek for himself the right course he has been advised to follow. Even groggy with alcoholic fumes, Gambara sees the poverty: "Here the music has weakened." He did not hear what he might have heard at the end of Gounod's *Faust* or Boïto's *Mefistofele*, "that cry of devine voices of which I have so often dreamed" (G 466).

Because of his tacit and overt reservations, Balzac does not seem the impassioned panegyrist of *Robert le Diable* he would appear at first glance, indeed the panegyrist his century would otherwise have made him. If we look into the artistic situation of Meyerbeer, we encounter praise everywhere during Balzac's years. Even the severe Berlioz, complaining about Italy, once wrote: "I am immured in this dreary and anti-musical country, while in Paris you hear the Ninth Symphony, *Euryanthe*, *Robert le Diable*!"[12] In *Le Rénovateur* of May 18, 1834, he called the latter opera "profound," "immense," and on September 14, "picturesque," "varied," "rich in contrasts," "felicitously bold," "orchestrally modern." Chopin called it the masterpiece of the new school and published with Franchomme a *Grand Duo* for piano and 'cello based on its themes. Liszt said it inaugurated a new era in the field of operatic music. The première on November 22, 1831, enhanced by the concurrence of the best voices of that time and the choreography of the famous signora Taglioni had taken the capital by storm and it held European imagination in its grip throughout the century. The *Cabinet de Lecture*, *Journal des Débats*, *Revue* and *Gazette musicale*, *Courier des Théâtres*, *Autographe*, *Eclipse*, *Opéra*, and *Journal des Artistes* waxed superlative until well after Balzac's death.[13] Gate receipts three years later were being totaled in five and six figures.[14] Méry could not avoid devoting the largest section of his poem *L'Art* to *Robert le Diable*.

The opera must be "situated" in order to understand the triumphant reactions of a public that had been abandoned by Rossini two years previously and that sought new, revolutionary expression. The Romantics in particular saw no banality in Meyerbeer's trivial themes; their epidermal psychology, as we now see it, likened the theatre to life. They facilitated the exteriorization of inner feelings by translating them into gestures, into starts and sighs. The music is such that Bertram, Robert, Isabelle, and Alice cannot sing without twisting their hands or raising cursing fists to the sky, a behavior which justified Louis-Philippe's bourgeois who said he was going to the *spectacle* rather than to the *théâtre*. Abetted by his librettists Eugène Scribe and Casimir Delavigne, Meyerbeer catered to facile ways.

Yet he contributed something too. If he did not invent the refrain, he found a way to multiply thematic incidents without allowing the musical action to scatter; if he did not invent transition, he enlarged and generalized its scope, as in the Introduction to the opera, by replacing modulation through relative tonality with omniphonic modulation. His was an art of distribution, of satisfying the listeners with a constant epigenesis of themes. He regaled them orchestrally as well, coloring a string background with woodwinds and brasses, treating violas in a novel way, combining 'cellos and bassoons, intermingling families of instruments, and endowing each with a psychological value. Bertram's demonic pride rings through trumpets and trombones; rarely does he speak without trombones, bassoons, and double basses. Rarely, too, does the naive Alice appear without flutes and clarinets, to which is added a chorus aided by a solo trumpet when she assumes the role of the tutelary angel.

Meyerbeer's *symphonie-action*, however, was not Beethoven's *symphonie-analyse*. Balzac's developed consciousness of the composer of the Fifth Symphony made him sense a difference. Besides, he did not favor endless roulades, too many ballets, and the declamatory requirements of a work which could not outlive those singers who found in its score opportunities to display their bravura. For him,

Bertram should have been more tragic and moving. Instead of being great, Meyerbeer's music revealed faulty construction and an eclecticism that used every musical idiom from Bach to Auber. Through the lenses of opera, the composer saw a world of poetry and sound with barbaric enthusiasm, but he always deferred to the wishes of his public. As one critic has said, "his music is that of an honest man careful not to deceive his client; but oh! how little artistic this honest man is!"[15]

All of this is condensed in Gambara's final words, conveying what he objectively thought of *Robert le Diable* as compared with what he had seen in it as a whole in his drunken stupor the night before. Now Gambara's head was clear; he made his remarks "very openly" (G 469). Not that Balzac did not respect Meyerbeer's merits or was not dazzled by his music. He loved it. But he understood its failings, and made this known in a work which only ostensibly eulogized the composer; at the end of *Gambara* we read of a "miserable opera" because it was made with "ordinary means, . . . mountains of notes heaped together, *verba et voces*; . . . chopped up phrases whose origin I recognized. The piece "Gloire à la Providence" resembles too much a piece by Handel, the chorus of Knights going into battle is related to the Scots air in *La Dame blanche*; . . . if the opera pleases so much, it's because the music belongs to everybody, therefore it must be popular" (G 469). These are the analyst's last words; this, then, is Balzac's verdict. Hence, even if Balzac himself says that his hero makes sense only when drunk ("He reasons better after some glasses of wine" [G 454]), we have to conclude at this point that he wrote from the point of view of Gambara's little society and that he did not say what he appeared obviously to be saying. Like Virgil, whose *AEneid* (though not usually thought of in this way) conceals a sharp criticism of Imperial Rome, Balzac's overt enthusiasm contains covert barbs. The wine was a stratagem which served him more than the Count, and we are ultimately led to apply the words of Schiller's Karl von Moor: "A curse on myself for what I said! But it was done in the fumes of wine, and my heart knew not what my tongue uttered."[16]

To be sure, while drinking, Gambara had also approved Marcosini's praise of Beethoven and discoursed intelligently on Idealism and Sensualism. On these occasions, however, he was not "plunged in one of those half-sleeps," nor was he yet under the systematic regime of wine that the Count administered to him. Tactfully, Balzac avoids giving a clear-cut definition of intoxication by making the difference involved here one of degree: the difference between being drunk or in a stupor and being merely "very animated" by wine, a condition which, according to Hoffmann, accelerates the revolution of ideas. Balzac suggests the difference in *Voyage de Paris à Java* when he says that "gross drunkenness disturbs the organism. . . . Yet, taken in moderation, this liquid imagination has effects which are not lacking in charm" (VPJ 198). In *Gambara*, we receive another hint: "*Without being drunk*, the composer was in that condition whereby all his intellectual forces were very excited . . ., whereby the soul flits about in the world of spirits (G 452: stress added). Balzac, then, lets his composer discuss Beethoven and future music when sober or simply "animated"; he leaves Meyerbeer for when he is considerably drowsier, thus conveniently having him tread the narrow path between rationality and irrationality in order to retain the desired ambivalence in his judgments, an ambivalence that will be resolved in the sober, negative assessment at the end of the tale.

We note that in the novelist's writings, Meyerbeer's name, compared with those of Beethoven and Rossini, makes rare appearances. Balzac tacitly assumed what we believe today, that the merits of *Robert le Diable* lie less in the music than in the drama, and less in the drama than in the dramaturgy. His praise bore the mark of that frenzy of admiration that took hold of Parisian audiences during the 1830s, but it never disassociated itself from his personal clairvoyance. Gambara thus became a critic, predicting in his own fantastic way that the new idol of Paris would become for posterity *magni nominis umbra*.

Balzac, Rossini, and Adulation

We learn how differently and how genuinely Balzac respected Rossini by juxtaposing not only the number of times his and Meyerbeer's names appear in his writings, but, more significantly, the frequency of the allusions to the composer's works and their tone. Balzac venerated Rossini's music. *Otello* figures in *Béatrix*, Matilda's duet from *Guglielmo Tell* in *Les Comédiens sans le savoir*, the beautiful chords of *Semiramide* in *La Peau de chagrin*; more references appear in *La Cousine Bette*, *Le Père Goriot*, *Modeste Mignon*, *Facino Cane* and, of course, *Gambara* and *Massimilla Doni*, to mention but a few novels and not to speak of Balzac's newspaper articles, correspondence, and other writings. Sometimes Rossini served as an analogy. In *La Maison Nucingen*, he makes humorous use of Basilio's "Calunnia" aria from *Il barbiere di Siviglia*, which Alfred Einstein has called "at once a piece of humor and demonism."[17] Its unearthly *pianissimo* before the final cadence especially impressed Balzac who transposed it into the shady setting of financial transactions: "The profiteers performed, financially speaking, the slander aria from the *Barbier de Séville*. They went along *piano piano*, proceeding by slight tittle-tattles about the worth of the deal, whispered from ear to ear. They exploited the patient, the shareholder, only in his home, at the Bourse, or in public, through that ably created rumor which swells up to the *tutti* of a quotation in four figures. . ." (MN 634).

While it is true that by the late 1830s Meyerbeer's operatic production was limited to *Robert le Diable*, *Les Huguenots*, and a few earlier dramatic works, and that *Le Prophète*, *L'Etoile du nord*, *Dinorah*, and *L'Africaine* were still to come, the unchallenged lordship he enjoyed at that time over critical opinion at large is not reflected in Balzac's utterances. The fact is that *Mosè in Egitto* drew from Balzac much warmer words than *Robert le Diable*, if only because its religious tone rang more solemnly. When, in *La Duchesse de Langeais*, Montriveau hears a nun playing the organ, we read: ". . . the organ music seemed to belong to the school of Rossini, the composer who has brought the most human passion to the art of music and whose works will inspire some day, by their quantity and quality, a Homeric respect. Among the scores for which we are indebted to this fine genius, the nun appeared to have studied specially that of *Mosè*, probably because the feeling of sacred music is expressed in it to the highest degree" (DL 129). Critics, including Stendhal, had duly chastised Tottola for a bad libretto, and in 1827 the opera was turned into an oratorio, rewritten for the Paris stage on a text by Balocchi and Jouy, which happily allowed more expressive and natural vocal lines, recitatives more varied and richer in inflexions in the Gluckian tradition, and a larger orchestra. Balzac saw fit to call the work "the most immense opera created by the finest genius of Italy" (MD 352).

A rhapsodic exposé forms the core of *Massimilla Doni*.[18] Allowances made for the heroine's patriotic frame of mind as she delivers her Pindaric account, we must nonetheless accept the view that Balzac's own estimation of the opera approximates what she says. After declaring that one must be both poet and musician to understand the import of such music, she begins by extolling the three opening C major chords of the Introduction, a "sublime symphony" (MD 357) which is indeed a good piece of writing. Without varying the basic tonality, Rossini channels his theme supplely through a series of keys that mount in intensity until the "explosion of all those collected sorrows in the cry: '*O nume d'Israel!*'"(MD 358). Balzac's style leaves no room to doubt his preference of Rossini's to Meyerbeer's music; the passage where he describes ray by ray the approach of dawn by means of the composer's consecutive tonecolor effects and successive groupings of violins, woodwinds, brasses, even a triangle, serves as an example. By comparison, Gambara is nowhere so lyrical.

> We recognize the power of that simplicity.
> The effect of that phrase, which depicts the
> sensations of cold and night in a people

accustomed to being bathed in luminous waves of sunshine, a phrase repeated by the people and the kings, is gripping. The slow musical movement has something relentless about it. That cold and doleful phrase is like an iron bar held aloft by some celestial henchman who lets it fall at regular intervals over the limbs of all those sufferers. . . . The sun appears first and pours its rays on the hilltops, then into the valleys. . . . The chord is first heard on the high string of the first violins with boreal sweetness; it spreads through the orchestra, animating each instrument in turn. It unfolds. Just as light colors by and by every object, it awakens all the sources of harmony until together they flow into a *tutti*. . . . Light, the source of harmony, has flooded nature; every musical resource has shown forth with the vehemence and the refulgence of the rays of an oriental sun. Nothing, including the triangle with its repeated C, fails to remind us of the song of morning birds with its piercing tones and sprightly rhythms. [MD 338, 360-361]

Rossini's sparkling "simplicity of means" (MD 375) captured Balzac's attention, foreshadowing Wagner's recommendation never to abandon a tonality so long as it has something to say. Gambara would have praised Moses' invocation "Celeste man placata" on the same grounds. The "Voci di giubilo" quintet, which got much praise in reviews, is not as "magnificent," despite its solemnity and its "ravishing vocal setting," as Balzac indicates (MD 361, 362). The novelist also stresses the situation represented by Osiris' and Elcia's duet "Ah! se puoi così lasciarmi" more than appears warranted in a work in which the individuals' love story is submerged by the collective drama of the oratorio. Rossini attains greater expressiveness in the religious situations.

One of Massimilla's observations deserves highlighting: "Rossini knew how to retain for each people its national identity" (MD 363), for the hymns of the Hebrews and the angry declamations of their oppressors do relate in spirit, if not in authenticity, to different backgrounds. But a subsequent observation, the "divine and delightful allegro" (MD 364) of the Hebrews marching off into the desert, errs when it pays tribute to a murky page of music characterized by jarring trumpets, clarinets, and bassoons. At another point, Balzac betrays some embarrassment in explaining Elcia's half of the duet "Dov'è mai quel core amante," intended to express a deep disturbance but achieving little. He admits to a "mistake" (MD 365), tacitly accusing Rossini of a lack of artistic integrity for bowing to the whims of prima donnas who demand occasions for vocal virtuosity. The Finale of the first act, however, is justly praised. The "muffled and grave phrase" expands to incorporate a variety of moods—anxiety, uncertainty, suspicion, irritation—which merge eventually into an octet placed above mixed chorus and full orchestra, piercing with primeval vigor: "The religious chalice of certain vocal scores, the way in which voices multiply and group themselves, expresses how we conceive the sacred marvels of that first age of humanity" (MD 366). From the complex musical architecture does not come what Balzac claims, a dramatic sense of severity required by both the descending hail of fire and the ascending imprecations by the Jews, but rather a musical sense of total euphony, of balance and physical health. Too enthusiastic over the historical situation, Balzac has Massimilla downgrade the Finale of *Don Giovanni*, where a mere libertine struggles with his divinely aided victims, and favor the nobler drama of earthly forces fighting with God. Here Balzac played with words to energize the heroine's patriotism.

Exercising Gambara's prerogative of silence with respect to those pages of *Robert le Diable* he did not want to discuss, Massimilla passes over much of the beginning of the second act, pages indeed of platitudinous recitative. Balzac points out that the score rests to a large extent on tonic to dominant progressions, though the I-V sequence need not be a formula for, or a justification of, simplicity. He does observe, however, that the opera can do without "Pace mia smarrita," sung by Pharaoh's wife Amaltea, again one of those bravura arias "which harm the general design of the poem" (MD 371).

The "climax of the score," the "king of quartets" (MD 371), is the concertato "Mi manca la voce," written in a canon form dear to Rossini. Balzac displays his knowledge: "the old mode of the canon in unison to bring in voices and blend them into a single melody" (MD 371-372). It is a classic in its genre, the only one of its kind following the purer canon quartet from Beethoven's *Fidelio* and before Verdi's famed quartet from *Rigoletto*, and well deserving of the novelist's respect. There are no modulations from one voice to the next; its broad melodic line expresses the new anxiety invading each character and is worked out over a simple harp accompaniment which serves to suggest a prayer. A crescendo (not the usual Rossinian device for orchestral elaboration but an expansion for dramatic intensity) underscores its emotional stress. "This 'Mi manca la voce' is a masterpiece that will resist everything, even time, the great destroyer of musical styles, for it is drawn from the language of the soul which never varies" (MD 371). Balzac did not realize that a quartet is much more vulnerable to time than a solo, and Rossini's fine canon has not enjoyed its deserved permanence.

The opera's second *Marcia* is more successful than the first. Yet, rich as it is in joyful energy, Balzac's nationalistic heroine overestimates its value when she equates it with the best in Beethoven. As a result, rather than applaud a good selection, Balzac demeans it with his comparison. He is more circumspect when he does not waste words on the ensuing parts—recitatives by Pharaoh and Moses, an aria by Moses, and a chorus—and when he considers the Finale of the second act with Elcia's superimposed "Porgi la destra amata" and "Tormenti! affanni! smanie!" Musically more stirring than studied, the Finale rings with grand tones. Balzac sensed the extrinsic quality. There, he comments, Rossini placed the whole responsibility on the soprano and on her ability to execute roulades artistically; "with a mediocre performance . . ., nothing would be left" (MD 373). Rather than discuss the music, he describes the audience's reaction to it, to La Tinti's impact, and takes this occasion to expound on the kind of music that can set Italy afire.

Only one selection occupies Massimilla's account of the third act: the Prayer, the climax of the opera and the beautiful invocation still remembered today. "Here . . . science has disappeared: inspiration alone has dictated this masterpiece; it has risen out of the soul like a cry of love!" (MD 374-375). The whole section consists of one phrase built along Moses' opening appeal in G minor, "Dal tuo stellato soglio, Signor, ti volgi a noi." The passage breathes irregularly, as if trying to accede to the throne of the Almighty, its imploring sighs translated by a chromatic ascension from C to C-sharp to D; they subside in the second part, only to rise again in the third and affirm themselves in the last. Amenosi, Aronne, and Elcia join in, supported by chorus and orchestra, as the theme expands into a crescendo ever more serene and radiant. The transition from G minor to G major is truly luminous. Technical knowledge has not "disappeared." Contrapuntal and harmonic intricacies carry the Prayer structurally, though a plain harp arpeggio eventually establishes itself through its own persistence, underscoring the beauty and expressiveness of the simple melodic lines. At this point, Balzac finds his apogeal occasion to praise Rossini:

> Never will Rossini soar higher than he does in this prayer; he may do everything as well, never better. The sublime always resembles itself. But this song is in addition one of those numbers that will belong entirely to him. . . . It seems that in rising toward

> the heavens, the chant of this population
> emerged from slavery joins with strains that
> have descended from the celestial spheres to
> meet them. . . . The roundness and fullness of
> those themes, the nobility of the slow
> gradations that prepare the outburst of
> thanksgiving and its doubling back onto itself,
> develop celestial images in our soul. . . . The
> secret of that harmony which refreshes our
> thought is, I believe, the same as we find in
> very few works of human beings; it hurls us
> momentarily into the infinite. We feel it, we
> glimpse it in those endless melodies, like
> those that are chanted around God's throne.
> Rossini's genius elevates us to prodigious
> heights. . . . [MD 375]

Balzac understood the meaning of the Prayer both historically and dramatically. Firstly, it stood as a hymn to freedom, reawakening the long suppressed national consciousness that fired the poet Giuseppe Giusti to deplore the *teste curvate*, or heads bent in servitude, in his poem "Sant'Ambrogio."[19] One character declares: "I feel I have witnessed the liberation of Italy" (MD 374). Secondly, it acted as a culmination: the shepherd Moses, whose symbolic significance had been sought throughout the preceding events but never realized musically until this late moment, and who finally emerges indelibly as the designator of the Promised Land. We finally read how, through the power of the music, "we perceive a promised land into which our eyes, caressed by celestial glowings, plunge without sighting a horizon" (MD 375). Massimilla finds it fitting to terminate her running commentary on this note[20] rather than on a description of the deglutition caused by the descending waves of the Red Sea, and of the tranquil motive of peace developed by violins and clarinets just before curtain-fall.

Balzac's account of *Mosè in Egitto* is one of the most extraordinary panegyrics ever penned. In the sheer momentum of its enthusiasm, we feel his readiness to excuse any of Rossini's faults. Europe agreed with him. France's paean surpassed even the one it accorded to Meyerbeer. The tenor of the acclaim may be assessed in various contemporary periodicals: *Pandore* on July 25, 1827: "No one can argue about the superiority of the talent of the author of *Moïse*"; *Le Journal des femmes* on November 9, 1833: "The final number is the most beautiful we have ever heard. . . . [It is] resplendent, overwhelming. . . . The introduction in C minor is one of those pieces which of themselves would establish Rossini's reputation even if he never produced another thing"; Berlioz himself in *Le Rénovateur* on May 18, 1834 wrote: "beautiful work"; and *La Revue musicale* on November 15, 1834 devoted lengthy statements to the opera: a few reservations are overshadowed by opinions such as "a profound and true feeling, admirable above all because of its constant loftiness of style. . . . A work of elevation which almost always stays in an ideal and poetic sphere. We breathe something of an oriental perfume; we feel that that music is sung in the Pharaoh's city, in the country of the desert and of the granite sphynx. Certainly no musician in the world was less concerned than Rossini with the character of his work; and yet, how is it that his music enchants you as if by magic. . . ? How is it that during the introduction . . . you are gripped with terror as if you were reading the pages where the Bible recounts the flood? . . . The reason is that Rossini's genius is endowed with a marvelous, instinctive force; that he rises suddenly through inspiration to summits that knowledge needs a century to scale; that he bears within him an innate perception of all the sources of color and life. . . ."[21] Even before the 1827 revamping, Eugène Delacroix had exclaimed: "Admirable music! One must go there alone to enjoy it."[22]

Rossini, we know, ranks high in music history, though not as high as the Romantics saw him. With more enthusiasm than perspective, Balzac coupled the names of Beethoven and Rossini (MM, FC), but at least he did not follow Auber, who placed the Pesarote above Beethoven, Mozart, and Weber. We must remember, however, that Beethoven declared Rossini supreme in his field, and that Verdi paid special tribute to him during the centenary of 1892 by conducting the Prayer. It is hard to find two more critical composers.

We must also remember to look at Rossini historically. Compared with his contemporaries, his music represented a wealth of ideas, of rhythmic devices, and of spontaneous inspiration that had rarely animated opera outside of Mozart and Gluck. Much needed change in the styles of his predecessors in vogue—Cimarosa, Paesiello, Spontini—with reference to orchestral color, tonal modulations, and a sense of effortless melody. He expanded melodic movement, loosened the rigidity of monotonal basses, shortened the prolix scenes, and imbued them with a richer supply of motives that did not depend on structural conventions. In accomplishing this, he was not the revolutionary that Mazzini saw in him, but the perfecter hailed by Stendhal in the vanguard of many Romantics. Although not consistently, Rossini tried to make vocal virtuosity fit musical requirements, and if he made use of roulades, which he disliked, he did so lest singers of bad taste improvised them in his operas. A comparison of the roles of Isabelle and Elcia illustrate this.

Balzac agreed with his friend that clean, direct melody should lie at the base of operatic creation. Intellectualism should not be bought at the price of spontaneity. Balzac enjoyed more the affective qualities of Rossini's melodies than the ingenuous sentiment of Paesiello or the witty capriciousness of Cimarosa. He did not, however, reach the point of distinguishing between the spontaneity of Rossini and the poetic elegance of Mozart. The Italian's music was tender and serene. It encouraged relaxation, and Balzac sought it as often as he could. To Mme Hanska he wrote from Paris: "Here we have *Mosè*, *Semiramide*, staged and performed as these operas will be nowhere else, and every time they give one or the other, I go. These are my only pleasures." He liked the "diamonds and pearls."[23]

There is little doubt, too, that in *Mosè in Egitto* he was overjoyed to discover that his venerated composer, who at times had been charged with frivolity, was capable of sound harmonic structures—a fact that gratified the budding "Germanism" of his aesthetics. Balzac loved the oratorio quality, its legendary richness absorbing into a heroic framework a world of reality and of fantasy through the convocation of musical symbols. And he loved its melodic harmony. For Rossini used the orchestra to intensify expressively the life of the vocal line. Whereas eighteenth-century Italian operatic music was essentially linear, Rossini, even with *Mosè in Egitto* which he wrote when he was only twenty-six, evidences a greater concern with the vertical concept. Serving less as a musical accompaniment, the orchestra approaches its future role as a commentator that identifies itself with the vocal melody. A dialogue between voice and orchestra or a superimposition of polyphonic parts creates not a sonorous sequence but a total architectural sonority. As a result, scenes of storms and rains of fire emerged less as external descriptions than as compendious, inherent narrations. For Balzac, this represented harmonic mass.

Rossini employed the vertical volume concept concurrently with his noted crescendo. Count Marcosini's criticism of this obvious device, to which Gambara offers no rebuttal, indicates that Balzac appreciated other forms of Rossinian expression more. Yet there was something attractive about the crescendo's orgiastically and triumphantly repetitive manner. Deep down, it complemented Balzac's impelling, high-mettled nature. He uses it metaphorically in several novels (e.g., PC) to describe an irresistible impetuosity that feeds on its own dynamic joy. In this regard, Balzac is a pure sensualist, the prey of Rossini's frequent aesthetic externalism.

But *Mosè in Egitto*, crescendos and all, afforded him far more than sensual pleasure alone; he saw "the loftiness, the grandeur of such music" (MD, 363) which excluded rabid passions, disorderly form, and pompousness. He saw in it a metaphysical design that even *Don Giovanni* did not have. Perhaps he heard in the score more than we hear in it today. Even so, much of what he heard is still well worth hearing. Besides, Balzac could not brush aside his intimate friend who had enriched his life with so many rewarding musical experiences. We are reminded of the letter in *Le Père Goriot* which reads: "No sooner loved, could I be neglected already? You have shown me, through all those heart-to-heart disclosures, too beautiful a soul not to be one of those who always remains faithful. . . . As you said while listening to the Prayer in *Mosè*: 'For some, it's only one note; for others, it's the infinite of music!'"(PG 1055).

Advice to Young Composers

Nowhere does Balzac proffer critical views with such concentration as in *Gambara* and *Massimilla Doni*. In the light of these two *contes philosophiques*, we should credit the "improvised melophile" with an authentic capacity for sustained speculation and corroborate Baudelaire's dictum that every truly creative genius is necessarily also a critic.[24] While it is evident that Balzac's comments and critiques of *Robert le Diable* and *Mosè in Egitto* rely heavily on literary narration punctuated by musical indications of rhythm and tonality rather than on a definition and study of the music itself, there are instances where he illustrates what Bourget meant when he spoke of Balzac's superior import. He grasped something of the nature and essence of what he discussed, and as a result we can extrapolate from his writings a series of precepts which he would have offered the young composer.

In the first place, the artist must be a savant whose creation should conceal, behind its spontaneity, an intellectual effort—the "cerebral maternity" (CBe 318) that procreates by means of a comprehensive, though not stifling, analysis. Balzac would extend this analysis to the structure and physical properties of instruments in order to pave the way for innovations in sound. Science and art must blend as complementary powers. "If each modified sound corresponds to a force, you must know it in order to wed all those forces according to their true laws. Composers work with substances which they ignore. Why do the metal instrument and the wood instrument, the bassoon and the horn, resemble each other so little though they use the same substances, namely, the gasses which make up the air? Their differences result from some kind of decomposition of those gasses, or from a perception of the principles that are proper to them and that they relay modified, through properties still unknown. If we knew those properties, science and art would gain. What advances science advances art" (G 435).

Secondly, the composer must ward off the excesses of both

harmony and melody, and at no time must he become, in the fever of creation, the slave of his subject. No music is made through idealism or sensualism alone; no lasting expression ever presumed an abdication of control. Without his faculties in balanced composure, the musician cannot attain the fundamental requirements of art: simplicity and unity. "Power can be recognized through simplicity"; "there is the seal of the great master: unity!" (MD 358, 361). Gregorian chant and a Beethoven symphony are models of lasting beauty stemming from simplicity.

Thirdly, he who writes music should employ the idiom which is most intimately his, but he should eschew such devices as would all but affix his signature to the composition—the weakness of Rossini's crescendo: "I know that each composer has his own particular formulas to which he returns again and again, but it is essential to avoid this defect" (G 458).

Fourthly, he must work constantly, for inspiration is elusive. The habit of creation assures the recurrence of inspiration and its occasional capture. After the initial insight, music is a process of thought as well as of will to surmount difficulties and facile expressions. In this sense, creation is a technical exercise whose goal transfigures the technique.

A fifth principle derives from the belief that a creator of music must think of himself historically. Similar to the novelist, the operatic composer should preferably draw inspiration from some lofty religious or social concern. The best constructed drama reveals the cause-effect relationship of events. In a more abstract way, the symphonist shares an equal responsibility, for mindful of his historical presence he must, like Gambara, devise a mode of expression superior to that of the past and envisage a future superior to the present. Aware that he inherits traditions through which he can spread new ideas, he must realize his contribution to progress. By making *Massimilla Doni* a tribute to the past and *Gambara* a salute to the future,[25] Balzac implies congeneric values.

Finally, the composer must aim at perfection without, however, being lured into over-indulgence. Thought creates as much as it destroys, and in the human context the not-quite-perfect is a magnificent achievement. "Isn't this the case won by a sketch over the finished canvas. . . ?" (G 452). The same holds in music, an art which in essence is transcendental and which will always live independent of our noblest endeavors. A measure of resignation is therefore a virtue, like that of Christ who, Balzac says in *Des Artistes*, accepted "death in exchange for the divine light he spread on earth" (Art 228).

Balzac's colleague Stendhal had much more to say than he about music. But we agree with Guichard that Balzac's vision of the world and of the musical phenomenon surpassed that of Stendhal because it was "more open, more generous," and because Balzac, despite his generally unsequenced critical comments and judgments, asked himself more questions about it, about what it was intrinsically and for others. His colleague preferred to study himself in relation to it; Balzac approached it more spiritually. Stendhal "treated music as an egoist; Balzac treats it as a visionary."[26]

Gambara at the Panharmonicon

PART THREE

BALZAC'S MAJOR PERSUASIONS

CHAPTER VII

RELIGIOUS MUSIC: AN INNATE AFFINITY

The sense of spiritual elevation Balzac experienced in the presence of Beethoven's "infinite," wordless universe reflected a religious disposition we know he had nurtured since childhood. This affinity manifested itself in his attachment to compositions and instruments associated with spiritual experiences: the Prayer from *Mosè in Egitto*, an opera turned oratorio; *Robert le Diable* viewed as a sacred drama; the overwhelming "Dies Irae" in *Ferragus* and *Melmoth réconcilié*; the organ in *La Duchesse de Langeais*. Chopin he compared to angelic perfection. It was indeed a form of mysticism that shaped his response to Beethoven, the composer who appeared to have renounced all material things and abandoned every earthly connection. Acquaintance with the final quartets would have drawn Balzac even closer to him. As Philippe Bertault has demonstrated, liturgical music always occupied a special category in his mind.[1] The critic has looked scrupulously into the multiple dimensions of Balzac's affinity, which we echo here, along with a few expansions, modifications, and shifts of emphasis. Bertault was one of the first to grant Balzac credit for a fine musicality. He saw that to the promptings of the religious spirit the novelist often entrusted his most intimate thoughts, and it is under this heading that we discover one of Balzac's two most profound persuasions about music.

Early Exposure to Religious Music

Balzac did not have as much opportunity as he would have liked to listen to the masses, requiems, oratorios, stabats, and the Saint-Simonian *chants religieux* that filled the French capital. Even so, he would not have heard performances of sterling quality. The first half of the nineteenth century was everywhere inauspicious for religious music. The critics Corbet and d'Ortigue lamented its decadence, and Lamennais condemned the complicity of its guardians.

As Countess d'Agoult wrote in her *Mémoires*, Liszt, a future man of the cloth, was seriously preoccupied with sacred music and wanted to restore it to the temple from which the profane tastes of his time had banished it, to render unto God the pure cult He deserves through the purest of the arts, to inspire the multitudes and permeate them with adoration and love. Most of his contemporaries wrote either a mass or a requiem, but too often a theatrical flair prevailed. In one respect, Liszt himself contributed to the secularized taste; when he conducted a mass in a Parisian church, it was a veritable *événement*. Rossini's *Stabat Mater*, Berlioz's *Requiem*, and perhaps Adam's *Noël* stand among the few works that approach the genuineness required by a depersonalized art like that of sacred music. But they did not constitute a movement. It was not until 1845 that a renaissance took place with César Frank's setting of the Biblical poem *Ruth*.

Of the earlier religious music, that of Mozart and Handel was performed, but that of the Italian schools of Naples, Rome, and Venice was virtually ignored. And Gregorian chant usually suffered under the florid imaginations of arrangers, losing its devotional character, its flexibility of scale, its conjunctive emphasis, its avoidance of chromaticism, and its staid vocal lines and coursing rhythms. Fortunately for young Balzac, the Cathedral of Saint-Gatien in Tours boasted of a master musician as organist, Sulpice-Philippe Lejay, who refused to adulterate with drums or Italian *fioriture* his renditions of "Super fumina Babylonis," the Psalms, the Christian "Gloria in excelsis," the "Stabat Mater," and other chants that were never to leave the novelist's memory. Under the Gothic vaults, he absorbed for the first time some of the sensations that later entered his aesthetics, in particular a sense of mystery and remoteness. "The simplicity of those rudiments, of those musical ruins," as he described folk music, also applied to plainchant and contrasted with the pompous styles perpetrated in Parisian churches by composers like Abbé Roze, Choron, and Niedermeyer. The mature Balzac's temperament and recollections made him respond to the hallowedness of Gregorian chant even through the transgressions of modernization. If the knowledge of other forms of sacred music, of oratorios, chorales, and cantatas, remained alien to him, simple liturgical music provided an adequate spiritual substitute. The impressions gained served as a suffusive yet vital background for, among others, the mystical pages of *Séraphita*.

The Sacred Hymns

Remembering the Cathedral of Tours, Balzac endeavored to convey a sense of divine ideality in *Sténie* when he wrote: "Everything there breathes *a scent of Heaven*, as we used to say once about Saint-Gatien" (St 148). Hence *Maître Cornélius*, a story beginning during pontifical vespers in the same church, speaks of the "inexplicable phenomenon of spirituality" arising from "the secret of the magical influences of priestly chant and organ melodies" (MCo 898). *Jésus-Christ en Flandre*, a religious tale, refers to "an old religious hymn" with which a young mother cradles her infant to sleep on a boat (JCF 253), and well in advance of Hugo's famous musical description of fifteenth-century Paris in *Notre Dame de Paris*,[2] Balzac animates the pillars, arches, stones of a convent church with references to music: "The dance of those arcades mitered with those elegant window-ribs resembled a combat in the lists. Soon each stone in the church began to vibrate, but without shifting position. The organs spoke and filled my ears with a divine harmony that was then joined by voices of angels—an unparalleled music, accompanied by the deep bass of the bells whose tolling revealed that the two colossal towers were swaying on their square foundations" (JCF 262).

Six years at the Collège de Vendôme, a school thoroughly unsuited for formal musical training, had left Balzac nonetheless with lasting memories of psalms and canticles that seed his novels: "Lauda Sion" (AP), "In exitu" (MD), "De profundis" (PG, B, CV, MD), "Super flumina Babylonis" (CD, FC, EM, FM), "In manus" (UM, EM), "Ut queant laxis" ("Hymne Saint Jean": UM), "Veni Creator" (C, UM: a chant for "pious effusion" [UM 335]), "Te Deum" (DL, ELV), "Magnificat" (DL: "this joyous chant consecrated by the sublime liturgy of Roman Christianity to express the soul's exaltation in the presence of the ever-living God" [DL 131-132]), "Libera" (PG), "O Filii" (LV, G, MD), "Dies Irae" (CD, WC, F, MR, MD), "Venite, adoremus" (EG). Balzac was consistently and romantically moved by the melancholy words of such music, as he once expressed it in *L'Israélite*: "The sad monotones of the church song have a certain melancholy about them that I find admirable" (Is 36).

Upon returning from Vendôme, he used to roam about the "desert of stones" of the cathedral in Tours, listening to "the grave and monotonic chant of the offices regularly celebrated at different hours of the day, a chant that echoes feebly, murmurs, and mingles with the breath of the wind" (PCa 41). Philippe Bertault compares this attitude with that of one of Chateaubriand's disciples who believed with their master that the Christian religion is essentially melodious for the sole reason that it likes solitude. Balzac took Chateaubriand's idea seriously, for he too saw the strongest bond between the Christian religion and music in their common denominators of solitary beauty and mystery. As a symbol of nature, music is the art that purifies the soul and inspires virtue. Such impressions pervade the religious settings of *La Duchesse de Langeais*, in particular Annette's periods of communion with the organ in the Carmelite nunnery on Maiorca to which she had retired. While Montriveau awaits the designated hour for the abduction he has planned, he hears the night and morning hymns that "caused unfathomable delectation in him," the organ music, the "vocal mass" that his ears distinguished only confusedly, the "suave harmonies in which defects of execution could no longer be heard, and from which the pure spirit of art was released to communicate with the spirit of the hearer, making no demands on his attention, causing no strain in the act of listening" (DL 251). Rossini's *Mosè in Egitto* is evoked because of the feeling of sacred music that permeates it. This is the Balzac writing who in Paris lived across the street from a Carmelite convent, whence he heard frequently "breaths" of divine hymns which occasioned him to be "singularly moved,"[3] like Montriveau before the nunnery or Chateaubriand's René before the monastery enclosing his sister Amélie.

The Easter motet "O Filii, O Filiae" appears in several novels thanks to "[its lingering] harmonies" (LV 824). Likewise the "Te Deum," whose first phrase "climbs toward Heaven like a sublime shout, like a hurrah of joyous acclamations" (FTA 820), conveyed many a nuance of both jubilation and severity to the ears of the devout novelist. If we listen to him describe it, we must agree with Bertault who finds his words superior to those of Chateaubriand in *Le Génie du Christianisme*; Balzac captures the dual quality of force and love, robustness and grace, through which the hymn magnetizes the listener, and he understands instinctively the device through which the qualities are communicated:

> When the hour of triumph had come, the bells awakened echoes in the countryside, and this vast assembly lifted to God the first cry of praise with which the *Te Deum* begins. Sublime cry! They were pure voices, voices of women in ecstasy, mixed with the sterner and deeper voices of men, thousands of voices so mighty that the organ did not dominate the whole, despite the bellowing of its pipes. Only the shrill notes of the young choir boys, and the broad tones of the bassi profondi, evoked glowing thoughts, visions of childhood and manly strength, in this ravishing concert of human voices all intermingling in expressing a single idea of love.
>
> *Te Deum laudamus!*
>
> From the depths of that cathedral dark with kneeling men and women, this chant sprang

upward like a light which breaks out suddenly in the night, and the silence was shattered as by a peal of thunder. The voices climbed with the clouds of incense that spread diaphanous, bluish veils around the fanciful marvels of the architecture. Everything was splendor and perfume and light and melody.[4] [ELV 320]

Another hymn of triumph to whose solemnity Balzac responded instinctively was the "Lauda Sion," about which he wrote in an early novel: "The song of joy and the mass of harmony spread by the vocal ensemble and something imposing about it" (AP 10). While it is difficult to determine what version of the original plainsong melody of the "Te Deum" he heard because of the various ways it had been arranged from Anerio, Handel, and Vaet to Benevoli and the Italian masters of the seventeenth century, we may suspect that the version of the "Lauda Sion" in question belonged to one of the polyphonists Palestrina or Gardano, possibly to the latter, who developed the former's technique of the unequally divided voices of two choirs. This might explain the "mass of harmony" and its "imposing" effect.

One of the most beautiful pieces in Roman Catholic liturgy, the "Dies Irae," occupies a place of distinction in *Ferragus*. Balzac sought to communicate to the reader the grand, sober, dramatic, and pathetic impressions he had received from it; like Maurice Barrès who trembled at the thought of man's feebleness (Leopardi more philosophically would only observe man's exiguity) before the endlessness of being, his mind and flesh quivered before the otherworldly visions presented by the music with which he highlights Mme Jules' funeral:

Terror rose from all parts of the church; everywhere cries of anguish responded to cries of dismay. This frightening music spoke of agony unknown to the world, of secret friendship lamenting the dead. Never, in any human religion, have the terrors of the soul, violently stripped of the body and tempestuously agitated in the presence of the thundering majesty of God, been rendered so vigorously. Before that clamor of clamors, artists and their most impassioned works must humble themselves. No, nothing can rival that singing that embodies human passions and galvanizes them into a life beyond the tomb by leading them, throbbing still, to the presence of the living and avenging God. Those shrieks of youth, joined to the sounds of deeper

> voices, which then, in that canticle of death, embrace human life in all its developments, recalling the pains of cradled infancy, swelling into all the suffering of later years with the broader tones of the adults together with the quavering strains of the old men and priests—all that strident harmony full of thunder and lightning, does it not speak to the most undaunted imaginations, to the most frigid hearts, and to philosophers themselves? Listening to it sounds as if God were thundering. No church vault anywhere is cold; they all quiver, they speak, they pour forth fear with all the power of their echoes. You think you see the countless dead rising with outstretched hands. It is no longer a father, a wife, or a child under the black pall; it is humanity emerging from its dust. [F 111]

The "Dies Irae" is a remarkable old ecclesiastical melody in mixed Dorian mode, in form not a liturgical sequence properly speaking because the tune was adapted to Tommaso di Celano's poem. At Saint-Gatien, Balzac very likely heard a version close to the original, possibly one by Asola, Vecchi, Anerio, or Pitoni. But in *Ferragus*, dedicated to Berlioz, there was also the recollection of the *Symphonie fantastique*, where the hymn of the dead resounds in an extraordinarily realistic setting. Balzac approaches the piece by combining earlier and more recent memories, stressing majestically what was for him its broadly imaginative and distinctively dramatic character. Bertault analyzes this background very accurately.

The chant is similarly evoked in *Melmoth réconcilié* when Rodolphe Castanier, attending the services for John Melmoth in Saint-Sulpice, is moved to tears and fear, despite his inability to understand the Latin text. Suddenly, he believes in God. "The *Dies Irae* frightened him. He understood, in all its grandeur, that cry of the repenting soul that quakes before infinite majesty" (MR 303). God made perceptible to the heart through liturgy and sacred music: this Bertault calls one of the most important facts of religious psychology, and this Balzac believes. For the words of the liturgy that tell of the Savior who is ready to forgive the sinner as he had Lady Magdalen and the thief, could not be understood by the uneducated cashier Castanier who had sold his soul to the Devil. Only the music could act upon his groping thoughts, and act subconsciously, somewhat similarly to the roulade that "awakens" in Capraja's soul "a thousand slumbering ideas." It startled his conscience with a simple contrast. After the terror of the "Dies Irae," he found his peace in faith, in the soothing promptings of a suave music that intensified his remorse, and by so doing opened up "the azure poetry and the distant luminosity of hope" (MR 304). The new melody, not in the cathedral but in his soul, as it were, might well have been "In Paradisium."

The question of the relationship of music to text in liturgical chant had provoked considerable discussion in Balzac's day (it dates back to a Renaissance controversy that only Palestrina resolved), with authoritative opinion favoring verbal emphasis over melody because of the chant's oratorical rhythm. Castanier's conversion, therefore, is also interesting because through it Balzac appears to decide in favor of the opposite view, a decision that places him in agreement with today's practice. Balzac was not alone, however: Lamennais, too, in his *Esquisse d'une philosophie*, spoke of the pure melody of Church hymns as bridging intimate feelings with the spiritual realities of man. Hugo, Liszt, and Vigny also favored Lamennais' position. But their opinion was nonetheless unique for their time.

Balzac's musical sensitivity reveals itself unarguably through his instinctive fondness for plainchant. He did more than Pétrus Borel who complained about the intrusion of profane music in churches.[5] We must credit Balzac with an attempt to rehabilitate the more and more forgotten dignity of the religious hymns, with possessing, as Bertault points out, a well developed sense for ancient, unisonous, unmetrical melody years before the Benedictines began their task of restoring its beauties. His prose becomes suffused with poetic eloquence at the mere hint of a hymn. He can distinguish between the exuberance of "O Filii," the tenderness of "Venite, adoremus," and the dramatic pathétique of "Dies Irae." In *La Peau de chagrin*, as later in *Le Médecin de campagne*, *Le Cousin Pons*, *Le Lys dans la vallée* and other novels, we continue to experience in different contexts Balzac's affinity for sacred music. Typical is Raphael's comparison of the murmur of branches by a lake with the voice of the cloister, "a monotonic voice resembling the psalmodies of monks" (PC 224). Once, in 1832, he had strolled with Mme de Castries along the outer walls of the Monastère de la Grande-Chartreuse in Aix, where he had listened soulfully to "those old men unknown to the world and dead to the world singing their prayers."[6] Balzac's words could not be more heartfelt.

The Organ

Balzac's fondness for the organ provides a further illustration of his penchant for religious music. Greatly affected by the grandeur of its symphonic force in *La Duchesse de Langeais*, he reserved for it nevertheless a quieter devotional role elsewhere. The subdued accompaniments of the instrument that humbles its power to become part of the unity of purpose symbolized by the altar stimulated the novelist's imagination. Bossuet might have said that it leaves itself in order to rise to God, or in order to lift our feelings and thoughts to God. It becomes the moving element of a trinity that conjoins religion and love. Lamartine's "Religion-God-Music" bespeaks a similar view. The inspired Carmelite organist, Sister Thérèse, read on the keyboard the text of her recollections: "Religion, Love, and Music—are they not the triple expression of a single fact, the need to grow with which every noble soul is travailed? These three poems all go to God. . ., Whom we never envisage without surrounding Him with the flames of love, the sistra of music, the light of harmony. Is He not the principle and goal of our works?" (DL 133-134). The nun's love harbors the exile's love of country, a religious sensibility analogous to the sinner's nostalgia for the heavenly home he has forsaken. From the "Te Deum" one day to the "Magnificat" the next, the organ's subtle and colorful commentary imbues her invocations with tenderness. Bertault describes them as rich and graceful developments, flourishes, lively phrases, changing modes, agitations, delirious and flexible fugues, prolonged melancholy, soft modulations, deep sorrow, lofty tones expressing angelic choirs, and echoes of torrential chagrin. This indeed was Balzac's intention. No surprise, then, that after such a troubled mixture of sentiments interpreted by the organ, the final chord of the *Amen* sounds as no other instrument could, like a "grave, solemn, awesome return to God" (DL 133), leaving behind a sepulchral silence. "As one follows this development, if one has been modestly initiated, one imagines oneself translating all these emotions. One sees oneself pulling and combining the appropriate registers, coupling the keyframes. And the organ is animated; it speaks. . . . Clamor of the reed-stops, moans of the violas, murmurs of the drones, chants of the flute-stops! . . . The hallucination is complete."[7] For Bertault, Lamennais's words on the organ fall short of Balzac's eloquence. We agree. In *La Duchesse de Langeais*, Balzac anticipates what he meant later in *Séraphîta* when the temporarily humanized angel, like Flaubert who will see the soul reaching God via the organ, refers to the instrument as the only one befitting the depiction of infinite horizons.

Mystical Essences

The liturgical chants of the Catholic Church represented for Balzac the origin and foundation of the art of music in all its forms. The novelist who claimed to write by the eternal truth of Religion never lost his affinity for religious music. His devotion presupposed his faith, and his faith, like love, represented an indispensable corollary to the understanding of music. Gambara implied it when he described the music he was analyzing as unfit for nonbelievers and for those who do not love. Again we read: "nonbelievers do not love music, the heavenly language developed by Catholicism, which has named the seven notes from one of its hymns" (UM 314),[8] Religious music may express human and divine love because all music favors our religious inclinations. Indeed, Balzac's inclinations ran so deep that he became very discriminating in his preferences. As late as 1846, while visiting St. Peter's basilica in Rome, he so preferred a "Miserere" by Pietro Guglielmi to one of Valentino Fioravanti performed in the Sistine Chapel that he returned to hear it: "Nothing surpasses the choir's *Miserere*, which is so superior to the one in the Sistine Chapel that I didn't want to listen to the latter. I preferred to hear twice the one in St. Peter. This one was a music of angels; the other, which was well crafted, seemed bad to me, despite the performance."[9]

If religion and music are to coexist, their prerequisite in human beings is pureness. The candid, child-like soul of any mortal, musician or not, can hear the voice of angels. So Pierrette, a humble peasant girl, can listen poetically to Weber, Beethoven, and Hérold (P); the naive Calyste can shed a tear in the presence of Conti's art (B); Eugène can glow with love at the words "My dear Annette, my beloved" which evoke "the divine notes of *Venite, adoremus* retold by the organ" (EG 576); a young and sick farmer can move the saintly Benassis with his folk melody (MC); and the simple, uneducated Etienne and Gabrielle, angels in their own right, can adopt music as the most delicate of languages (EM). Similarly Pons, a "pure soul," and Schmucke who had retained "his child-like naïveté," believed firmly that music was "the language of Heaven" that plunged them into private, ecstatic experiences (CP 536, 538, 539).

The mysticism that penetrated Balzac's emotions at performances of religious music, like the "Miserere" of Guglielmi, found its counterpart in his readings of Swedenborg, as recounted in *Séraphita*. In order to write this novel, he confessed to Mme Hanska that he would have to "hear the music of the angels."[10] His inspiration shaped poetically the soul's constant aspiration toward Heaven whereby Wilfrid and Minna rose to the summit of Mount Falberg in Norway. "Leaning on that nature subtilized by space, one feels inside more depth than mind, more grandeur than enthusiasm, more energy than will; one experiences sensations whose interpreter is no longer within us" (S 473). Such is the background of his definition of music: "the art which penetrates most into the soul. . . . It alone has the power to make us draw into ourselves . . . [and] . . . this power over our inner being is one of its grandeurs" (G 436; MD 356). What he sought in Beethoven he found in religious music: feeling elevated into limitless spheres—to paraphrase his words—where sensations of all kinds become abstractions and where the most commonplace works of nature are transmuted into divine symbols. Music, in this sense, is a means of self-sanctification, conferring on the human being humility, repentance, and eagerness for purification. It enhances the language of exhortation, stirring man's feelings which then become more susceptible to the act of grace. How else may Castanier's salvation be explained? Even a simple romance in *Robert le Diable* is galvanized by its religious context. The holy music of the Church provides this opera with an electrifying climax (G). *Séraphita*'s divine expanse, its revelation of creation, rests on the spiritual analogy Balzac makes between mysticism and music, "like an organ which . . . reveals the musical universe" (S 560). A higher place could not be accorded to music, for *Séraphita* represents philosophically one of the culminating novels of *La Comédie humaine*.

When it came to religious music, Balzac surpassed his contemporaries in sheer intensity of feeling. And in vision. There was no Strunz, no Berlioz, no Liszt, no vogue to guide his thoughts where plainsong was concerned. Recognizing its meditational essence, he saw through the aesthetic transgressions of his day and understood the music's linear melody, transparent rhythm, and elevated monotones, aversion to agitation, and suspended construction in space and time. Through it Balzac expressed the many ethical ideas that moved his intellectual and moral conscience, its aspirations and convictions. Bertault's concluding remarks are apposite: ". . . it is to his credit to have treated plainchant with intelligent admiration, sympathy, and respect at a time when those who were its official custodians charged with attending to its honor vilified it. Here again, Balzac shows himself as a forerunner; a kind of divination inspires him. In explaining the sense and the richness of liturgical chant and of religious music, he contributed enthusiastically to restore favorable opinion about the Church and its institutions, to rally around the sanctuary those souls who were sensitive to beauty and harmony."[11] No praise is more fitting for the man whose supernal philosophical leanings made him value Dante's *Paradiso* above his *Inferno*.

CHAPTER VIII

BEETHOVEN: THE GROWTH OF A CONCEPT

Beethoven's Reception in France

Ludwig van Beethoven's acceptance by the French public was slow and far from complete even by the end of Balzac's life. If a few connoisseurs recognized the transcendent power of the composer's symphonies, many more expressed diffidence and dislike for them, and his chamber works, according to Romain Rolland, had to wait until well after his death—and Balzac's—to make a definitive inroad into French musical consciousness. In 1811, at a time when the first six of Beethoven's symphonies had reached the European public, one read the following opinion in the musical periodical *Tablettes de Polymnie*: "This composer Beethoven, often bizarre and baroque, sometimes sparkles with extraordinary beauties. Now he flies majestically like an eagle; then he creeps along grotesque paths. After penetrating the soul with a sweet melancholy, he soon tears it apart with a mass of barbaric chords. He seems to harbor doves and crocodiles at the same time."[1]

Conductor Habeneck's grand effort, six to ten times a year from 1828 onward, to install Beethoven's music in France made it possible for Parisians to hear all nine symphonies by March of 1831.[2] Had it not been for his genial baton, which revealed the Ninth Symphony to Wagner in Paris when Leipzig and other German cities had been unable to hear it performed, not many Frenchmen would have been shaken from their torpor. The Société's little concert hall was filled to capacity with cheering audiences, tickets had to be purchased months in advance, Malibran swooned the first time she heard the Fifth Symphony, Vigny began an unfinished poem in an epic mood entitled *Beethoven*, and beginning in 1834, *La Gazette Musicale* praised consistently the master from Bonn. In addition, there were the literary interpretations of Beethoven by d'Ortigue, the determination of Castil-Blaze to reconcile the

German's scores with Romantic trends, the crusading zeal of Berlioz, Liszt's piano transcriptions of the symphonies, and the praises of Hugo, Sand, Nerval, Lamennais, Deschamps. . . .[3] All these plaudits, not to speak of the earlier panegyrics of Hoffmann, reached Balzac in the middle of his long standing and fervent adherence to Rossinian music. We cannot say, however, that his attraction to Beethoven followed the common manner of a fad, or that what he heard about the composer represented anything like a fad. The stirs that Habeneck's concerts provoked resembled little more than ripples in the wider pool of animosity and uncertainty that characterized French reaction. If a chronicler in an 1837 issue of *L'Artiste* congratulated the Société because "now we want to hear Beethoven symphonies every evening," whereas about decade before people had declared "that Beethoven was a maniac and that his symphonies would be hissed by our public,"[4] we should not overlook Berlioz's lament of that same year: "Many people are beginning to talk with a certain disdain about these immortal productions. Well, gentlemen, truthfully, when you see daily and without surprise the announcements of the fiftieth performance of some dramatic platitude, is it abusing your patience to offer you with such discrete persistence masterpieces of such breadth?"[5]

The cultural mood of the country, dominated by Italian or Italianate music (a rubric which included Mozart and Haydn) tended to oppose the incursion of the German school. Mme de Staël herself, in her Teutonic-minded *De l'Allemagne*, had not mentioned Beethoven, and Chateaubriand had found only one brief moment to refer to him, in *Mémoires d'outre-tombe*. Albeit with reservations, Stendhal preferred Rossini, and if he manifested some respect for the German, he did so on the basis of his "scientific and almost mathematical harmony" insofar as it elicits thought, which for him remained only second to feeling.[6] Lamartine, although lured by the dreamy exercise of the imagination that Beethoven occasioned in him, indicated nonetheless in his *Entretien* on Mozart that he would like to be Mozart or Rossini. Chopin expressed himself with cautious disapproval, and Adam, in adopting Rossini's style for *La Muette de Portici* in 1828, showed he conferred the honor of primacy upon the Italian composer. The larger public agreed with this, with its reactionary critics like Paul Scudo, or with its musical historians like Fétis, who might grant that Beethoven was a philosopher and thinker but refused to acknowledge him as an artist and musician: "if he is undoubtedly a man of genius, even of immense genius, he is not a man of taste."[7] When his *Revue Musicale* passed into his son's hands in 1833, Fétis Jr. continued in the family tradition.[8] The uncertainty needed many more years to dissipate, and while the process began during Balzac's lifetime, four years after his death readers of *La Revue des Deux Mondes* could still find none other than the usually perspicacious Delacroix stating reservations, accusing

Beethoven of want of "correctness" and lack of "rigorous proportions," and concluding with uneasy approval: "I shall, however, agree with him even against my feeling."[9]

Beethoven's Gradual Ascendancy

Balzac did not oscillate. The earliest documented encounter between him and Beethoven's music is recorded in an article of 1831 which refers to "a piece by Beethoven, a score full of charm and glitter."[10] In January of 1834 in Geneva, he heard a selection from the Sixth Symphony. Then—again in terms of the record we have—he heard the Fifth, one of Habeneck's brilliant performances which brought the entire audience simultaneously to its feet.[11] This time the novelist was thunderstruck. We cannot determine, however, exactly how many works by the master he heard during the course of his musical evenings, and to go by his own account, we are left with a disarming statistic. "You understand," he wrote to Mme Hanska toward the end of 1837, "that I still only know the Symphony in C minor and the little excerpt from the Pastoral Symphony which together we went to hear butchered on a third floor in Geneva. . .?"[12] But it is difficult to accept this as the truth, because, as we have noted, for a year Balzac had sought many ways in his correspondence to dispel his Polish lady's suspicions about his private life with declarations of hard work and of an uneventful social and cultural existence.[13] Then, too, as one of Liszt's favorite listeners since the beginning of their friendship about a half decade before, he certainly had heard, along with sonatas he grew to appreciate, like "Les Adieux," at least the piano transcriptions of the symphonies. Definitely the *Eroica*. The evenings at Fétis' and Erard's, which he sometimes attended, featured works by Beethoven, not to mention the Concerts du Conservatoire. This is the background which permitted him to refer to the Seventh Symphony in *Ursule Mirouët* and to compare the Fifth with its "brilliant sisters" in *César Birotteau*.

Compared with his immediately enthusiastic response to Rossini's music, Balzac's response to Beethoven's was gradual. We witness here the growth of a concept which, for all its attractiveness, he was never able to express meaningfully in words. The music was impressive, but remained enigmatic. His earliest reference in a novel to the composer appears insignificantly in 1829 in *La Physiologie du mariage*. Then in 1831, in the description of an orgy in *La Peau de chagrin*, we come across an insecure allusion to the occasional lulls in the party's movement: "Those alternations of silence and noise resembled vaguely a Beethoven symphony" (PC 65). Balzac missed completely the charged pathos of such silences which, as Rousseau had prophesied, come within the orbit of musical descriptiveness. After a few pages, the novelist abandons objective analogy in favor of subjective meaning: "I exhaled my unhappiness in melodies. Beethoven or Mozart were often my discrete confidants" (PC 76).[14] That was the year in which he had referred to a piece by Beethoven with the vague nouns "charm" and "glitter." In *Louis Lambert* in 1832, he was content to place Beethoven's name in music alongside the names of those who represent the summits of achievement in other fields: Columbus, Raphael, Napoleon, and Laplace.

Two years later the concept begins to mature; Balzac refers to the Fifth Symphony with reverence: "After that sublime musical poem, there is nothing left to say; we can only lower our heads in meditation. . . ."[15] Then in *La Recherche de l'Absolu* Beethoven is a great figure who is misunderstood and whose simplicity of means alienates the intricacy-minded public: "The crowd prefers generally an abnormal force that overflows to an equal force that persists. The crowd has neither time nor patience to notice the immense power hidden under a uniform appearance" (RA 475). That same year, between the 28th of April and the 10th of May, after hearing a performance of the Fifth Symphony—his sole distraction, he claims—the theme of jealousy, as tangible an indication of his fascination as there is, appears in his correspondence in a letter to Mme Hanska: "I am jealous only of the illustrious dead: Beethoven, Michelangelo, Raphael, Poussin, Milton . . .,"[16] and in 1835, in *Séraphita*, his emotional agitation continues before the composer's "palaces of harmony" which he can only compare with one of his most respected literary figures, Dante. Here he attempts to formulate an appropriate analogical vocabulary to describe his feelings, relying on visual images like "a river of light" and "waves of flames" to express what he views as the unseizable immensity of the two artists: "You roll in endless whirls, where your mind cannot always sustain you; certainly! you must of necessity have a powerful intelligence to come out of it all safe and sound. . ." (S 513).

One senses a crescendo in Balzac's reaction, an increasing fondness for the music: among his recent winter pleasures he includes, in March of 1835, "the Beethoven performed at the Conservatoire as it will never be performed anywhere else."[17] As the term "metaphysical genius," with which Beethoven was frequently described by admirers as well as by some uneasy detractors, acquired innuendoes of magnitude, Balzac focused more and more on the spirit of the composer's music, on the mystical beauties it revealed and the gigantic ideas it inspired, ideas in fact so gigantic that they defied definition. A French musician around 1840 said retrospectively: "Beethoven taught us the poetry of music; his work awakened in us for the first time a consciousness of the dignity of our profession, and after having partly grasped him, we soon recognized the duty, entrusted to us, of becoming the promulgators of his idea. He is our delight, but our despair too whenever we endeavor to emulate him."[18] Unable to seize the "idea," Balzac turned to conquer the "poetry." His was a Romantic reaction, to be sure, like a religious response that raised the composer onto a remote sphere from which he threatened all who approached, and that enabled him to achieve formidable size and forbidding aloofness. Those to whom Beethoven spoke could not speak of him in turn except with a vocabulary of awe. Berlioz above all, and the isolated, intellectually aristocratic members of La Jeune France who identified the great symphonic composer's work with the fulfillment of their own artistic cause, referred to him as a poet-superman and fired their comments with poetical images, transforming a musical composition into a tableau of quasi-allegorical significance. Typical is Berlioz's comparison: Beethoven is "like those eagles of the Andes who wing through space at heights below which other creatures would find nothing but asphyxiation and death." Again, he describes a movement that seemed "as if it had been sadly murmured by the Archangel Michael on some day when, overcome by a feeling of melancholy, he contemplated the universe from the threshold of the empyrean."[19] Or he praises the Pastoral Symphony in accordance with varied passages: "These living pictures! These perfumes! That light! That eloquent silence! That vast horizon!"[20] D'Ortigue's descriptions of the Fifth Symphony were thoroughly "unmusical" and just as literary as those of the music chronicler of *Le Rénovateur*.[21] It was Berlioz who taught those around him—Castil-Balze, d'Ortigue, Berthé, Chrétien Urhan—to speak of Beethoven in imagistic language, establishing a glossary of interpretation that relied on the poetic imagination and on seemingly unrelated ideas to render better the impressions of what Countess d'Agoult called "the most intimate depths of the self,"[22] and Vigny "the echo of another world."[23] Indeed, albeit for different reasons, as Berlioz chose never to speak of Beethoven as a "musician" because the terms can be misleading and belittling, or as he refused to refer to his "compositions" because the word "poems" could embrace much more, so Balzac gravitated conveniently toward the sense of poetry that wafted from the idea rather than toward the idea itself, which he felt incapable of transmitting. He concealed his inability under inventive images and a selective vocabulary that echoed the Romantic view with lofty feelings; these longed for remote regions of ecstasy and compelled the soul to gaze steadily into the infinite. For the esoteric élite that felt itself drawn to the great symphonies, the word "infinite" solved the enigma of Beethoven.

Beginning with *Le Lys dans la vallée* of 1835-36, a lyrical novel pervaded by a fragrance of country blossoms, Balzac's references to Beethoven acquired poetic hues. One thing that struck him about the Fifth Symphony was the way in which the last movement recalls rhythmically the first and transforms melodically and harmonically the opening theme. About the bouquets gathered for his Platonic mistress Mme de Mortsauf, the narrator Félix de Vandenesse writes that they resembled "symphonies of flowers, in which my unsatisfied desire made me deploy the efforts that Beethoven expressed with his notes: profound doubling back onto itself, prodigious flights toward heaven." As Mme de Mortsauf "nourished herself" looking at them intensely and fondly, their lovely presence instilled in her the very feelings he had had while picking them, transforming the flowers into "all the thoughts I had placed in them"(LV 857). A letter to Mme Hanska in 1836 speaks of "the feeling that a beautiful Beethoven passage gives us by presenting, in its purest expression, a whole feeling, a whole nature." It bespeaks the loftiness of this feeling with the addition "in heaven, everything is infinite."[24] Balzac's poetic impulse intensifies. So when the theme of jealousy returns in another letter one year later, Michelangelo, Raphael, Poussin, and Milton have been superseded by the sole and "illustrious" personality of the composer: "Beethoven is the only man who makes me know jealousy." There is no doubt of his ascendancy in Balzac's mind when we come to the next sentence: "I should have wanted to be Beethoven rather than Rossini and Mozart." The apogee has been reached. Even his friend from Pesaro must step down in favor of the master from Bonn, for "there is a divine power in this man." And with this, the novelist plunges into a flowery description of the Finale of the Fifth Symphony: "In his *Finale*, it seems that an enchanter lifts you away into a world of wonders, amid the most beautiful palaces that contain the marvels of all the arts, and there, at his command, doors like those of the Baptistry [of Florence] turn on their hinges and permit you to perceive beauties of an unknown kind, the fairies of fantasy. They are creatures who fly about with the beauties of woman and the variegated wings of angels, and you are immersed in a superior air, that air which, according to Swedenborg, sings and spreads its fragrance, which has color and feeling, and which abounds, and which beautifies you." Then Balzac asserts the supremacy of music over literature, and terminates the letter with a brief allusion to his correspondent's city in Ukraine "where there is no Beethoven symphony."[25]

Beethoven's Fifth and *César Birotteau*

During the "twenty-five nights and twenty-five days"[26] of November and December, 1837, in which Balzac labored to meet the publication deadline for *Histoire de la grandeur et de la décadence de César Birotteau*, he inserted into the novel a similar, but longer and more ecstatic description of the Finale of the Fifth Symphony. Again Balzac listens to this "ideal" music through the earphones of literary images, following the pattern of those who, like Lamennais, tried to fathom mystically the depths of those "marvelous poems by Beethoven."[27] The Finale represents by analogy what the ball of Birotteau, celebrating his new apartment decorated by Grindot and his own decoration with the star of the Legion of Honor, represents in his life. His long-cherished ambition realized, the virtuous perfumer has reached a culminating moment of grandeur. The first part of the novel, "César à son apogée," ends with a recollection of the symphony's final Allegro:

> In Beethoven's eight symphonies,[28] there is a fantasy that is as large as a poem; it is the culminating point of the Finale of the Symphony in C minor. When, after the sublime magician's slow preparation so well understood by Habeneck, a gesture by the enthusiastic conductor raises the luxurious curtain on the scene, summoning forth with his bow the resplendent theme toward which all the musical forces have converged, then poets with palpitating hearts will understand that the ball produced in Birotteau's life the effect that was produced in their own souls by that fecund theme, which probably makes the C minor Symphony superior to her brilliant sisters. A radiant fairy leaps upward lifting her wand. You hear the rustling of the curtain's purple silk which is being drawn by angels. Golden doors sculpted like those of the Florentine Baptistry turn on their adamantine hinges. Your eye sinks into those splendid sights; it encompasses a vista of marvelous palaces about which glide supernatural forms. The incense of prosperity burns, the altar of happiness is aflame, a fragrant air circulates! Beings with divine smiles, donning white tunics edged in blue, float lightly before your eyes, disclosing their unearthly, beautiful faces and their infinitely delicate shapes. The Loves hover about, spreading fires from their torches! You feel loved; you are delighted with a happiness that you inhale without understanding it as you bathe in the waves of that harmony that streams downward and pours for everybody the nectar of his choice. Your heart has been touched in its secret hope, now momentarily realized. After having strolled in the heavens, the enchanter, through some deep

and mysterious movement of the basses, plunges you once again into the marshes of cold realities, only to remove you from them when he has awakened your thirst for his divine melodies and when your soul implores: More! [CB 463]

If this lavish and languorous cascade of visions suits M. Birotteau's euphoric mood, it does not suit Beethoven's compelling, energetic mettle. Instead of being overwhelmed by the almost martial pounding of the Finale's rhythm, the protagonist is lifted on heavy wings to a beatific fairyland of harems. In this singular failure, Balzac outdoes descriptively the literary habits of his contemporary melophiles. His optical orgy forsakes the permissible language of lyrical emotion which leaves the image fugacious and transparent, and indulges in an idiom of relief and color. By using an overly rich brush, he fails to subordinate the elements of his description of the logic of the musical form and to intellectual clarity. Too much "observation" strangles the dream he wished to communicate, and the auditive impression becomes visual ludicrousness.

Balzac's poetic debauch has nonetheless its psychological interest. That he abandoned himself to such an ungermane cascade of visions betrays a lack of control over the subject matter, and a resultant dramatic struggle with himself, with his inability to match verbally the music's beauty. We are touched and smile in sympathy. Balzac confessed his apprehension that same year: "No, the spirit of a writer does not provide such joys because what we depict is finite, determinate, whereas what Beethoven hurls at you is infinite!"[29] So he released his copious images in the hope that their sheer number would constitute a form of tribute to the source that inspired them.

In the long novel, Birotteau's ball represents but an instant of attainment as the fateful knocks on the door by his dishonest subaltern, Crevel, announce a sad unfolding of events. The Finale is also a finale of the "grandeur," a commencement of the "fall." The Fifth Symphony makes a second appearance at the end of *César Birotteau* when the merchant, though almost on his deathbed, has emerged from ruin after an epic struggle of honesty and smiles at the rehabilitation of his finances. Here, as if he had just reheard the work, Balzac's characterization of the music is more exact. He speaks of "the heroic movement of the Finale of the great symphony" which "in the head and heart" of the perfumer rang like a "grand finale," or of "that ideal music [that] made its clarions sound" (CB 590). In retrospect, the suggestive language used to describe the music at the ball served to convey merely an impression of grandeur; now the more precise vocabulary asserts its realization. Berlioz found the key to the Finale's prodigious effect not only in its dynamic swelling but also in its modulation from minor to major.[30] Something similar occurs in Balzac's novel as it moves from the major of the "grandeur" to the minor of the "fall" and back to the major of the triumphant restoration.

In this respect, Balzac may have emulated the structure of Beethoven's movement. There is no doubt that the impressiveness of the musical insertions in the novel lies not in what the descriptions say but in what they do. A vast sweep of events climaxed by two dramatic musical appearances bespeaks an architectural purpose which, in this case, is highly successful. The Finale is not evoked only as a comparison with two moments in the merchant's life,[31] the way the finale of Mozart's *Don Giovanni* is introduced in *Le Cabinet des antiques*. It serves a powerful structural function, the second evocation acting like another "profound doubling back onto itself" that unifies the novel through its cyclic force. Théophile Gautier was to remark that one of music's superiorities resides in its "facility to express simultaneously a complex feeling, a scene with several facets."[32] He uses it accordingly, in *Jettatura*, to advance the action. So do Stendhal, Musset, Mérimée, and Sand. But none ever "produced the effect invented by Balzac to prolong and enlarge states of paroxysm.[33]

Beethoven's Presence in *Gambara*

While Balzac was writing *César Birotteau*, he was also writing *Gambara*, a work in which we find his first and only attempt to understand musical method technically. Although its purpose centered around an analysis of a Meyerbeer opera and an explication of one of the protagonist's own, many clues point to the presence of Beethoven in the background of the whole tale. To begin with, it expounds theses which come more within the orbit of symphonic than of operatic music. There is what Balzac considered a Germanic sense of harmony in Gambara's aesthetics and in his consciousness of instruments, qualities which the novelist associated with Beethoven. Gambara himself, the composer of new music, is a misunderstood artist. He compares his music with Beethoven's, and happens to begin the Overture of his opera in the key of the Fifth Symphony, Balzac's favorite. Then there is a subtle implication: we know that Gambara's music met with no success in Italy, and we are forced to make a telling association when he exclaims that if one gives the Italians some Beethoven, "they are no longer with you" (G 437). Furthermore, one of the characters, the conductor Gigelmi, "one of the greatest musical celebrities" (G 424), who makes perceptive remarks about his art, is deaf. And finally, there are many and obsessive references to Beethoven, including an association with a "prodigious doubling back of the whole opera onto itself" (G 449). One exchange in particular between the conductor and Count Andrea Marcosini arrests our attention. Gigelmi's comments still bear the poetical imprint; though deprived of his auditory sense, he hears—or sees—the music, because "Music exists independently of execution. . . . During the opening measures of Beethoven's Symphony in C minor, a musician is soon transported into a world of fantasy on the golden wings of the theme in G natural, repeated in E by the horns. He sees all of nature, illuminated in turn by dazzling sheaves of light, darkened by clouds of melancholy, and enlivened by divine hymns . . .; Beethoven has extended the limits of instrumental music, and no one has followed him on his course. . ." (G 430). In contrast, the Count's comments are surprisingly exact:

> Above all, his works are remarkable in their simplicity of design, and in the way the design is followed. With most composers, wild and disordered orchestral voices interlace only to produce a momentary effect; they do not always make the regularity of their pace coincide with the piece as a whole. With Beethoven, effects are distributed in advance, so to speak. Similar to the various regiments that contribute to the winning of a battle by regular movements, the orchestral voices of Beethoven's symphonies follow the commands given in the general interest, and are subordinated to admirably conceived designs. . . . At a given moment, the themes farthest removed from the action join in the development, as if pulled by strings woven into the fabric of his composition.[34] [G 430]

Alfred Einstein has pointed out that, characteristically, the Romantics misunderstood Beethoven. They admired his symphonies not for the clarity of their form, the taming of all excessive impulses, but because of the manifold possibilities of interpreting them. Hence the encouragement to talk of "poetry" for those who felt that the composer was especially "deep" because they did not quite understand him,[35] or could not comprehend purely instrumental music in general. With or without Strunz's help, Balzac shows by his approach and the accuracy of the Count's observation that this time he may have succeeded in glimpsing, however briefly, "beauties of an unknown kind." His analogy with the instrumental order of battle, recalling the brief implication in *César Birotteau* of the "musical forces" which "converge," bespeaks a growing awareness on his part of pure music and of the abstract calculations upon which a large part of the moving power of music depends. To be able to sense—we do not wish to say distinguish—the organized forces of a score requires a listening attitude different from the one required to appreciate program music or opera. Hoffmann had already asked in his comments on Beethoven's instrumental music: "When one speaks of music as an autonomous art, should one not always think only of instrumental music, which, disdaining any help, any admixture with another art, gives pure expression to the peculiar and otherwise unrecognizable nature of the art?"[36] Such music is formally and essentially untranslatable into another idiom. As Liszt professed, words tend to destroy the magic, to desecrate the feelings. Something of this attitude permeates the would-be eccentric infatuations of Cataneo and Capraja with wordless musical expressions, the roulade and the blending of two tones. The analyses of *Mahomet* and *Robert le Diable* notwithstanding, *Gambara* represents a claim on behalf of instrumental music against the existing supremacy of opera. And it was Beethoven who, while initiating Balzac into the vaporous sphere of the infinite, also offered him his first key to the citadel of symphonic music.

Dénouement of the Concept

The year 1837 marks neither the end of Balzac's Beethovenian passion nor the beginning of his admiration.[37] It marks, rather, a culmination, after which a dénouement occurs. After this year, Balzac endeavors to put the composer of the Fifth Symphony and the composer of *Mosè in Egitto* into perspective. Not even a "divine power" could usurp the prominent position which Rossini had held for so many years. In 1839, *Massimilla Doni*'s patriotic exhortation before "triumphant Italy" (MD 357) and the heroine's faith in the Homeric respect that Rossini would some day enjoy, rehabilitate his friend; Beethoven and the *tedeschi* are made to genuflect. Elsewhere in the tale, however, Beethoven is treated with reverence, as by implication in the paragraph where the *entirety* of the Fifth Symphony is declared eternal while the supreme accomplishments of other composers are measured only in short selections (Mozart's Finale of *Don Giovanni*, Marcello's "Coeli enarrant gloriam Die," Pergolesi's "Pria che spunti," Cimarosa's *Stabat*, and Rossini's "Mi manca la voce").

Beethoven reappears in novels and correspondence in sentimental settings: In *Béatrix* (1839) as a favorite composer to whose works Félicité des Touches returns with affection after a venturesome episode, and as an inspiring symphonist in a letter to Marceline Desbordes-Valmore (1840), whose finely written messages Balzac likened to "the most beautiful passages in a symphony by Beethoven."[38] Then in 1841, *Ursule Mirouët* portrays another heroine who confides in the composer, this time in his Seventh Symphony which she plays on the piano, and which Balzac imagined undoubtedly in the form of one of Liszt's accomplished transcriptions. Aware of the technical difficulties involved, the novelist wished to enhance Ursule's talent, which had been "brought to perfection" (UM 384) by her teacher, Schmucke. Always amazed by Liszt and by the digital intricacies of Beethoven's music when performed on the keyboard, Balzac could not help exclaiming once to Mme Hanska about her pianist daughter: "Tell me how old Anna is, who understands Beethoven!"[39] The very tone the last word acquires in this exclamation registers awe. His music is "grandiose," and the Seventh Symphony "has to be studied in order to be understood" (UM 364).[40] Therefore, if Gambara was correct when he stated that such great music can only invite the attention of genial listeners, then Ursule may well use it as a godly weapon with which to rid her home of unwelcome, boorish visitors who have nothing in common with grandeur.

Yet Rossini is not forgotten. A letter to l'Etrangère in 1845 shows that Balzac's esteem has not waned: "Last night I went to hear the *Desert* symphony, and I was stunned. Nothing better of its kind has been done since Beethoven, except for Rossini, of course."[41] Indeed, when the name of the German master is absent, Rossini enjoys the enduring devotion of a man whose heart, Pascal would say, has its own reasons. But when it is Rossini's name which is absent and that of Beethoven stands magically alone, then Balzac's reason pays tribute to an artist whom he can only associate with the adjective "sublime": "the sublime productions" (G 430), "a sublime symphony,"[42] "the sublime magician" (CB 463), "that sublime musical poem,"[43] and, in December of 1845, the ecstatic declaration: "the genius of Beethoven, it's sublime!"[44]

For while Beethoven did not cause a change in his musical evolution but rather entered it as an addition, Balzac remained in the long run convinced of his ultimate and absolute greatness. As such, he represents Balzac's second important musical persuasion. "He still has not been understood," he wrote, "so how can he be surpassed?" (G 430). Self-confession, historical truth, and admiration make these words a welcome shift from those of less perceptive, Stendhalian intellects, Balzac's contemporaries, who remained eternally mistrustful of the message from across the Rhine, not to speak of those of ill-disposed spokesmen who even later maltreated Beethoven, the various Tolstoys in their ascetic detestation of superiority. More than that of anyone else, Beethoven's music, as Hoffmann had declared about the Fifth Symphony, confirmed the alliance of genius and art in the highest degree. And this art embodied an important Balzacian principle, that of passing, as Gambara puts it, "from sensation to idea" (G 472).

But what "ideas" did Balzac grasp? The sense of the infinite that emerges from Beethoven's developments which, however concise, leave us with the ring of endless other possibilities? The suggestive power of the orchestration, its discursive motives and harmonic implications which prompt bright or dark dispositions toward life and nature? Romantically, the Faustian dimensions of the composer's independence and originality which "draw from the fluids and saps of universal life . . . in order to seize infinite Nature, or more correctly to communicate with her, to lose oneself in her"?[45] Aesthetically, did Balzac understand how Beethoven's pure form incarnates such abstract ideas, or philosophically in the Schopenhauerian sense, how a serious and complex thought like the expression of man in his highest powers can remain essentially symphonic? We must answer: no. Between Balzac's reaction to Beethoven and his expression of it, *Gambara* notwithstanding, lay an unbridged gap across which the living energy of meaning did not pass. But our negative reply should not be categorical. For Balzac recognized now that instrumental music could be more than the marvelous divertissement and ornamental art the symphonies of Mozart and Haydn represented for so many listeners. Now he realized the difference between the open quality of seductiveness of Rossini's music and the more intimate quality of poetic sensibility of Beethoven's. He felt a presence, something he could not verbalize, something which left sensation behind and, through the incalculable force of sounds, shaped his concept of Beethoven.[46] And his was a reaction as genuine as it was legitimate, for Beethoven, more than anyone else, had fused great thoughts—liberty, equality, heroism, struggle—as well as the more personal experiences of life, with musical expression. Quite naturally, Balzac shaped his concept by using attributes he admired, bestowed upon some of his favorite characters, and liked to ascribe to himself: temerity, power, excellence in mastery of the art, overtones of Promethean pride, perhaps some immoderateness, Dantean universality, and a capacity for a frenzy of feelings; in short, it was the concept of Titanism, the source of Tolstoy's grievances against the German composer.

Heroic will stirred Balzac, even in a modest creature like César Birotteau, and this attraction constituted his first step toward understanding Beethoven. Therefore we agree with Thérèse Marix-Spire that if Balzac had lived longer (or had had more time), Beethoven would have held eventually his exclusive esteem.[47] Although he continued to be a rhapsodist for Rossini, he presents himself also as a psalmodist for Beethoven, and ultimately is secretly persuaded by him. He opts for the Master from Bonn. A fundamental affinity existed, approaching but not attaining revelation. Did he not—unwittingly?—envisage a famous scene from *Fidelio* as early as 1833, one which curiously sums up his own situations: "I am like a prisoner who, from the depths of his dungeon, hears from a distance the ravishingly sweet voice of a woman. His whole spirit is borne in the frail and forceful perceptions of that voice. . ."?[48]

Massimilla Doni at the Fenice

PART FOUR

BALZAC'S MUSICAL TALES AND THEIR IMPLICATIONS

CHAPTER IX

GAMBARA: PRESERVING IDEALISM

Genesis of the Tale

The genesis of *Gambara*, marred by a complicated transaction between an undecided author and an eager publisher, is in itself a tale. The work was written concurrently with *Massimilla Doni*. Schlesinger felt honored to list Balzac as a collaborator on *La Gazette musicale* when he announced "*Gambara*, a musical novelette" in 1836; but Balzac delayed and the editor tried to force matters by reannouncing "*Gambara*, or the human voice" in the first issue of 1837. "Schlesinger is showing his teeth,"[1] reported the author, who then submitted a few pages, only to learn later that they disappeared in a fire that destroyed the printing establishment in February of that year. "The head and the tail" survived "without the middle."[2] Making the most of this new excuse for an extension of time, Balzac left for Italy, claiming a need for further documentation in the land of music. In the meanwhile, Marquis de Belloy, his secretary, sketched for him a Hoffmannian story with which he hoped to assure Schlesinger of his good will, but upon returning to Paris he withdrew it, dissatisfied with its content: it contained no music. He then proposed another *Gambara*, in fact something more consistent with the question of the human voice, and something that would be "a study on the same subject, and more within the reach of my weak knowledge of music."[3] The cell of the original idea fissioned, producing what were to become shortly the two organisms of *Gambara* and *Massimilla Doni*.[4] It was a convenient division, for now he could dedicate one to de Belloy,[5] the other to Strunz; he could treat the subject of German music and the orchestra separately from that of Italian music and the voice; and he could include analyses of two of the most discussed contemporary operas, *Robert le Diable* and *Mosè in Egitto*, without encumbering a single work with both. One novella would ostensibly honor a commitment to Meyerbeer, that this composer would be "the keystone"[6] of a work;

the other would justify his trip to Italy. Balzac explained the dichotomy more impressively: "*Massimilla Doni* and *Gambara* represent, in the *Etudes philosophiques*, the appearance of music under the dual form of performance and composition, submitted to the same test as *Louis Lambert*'s thought, that is to say, the work and its execution killed by too great an abundance of the creative principle, the very idea which prompted me to write *Le Chef-d'oeuvre inconnu* in the realm of painting."[7]

But the complications were not about to end. Balzac shied away from plunging into *Gambara* because he did not feel as prepared for it as for the companion tale. Yet, because he had sold some rights to another editor, Lecou (a partner of Delloye and Bohain), who refused to permit the publication of *Massimilla Doni* in *La Gazette musicale*, he had to take cognizance of this review's anxiously awaiting readers and concentrate on the long postponed *Gambara*. Again stalling for time, he composed a long letter to Schlesinger, published in the periodical on June 11, 1837, in which he joined to the history of the recent comedy of errors a few facetious observations on his ignorance of music:

> I belong to the *gens de lettres* . . . ., writers given nowadays to *artisticize*. . . . An orchestra has never been more for me than a misapprehended and bizarre assortment of crooked woods, more or less garnished with twisted catguts, with more or less young heads above it, powdered *à la Titus*, surmounted by bass necks, or obstructed with spectacles, or adapted to spheres of brass, or attached to barrels improperly called bass drums, the whole interspersed with reflector-bearing lights, interlarded with notebooks, a place where unexplainable movements take place. . . . [This] visible monster, born during these last two centuries, due to the coupling of man with wood, begot by orchestration which has ended by stifling the voice, in short, this hydra with one hundred bows has complicated my pleasures with the prospect of a horrible amount of work.

It was George Sand's encouragement that eventually injected confidence into the recusant novelist. "You proved to me with palpable and peremptory reasons," he continued humorously in his letter to the editor, "that I was capable of writing on music in your *Gazette*. Ever since then I have looked upon my initiation as complete, inasmuch as the possibility was sealed by the declaration of George Sand." After that, Schlesinger's urging reaped its dividend. "Your desire," added Balzac, "grew proportionately to my resistance: all of this made me believe in my ability." His ability lay chiefly in philosophical interpretation, and this he counted on exploiting, especially since Schlesinger had spurred his vanity so cleverly by mentioning, as de Belloy had suggested, a parallel with the great Hoffmann. In conclusion, Balzac asked the editor for an extension until July 20, in order "to crystallize my ideas on music, providing I can convert my sensations into ideas and extract from them something resembling a philosophical system." And with typical fire, the formerly hesitant author, who had cringed at the idea of seeing himself "posted in *La Gazette musicale* like a future authority," asserted solemnly: "From that day forward, *Gambara*, that Louis Lambert of music, shall be cast regularly in lead, braced by the iron frames that support the columns of *La Gazette musicale*, for . . . the publication of *Gambara* becomes a matter of self-respect before becoming a matter of business." He kept his word: the tale of the Cremonese musician who slept in a bed fashioned from a harpsichord began appearing in the July 23rd issue. And he could well keep it, fortified as he was technically by the lessons of Strunz and psychologically by his various musical friendships.

The Hoffmannian Dimension

Gambara is a fascinating figure. It is not true, as someone has suggested, that he is "completely of Strunzian inspiration" simply because some of the old German's dreams and failures appear romanced in Balzac's fantasy. And it would be very unwise to accept what the same critic maintains as she continues: "this means (and there is piquancy in it!) that all Balzac's ideas belong to no one else but to that obscure jobber Strunz."[8] There may have been a good measure of Berlioz in the harangues of both Count Andrea Marcosini and Gambara, and surely the influence cannot be overlooked of a man whose works, moving in an atmosphere of irrationalism and fantasy, Balzac had read from cover to cover: Ernst Theodor Amadeus Hoffmann. By coincidence, Balzac was the editor of the review, *Le Gymnase*, which published the first French translation of a work by the Berliner.[9] Forever lured by ideas of the supernatural, of animal magnetism, telepathy, somnambulism, talismans, and the like, he never lost contact with Hoffmann, and in 1833 declared to Mme Hanska: "I have read Hoffmann in his entirety."[10] He suggested him to Stendhal in 1839 as an example of balance between reality and imagination, and gave every indication of listening to his own advice. *La Peau de chagrin*, *L'Auberge rouge*, and *Le Chef-d'oeuvre inconnu* bear resemblances with *Der Artushof*, just as *L'Elixir de longue vie*, *Sarrasine*, and *L'Adieu* may be compared with *Die Elixiere des Teufels*, *Agrafia*, and *Das Gelübde*. Hoffmann hovers somewhere in the background of *Les deux rêves*, *La Comédie du Diable*, *Jésus-Christ en Flandre, L'Enfant maudit, Le Réquisitionnaire*, and of the Preface to *La Physiologie du mariage*. He is mentioned in various writings: in the prospectus of *Caricature*, in the Preface to *La Peau de chagrin*, in *Le Cousin Pons*, as the songster of the unknown in *La Physiologie de l'employé* as in its later form of 1846 *Les Employés*, and in *Une Fille d'Eve* where he appears as a friend of Schmucke, presenting him with a gift, a cat called "Murr."

Balzac discovered easily within himself multiple affinities with the author of the *Kreisleriana*. For one thing, they liked to think of Italy in terms of the same stage-set: theatres, romance, aristocrats, adventures, song, wine, and lovely women. But the rapprochement ran deeper. Though possessed with a keen sense of the reality they observed, both were so enticed by strangeness, impossibility, and incomprehensibility that they transfigured that same reality, a process they applied conveniently to their understanding of a musician's tribulations when operating under the fury of creation. We could be misled by Balzac's criticism of Hoffmann in which he seems to diminish his influence: "He is beneath his reputation. There is something there, but not much. He talks well about music. He understands nothing about love and women. He doesn't create any fear; it is impossible to create any with physical things."[11] The underlying realism of *La Comédie humaine* enables us to understand these remarks, for while Hoffmann sometimes appears interested in the fantastic for its own sake, Balzac always applies it and its consequences or its moral to humanity. The former likes to describe the ridiculous traits of his characters like, for instance, Baron von B.; the latter seeks the inherent tragedy of genius. For him, fantasy expresses phenomena still inscrutable by human intelligence, but on their way toward becoming a matter for science and for serious thought. We should not forget the difference suggested immediately by the titles *Fantasiestücke* and *Contes philosophiques*. But the fact remains that Balzac admired *Ritter Gluck, Kater Murr, Don Juan, Rat Krespel, Die Fermate, Der Baron von B. (Der Schüler Tartinis)*, and that he read carefully *Höchst zerstreute Gedanken* and *Der Dichter und der Komponist*. He agreed with Hoffmann's view of the world and of the artist, and liked the idea of the "poetic truth" which permits us to escape from ourselves. And—most important—the German "talks well about music." Together with Hoffmann's Kreisler, Balzac liked the idea of considering music still in a state of infancy, strengthened in its growth by Mozart, Haydn, Gluck, Beethoven, and, of course for Balzac, Rossini.

Gambara, by the novelist's own admission "that character worthy of Hoffmann" (G 415), is a fit descendant of conductor Kreisler and of Knight Gluck. Diderot's Nephew of Rameau and Cervantes' licentiate Vidriera may also claim ancestry. Each refuses to reconcile the immediacy of an ill-adapted reality to the immanence of his dreams. Gambara occupies a medial position between Rameau's extravagance and Gluck's folly, which includes an attempt at a personality transference, and between the loquacious congeniality of the one and the geniality of the other as proved by his enlightened understanding of the composer of *Orfeo ed Euridice*. All fascinate their listeners with original views expressed with excited confusion; all can hear whole instrumental ensembles by reduced means—a mere handful of musicians, an imaginary violin or clavier, a Panharmonicon; all interlace variations and develop rhythms with weird ability and are exhausted after their renderings; all are destined to a form of spiritual exile in their respective capitals. But Hoffmann's maniac does not progress beyond the stage of variations on Gluck's or Mozart's music, and Diderot's bohemian, who has much to say about his uncle, his contemporaries, and music in general, does not create beyond his immoderate pantomimes. For them, irrationality fashions genius, and to this extent they remain elusive. Balzac's hero, on the other hand, is more tangible, however wild. He does not remind us, cautions Balzac, of one "of those grotesque characters brought forth by German storytellers and librettists" (G 426). On the contrary, Gambara reaches rationally, albeit adventurously, into the physics of music and the psychology of musical creation, and also writes an epic opera, a symphonic, dramatic, psychological, historical, occasionally hysterical synthesis of human and divine emotions, or, in resoundingly simple terms, "a portrayal of the life of nations" (G 443). Gambara appears more inordinate than Rameau and less demented than Gluck, and generally more provocative than both.

Johannes Kreisler, too, is suffocated by a philistine milieu; a wine-drinking, unsociable, inspired bohemian tortured by a musical *mal du siècle*, by the artist's maladive sensibility, he is absorbed in the auscultation of his inner music and the thousand voices of nature. Gambara is less virulent and combative, and in temperament resembles more the genial and suffering composer of Wackenroder's *Das merkwürdige musikalische Leben des Tonkünstlers Joseph Berglinger*, and the dragoman in Tieck's *Phantasien über die Kunst*. He is like the conductor in his excess of sentiment and imagination and in his lack of phlegm. With Kreisler, he implies that the artist who perseveres in his art must be a madman who believes he rises above vulgar reality by his initiation to the arcana of the temple of Isis. But if the irony turns to humorless sarcasm, the satirical intent is ultimately transcended by the musicians' deeply human aspects as these are brought into relief through the sorrowful realities of their lives and the sincerity of their dedication.

In Krespel Balzac found another Kreisler, an originator of ideas whose eccentricities are franchise and extravagances common sense. In the romantic Spaniard of *Don Juan* he saw how an insatiable zeal for the transcendental plunged a man into sensuality, delinquency, misery, and isolation. He read of the young apprentice Theodor's acquisition of the three most important aspects of the art of music: harmony, German polyphony, and Italian melody under the double form of opera and religious hymn. He discovered in Baron von B. a violin fanatic who discoursed learnedly on music and fed on imaginary masterpieces. In *Signor Formica-Salvador Rosa*, he encountered the old Pasquale Capuzzi who, like Gambara, with abominable music thought he wrote magnificent operas; the latter, whose lady—who eventually leaves him—is also named Marianna, becomes drunk and drained of energy, again like Gambara, as he attacks the keyboard convulsively. Furthermore, in *Ombra Adorata*, Balzac listened to the narrator explain beauty in music through technical media, just as in *Die Automate* he faced the problem of envisaging a mechanism that would imitate perfectly the sounds of instruments and the human voice. And he was reminded of the idea of the self-destructiveness of genius, in other words, of the usury of art, in the cases of the painter in *Die Jesuiterkirche* and of the poet in *Der Sandmann*. Each of these themes contributed an important metal toward the forging of *Gambara*, in which Balzac, far from sketching a synthesis, braces his Hoffmannian inventiveness with some of his own favorite philosophical supports.

Gambara's Mahomet

Two common denominators underlying the thinking of Hoffmann and Balzac relate to the nature of the composer and the role of the human voice in opera. Grétry's notion of the artist-philosopher who must "consult the great book of nature"[12] is shared by Balzac: "in order to be a great musician . . . one must also be very learned" (G 443). Hoffmann's idea of the supernatural merely added an extra dimension to the nature of the composer without replacing the fundamental concept of Grétry. Wrote the author of *Der Dichter und der Komponist*: "the poet who wants to seize the marvelous must be endowed with that magic power of poetic truth, for this power alone can transport us away from ourselves."[13] In his ecstatic moments, Gambara relegates analysis to a secondary position in the quest for knowledge and its natural principles, preferring to leave it up to his intuition to penetrate the superior realities that concerned his Mohammed as well as the music that described him. In the long run, the Wagnerian concept applies, namely, that music is not to be comprehended by logical examination but as a power of nature which men perceive but do not understand, and which the composer interprets. Balzac liked to think of his composer as a seer, a magician, wedded to an ideal and to a mission. Furthermore, he felt that opera as a form encompassed all the possibilities for transcribing ultimate concepts. If, as the Italians thought, the form existed essentially to display the human voice, then its most magnificent potential of uniting equally words, action, and music was lost. "The composer who sings for the sake of singing is an artisan and not an artist," claims Gambara (G 443). Hoffmann praised Gluck for making music grow intimately and organically out of the poem, appending his own metaphysical assertion that the poet and the composer alone possess the key to the supernatural. Through Gambara's *Mahomet*, Balzac too maintained the primary role of the subject in guiding the musician toward a vision of poetic truth.

When he included the fictional opera in his tale, Balzac found the vehicle through which to surround his protagonist with an epic aura, to engage in a character study set in an evocative framework, and to fashion a human but also visionary drama in which music and symbol merge. Now more manifestly than in 1819, Laure de Surville could have said "He saw, he heard that opera." He indicates practically each measure and tonality[14] of the unpremièred masterpiece, act by act, aria by aria, with one eye on the glossary of nomenclature, and with a strong determination sometimes unmatched by sound musical judgment. Gambara performs the work on his special instrument, attacking it the way he will delve into *Robert le Diable* later, "with a kind of discharge of the soul in the manner of Liszt." Having written his own libretto, he outlines for Count Andrea the basic purpose: "Here the people who receive musical impressions do not develop them in themselves, the way religion teaches us to develop sacred texts through prayer. It is therefore quite difficult to make them understand that an eternal music exists in nature, a suave melody, a perfect harmony, disturbed only by the independent revolutions of divine will, just as passions are by the will of men" (G 442). Gambara envisions not one opera but a trilogy: Mohammed's love for Cadhige in *Les Martyrs*, his founding of a warrior religion in *Mahomet*, and in *La Jérusalem délivrée* his disenchantment and exhaustion after a lifetime of trying to steal the secret of death in order to become a god, the final presumption of human pride. Hence the god of the West and the god of the Orient engage in a religious struggle around a tomb. The concept suggests the unfulfilled aspirations of the composer and of the novelist himself, both Titans only too conscious of the Divine Tragedy that is in store for those who seek to best the Human Comedy. As for *Mahomet* itself, the three acts which comprise it, symbolizing toil, triumph, and tedium, embrace in smaller compass the broader pattern of the trilogy.

Balzac regarded an overture not as a free interpretation of the opera's moods but as an announcement, a "sample" (G 445) prefiguring symphonically and synthetically the actual thoughts of the whole drama. As far as it goes, the concept is acceptable, but the itemized account that follows is implausible and must have elicited many a smile from Balzac's friends. The Overture contains an andante, an allegro, a cantabile, a maestoso sostenuto, a stretta, a crescendo (Rossinian?), fanfares, and tutti eruptions. It strides from 3/4 time to 4/4 and 6/8 and back again, modulating from C minor to E-flat major to A-flat major to F minor to C major to G major to B-flat major to G minor—reasonable tempos and modulations, to be sure, but all expected, despite their congestion, to express the hero's melancholy, epileptic, and joyous cries of war, Cadhige's love plaint, an angel's pronouncement to the populace, the arrival of knights and people to hear the false prophet, their belief in him, the conquest of Medina and the march on Mecca, a devoted cantilena by Cadhige, the disgust and fatigue of a man who wants to die a god, and the high esteem in which he is held throughout Arabia! The symbolic intricacies of *Götterdämmerung* are outmatched by this multiplicity of events. Balzac's method of conveying variety and movement consisted in little more than constant key changes and "torrents of harmony" (G 444), interrupted now and then by a calm motive in the Italian style. Hardly even literary, let alone musical, the Overture can best be described as a sensationally hysterical avalanche.

The same oriental exoticism that regaled the listeners of David's *Le Désert* less than a decade afterward was to impress the audience from the very first scene of *Mahomet*. By a picturesque well, a chorus of cameleers embroidering a "majestically sorrowful" aria by Mohammed opens the first act. Unlike the overly ambitious Overture, the act shows more restrained calculations; its forces deploy more organically around a unified concept. After a symbolic duet between the leader and Cadhige—will and intelligence respectively—during which the former's epilepsy is sanctified as evidence of communion with angels, a quintet composed of his wife, two young ladies he is to wed, and their fathers, brings the plot down to a more human plane. The strife which ensues in a choral section between Mohammed's followers and the persecuting forces underscores the human dimension, climaxed by the protagonist's flight. The act ends with the three women foretelling their master's triumph, a musical idea that will serve as a leitmotiv in the final act. Although Balzac's verbal synthesis necessarily blocks the scenes too obviously, the overall organization remains logical.

Irregularities mar the second act. While Gambara is proud of a prayer in F major for bass because of a "brilliant and majestic harmonic structure fixed under this song in which I may have extended the limits of melody," Balzac makes him guilty, from our standpoint, of misusing vocal flourishes to express by themselves the poetry of Mohammed's gallant and militant religion as well as to accomplish something of highly questionable feasibility: to depict the "delightful Moorish architecture" (G 447). This may reflect too literal a recollection of Friedrich von Schelling's *Philosophie der Kunst* where architecture is likened to frozen music. Following a section sustained by brasses (possibly Strunzian in conception) that vibrantly announce Mohammed's conquest of the three Arabias, Gambara, with confessed inconsistency, has inserted "one of those ignoble ballets that cut the thread of the most beautiful musical tragedies" (G 447). Why Balzac permits his unconventional composer to submit to convention remains unexplained, unless this was Balzac's way of criticizing a common excess. Then with the proclamation of Mohammed's polygamy, the opera reaches a high point of pathos: the anguish of his faithful wife who, having insured her husband's ascent to glory, now must suffer its consequences. When the leader becomes prophet, he can have no equal. "Cry, rejoice! Triumphs and tears! That is life!" (G 448) exclaims the composer spasmodically.

A quartet of houris and more ballets introduce the third act. This time the dances find some justification, however unoriginal, in the layman's conventional way of envisaging a seraglio. Mohammed sits there, afflicted by the ills of polygamy and lamenting his first love, Cadhige, singing an aria in F minor. The key fits such a purpose well: it lies comfortably within the bass's range, and lends itself to an expression of melancholy. Gambara's enthusiasm revolves around the unity of his inspiration, its signal theme, and its symbolic purport: "Never has a musician had a similar theme. Orchestra and women's chorus express the joys of the houris, while Mohammed reverts to the melancholy with which the opera began. —Where is Beethoven, that I may be correctly understood with this prodigious doubling of the whole opera back onto itself. . . . Beethoven constructed his symphony in C in no other way. But his heroic movement is purely instrumental, whereas here my heroic movement is supported by a sextet of the most beautiful human voices, and by a chorus of believers who watch by the DOOR of the sacred house. I use all the wealth of melody and harmony, an orchestra and voices. Listen to the expression of all those human existences, whether rich or poor! 'Struggle, triumph, and weariness'" (G 449). Wishing death as a final consolation, Mohammed bids farewell to his people. A grand triumphal march is heard, but instead of terminating the opera at this point, Balzac preferred to lower the final curtain after one of his favorite forms: a solemn prayer, intoned here by a chorus of sixty before the holy casbah. The idea of closing such a drama on a gentle note is in good taste, but how effective it would sound immediately preceded by the bombastic clamors of a march is another matter.

Balzac would have done better not to draw so liberally on his thesaurus of musical terms or to rely so patently on stereotyped patterns of composition. He cannot move from joy to sorrow without modulating from major to minor. He cannot manipulate tonality and construct a musical phrase sequence without adhering to the rules of neighboring tones, generally applied to relative majors and minors. His tempos are so commonplace that in stating them he risks redundancy. When, then, he wants to characterize Gambara's extraordinary effects, all he does is have him violate the classical rules, such as moving "fourths without sixths in the bass" (G 450), instead of abiding by the safe and pleasant major thirds. The musical result of the novelist's exposé is amiable ingenuousness.

In one respect, however, "Balzac's" *Mahomet* is felicitous. While it reflects the era which produced *Mosè in Egitto* and *Robert le Diable*, it implies something broader: a synthesis of musical styles, past, present, and future. Its classical structure, characteristic of many of the operas to which the novelist had been exposed, echoes Gluck's insistences on a logical denouement of the plot and on a veracious human drama. The divine prompting of Mohammed's destiny, alternating with the human pathos of Cadhige's plight, reflects the Romantic tendency of embracing all of life in its broadest possible aspects and of delineating the conflict through the manipulation of contrasts. Balzac expected such "rendings" (G 448) to give the text more meaning as well as the music an added occasion to display its vast powers. And finally, his poorly implemented suggestion of the unhampered liberty of the composer in matters of musical grammar and theory nonetheless forecasts coming innovations in aesthetics. "Musicians who write grammars . . . can be detestable composers" (G 467). Gambara's anarchy enlarges the horizons of his art even if his extremism might outride his intentions. He cannot abide the restrictions of the imperfect musical language which he has inherited and heads toward the *Wort-Ton-Drama* of the second half of the nineteenth century, the century, if we leave Verdi aside, of Richard Wagner.

Pre-Wagnerian Visions

"At first an inventor only glimpses a kind of dawn" (G 436). The statement serves as a key to the secret of Gambara's attractiveness, the most enticing facet of which being his far-ranging aesthetics. Whether or not inspired by the dreams of Hoffmann and Strunz, the words of Liszt and Fétis, or the works of Berlioz and Weber, Balzac did put into his composer's mouth and deeds adumbrations of a "music of the future," the flares of a Wagnerian before Wagner. We cannot dismiss the practices of Berlioz, for if Wagner conceived an immense production in the *Niebelungenlied* tetralogy, so had Berlioz in *L'Enfance du Christ* and *Les Troyens*; if Wagner scorned librettists to the extent of writing his own texts in order to strengthen their integration into the score, so had Berlioz, whatever the thrust of Nerval's remark that great poets cannot be librettists; if Wagner replaced the overture not intimately bound thematically to the opera with a synthesizing prelude, so had Berlioz, in agreement with Gluck's notion of "expressive overtures." So to say that *Gambara* (and *Massimilla Doni*) spoke the language of *Zukunftsmusik* would encourage unwarranted, Procrustean parallels. But that there are Wagnerian overtones in much of what the tale says is undeniable; the music which concerns Gambara/Balzac is philosophical. "He is a true visionary" (LL 359), says Mme de Staël about Louis Lambert, ostensibly Balzac himself, and the same may be said about his Cremonese composer. The novelist demonstrated what Diderot had illustrated by personal example: that in the long run a writer's technical learning, while indispensable up to a point, is of marginal relevance from the moment he has supplanted it with an aesthetic vision.

Balzac has his musician write a drama,[15] exactly as Wagner will do and explain in *Oper und Drama*.[16] And the novelist has him adopt the same method of composition, namely, first the dramatic poem, then the music which translates it into action. Gambara is above all the *Dichter* that Wagner wants to be before becoming the *Komponist*. Music must speak. During the previous century, Rousseau had based his theory of dramatic music on a successful solution of the problem of making speech sing and music speak, and Calzabigi, in his Dedication of Gluck's *Alceste*, had talked of reducing music to the function of seconding the poetry without superfluous ornamentation. Grétry, too, had foretold that some day all that did not conform strictly to the poem would be rejected. These views disagreed with those of Mozart, who showed little concern for the mediocrity of libretti, maintaining that the central preoccupation of opera was that the music should please. Gambara's conviction, therefore, takes a definite step in the direction music will take under Wagner, especially when he asserts that this art must rise above the production of mere sensations. He narrows the limits of the impressions that sounds produce on us and tries to express by these same sounds a pure concept, unmarred by sensation or emotion. The same notion appears in *Massimilla Doni*: music "awakens ideas" in their "essential form" (MD 356); it strikes at the very "elements of thought" (MD 350). In this respect, and by virtue of his exaggeration, Balzac goes beyond the Bayreuthian himself. Gambara is bent upon "pushing the musical principle to the extreme" in order to "exceed the goal" (G 467).

Refusing to be tied to the boxed form of an eight-measure melody "with geometric patterns" (G 430), Gambara demands a symphonic style in drama with melody as the "golden thread" that weaves through the fabric of the score (G 457, 463). Puccini,

Moussorgsky, and the later Verdi come to mind, but even more so Wagner and his "endless melody." In this way Gambara's music speaks, and by doing so, it speaks the unconventional idiom of revolutionary innovation. The result of intermingling dramatic and musical thought and of replacing the antithesis of voice and orchestra with synthesis is in Gambara's exposition, a chaotic explosion:

> There was not the semblance of a poetical or musical idea in the deafening cacophony that smote everyone's ears. All the principles of harmony, the rudimentary rules of composition, were completely foreign to this amorphous creation. Instead of the intelligently sequenced music that Gambara had indicated, his fingers produced a succession of fifths, sevenths, and octaves, major thirds and progressions of fourths without sixths in the bass, a union of discordant sounds hurled about haphazardly, that seemed to have been combined to rend the least delicate ears. It is difficult to describe this bizarre execution, since we should need new words for this impossible music. . . . The strange discords that rattled under his fingers had evidently produced the effect of celestial harmonies in his own ears. [G 449-450]

Gambara senses that a Debussy, a Richard Strauss, a Scriabine, a Schönberg, and a Stravinsky would not be long in coming, and that the tendency would be toward atonality and the suppression of the notion of dissonance as a negative value. *Gambara* presents a fictional illustration of an original composer who, by writing what seems to be an "undigestable amalgam of notes" (G 445) demanding a new mode of sensitivity, scandalizes and revolts his unenlightened public—a situation as true for Monteverdi and Beethoven as for Wagner.[17]

Through the process by which "music forms thought" (G 436), Gambara's maxim for combining ethical and aesthetical emotion, he "glimpsed a kind of dawn" where pure instrumental expression without reference to any subject may have a highly emotional impact. But he did not refine the idea further; its wide implications remained mere potentialities, and we are left solely with a hint that whispers to us about Wagner's productions or Debussy's *Pelléas et Mélisande*, even Berg's *Wozzeck*. The implications that exceed musical principles clearly leave behind Wagner's desire to render as sensually as possible the sensation expressed in speech rather than the exposition of ideas.

On other accounts, there are more substantial indications of theories we normally associate with the author of *Oper und Drama* as well as with Schopenhauer. Through one such theory, music, as one of the arts, "joins outer nature in agreement with a marvelous nature, . . . our inner life" (MD 353). Through another, music reveals to man the essence of the whole world, "the entirety of nature which it has the power to express" (MD 356). Through again another, music alone has the power to make us commune with ourselves, "whereas the other arts give us defined pleasures," and "this power over our inner selves is one of the grandeurs of music, [for] the other arts impose defined creations upon us, while in its own creations music is infinite" (MD 356). Even the vocabularies gravitate toward each other. For like Balzac, Wagner too dreamed in music of the ideal, purely human form that appeals less to the mind than to a sensitivity which understands without intermediary, which blends instinctively outer form and inner truth, and which to that extent recognizes music as the most central of the arts, the most privileged in interpreting life.

The leitmotiv, which flows with structural ease into the pattern of "endless melody," is a most effective device for suggesting meaning. Balzac includes something similar to it in Gambara's imaginary opera, where the symbolism of the characters needs to be strongly linked to the evolution of the drama. Not only is the motif of triumph echoed from first act to third, but the even larger C minor theme of melancholy, "this prodigious doubling back of the whole opera onto itself" (G 449) frames *Mahomet* structurally and symbolically. It is intended to give evocative relief to its textual association, to Mohammed, his greatness and his failure. Again, when Gambara talks about his other opera, *Les Martyrs*, we are reminded of *Götterdämmerung*: the composer had striven for "an effect prepared by different motives sounded by each instrument, motives which were to join together in a great ensemble" (G 437). Wagner was surely not the first to apply the technique of the leitmotiv in his works, although no one has ever done it so characteristically. His venerated master Carl Maria von Weber had used it long before, as had Mozart in *Don Giovanni*; Berlioz called it an *idée fixe* in *Harold en Italie*, and Liszt referred to a "metamorphosis of themes." Strunz, a fond Weberian, most likely made allusion to it during his chats with his student. Balzac does not imbue his leitmotiv with the subtle and multiple associations it acquires in the tetralogy, but he remembers how strikingly the opening theme of Beethoven's Fifth Symphony recurs in the final movement, and makes Gambara adapt it operatically. To that extent, it testifies to his musical imagination. He recognized a signal possibility, one of the first essays in musical psychology strictly through narrative, expositional means.

Before Beethoven's Ninth Symphony had become familiar to French audiences, and when Debussy's *Sirènes* was many years away, Balzac echoed Mazzini's suggestion that the chorus assume more ample proportions in musical drama, that it be removed from its passive position and placed in one of solemnity. Gambara spoke of more intense choral support of the melodic line, of an "aria broken by choral accompaniments, gusts of voices bracing the melody . . . by joining it contrapuntally" (G 446). *Mahomet* ends with a gigantic combination of voices, mainly feminine. For its composer, Beethoven's Fifth Symphony represents one of the pivotal points in the history of music, a composition whose heroic movement would attain the ultimate in expressiveness if crowned with human voices. Therefore, like Wagner, he is conscious of the interplay between chorus and orchestra as one of the most exhilerating of musical experiences. We are reminded that, when Wagner commented on Beethoven's Ninth Symphony (which Balzac did not know), he wrote with admiration: "We are witnessing a real awakening in the evolution from instrumental to vocal music."[18]

Gambara, "the unknown Orpheus of modern music" (G 472), prefigures Wagner through a coincidence of Romantic attitudes, but also through his creator's own visionary purpose. The parallels we can make between the fictional composer and the historical composer relate just as much to the Romantic atmosphere of an epoch as to Balzac's independent invention. The constructive principles of a Beethoven symphony, the nationalistic feelings and love of nature that one associates with Weber, the operatic amplitude of Meyerbeer, the grace of Rossini, the orchestral virtuosity of Berlioz—these form the common patrimony of a period that sought beauty of style and grandeur of utterance. Eleven years before Wagner thought of treating the story of Siegfried in *Das Rheingold*, *Die Walküre*, *Siegfried*, and *Götterdämmerung*, Balzac spoke of a related sequence of operas in the same spirit that Hugo envisaged *La Légende des siècles* or *La Fin de Satan* or *Dieu*. Hugo considered the links between man and God, Balzac between humanity and divinity, Wagner between mortals and immortals, each of them grounding his views in imaginative formulations and intellectual precepts. An extensive reader of Balzac, Wagner undoubtedly read *Gambara*.[19] The tale need not lay any claim to his musical formation, but it does serve as an example of how, according to Nietzsche, France began to Wagnerize before knowing the meaning of the word. The more French music learned to adapt itself to the actual needs of the *âme moderne*, claimed Nietzsche, the more it would "Wagnerize." The question is not whether Balzac is a precursor or from whom he may have received his futuristic ideas. Rather we should ask how he perceived those ideas, to which the answer is: not eruditely, as a committed philosopher would perceive them, but excitedly, like an artist who has fashioned a new dimension of experience, who has discovered a new facet of his own personality. Olin Downes has stated it poetically: "Thus did the poet of the modern age [Balzac], from the mysterious fastness of his consciousness, perceive 'the shadow' cast by the present into the soundless future of thought and art; and so did he record another coming of the truth, another rustling of its wing in the night."[20]

Demonic Visions

Gambara contains an apology of Meyerbeer's *Robert le Diable*, a work which, coincidentally, influenced Wagner through its macabre and demonic elements. While what Balzac's character says about the opera is largely a matter of musical criticism, how he says it is central to an understanding of the tale. Balzac's train of vision is too inventive to be limited to the simple outline of a normal musician. To borrow words from *Louis Lambert*, he makes his hero's intellectual "acuteness" place him on the threshold of "folly." We cannot overlook the demonic overtones of this folly. Interpretations have relied heavily on Balzac's own declaration and alluded to the narrative's two purposes: to illustrate the psychic law of failure, or the fiasco, and to elevate Art, or the Ideal, to a level above reality. The way in which the concept of Satan insinuates itself into the story has not been mentioned. Yet Balzac's fascination for the occult colors one whole area of his interest in music and must be treated in analyzing this *conte philosophique*. From the earliest gestating moments of *Gambara*, he had said in his letter to Schlesinger: "following Hoffmann's favorite word, the devil had stuck his tail into this seduction."

The compromises that dilute ethical standards in the world of economics and politics are expected and therefore tend to find general acceptance in society. Though frequently attempted, in the world of art and of artistic creation, they are inadmissible. When reality, as fallen man has fashioned it, struggles with divine perfection, the protagonist in the contest who is preordained to defeat, or at least to incompletion, emerges as the true hero of a noble endeavor. In the tragic juxtaposition of reality and the spirit, the latter's demands exhaust life, even deny it, without ever suggesting either acquiescence or resignation. Frenhofer, the painter in *Le Chef-d'oeuvre inconnu* who strives to create the perfect masterpiece, and Claës, the scientist in *La Recherche de l'Absolu* whose quest is fundamentally as aesthetic as it is scientific, are kindred souls. The Cremonese composer joins them in refusing to recognize the boundaries of human limitation and the compromises that would have made their lives less agonized but also less great. "This soul is so distant from us only because it is close to Heaven" (G 441). Balzac admired his composer, in whom he

saw his own reflection, the man who tried to free himself from the
popularity of mediocrity not in a merely temporary imaginative
fantasy but in the creation of angelic concerts which, Horace would
have said, would enable him not to die completely.

We cannot agree with the opinion expressed by Léon Emery that
in the parable of *Gambara* "we are advised not to take anything too
seriously" because "music is a sylph with mad eyes, sparkling and
charming in turn. To abandon ourselves to it means certainly to join
the ranks of those who wish to exceed the goal, but in a less
Promethean fashion, for a far larger measure of abandon to the
powers of the philter enters then into the idolater's attitude."[21]
Nor can we stress the satirical hoax which for some the tale
represents, and to which Berlioz supposedly contributed. Some sense
of parody may emerge from the contrast between the grandeur of the
exposition of *Mahomet* and the fact that the protagonist was a *false*
prophet. Even so, the subject carries with it more seriousness than
comedy, for, as Nerval reportedly said, "One must be convinced in
order to win others over to a new idea; . . . the man who subjugated
half a world by the force of his enthusiasm was perhaps a false
prophet, but he was also Mohammed."[22] More sense of parody arises
from the seeming similarity between Giardini and Gambara, especially
when the astounded Marcosini comes to look upon them "as two
abstractions" (G 432). But the similarity is deceiving; we realize
it the minute we study the juxtaposition of the cook and the
composer, of vulgarity and nobility. Balzac underscores the
disparity subtly, by planting Giardini in almost every scene of the
tale, making them both drink and both fail. They are different:
Giardini is Hoffmannian; Gambara is Balzacian, not one of those
Germanic "grotesque characters." If there is grotesqueness in the
composer, it is there by what Curtius calls the constancy of the
"grotesque-ideal"[23] in Balzac, which Balzac admitted when he wrote
into his story: "sublimity and parody, those two faces of all human
creation" (G 432). But the fantastic elements merely provide a
favorable terrain for the exposition of his ideas; they are, for
Bardèche, "a secondary and accidental"[24] part of his art. Gambara is
a creator, whose characteristics Balzac took seriously. "Genius is
a manner of being of the brain" (SPC 36), says Princess de Cadignan;
it is a monstrous sickness about which we ask: will it defeat the
man or will the man defeat it? (IP). Gambara is "sick"; he is sick
when he thinks and dreams, when he shows what Ballanche called the
gift of reading in the future, when he agonizes to convert his
conceptions into execution and, rather than "be repelled by the
convulsions of this insane life," create instead "an animated
masterpiece that is meaningful to all eyes in sculpture, to all
minds in literature, to all memories in painting, to all hearts in
music" (CBe 318). In the portrayal of Gambara, there is no intention
of levity.

The quest for perfection, or the Absolute, filled Balzac with the ecstasy of divinity, but what concerned him—and fascinated him—more was the chill of profanation he felt concurrently.[25] Prometheus' goal was both noble and criminal, as was that of Dante's Ulysses or Milton's Satan, "the first that practiced falsehood under saintly flow."[26] Gambara's "falsehood" was his mistake, his overintellectualization of his art which destroyed any possibility of communication with ordinary mortals. "Often perfection in works of art prevents the soul from enlarging them" (G 452), writes the novelist, but his character could not stoop to using the imperfect language of man when he held "the key to the *celestial Word*" (G 467). He failed on three levels: intellectually, psychologically, and artistically, but on all three, like Don Quijote, he failed as an idealist. His most painful admission comes at the end when he declares: "My music is beautiful, but when music passes from sensation to idea, it can only have geniuses as listeners, for they alone have the power to develop it. My misfortune comes from having listened to the concerts of angels and believed that men could understand them" (G 472). The notion of "execution killed by an overabundance of the creative principle"[27] existed so prominently in Balzac's mind that he stressed it even in the Preface: ". . . this pilgrim seated at the gates of Paradise, having ears to listen to the songs of angels and having no tongue to repeat them, exciting the ivory keys with fingers broken by the contradictions of divine inspiration, and believing to express the music of Heaven to dumbfounded listeners" (G 415). It is appropriate to compare this to similar ideas formed in Jacob Böhme's *Beschreibung der drei Prinzipien göttlichen Wesens* of 1816: "Therefore should I speak and write that which is purely heavenly, and altogether of the clear Deity, I should be as dumb to the reader, who hath not the knowledge and the gift"; and Emanuel Swedenborg's *De Coelo et inferno ex auditis et visis* of 1758: "The wisdom of the angels of the third and inmost heaven is incomprehensible even to the inhabitants of the ultimate (outer) heaven."[28] Both mystics were well known to the author of *Séraphita*.

Balzac loves Gambara for his very mistake, for his thirst for eternity, and is compellingly drawn to join his cause. An organic sympathy vibrates between the author who feared to become the victim of his own imagination,[29] and his character; both are united in the awareness that dedication is dangerous to the degree in which its promises are infinite. Even human love is at stake. The incompatibility between an artistic vocation and marriage, which receives subtle treatment in Sand's *Les Maîtres sonneurs* and *Consuelo*, is set forth dramatically by Balzac. "Great men belong to their works" (CBe 323); Louis Lambert's chastity prefigures Gambara's, who is firstly wedded to solitude and only secondly to Marianna, whom he loves. His dream anchored in the Absolute, he loses contact with objective reality to the point of not seeing the obvious connection between the story of his opera and the cause of his wife's grief, between Mohammed's impassioned loyalty to his calling which isolates Cadhige, and his own absorption in music which estranges Marianna's affection. When he detects tears of sorrow in his listeners' eyes, he mistakes them for approbation: "Finally you understand me" (G 448), he exclaims, and so encouraged, he continues his performance of *Mahomet* with throat contractions, canine utterances, spewing mouth, smiles and lingual grimaces at the piano, irate glances, rapt swoons, and an incomprehensible, private gibberish. In paroxysmal form, these are the labor pains of creation, its expectancies and frustrations, which govern the forging of new worlds, finer humans, and nobler art. Balzac, himself a shaper of worlds, understood the process. Prometheus had to leave life behind in order to discover its secret, and even the gods did not appreciate the nobility of his endeavor.

Gambara's dedication exacts a heavy price; he too must receive his punishment for his attempt at *lèse divinité*. Has he not reenacted Adam's sin? The offerings of Heaven are free for anybody's contemplation but not free for anybody's possession. A mortal who tries to possess them is being unconsciously inveigled by the infernal forces to which Faust also fell prey. Gambara's is a similar rebellion, the innate rebellion of genius against the imperious limits of the earthly condition. Raphaël de Valentin had verbalized it in *La Peau de chagrin*: "One must understand the runaway ecstasy of work, the tyranny of ideas and the instinctive repugnance that a man who lives by thought feels for the details of material existence" (PC 94).

The limits force the composer's creation to be nothing more, ultimately, than a pretense. Where perfection is the aim, the result of art is false. Gambara's tragedy is the tragedy of any true artist—D'Arthez, Bridau, Frenhofer—whose singlemindedness makes impossible any compromise with imperfection. But while D'Arthez and Bridau discipline themselves within the framework of a saner, more proportioned sense of aesthetic and moral values, Frenhofer and Gambara seek greater liberty while making at the same time impossible demands upon themselves. Upon such a temperament the Devil pounces. Spirit may well be superior to matter, yet, as Béguin says, "spirit bears disturbing resemblances to the powers of Darkness," and "to the angelic harmonies respond the sneers of the demons."[30] Rather than elevate, passion reduces inspiration to terrestrial proportions and taints it, however magnificent, with mania and monstruosity. Gambara, who lives passionately by his art, is as much a maniac of music as Goriot is a monster of paternity or Claës a madman of chemistry. "The artist," we read in *Des Artistes*, "is a puppet of an eminently capricious force"; he "has a mind only for extravagances," for "genius is a deformity of the brain, . . . a human sickness, the way a pearl is an oyster's sickness" (Art 223). An overwhelming phenomenon devours him. Gambara has felt "the vigorous attacks of an evil spirit that disorients the goal when you aim for it, that brings the most beautiful hopes to a sad end; in a word . . . the tail of the devil wriggling in this world" (G 459). When he begins to analyze Meyerbeer's opera, his "I hear Hell!" assumes both a literal and symbolic meaning, and when he comments on the human passions described, he sees "all the strings by which the devil manipulates us" (G 460).

We have noted earlier that Gambara makes these statements after having drunk; that he experiences seraphic emotions when, sober, he explains his music; but that the clashes of dissonance and the chimerical aberrations which characterize it elicit nothing but bewilderment and irritation from his friends. When they discover that his genius, as far as they are concerned, attains a more proportionate and comprehensible relationship with life and art under the influence of wine, the Bacchic nectar of the Underworld, they submit him to the bizarre hygiene of methodical intoxication. Most references to the Devil come in the second half of the story where the wine regime is applied and where the discussion centers, not coincidentally, around *Robert le Diable*. Contrary to what Hoffmann says in *Höchst zerstreute Gedanken* (that wine accelerates the revolution of ideas when one must pass from incubation to creation), Gambara, while matching the delirium of the Berliner's characters, loses sight of his ideal and of his mission. He creates and performs beautifully nothing more than little cavatinas. He plays into the hands of the Fallen Angel who grants him the satisfaction of communication, and who, locked out of Eden, works vigilantly for the ineffectiveness of any idealism.

We have also noted that Gambara counters Count Andrea's criticisms of *Robert le Diable* with arguments that show some understanding of the opera but also betray a sinister weakness of mood. There is something of an illustration of the law of attraction and repulsion in his excited defense of a work where the spectator comes "face to face with demons," where "the devil is under there, . . . hiding, . . . wriggling," and where "the infernal powers, [having] seized their prey, hold it [and] dance" (G 463, 461, 464). To these last words he adds revealingly: "This fine genius, destined to win, to rule, is now lost! The demons rejoice" (G 464). The Count's remark, that Meyerbeer gave the Devil too good a role, prompts his interlocutor in his drunken stupor to retort curtly: "Be quiet," after which he recalls the performance admitting that he is still "under the spell of a supernatural power" (G 457). He would almost place the opera on an equal plane with Mozart's *Don Giovanni*—appropriately, another musical drama in which the Devil, though unseen, plays no small part. And when "this devil of a man" had sat at the piano earlier to perform his composition for the Count, "his fingers had equalled in nimbleness the forked tongue of a serpent" (G 422, 450).

So many implicit and explicit references to the demonic powers cannot go unnoticed. In the aggregate, they create an atmosphere in which music, as Nietzsche would say, exalts or should exalt the tragic experience of man. The ambiguity evident in the juxtaposition of exaltation and tragedy is manifest in Gambara's heroic anomaly, the fiasco of his attempt to escape the natural condition in order to sublimate his art. Ambiguous, too, is his paradoxical oscillation between a heavenly invitation and an infernal prompting. He would like to accept the former, but finding this impossible, he is tempted to gamble on the Fiend's resources. Sober, the composer of *Mahomet* supports his lofty inspiration with a rational search into the mathematical and physical underpinnings of music and its causes. He is derided. Drunk, the critic of *Robert le Diable* leaves his hermitic temple and descends to the crowd that delights in his cavatinas and in what it considers "music worthy of angels" (G 452). He is applauded. He is great when considered mad, and mad when considered great.[31] "Balzac never ceased to fear . . . that there was something demonic in this multiple reality that he found in himself"[32] and with which, surely, he endowed Paolo Gambara. The questions Balzac asked of Frenhofer he could have asked just as easily of his composer: Was he rational or mad? Was he the slave of an artist's whim, or were his ideas the result of that incredible fanaticism produced in us by the long gestation of a great work? No answers are required where none exist.

One implied question comes to mind and may be studied: Is music, for Balzac, the demonic art par excellence? Goethe had mentioned it in his *Gespräche mit Eckermann*, and Hoffmann, reflecting Leibniz's concept of music as a mathematical and occult exercise of the soul, had declared it. For him, Bach's music, so generally accepted as religious, contains numerical proportions and mystical rules of counterpoint which awakened in him, as they had in Wackenroder, "an inner horror."[33] Berlioz asks it another way: "Is it because certain people are mad that they cultivate music, or is it music that makes them become mad?"[34] And Balzac gives us a hint when the vexed listener exclaims after Modeste's romance: "She has the devil in her . . . *she* is in love, that's sure, and the devil knows the rest" (MM 454). Are we permitted a Satanic interpretation for the word "maybe" in the sentence: "God . . . gives . . . the musician [the faculty] of arranging sounds in a harmonious order whose prototype is up above, maybe! . . ." (PC 216)? The finest artists in *La Comédie humaine* work in the tacit presence of evil shadows, but no narration of their vicissitudes is so surrounded by allusions to the Devil than the story of Gambara. There is much which remains unexpressed in Balzac's implication. As is frequent with him, he likes to expose certain questions rather than probe them; in preference to solving a problem that eludes him he likes to disclose its mystery. Other writers during and after his time have been more explicit. In *Doktor Faustus*, Thomas Mann's Adrian Leverkühn replies to the question in the affirmative, especially when he looks ahead to the kind of music that will be a rude game of "progressivist barbarism," not devoid of the magic fascinations of alchemy and necromancy.[35] The true enigma of the modern world is music, in its many guises and in its function as a connecting artery with the obscure, vitalistic forces we call demonic. In *Don Juan*, Kierkegaard confirmed the demonic principle, adding, however, the element of eroticism,[36] which does not figure as much in *Gambara* as it does in *Massimilla Doni*.

Through his Romantic attachments, Balzac equates artistic fanaticism with the darker forces of existence, and one interpretation may hold that whatever demonism plagues his composer is to be sought not in the nature of music itself but in his own fanatic passion. We need only recall Robert Schumann who similarly "experienced the horror that the genius of music awakens,"[37] but felt it dissipate in the different context of his private emotions in Italy, in the candid radiance of Italian music, particularly of La Pasta performing Rossini. In *Séraphita* we observe that, far from being a bedeviled art, music is in essence the celestial art composed of air and light, the mystic expression of the final Unity that derives from Number—an elaboration of Gambara's belief that "sound is modified air" and "light under another form" (G 434). But there are too many demonic implications in *Gambara*; there is too broad a Hoffmannian background to stress this interpretation. The lure of occultism was just as strong in Balzac as the longing of mysticism. *Gambara* and *Séraphita* complement, rather than complete, each other. If the novelist has his composer exclaim: "[I] groan under the repeated blows of the demon" (G 459), it is difficult to assume that the blows are purely self-inflicted. They stun him because the nature of both his temperament and his art have insisted on his taking the Promethean risk, on his following in the footsteps of Misenus.

Balzac defined the complete genius—a Raphael or a Michelangelo—as the person who combined high artistic and moral qualities, "the man whose heart and character are the equal of his talent in perfection" (MM 407). It is significant that, of all the arts in *La Comédie humaine*, music is the only one not represented by a non-fanatic, by a *beau talent-beau caractère*. Literature has its D'Arthez, painting its Bridau, sculpture its Steinbock; music has only Gambara, more a *fou génie* than a *beau génie*. The margin of difference may well betray the measure of the art's demonism. This, of course, may make him more attractive, for the very reason that Vautrin fascinates us more than Bénassis or Popinot.

In a philosophical sense, Gambara's quest for the Absolute is a Faustian quest for freedom. A degraded human being whose work is interlaced with unhappiness, he becomes what Goethe said of Diderot's Nephew, an accomplice of his destiny. He, too, is several people because he cannot be one, his second manner of drunkenness, whether or not induced by Count Andrea, representing his disgust at his inability to communicate or at the inability of others to understand him. It appears a masochistic revenge. It was his compromise, through the temptation to sign a pact in blood, the only way to meet the world on its terms. "A madness that borders so closely on genius must be incurable in this world" (G 441), comments Andrea. Life does not permit him the benefits of his seraphic talent. Even a fellow madman like Giardini, whose ingenuity serves a transcendent culinary art, rejects him as crazy. The contrast between the cook's grotesque folly and the composer's sublime folly, we said, is one of the keys toward an interpretation of the work. Gambara shunned the values of disbelievers: "He felt himself placed in so superior a sphere that he no longer took the trouble to repel their attacks" (G 427). Should he be able to appraise himself frankly through the eyes of his friends and of society, he still would never feel as honest with himself as he does in his characteristic moments of exalted removal from the human sphere. Hegel would call it eternal self-deceit; but this it is not. Balzac, who poured so much of himself into characters like this one, could never permit his composer to appear more deceiver than deceived where his Platonic lie is concerned. Though he sees in Gambara's disintegration through wine an acquiescence to social pressure—the duty that genius pays to evil, according to Balzac's hero—he makes the compromise momentary and has him abandon the demonic drink in favor of his ivory prison where he is at least free to distinguish perfect knowledge from the imperfection of mortal life. "I renounce forever the use of wine," and in so doing, he denounces his attraction for *Robert le Diable*, "music made by ordinary means . . . [whereas] it's the dregs of ambrosia that I drink with long gulps in transcribing the celestial music I hear" (G 469). Just as he had once briefly put aside his goal when, newly wed and before returning compulsively to his mission, he had behaved more as Marianna's husband than as a composer, so now he forsakes the earlier lure to re-embrace the suffering that stems from his projected "musical regeneration, whose Messiah he believed himself to be" (G 433). His final word in the diabolical parenthesis of wine is heard by Andrea: "The Count . . . looked at Gambara who, his eyes fixed in the manner of a man who has taken theriaca, stuttered the word 'God!'" (G 467). In this respect, *Gambara* differs from *Le Neveu de Rameau*. The tension between the knowledge of failure and an obdurate will for ascension is relieved when Princess Massimilla di Varese can say of the composer on the final page: "This man has remained faithful to the IDEAL" (G 473).[38]

In *Robert le Diable*, Robert also rejects the Devil, Bertram: "he spurns disdainfully the infernal power" (G 465). Gambara's reservation about the ending—"I saw a cathedral instead of hearing the concert of joyous angels" (G 466)—is compensated by the novelist. The reader of *Gambara* is not left "under the weight of Hell's enchantments"; he emerges from his reading "with a hope in his heart" (G 466). In the long run, Gambara's toxic illness is powerfully tonic. The Princess who confesses nostalgically to her society's destruction of the Ideal makes this clear. The madman breaks the fastidious conformities that stifle freedom and level the body social, and the artist scowling under the "blows of the demon" ends by demonstrating his liberty. Does the answer to Gambara's secret attraction to the force that bludgeons him lie in a need for rebirth and for a final affirmation of principle, whatever the means? Good has a mysterious way of emerging from evil. A central sentence in *Melmoth réconcilié* lends itself to this paradox: "The infernal power had revealed divine power to him" (MR 303), a notion similar to the one through which Thomas Mann can speak of "the dialectical association of evil with goodness and holiness."[39] It restates the moral problem of Goethe's *Faust* where Mephistopheles serves God's purpose. Conscious of his genius, Gambara complains to the Count who has applied his "cure": "Ah, sir, you should at least have left me my folly!" (G 468)—a complaint that does not ring with dejection the moment "folly" is identified with "Ideal." Besides, folly represents an ambiguous concept; the average person refers to it arbitrarily using criteria open to question. The overtones of Marianna's lament to the Count—"My friend, my friend, it's not our fault; he does not want to be cured" (G 469)—acquire a positive ring for the reader. Without the beclouding interlude of drink, the Ideal would not have shone later with such luster. In this way, the demonic prompting lifted Gambara's ideal from the pathos of impurity to the ethos of purity. If he sips some wine at the end, he does so in order that he and his wife may eat a crumb of bread and because he is hurt, not because he has compromised or is vanquished. The gold coin he receives is significant in that it comes from the hands of a willing protectress, and in reminding him of his early scientific work, it should give him reason to believe that his principles were not wrought in vain. And the passer-by who, hearing him sing fragments from *Mahomet*, exclaims: "That is certainly beautiful music" (G 472) suggests an eventual, though posthumous, reward. He becomes the audience of the future.

Gambara willingly assumes the consequences of his Ideal. This is his anarchy. This is also his self-sacrifice, according to the Balzacian axiom that genius is the usurer of energy. The downtrodden composer, however, exacts his own dividend: he retains his individuality in its purest state, like a shadow of Rousseau's "original genius." He shows something of what a reader of *Don Quijote* might call the power of illusion to reveal a real, transcendent reality. In his romance to woo a secret beyond the ken of ordinary mortals, he is to that extent unfit for life and, like Claës's equating of life and combustion (RA) or the old man's allusion to the will that burns us (PC), can sigh alluding to the consuming tears of his sorrow: "Water is a body that has burned" (G 473). But he leaves an indelible mark in *La Comédie humaine* through his conviction, as Louis Lambert would say, "that life exists within us and not without us, . . . and that those who are strong enough to climb to the spot from which they can enjoy a glimpse of worlds must not gaze at their feet" (LL 414). In this sense, Gambara's presence in Balzac's epic can only have broadly liberating consequences. He inspires us because he refuses to gaze at his feet, absolutely loyal, in the end, to his inner experience. To him was given a glimpse of the Absolute, and upon him, consequently, lay the duty to pursue it. One of the passionate needs for genius is to believe in itself and to be devoted to its failures, even to its falsehood. Hence there is no fundamental negativism in Balzac's creation of Gambara. Marxist criticism, supported by Hegelian interpretation, might dilute the true significance of the work with assorted concepts of historical malaise, a bankrupt society, and the dawn of inescapable revolution. Although much of Balzac can be interpreted on the level of dialectical materialism, an assessment of a visionary's work cannot be throttled by the simple notion of a historical juncture. *Gambara*'s inactuality, as in the case of Dostoievsky, goes deeper than local time; it conceals a challenge to life.

At this point, we may aver that, through Gambara's ultimate and painful refusal to compromise, Balzac rediscovered the beauty of imperfection and of unsatisfaction, a "flower of evil" before Baudelaire, the reverse of the coin of the "hypocrisy of beauty" (one of his favorite aphorisms). This aspect of the Satanic presence has been known since the days of Faust, who learned eventually that the supreme instance of life is not a pact with Mephistopheles but a mystic sacrifice. As Novalis claimed, it is so much more distinguished to conceive than to realize. Gambara claims such distinction. In the throes of his folly, he espied God, though he remained unconscious of his beatitude.

CHAPTER X

MASSIMILLA DONI: TRANSCENDING SENSUALISM

Balzac's first instalment of *Massimilla Doni*, then entitled *Une représentation du Mosé de Rossini à Venise*, appeared in *La France musicale* on August 25, 1839, and not in Schlesinger's *Gazette*. The tale balances, on the side of Italian music, some of the attacks leveled against it in *Gambara*. If the latter cost Balzac six months of hard work, the Venetian story demanded an equally assiduous preparation. On May 24 of 1837, Balzac had declared with anxiety: "If I can realize all the ideas that cross my mind, this book will certainly be as stunning as *La Peau de chagrin*, better written, perhaps more poetical."[1] Months later, he expressed reservations to Mme Hanska about the public's ability to understand it apart from its piquant, shifting relationships:

> *Massimilla Doni*, another work which will be quite misunderstood, gives me enormous tasks because of its difficulties; but I have never caressed anything so much as I have these mythical pages, for the myth lies buried very deep under reality. . . .
>
> You cannot imagine with what a sense of resignation I foresee the bad and mean stupidities that this *Massimilla Doni* work will direct against me. Taken from one point of view, the subject plays into the critics' hands; they will call me obscene. But look at the psychic subject; for me, it's a marvel. . . . In five years, *Massimilla Doni* will be regarded as a beautiful exposition of the most intimate processes of art. In the eyes of its first readers, it will be what it appears to be: a lover who cannot possess the

> woman he adores because he desires her too much, and who possesses a pitiful girl instead. Let them figure out from that how works of art are brought to light![2]

There is a possibility that Jules Janin's *Gabrielli* served as a basis for the story, but the similarities reveal only surface relationships and do not go beyond a few minor incidents of plot.[3] More likely is the supposition that some of the more bizarre aspects of the tale were drawn from the repertory of anecdotes of Jacques Strunz, to whom the work is dedicated and who schooled Balzac extensively for the opera section: "*Massimilla Doni*," wrote the novelist, "demands a long study of the score; . . . I must do this with a consummate musician. . ."[4] One such anecdote had become the story of the sudden fortune of the flutist Schwabe in *Le Cousin Pons*. In *Massimilla Doni*, Clarina Tinti's carefree combination of a beautiful voice with sexual wantonness, Capraja's fanatical pleasure in the roulade and in arabesques, Duke Cataneo's odd background of overstrained sexualism joined with his current interest only in the perfect conjunction of two sounds, Prince Emilio Memmi's too ideal love for the heroine, Genovese's inability to sing in the presence of his lady love, and Marco Vendramini's patriotic despair that seeks refuge in opium—all these abnormalities thrown together make the tale sound like a compendium of eccentricities. In addition, the reader finds a number of possible Strunzian elements, ideas the teacher and his pupil held in common. The story's action takes place in Venice, not only because Balzac had discovered the city rapturously from February to May of 1837, but also because—Balzac and Strunz agreed—only Italians and Germans can be musicians, the French being incurably frivolous. There are romantic theories about music expressed by Massimilla: music as the most powerful of languages, conveyor of the infinite, penetrating the ages with the lingering force of melody. There is, finally, an opera by Rossini, the composer so admired by the two men. Balzac intended more than a simple report or remembrance of a performance in La Fenice. He wanted to transpose creatively what his teacher had explained to him at the piano and arrive at a transfigured interpretation of *Mosè in Egitto* as a tribute to his good friend from Pesaro.

The tale contains structural weakness, but these do not explain why it was not widely read—except perhaps in Italy where pre-Risorgimento readers heard in its pages an echo of their long and painful struggle for national unity. Nor does it suffice to accuse the hurried writing conditions under which the author labored (with such conditions he was well acquainted), or the threats made to him, such as the letter relating to his editor-in-chief: "Sir," a subaltern had written, "definitely Souverain does not want to settle before having received *Massimilla Doni*. The delay you are causing in giving us this story is so prejudicial to us that I am forced to advise you that, from this moment forward, I shall prohibit any insertion of your works in the newspapers until such a time as you shall have finished this work."[5] Yet, notwithstanding its irregularities, *Massimilla Doni* fascinates the thinking reader, less for the analysis of *Mosé in Egitto* that was to be its mainstay than for its psychological piquancies and its advanced synaesthetic theory, let alone its sparkling depiction of a soirée at La Fenice during which Italy and Mediterranean art pulsate before us. Balzac fashions a system of images (for which he has been reproached) whose end is to shape poetic essences, reach a reader's response with sensations that must necessarily remain abstract, yet create a recognizable phenomenon. He labors with a relatively new language, and becomes awkward as well as significant—and prescient—only to the tutored reader. Like a Pirandello play, the story seeks not to entice our curiosity in a plot but to expound a thesis, a cerebral thesis that molds an inner drama whose amorous vicissitudes represent merely an externalization, thus forcing reality into a position subservient to the imagination. Hence Balzac's prediction that his public was not ready for *Massimilla Doni*, and that it would be in (at least) five years.

The Problem of the Fiasco

Massimilla Doni sustains a mood of paradox from beginning to end. On this level, it appears homogeneous. Emilio Memmi offers us an early glimpse into the theme of antithesis: a prince with little income, possessor of a beautiful palace with no rights over its contents, owner of sumptuous galleries and living in a single room: "He then saw the present as it really was: a palace without a soul, a soul without influence on the body, a principality without money, an empty body and a full heart, a thousand despairing antitheses" (MD 320). The very cultural situation of Italy offers another contrast: "From the depth of her misery, Italy reigns through the elite people who abound in her cities" (MD 346). As for the Verdi of *I Lombardi* and *Nabucco*, Italy signifies a moral presence. Even Rossini's opera fits the pattern, a work in which "a sobriety of means makes the music's fertility that much more startling" (MD 371). These paradoxes, however, are peripheral to the central paradox: the bizarre or incongruous amorous relations among the characters. The Prince strikes a telling note when he remarks to himself: "The joke that fate permits itself to play on me may also be found in my love" (MD 319). One love situation—impotence derived from excessive passion—that Balzac did not treat in that merry-go-round of human relationships called *Béatrix* he treated in *Massimilla Doni*. Here, love is the instrument of a mysterious synthesis of spirituality and sensuality. The carnival atmosphere of Venice reflects what for the reader is the private carnival of the characters, although their strange inhibitions make them suffer and their involvement with each other's troubles is not merry. La Tinti, the *prima donna assoluta*, is enamored of Prince Emilio Memmi who passionately loves and is loved by Massimilla Cataneo, except that her absolute beauty and purity induce impotence in him. He can satisfy his male urge only in the arms of the prima donna, whom he resents, and who is adored by Genovese, the tenor whose beautiful voice turns to braying and bellowing whenever he sings alongside her. Our credulity continues to be taxed when a French doctor rescues the frustrated little society with the simple stratagem of substituting Massimilla for La Tinti under the cover of darkness—an old Renaissance stage trick used in salacious comedy, such as Machiavelli's *La mandragola*. Somehow the recalcitrant knot unties to the relative satisfaction of all and to the news of the heroine's pregnancy.

Balzac's untutored reader, therefore, sided with the critics whose raised eyebrows and accusations of twaddle and foolery he fully expected. It was difficult to approach the story from Balzac's point of view and accept his gross unconventionality on grounds not of his realistic but of his illustrative purpose. Though the unlikelihoods of the plot become ancillary to the underlying "psychic" principle, one might still wish that Balzac had lodged his theory in a more credible, palpable psychology; but he did present it in a discernible way. Still, the exaggerations remained glaring. A lovely and cultured lady like Massimilla would not find herself playing the courtesan, except on the author's Romantic assumption, shared by Stendhal, that a passionate Italian will not hesitate to degrade herself for the sake of the man she loves. Nor would she expound a pedantic musical lesson at a time when she is more interested in Rossini's music for the way in which it arouses her passion for someone in the next loge. Then, too, the extreme vitiation of Memmi's and Genovese's finest impulses is not warranted by logic and produces situations that border on the risible. The most Balzac's contemporaries could do was to count on this hyperbole of the senses to balance the equally extreme hyperbole of the intellect in *Gambara*.

The similarities and the differences that join and separate *Massimilla Doni* and *Gambara* become important. Whatever Balzac's intention to create analogous situations, the two stories differ strikingly on an ethical plane. With *Massimilla Doni*, we descend from the celestial level of the seekers of the absolute to mix with a society that, however exceptional its energy, roots its desires in the common soil of earthly, and earthy, love. Indeed, this love is so physical that it besieges the animal being, causing one character to sound like a deer and an ass and another "to hear in his ears the precipitated movement of his blood rising in waves and threatening to burst the vessels of the heart" (MD 314-315). Though honest in their struggle, Massimilla's group cannot be classified as paradigms of thought. These skirmishers wage an inner battle that reveals itself in tragic dimensions; it finds no equivalence with the conflict of those who face outside rivals and the material complications of their own sensuousness. Memmi's and Genovese's battles are acted out in the presence of concrete facts. For them, to conquer means to surmount a psychic phenomenon induced by an external obstacle, while for Gambara it would mean, if it were possible, to accede to an angelic, private dream. The Prince and the tenor eventually reap the benefits of their actions; they can count their successes without ever fearing to lose themselves in meditation. There is no question of a divine prompting when instinct leans toward a material object. Gambara lives through his aspiration to an Idea; Massimilla's friends exist through their appetites for their rather base egos. Only Capraja and Cataneo escape moral censure. Like Gambara, they remain faithful to their ideals, although, because their social status allows them to pursue them as a hobby, their idealism reveals no traces of heroism. It is in no way paradigmatic.

If we stress Balzac's declared intention to show by example how the problem of the fiasco affects creation (*Gambara*) and performance (*Massimilla Doni*) and consider the instances of physical love merely as illustrations of the broader theory of failure, then certain similarities between the two *contes philosophiques* do emerge. In this case, we too may be in the presence of "a work of poetry far removed from the goals of brutal nature" (MD 313). The similarities run deeper than what we might call the purely medical, schizophrenic aspects of the two stories.[6] Both tales suggest the theories of psycho-physiologists like Dessaignes, who regarded thought as an ethereal fluid that worked in people according to laws as yet undiscovered but partially recognizable. But they likewise suggest the theories of "physiologico-mystics" like Baader. Wrote Balzac: "Baader, who in his lessons used to explain celestial things using erotic comparisons, had probably noticed . . . the great resemblance that exists between human love and heavenly love" (MD 333). Yet, even more distinguishable than that of Baader, the shadow of Hoffmann again lurks in the background of the novelist's thought, especially in what pertains to the fiasco in music. An artist like Genovese fails because he cannot forget himself as signor Genovese and position himself through his imagination and, as Diderot had urged in *Paradoxe sur le comédien*, through an objective intellectual effort, in the character he is portraying. Hoffmann called this complete detachment from the daily ego the ironic ecstasy that befits the manner of artists. It permits them to escape contingency in order to gain a deeper and less subjective understanding of themselves and of nature. As the magician Magnus Hermod intimates with nebulous allegory in *Prinzessin Brambilla*'s story of King Ophioch and Queen Liris, it represents both intuition and thought about the intuition: "Thought destroys Intuition, and, torn away from the Mother's bosom, one totters homelessly around in a strange land and in a blind stupor, until the reflection of Thought [Intuition] furnishes to Thought itself the Knowledge that it [Thought] exists, and that, deep in the richest mine which the motherly Queen has opened for him, Thought rules as mistress, though she might obey as a vassal."[7] Genovese would have to get in touch with reality, the true artistic reality from which he has turned, through such a process of thought-regeneration. He would then be his own master, for he would not strive to express, through his singer's art, the incandescence of his own love. Rather, he would express Love. And he would be able to sing even when his self-respect was injured. To use the role of Rossini's Osiride to express his love for Tinti and expect it to convey to his audience the protagonist's love for the opera's Elicia is as fraudulent in its technique as it is disastrous in its result. The French doctor, more likely a psychiatrist, summarizes the situation accurately: "When an artist is unfortunate enough to be full of the passion he wants to express, he cannot portray it because he is the thing itself instead of being its image. Art stems from the brain and not from the heart. When your subject dominates you, you are its slave and not its master. You are like a king besieged by his people. To feel too intensely at the moment of execution is tantamount to an insurrection of the senses against the governing faculty!" (MD 381). Otherwise stated, an artist can "feel too fully to translate" his ideal (Art 225).

In these few words we have Balzac's psychology of failure, a variation of the crisis that overwhelmed Racine's or Alfieri's heroines. As in the case of Hoffmann, it applies not only to music but to all the arts and sciences, paralyzing equally a philosopher like Louis Lambert, a chemist like Claës, and a painter like Frenhofer. Also as in the case of Hoffmann, it is especially applicable to music, for, according to the author of *Johannes Kreislers Lehrbrief*, musicians are those who say that their kingdom is not of this world: "Where do we find in nature, as painters and sculptors find, the prototype of our art?"[8] It is that much more difficult to maintain a proper, objective perspective and not to become overinvolved, like Gambara. Music is a mysterious language, echoing a distant sphere of existence in our souls, whereby their movements are lofty though often of destructive intensity. Genovese sounds like Gambara when he exclaims: "*Per dio*, don't you understand me? The feeling which animates me has pervaded my entire being, my heart and lungs. My soul and my throat have but one life. Haven't you ever listened, in a dream, to that sublime music imagined by unknown composers who make use of the pure sound that nature has put into all things and that we call forth, more or less successfully, by means of the instruments with which we compose colorful masses—pure sound that emerges, in those marvelous concerts, free from the imperfections of performers. . .? Well, such are the marvels I give you, and you censure me!" (MD 384-385). The tenor and the composer would profit by understanding the law formulated by Vendramin: "When the principle is stronger than the result, nothing worthwhile is produced" (MD 369-370).

Balzac is really opposing two emotive theories: self-expression, with which Genovese founders, and logical expression, with which he would have triumphed. C. P. E. Bach had insisted that the musician must be himself moved in order to move others, that he must "induce in himself all those affects which he would arouse in his auditors."[9] On the other hand, Balzac along with Diderot would have agreed with Ferruccio Busoni, who insisted with as much conviction that sympathetic emotion is a faulty principle, that to move his audience an artist "must never be moved himself—lest he lose, at that moment, his mastery over his material" and lest the auditor's appreciation "be degraded to mere human sympathy."[10] Edward Bullough called the degradation a loss of "psychical distance."[11] The only difference between Balzac's stand and that of Diderot lies in the kind of objectivity each would assume necessary for an artistic performance. Diderot would have urged Genovese to adopt an impersonal objectivity, nothing beyond an intellectually interested manner, while Balzac would advise a personal objectivity, an emotionally interested yet uninvolved manner that is free of sympathetic ties by being "filtered," as Bullough describes it, "cleared of the practical, concrete nature of its appeal."

The same overinvolvement which destroys the musician's performance destroys also that of the lover. Prince Memmi provides the example. His creative "principle"—the power of his worship—suffers from overabundance. He idolizes Massimilla to the extent of imagining her "with the white wings of angels . . . to whom painters give only a head and two wings" (MD 316-317). Balzac drives his point repeatedly: "Emilio and the Duchess love each other too much," "Emilio placed his mistress too high up to reach her," Emilio's was "a noble malady that afflicts only the very young and the old" (MD 314, 316). He is "frozen" by "celestial sensations," exists as if "married in Heaven only," and his love planes on "ethereal summits" because it is "the pure love of angels" (MD 319, 334, 368, 369). Sybil Vane loved Wilde's Dorian Gray this way,[12] and Octave de Malivert, in Stendhal's *Armance*, committed suicide in the throes of a similar dilemma. Memmi attains at best a vicarious consummation through the "diabolical voluptuousness" (MD 369) of La Tinti, an ambiguous satisfaction, one might say, rent as he is between the contemplative, spiritual pureness of the Duchess and the impetuous, rounded carnality of the soprano. Dante, evoked by Balzac in referring to the Prince's adoration of his lady, and even the more sensuous Petrarch, succeeded in their Platonic passions in the sense that they kept intact the angelic essence. The characters in *Massimilla Doni*, including the protagonist, do not succeed. Their "cure" is achieved only within the framework of human frailty—the same cure Gambara would have contrived if he had abided by the regime of wine. Massimilla's little society abdicates, and, like the Prince, disappears "like a needle in the slime" (MD 386) of its vapid carnival. Only Vendramin dies; he is a patriot. Excluding Capraja and Cataneo, the other toasters of the "Ideal" end by betraying it, by killing it, to use the words Massimilla utters with grieved nostalgia when she meets her compatriot, Gambara, who had kept his heroic faith in it. Only seemingly paradoxical, Vendramin the drug addict, derived from De Quincey's *Confessions of an Opium Eater*, remains faithful to his ideal. Like a brother of Gambara, but one whose dream or political exaltation leads him to suicide instead of perseverance, he sees not fuzzily but clearly in his excited state, and through love, music, and country, gathers unto himself the tale's many motifs. Indeed, he stands for the entire Venetian society (the French doctor must be excluded) that falls victim to thought. As one commentator notes: "[These] characters of *Massimilla Doni* [are] beings whose exclusive cult of an ideal—love music, country—has occasioned simultaneously a mutilation of the human being, a deep-seated inability to adapt to real existence, and the kind of exaltation that metes out sharp enjoyments . . . [This is what Balzac meant by 'a beautiful exposition of the most intimate processes of art.'] This dangerous privileging of dream over reality, this need of an impossible incarnation that gives rise to the despair of impotence, this mystical desire to concentrate on the object of one's love, to fuse with it even if it means death—what else is the eternal condition of the artist?"[13] But the artist, even a Gambara or a Frenhofer, redeems himself through creation, and no one in Massimilla's society is a creator. Hence the difficulty, for Balzac, in writing such a tale. Hence, then, the focus on musical theory, making *Massimilla Doni* a true *conte philosophique*.

The Process of Synaesthesia

The paradoxes that move along the timid plot of the tale serve as metaphors transposing physiological events into concepts. A correlative side of the same coin delineates correspondences that allow us not to transpose but to infer profound analogies between music and the visual arts. Capraja, who knows Gambara and "shared the opinions of that instrument-maker," declares that man has "inner fingerkeys that correspond to our nervous centers from which our sensations and our ideas spring" (MD 353). In terms less neurological than occultist, Hoffmann had suggested that the musician is to nature as a mesmerizer is to a seeress (*Somnambule*), "his energetic will being the question which nature never leaves unanswered."[14] Balzac arrived at an adumbration of the theory of synaesthesia through his conversance with the Illuminist creed and its Hoffmannian overtones, and through his Swedenborgian bent. That he voices such an important process, which became seminal for Baudelaire, in a musical novelette gives us an indication of the centrality of music, as he sensed it, in the realm of the fine arts. Since all of them communicate through the sensuous percept, their pure meaning should be most accessible through music. It should not be surprising, as it has been to some,[15] to hear Massimilla say: "When I spoke to you of the somber colors, of the coldness of the notes used in the introduction to *Mosé*, was I not as correct as your critics are who speak to us about the color of such and such an author?" (MD 376-377). In this statement, the heroine has struck those "inner notes" and enhanced her listener's musical appreciation by evoking similitudes, or interchanges, in sensory perceptions. Hers is a prose equivalent of the famous verse in *Les Fleurs du mal* which set a style: "Perfumes, colors, and sounds correspond," itself an echo of Hoffmann's comment on the intimate union in life of colors, sounds, and smells[16]—a willful distortion of aesthetic categories.

Balzac's synaesthetic comments extend the tale's tone of contrasts. Vendramin, as the embodiment of his lethargic patriot who cradles his energy and inflates his hope in the "brilliant vapors of opium intoxication" (MD 340), becomes central to the mood out of which allusions to synaesthesia grow. What the Venetian says to Memmi about Capraja's and Cataneo's melomanias places him among the forerunners of the symbolist poets and their recourse to the enchantments of their "artificial paradise": "Those two men belong to the legion of pure souls who can shed down here their larvae of flesh and who know how to vault astride the body of the queen of sorceresses, in the blue skies where the sublime marvels of moral life unfold; they reach through Art the place toward which your extreme love leads you and toward which opium pushes me. They can only be understood by their peers. I, whose soul is exalted by a sad means; I, who condense one hundred years of existence into a single night, can understand those great minds when they speak of the magnificent country called the country of myths by those who deem themselves wise, and the country of realities by us who are considered mad" (MD 352).

The aesthetic concern with unity which distinguished in Balzac's mind the Introduction of *Mosé in Egitto*, grounded as it is in the C major chord, made him regard the musician's language as special, and the artist's role as a unifier, as a mediator between man and nature, nature and God, God and man. Both Hoffmannian fantasy and Swedenborgian mysticism adduced in the author of *Louis Lambert* an aversion for all that meant separation or fragmentation, and in his effort toward universal reconciliation he fell happily upon the idea of sensory similitude, the kind that stimulates an alliance among the arts. In 1830, John Herschell had published an influential *Traité de la lumière* with a reference to Louis-Bertrand Castel's description of his optical clavichord in *L'Optique des couleurs* of 1740. Hoffmann had said that "the musician is not using an empty image or an allegory when he says that, for him, colors, perfumes, and beams of light appear to him as tones, and that in their intertwining he perceives a marvelous concert."[17] Balzac goes beyond Hoffmann. Indeed, he reproaches him for not having carried his theory to its logical conclusion: "Read what your dear Hoffmann the Berliner has written on Gluck, Mozart, Haydn, and Beethoven, and you will see by what secret laws literature, painting, and music hold together! Some pages are stamped with genius, above all Kreisler's *Master's Letter*. But Hoffmann was satisfied to talk about this alliance like a man who has taken theriaca. His works express admiration; he felt too strongly and was too much a musician to engage in discussion. I have the advantage over him of being French [according to Balzac, Italians feel music, Frenchmen judge it, and Englishmen pay for it] and a musician only very slightly. I can provide the key to the palace inside which he drank elatedly."[18] And the key is Balzac's fusion of scientific and mystic theories. "[Hoffmann] felt too strongly"; Memmi and Genovese come to understand the liability. Balzac, on the other hand, assumes the pose of the objective investigator who gives body to Hoffmann's allusions, completing them through an aesthetic utilization of them that borders on the supernatural.

Massimilla becomes her creator's mouthpiece: "In the language of music, to paint means to awaken through the use of sounds certain recollections in our hearts, or certain images in our minds, and these recollections, these images have their colors; they are sad or gay. . . . According to Capraja, every instrument has its mission, and addresses itself to certain ideas just as every color corresponds to certain feelings within us. Looking at golden arabesques on a blue background, do you find you have the same thoughts that red arabesques on a black or green background stimulate in you? In a given painting, there are no figures, no feelings expressed; it's a matter of pure art, and yet no one will remain cold looking at them" (MD 376). The implications of this last statement are boundless, relating not only to Cataneo's puristic notion of the perfect blending of two sounds or to Capraja's equally puristic emotions before a wordless roulade, but also to the expectations of what today we recognize as non-objective or non-representational art.

Balzac surpasses Hoffmann in the matter of the correspondence of sound with other senses. Hoffmann gives one example, suggesting that the aroma of dark red carnations makes him hear the "deep flowing tones of a tenor clarinet."[19] Balzac adds more substantially the factor of thought. "[Music] communicates its *ideas* immediately in the manner of perfumes" (MD 350). In *Les Amours de deux bêtes*, he stresses the factor of smell when he speaks of the "ecstasy . . . [of] sweet melodies" as Anna "breathed a concert of perfumes" (ADB 337). But he attempts to embrace even more in his interchanges. Seizing upon a different alliance, he has Massimilla categorize a whole orchestra when she asks: "Doesn't the bassoon have the power to evoke campestral images in everyone's mind, just as almost every wind instrument has? Do not the brasses possess something warrior-like, and do they not develop within us excited, rather furious sensations? Do not the strings, whose substance derives from live organisms, lay hold of the most delicate fibers in our constitution, and do they not penetrate to the very depth of the heart?" (MD 376). Balzac's associations, perfunctory even in his day, do not compare favorably with his model's single but provocative illustration. But he does outdo him in one important respect: Hoffmann made too abundant a use of sensory transpositions with the intention of tinting his *Kreisleriana* with the hues of a fantastic and mysterious reality. Balzac, says one critic,[20] is more discreet, and, we might add, more subtle in the employment of non-sensory realities. Massimilla translates her love for Emilio into her paean to Rossini's music; Genovese attempts to metamorphose La Tinti into a transcendent music; Cataneo and Capraja transfigure, through their respective musical idiosyncracies, their pleasure into ecstasy; Vendramin fashions the opera with his dream.

More often, however, in more common synaesthetic associations, the sense of sound melds with the sense of sight. The larger part of Massimilla's analysis of *Mosé in Egitto* transforms musical impressions into visual suggestions. Berlioz and Hoffmann specifically employed visual equivalents in their musical analyses to elicit a "tangible" response from a sensitive listener. Balzac, as we know, followed suit, but makes much more frequent use of art history. As Balzac intermixes instruments and colors, so Massimilla compares musical compositions with paintings. Rossini's "musical palette" brings to Massimilla's lips the names of Poussin, Titian, and Giotto, not to speak of the names of other painters that seed the tale: Leonardo, Andrea del Sarto, Raphael, Zurbarán, Dolci, Tintoretto, Murillo, Tiepolo, Bellini, Orcagna. . . .[21] A genuine synaesthetic experience occurs in the "brilliant" and "animated" stretta, "Voci di giubilo," about which that indefatigable commentator, Massimilla, remarks: "I would compare [its] color to the one Titian applies in surrounding his divine personages" (MD 362).

Temperamentally more inclined toward the visual than toward the auditive, Balzac's sensitivity to color made him approach music through painting. The painting vision lends itself conveniently to verbal communication involving the nature and feeling of sound. In addition, like Locke, Dickens, and Gide in their concern with blindness, Balzac also reverses the process. Color may be imparted through sound. Moreover, it may relate to certain "agitations of the soul" (F 66). Balzac alludes to Locke in *Ferragus*: "If, as Locke's blind man said, scarlet must produce in the eyes the effects produced in the ears by a fanfare, it would be possible to compare with gray hues" (F 66) an undefined melancholy which at a point tinges the relationship between M. and Mme Desmarets. The author of *Massimilla Doni* felt strongly the transcendent unity that privileges Art in all its aspects and in its relation to nature: "Art paints with words, with sounds, with colors, with lines, with forms; if its means are different, the effects are the same. . . . In their grandiose efforts, the arts are but the expression of the great spectacles of nature." But of all the arts, says his heroine, music enjoys a noticeable primacy: it is "superior as a language to color which is fixed, and to the word which has limits" because it is "infinite" (MD 377).

Swedenborg, though not an aesthetician, aided Balzac in crossing the boundary—not reached by Hoffmann—between sensory analogies and universal unity. The Swedish mystic based his doctrine on the idea of relationships not only between men and things or the physical and the moral, but also between the natural and the spiritual universe. These relationships are correspondences: "The whole natural world corresponds to the spiritual world, and not merely the natural world in general, but also every particular in it; and consequently, every thing in the natural world that springs from the spiritual world is called a correspondent."[22] Elsewhere, he suggested more subtly that color corresponds to opinion, because it is light diversified in different ways, and that modification in the natural world corresponds to sensations in the animal world and to affection in the spiritual world[23]—a notion that tinges the adventures of Memmi and Genovese. However, while Swedenborg sought in correspondences a means of knowledge geared to reveal the hidden messages of the Scriptures, Balzac made them serve his artistic ends and contribute to life's sense of mystery and marvel. Contrary to popular belief, Balzac's world is charged with more wonder than its deterministic society leads one to believe.

In *Massimilla Doni*, Balzac again leaves Hoffmann behind when he expands the concept of Swedenborgian correspondences in the direction of the "infinite" and blends music with the source of color: light. Massimilla admires the Introduction of Rossini's opera with its repetition of the C-major chord because it depicts the coming of light, the source of harmony, conjoining synaesthetically sonorous and luminous sensations, music and dawn, but, not being a philosopher, her appreciation reflects pallidly a more profound theory that Balzac developed in *Louis Lambert* and in *Séraphita* when he spoke of the unity of substance found in sound and light and thought. "Light engendered melody, melody engendered light, colors were light and melody" (S 584). The musical exponent of this idea is Gambara, quoted in *Massimilla Doni* as believing that "sounds meet within us a substance analogous to the one that engenders the phenomena of light and that produces our ideas" (MD 352-353). The background of the theory and all it encompasses must be sought in *Gambara* itself where the intellectual composer offers a scientific explanation of correspondences and urges the development of harmony through an understanding of the physical and mathematical roots of music:

> Sound is modified air; air is composed of principles that probably find in us analogous principles that correspond to them, sympathize, and grow through the power of thought. Thus air must contain as many particles of varying elasticity, and be capable of as many vibrations of diverse duration, as there are sounds in sonorous bodies; and these particles perceived by our ear and set in motion by the musician correspond to ideas according to our constitutions. I believe that the nature of sound is identical to that of light. Sound is light under another form: both proceed by vibrations which end in man and which he transforms into thoughts in his nerve centers. Music, like painting, employs bodies that have the faculty of releasing this or that property from the mother substance, in order to compose pictures with them. In music, instruments serve as the colors that a painter uses. . . . What I am saying is that music is an art woven into the very entrails of Nature. Music obeys physical and mathematical laws. The physical laws are little known; the mathematical laws are understood more. From the time we began to study their relationships, we created harmony, for which we are indebted to Haydn, Mozart, Beethoven, and Rossini—wonderful geniuses who

> certainly produced more maturely advanced music than their forerunners, people whose genius, to be sure, is irrefutable. The older masters sang instead of availing themselves of art and science, the noble alliance that permits us to fuse beautiful melodies and powerful harmonies into a single whole. Now, if the discovery of the mathematical laws gave us those four great musicians, where could we not go if we found the physical law by virtue of which—understand this—we could muster, in greater or lesser quantity and in proportions to be determined, a certain ethereal substance permeating the air, the one that gives us music as well as light, the phenomena of vegetation as well as those of zoology! [G 434-435]

The antecedent of part of Gambara's theory, proceeding from the physics of sound to the psychology of hearing, may be traced to Swedenborg's postulate that thoughts are undulations of fluid which transform themselves ulteriorly, thanks to our sensory organs, into vibrations in the air, hence into sounds.

Synaesthesia and the nature of music and air may ultimately find a more ascertainable explanation, but the "ethereal substance" that is common to colors, sounds and light, whatever its scientific implication, contains a valid aesthetic implication destined to make the synaesthetic process meaningful. Massimilla's analysis of *Mosé in Egitto* implies that music corresponds in its sounds to the innermost workings of our subconscious. It is, in otherwords, a symbol, for the concept of correspondences is inseparable from that of symbolism. The Duchess repeatedly finds passages of the opera symbolic of existences or realities outside of music. Gambara does the same. Balzac shared Hoffmann's and Swedenborg's idea that everything is symbol, that nature is a symbolic language to be deciphered, and that if all has a common cause—the "ethereal substance"—the synaesthetic process becomes the most suited to unravel the mystery of creation. And music, as the universal language, provides the key, explaining creation better than any other process or art. The "simple C chord" of Rossini's Introduction, like "light [which] is a single and same substance everywhere resembling itself, whose effects vary only according to the objects it encounters," tells us more about the sun and the "luminous waves" of sunrise than any other language. "It awakens each source of harmony" (MD 360-361). It symbolizes the phenomenon that we try otherwise vainly to enclose in signs or words, the phenomenon that a few privileged beings—the inner man, for Swedenborg—may have perceived in the unconsciousness of ecstasy.

So did Balzac take some steps in the direction of symbolism, symbolism suggesting the manner in which the material and spiritual worlds correlate by analogy, as well as the manner in which poetic intuition associates abstractly the two worlds, giving the former a soul and the latter a substance. We may conclude with Laubriet that "in trying to explain scientifically the intuitions of the story teller, . . . Balzac enriched the symbolic range of Hoffmann, pushing beyond the stage of synaesthesia to attain the level of profound correspondence, the level of that 'reciprocal analogy,' as Baudelaire will say, where everything corresponds to all other things with mathematical exactness. It seems that Balzac could not be satisfied with Hoffmann's more-or-less, and that he was spurred by his desire for the absolute—aided by Swedenborg—to construct a complete theory. . . . Before Baudelaire, Balzac, having loved to escape into dream, endowed the heavens of art with a new shimmer."[24] Given the intensity of Balzac's presentation, not of the amorous plot but of the theoretical concepts, it is difficult to believe that he was merely reacting to the dramatic situation he had set up without the benefit of genuine musical sensibility on his part. As he does inside *Massimilla Doni* in the way the tale transcends sensualism, as he did in the case of the spiritual growth of the Beethoven concept in his mind, and as he did in his maturation as a literary artist progressing from the realistic to the visionary in his world view, in matters musical, outside of the religious context, Balzac modulated from bare hedonism to authentic mysticism.

CHAPTER XI

AN ANIMATING PSYCHOLOGY

Music as Inner Force

In his writings, Balzac relied on the seductive powers of music, not unlike the driving energy of money, to move his characters, normal or abnormal, in and out of their realities and fantasies. In his pervasive concern for its causes and effects, the novelist viewed the former as a mystic, allowing his thought to alight upon the farthest edges of actuality and sense the mysterious vibrations of the beyond; and he viewed the latter as a student of human motivations, observing an art which, he believed fastly, makes our hidden feelings surface, restores us to ourselves, and reveals to us on occasion secrets of sex long buried in our subconscious. Music, in *La Comédie humaine*, acts as an inner force; it provides the intimacy that permits tacit or personal disclosures, conveys meanings that words would only mar, and excites or relaxes the psyche, prompting action or inducing contemplation. Through it, human beings take conscience of themselves, measure their surroundings with greater subtlety, and divine concealed feelings—Romantic conceptions which Balzac tempered with a scrutiny at once delicate and overt.

In one speech, Gambara, as Balzac's mouthpiece, discloses some of the art's psychological stimuli:

> Does it not form your thought? Does it not awaken benumbed remembrances? There are a thousand souls in a hall; a theme darts forth from La Pasta's throat, whose execution corresponds well with the thoughts that burned in Rossini's soul and when he wrote his arias. Transmitted to those souls, Rossini's theme develops many different poems in them: one sees

> a long dreamed-of woman; another sees some bank along which he has strolled and whose trailing willows, clear waves, and hopes that once wandered beneath the leafy bowers now appear to him; one woman recalls the thousand feelings that tortured her during an hour of jealousy; another thinks of her heart's unsatisfied longings and imagines an ideal being to whom she surrenders herself, experiencing the delights of the woman who caresses the chimera in a Roman mosaic; still another dreams that that very evening she will realize some desire, and plunges in advance into a torrent of pleasures, receiving its buoyant waves on her flaming breast. [G 436]

Music's "power over our inner beings," summarizes Massimilla, "is one of [its] grandeurs" (MD 356).

As such, Balzac surrounds it with a religious aura, consistent with its mystic principle or cause. Philosophers like Saint-Martin and Swedenborg contributed to the spiritual associations he makes. Was it not the Swedish mystic in particular who joined music and love, happiness and the world of the spirit, in an idealized transcendence? Three inseparable threads highlight Balzac's musico-psychological fabric: dream, remembrance, and love. Each comes to life in the presence of sounds. Music predisposes a listener to a state of reverie, conjuring up thoughts or sensations pertaining to any given moment of his life and unraveling them with uncommon clarity and intensity. Man seeks "the pure pleasure of listening to music and what one loves. . ." (AP 27). Our emotions are, after all, a form of music in that they flow like movement. Balzac's heroes, and especially his heroines, dream not necessarily *of* music but *through* music. As is implied in some of Grétry's *Essais* and stated in Stendhal's *Journal*, one of the art's functions is to reveal us to ourselves and to confirm our feelings so as to detect their movements that much better. Another is to purify our feelings, divesting them of all the vulgar circumstances that envelop them in life. In this manner, Balzac does more than all of his predecessors and most of his contemporaries who sentimentally made music the attribute of sensitive individuals. He associates it not only with the impressions of nature or with the heart's emotions, but, anticipating D'Annunzio and Proust, also with the mind's aspirations, self-revelation, and the drift of memory. As these are all expressions of love ("Only music expresses love," exclaims Massimilla after the final duet of *Il barbiere di Siviglia* [MD 347]), it is difficult at times to distinguish whether love gives rise to music or music to love. "If you need the heart of a poet to make a musician, do you not need poetry and love to listen to and understand great musical works?" (DL 133). Lope de Vega had averred long before in *El Perro del hortelano* that music and love agree well together. Both seem to exist in perfect accord in Balzac, as they do in Sand's *Consuelo* where music manifests a high order of ideas and expresses the humanly inexpressible. Rimbaud will allude to the language "of the soul for the soul"; Balzac anticipated him when he wrote: "That song entered the soul like another soul" (B 428), one of his most exquisite remarks.

Following the synaesthetic principle, Balzac speculated: "In the language of music, to paint is to awaken through sound certain memories in our heart, or certain images in our mind, and these memories, these images, have their colors. . ." (MD 376). He completed the statement elsewhere when he said: "The soul has a certain attachment for white, love likes red, and gold flatters passions because it has the power to realize their fancies. Therefore, everything that is vague and mysterious in man, all his unexplained affinities, were caressed by their involuntary sympathies. There was in that perfect harmony a concert of colors to which the soul replied with voluptuous, irresolute, elusive ideas" (FYO 302-302). Such power emanates from music's very worldlessness, from its ability to become a rarefied expression of feelings, impelling vibrations that move behind our innermost desires. Hence Schmucke submits that music is to ideas and sentiments what these are to words (CP). With melody and harmony acting respectively on the imagination and the soul, we are not surprised that together they produce in the listener all the effects of voluptuous or hyperphysical, psychical or subliminal hallucination. As one critic claimed, Balzac easily enchants us with whirling images, intoxicates us with heady perfume, makes us enter the supreme marvels of music.[1]

Music to Dream, Remember, and Love

Anticipating Proust,[2] Balzac will refer time and again to music in terms of his trinity. His letters to Mme Hanska contain numerous allusions like: "For me, music is remembrance [and] to listen to music is to love better. . ."; "[The] happy remembrances which invade me when I listen to good music"; "*La sonnambula* . . . reminded me of two of our evenings together"; "Throughout yesterday evening, at the Opéra where I heard Duprez sing in *Guillaume Tell*, I was in Switzerland, and Switzerland means the Pré-Lévêque and the shores of the lake we visited together."[3] On this level—his most instinctive—Balzac found music abetting his sensual inclination for the "voluptuousness of sound" which lay at the origin of his, and Stendhal's, appreciation. Here the effect of music is fundamentally physiological. Dream excitement, frequently erotic, characterized much of the Romantic century's interpretation of music. The way Emilio is aroused by Massimilla illustrates the voluptuary side, as Capraja will describe it talking about his reaction to the cavatina in *Il barbiere di Siviglia* ("My heart filled with fresh blood, a thousand desires fizzed in my veins. Never did more angelic sounds better extricate me from my corporeal bonds, never did the fairy reveal arms more beautiful, smile more amorously, better lift her skirt half way up her leg, raising for me the curtain behind which my other life throbs" [MD 351]). The brightness of her eyes caused inside him "nervous, voluptuary sensations" bordering on a "spasm," and her beautiful black braided hair made him hear "his rushing heartbeats swelling in waves and threatening to burst the vessels of his heart" (MD 314-315). So their kiss, excited by mutual meditation, becomes metonymic for music: "Their thoughts developed that kiss the way a musician develops a theme by virtue of the infinite modes of music" (MD 334).

But in the end, Balzac focused more intently on the "involuntary sympathies" brought about by the art, abandoning the exterior and often soulless analogies of his contemporaries and making music, "the only art which speaks to thought through thought itself" (UM 384), *the* element of passion and evocation, *the* mechanism of love. The musical art, Swedenborg had mentioned, is skilled to express various kinds of affections.[4] Because love sees its double in music, both are analogous through the psychic phenomenon of correspondences and may thereby be triangulated with memory and rise above carnality to the infinite, to the three infinites of boundless desire, incalculable feeling, and illimitable personal time. All subjective passions because they stem physiologically from the body and are emanations of the brain—in fact, of the nervous system—they allow Balzac, via Clara Tinti, to bring the elements together in one breath: "The soul, the mind, the heart, the nerves, all that in man produces an outburst and links him up with the heavens through desire or the flame of pleasure, results less from music itself than from an effect derived from the numberless effects of music. . ." (MD 329). In line with this analysis, Vendramin elucidates to Emilio Capraja's theory relating to light and ideas: ". . . sound [—music—] encounters within us a substance analogous to the one that generates the phenomena of light, which inside ourselves produces ideas. According to him, a person has inner fingerkeys that are affected by sound and that correspond to our nervous centers from which our sensations and our ideas spring. Capraja, who sees the arts as a collection of the means by which man can make external nature agree inside himself with a wondrous nature—what he calls his inner life—has shared with me the views of that instrument maker [Gambara] who is writing an opera [*Mahomet*] at this moment" (MD 353). In this elucidation,

Emilio sees an explanation of his love for Massimilla, thus equating the felicities of love and music, conjoined by an act of memory and divulging Balzac's adherence to the philosophical principle of Unity. Hence the inwardness of the effect of music and the subjectivity of our response to it. "Enchanting sensations," exclaims the opium-animated Vendramin (MD 369).

Berlioz liked to say that great music is only inferior to great love, and conversely, that a passion for music is as complete a dedication of one's whole being as love or religious vows.[5] Balzac agreed: religion (which may be construed as the memory that guides our conscience), love, and music are the triple expression of a single fact (DL). Indeed, an intimate relationship of music and love pervades La Comédie humaine, not just the two musical tales, like a leitmotiv, appearing with regularity in the utterances of his most endearing heroines. Metaphors involving harmony and melody automatically color matters of the heart, as if the author were unable or unwilling to make a more apposite analogy. "I know what purpose the divine harmony of music serves," writes the gentle Modeste; "it was invented by angels to express love" (MM 469). This is the notion that echoes in Massimilla's words professing that music alone can "express love" (MD 347). Balzac's favorite theory appears in La Peau de chagrin, after a reference to Foedora's melody: "Women-musicians are almost always in love. The one who sang so beautifully must have known how to love well" (PC 136). Certainly Pauline, Luigia, Modeste, Ursule, and Félicité prove the novelist's consistency on this point. L'Enfant maudit presents the theory more succinctly: "music is the most sensuous of the arts for souls in love" (EM 735). Again Swedenborg comes to mind, who in Apocalypsis explicata stated that musical sounds signify affections with their gladnesses and joys.[6]

When we scrutinize La Comédie humaine from the vantage point of music we note first how music plays the role of confidant and interpreter. Raphaël, who finds release from his unhappiness in melodies, declares that Beethoven and Mozart were his "discrete confidants" and "communicates his soul" to the keyboard (PC 76), exactly like Modeste who sits at the piano, "that confidant of so many young ladies," to relate her angers and desires through the varied nuances of her playing (MM 448). For her, music, like nature and poetry, is "the soul's ornament" (MM 422); hence she can sing and compose purely melodic ballads, though she has never studied voice or composition, the way a flower can bloom spontaneously. Félicité, on the other hand, is an accomplished musician who can hold long conversations with the piano to which she confides her melancholy, like a "De Profundis" from the tomb, "a prayer of love and despair, tenderness and repressed lament, the wailings of contained affliction" (B 389).

Functioning as an interpreter, music translates secrets and reveals the troubled consciences of Mme de Bargeton and Lucien de Rubempré while the former plays Beethoven and Mozart to the latter in *Les Illusions perdues*. A modification of the introduction to the cavatina "Grâce pour toi, grâce pour moi" from the fourth act of *Robert le Diable* permits Camille Maupin to convey lamentation and grief (B). Sténie, who alone knows "the secret of that harmony" (St 116), interprets Job's stirring improvisations on "Le Songe de Rousseau." Music serves as Ursule Mirouët's interagent to Savinien de Portenduère, whom she wishes to please, and who drifts into the "delightful realm" of love on the current of her piano playing which, by harvesting its power from an art needing the assistance of neither words nor colors nor forms, interprets her to him unmistakably. "By means of a game both suave and dreamy, her soul spoke to the young man's soul and enveloped it with almost visible ideas in something of a cloud" (UM 384). Savinien *knows* her after this, even as Raphaël in *La Peau de chagrin* knows that he must leave a mistress who had reacted so phlegmatically to the beautiful music of Rossini, Cimarosa, and Zingarelli performed at the Opéra. Shakespeare's passage in *The Merchant of Venice* comes to mind:

> *The man that hath no music in himself,*
> *Nor is not moved with concord of sweet sounds,*
> *Is fit for treasons, stratagems, and spoils. . . .*
> *Let no such man be trusted.*[7]

The idea was modified and spread by Lavater, who would know men by their singing as others would judge them by their handwriting or their physiognomy. Grétry had gone so far as to say that some young ladies refuse to sing in order not to disclose their personalities. Modeste, therefore, sings to accomplish the opposite; Ursule plays for the same reason. From this, Modeste's blind mother understands that her daughter is in love. Music, then, has disclosed a meaning also to someone not directly involved in the sentimental relationship. And the third party need not be a character at all but indeed the reader himself. Similar to the commentary implied by the placements of Beethoven's Fifth Symphony in *César Birotteau* is the use of the Finale of Mozart's *Don Giovanni* in *Le Cabinet des antiques*. Here the music interprets by analogy, explaining to us the parallel between young d'Estrignon's life of debauchery and that of the famous Spanish lover.

Balzac thus makes music an intermediary and transmitter, a vehicle for the transference of thought. Raphaël offers "to complete Pauline's education" by giving her piano lessons, which encourage the development of a little suspected love (PC 95). Eugénie and Landon show their affection through music (JP). The protagonists of *Le Bal de Sceaux*, Maximillien de Longueville and Emilie de Fontaine, being too proud to confess their mutual love, entrust its transmission to duets from Pergolesi and Rossini which they sing and under which "they concealed their happiness" (BS 116). Through the agency of "Fleuve du Tage," a romance from which Rossini had derived inspiration while composing the oratorio *Ciro in Babilonia* in 1812, a sighing but discreet Duchess de Langeais communicates her love to an eager but unsuspecting Montriveau. "Often, here and there in life," explains Balzac, "a young lady expiring under the weight of an unknown grief, and a man whose soul becomes disabled under the goading of passion, take a musical theme and have a secret understanding with Heaven, or converse inwardly with each other in some sublime melody, a kind of lost poem" (DL 191). Mme de Staël's Delphine had used the same method to reveal her love to Léonce.

In *La Peau de chagrin*, the cold Foedora can only disclose the movements of her heart by calling upon her singing, and *Béatrix*'s Félicité improvises on the keyboard to indicate her "excessive melancholy" (B 448). Music does not transmit only happy thoughts; Conti, for instance, takes advantage of Cimarosa's "Pria che spunti l'aurora," a number "Rubini himself never begins without trembling," to convey a "cruel meaning" to his mistress (B 506). But the lengthiest and most concentrated example of transmission appears in *La Duchesse de Langeais*. Here Balzac demonstrates with great subtlety both the "unexplained affinities" that had troubled the former Duchess' sentimental life and the "involuntary sympathies" that trouble the emotions of Montriveau when he visits the nunnery of her retirement. The Carmelite organist allows the General to infer from music that she is the woman he has been seeking for five years. By improvising on the "Magnificat" with the theme of their "private" tune, "Fleuve du Tage," the romance through which she had once revealed her love as well as her inability to offer herself to him, she conveys a multiple message. The air belonged to the *genre croisade* which often expressed the regrets of an exile. Now a cloistered exile, Sister Thérèse, through her fiery yet suave rendition, summarizes the history of her passion and confounds Montriveau with a variety of reminiscences and expectations ultimately held in solemn check by the authority of the holy site. Her playing translates first the joy of a woman who knows her lover has returned, then by modulating from major to minor describes her profound sorrow over the present circumstances relating to her consumed heart, and finally, in the "Amen," bespeaks the belief that their souls can only be united in the hereafter. Love is spiritual conjunction, whence is heavenly harmony, Swedenborg had suggested in *Arcana coelestia*.[8] Balzac places himself alongside Montriveau and observes:

> The sensations that those different selections stirred in him . . . belong to that

> small number of things whose expression is forbidden to words . . . but which can only be appreciated in their one point of contact with humanity. . . . The suspicions awakened in the General's heart were all but justified by the vague reminiscence of a sweetly melancholy air, that of *Fleuve du Tage*. . . . Terrible sensation! To expect the resurgence of a lost love, to find her still lost, to perceive her mysteriously. . . ! At the *Magnificat*, the organ seemed to give him an answer which the vibrations in the air bore to him. The nun's spirit found wings in music and flew toward him, throbbing with the rhythmical pulse of the sounds. Music burst forth in all its might; it warmed the church. This chant of joy, consecrated by the sublime liturgy of Roman Christianity to express the soul's exaltation in the presence of the splendors of the ever-living God, became the expression of a heart almost frightened by its happiness, in the presence of the glory of a mortal love, a love that yet lived and inspirited her beyond the walls of the religious grave where women inter themselves in order to be reborn as the brides of Christ. [DL 129-132]

Sand's *Les Maîtres sonneurs* does not describe the subtleties of musical communication more sensitively. To be sure, such fleeting intangibles of meaning flashing forth from the sound-centers of music require an atmosphere propitious for their transmission. Balzac suggests this in *L'Enfant maudit* as Gabrielle and Etienne adopt music as their language of love, and like Nerval in *Jean Sbogar* he insists on it in *Ursule Mirouët* by demonstrating the principle in two antithetical scenes. First we read of the plight of the heroine who is forced to play the piano for a company of greedy, insensitive bourgeois who say "Bête à vent" for Beethoven and "sonacles" for sonatas. Fortunately, the arrival of Abbé Chaperon puts an end to everyone's discomfort, after which Ursule declares that she cannot perform before people who have no affinity for music. The priest explains her inhibitions: "In richly organized beings, good feelings can develop only in a friendly atmosphere. . . . Even as a priest cannot bless in the presence of the Evil Spirit . . ., so a musician of genius experiences an inner defeat when he is surrounded by ignoramuses. . . . In the arts, we must absorb, from the souls that provide an environment for our own soul, as much strength as we transmit to them" (UM 365). In contrast to this, we read later of Ursule's playing not Beethoven's Seventh

Symphony on the piano but little more than Cramer's "Le Songe de Rousseau." Yet, even a modest romance communicates a message expressively, as is the case here, between two people whose beings are in fine accord.

Balzac gives music numerous functions; it acts as a catalyst and a comforter of emotions, as an exciter of memories, as a tempter of desires, as a therapeutic and spiritual appeaser of tensions. "Son regina, son guerriera" from *Semiramide* avails Julie d'Aiglemont to attract a young army officer and thereby triumph over a rival (FTA); Ursule allures Savinien with her song, for she was certain that her voice "would reach his ear" (UM 326). Julie's daughter Hélène runs off to the sea to accompany a pirate whose voice was "sweet and melodious like Rossini's music" (FTA 823). A duet from Zingarelli's *Romeo e Giulietta* sung by Félicité and Conti to Béatrix and Calyste bestirs everyone, especially Calyste who is drawn to "the divine wand" of music (B 428). These functions, exercised at love's waxing, acknowledge music as a catalyst of gentle emotions. It can, however, arouse bitter emotions as well, especially when it appears at love's waning. This becomes evident when the kindly Sabine, who has married Calyste but suffered the deception of his unrequited attraction for Béatrix, must dash out of her opera box during Rubini's rendering of "Il mio cor si divide" from *Otello* (B). With equal poignancy, Massimilla represses a convulsive movement induced by music that complemented her suffering (MD), and the hero of *Sarrasine* is so overwhelmed by a lovely voice that he leaves the theatre, "weak . . ., an emptiness within him . . ., his trembling legs almost [refusing] to support him. . . . Invaded by an unexplainable sadness, he went to sit on the steps of a church. There, leaning against a column, he abandoned himself to a meditation as vague as a dream" (Sa 97). And let us not forget the colorful example of Gambara, for whom music is an excitant, providing an artificial paradise by whipping the brain into a state of tension or of irritation that conjures up lovely images. Indeed, Stendhal had compared its effect to that of belladonna.

By nourishing love, music animates desires and memories. Those who are not musicians capable of producing their own melodies to abet their emotions sometimes despair when the musical flow is interrupted. In *Mémoires de deux jeunes mariées*, Louise de Chaulieu sighs when the season's performances at the Opéra and the Italiens stop: "Alas! . . . what will happen without that wonderful music when one's heart is filled with love?" (MJM 194). But the same young lady writes happily to a friend, after the resumption of performances and of *Romeo e Giulietta* in particular, about "the felicity of two neophytes of love listening to that divine expression of tenderness" (MJM 197). Those, however, who are musicians, like Modeste Mignon recalling her young man or Facino

Cane recalling his native Venice, can supply their own melodies, automatically recharging their emotions. Balzac everywhere insists that love acquires greater meaning through music, just as the reverse is also true. Massimilla and Emilio, Calyste and Béatrix, Gabrielle and Etienne generate their love in the presence of sounds, and Louise, her "soul brightened by the pleasures provided by a happy marriage," now finds much more meaning in Rossini's music than she had on a previous occasion when she had been nervous and aggravated (MJM 160-161).

Music achieves its most haunting effect when it opens the doors of memory, surrounding the human being with quietly seductive murmurs from his own past, like Raphaël when he declares that Rossinian themes can transport him "to the divine regions of [his] first love" (PC 107). His is an instance of direct recall, as is that of Countess d'Héronville in *L'Enfant maudit* who remembers Georges de Chaverny through the rebec-accompanied romance she used to sing to him, and through her child who likes the same music and becomes, therefore, "the accomplice of her dreams" (EM 686). More involved is Louise de Chaulieu's instance of indirect recall. As the story goes, she is morally responsible for her husband's death by not having reciprocated his love to a degree that matched his, and when she experiences the reverse of the situation in her second marriage, she falls into fits of agony and delirium, during the last of which, involuntarily recalling the atmosphere of her earlier happiness, she sings "with feeble voice some Italian airs from *I puritani*, *La sonnambula*, and *Mosè*" (MJM 326)—a psychological raving reminiscent of Lucy of Lammermoor's. These examples make it clear that the faculty of memory to respond to musical incentive depends on the mood of the listener, as Fétis had written in the *Revue musicale* seven years before *Massimilla Doni*, where he spoke of how "each one of us translates [a musical idea] for himself according to his own impressions."[9] Capraja probes the phenomenon on a psycho-intellectual level—that of thought—rather than on a psycho-sensual level, as his friend Prince Emilio would be likely to do. But even he agrees with the critic when, forgetting his maxim that music penetrates less down to our thought or memory of happiness than down to the very "ingredients" of thought (MD 350), he plunges into a lyrical description of "springing recollections, . . . the roses of the past, divinely preserved and still fresh," as harmonies and melodies under a goddess' "magic baton" emerge "from the depths of the brain" at an "organist's striking of his instrument's keys" (MD 351). And Massimilla, we have seen, is eloquent about how "certain memories" are awakened through sound (MD 376).

Better than Fétis, however, Balzac recognized therapeutic virtues in the art of sounds. A listener's receptivity is not necessarily impaired by an adverse mood; on the contrary, it can relax and comfort the depressed. The motif of comfort through music is best elaborated in *Un Drame au bord de la mer* when the love shared by two persons, the "unspeakable softness of a harmonic ecstasy," prompts Balzac to insert the following remark: "[their souls] were full of that pure pleasure that we could only describe by comparing it with the one we feel when listening to some delightful music, like Mozart's 'Andiamo mio ben'" (DBM 886). The tranquility and restfulness music affords is what the tired novelist himself sought when he went regularly to "bathe" in the sounds that filled the Opéra and the Italiens. With the conviction of experience he wrote that Modeste relaxes her tired mother and makes her cheerful by singing old German airs (MM 388), and that Raphaël, disturbed but deeply in love with Foedora, abandons himself leisurely to the charms of music, "draining [his] soul in the double happiness of loving and of discovering the movements of [his] heart beautifully rendered by the musician's phrases" (PC 127). It is in the context of comfort or solace that Balzac becomes most aware of the religious influence of music. Though an atheist who does not consider musical training at all necessary for his ward, Dr. Minoret, Ursule's tutor, relents under the power of sounds and follows the religious promptings of his spiritually oriented daughter (UM). Materialists can only be impervious to the language of music, which is the language of the soul, while believers, who open their souls to blessedness, are instinctively musicians. Philippe Bertault offers an explanation: "In all religions, music plays a preponderant role: it *binds* men together very tightly and strongly; in an agitated and motley crowd, almost unknowingly, it fosters fraternity by imposing unanimity of feeling. This mysterious power transports the soul to the very summits where faith encounters its divine object, the Eternal, and joins with it."[10] Under the sway of music, the conversion in *Melmoth réconcilié* is effectuated no differently. Such examples bear the imprint of Swedenborg's *Diarium spirituale* in which we are told that, for spiritual felicity to be understood, an idea of it may be conceived from the harmonies of sounds. These belong to spiritual harmony, and the gladness resulting from it is spiritual felicity.[11]

Surrounded by "devouring ascetic ideas" and various forms of pettiness, Marie-Angélique and Marie-Eugénie de Vandenesse find serenity and exaltation by escaping to the art of music and its rewards through the private joys of accomplishment. "Mozart, Beethoven, Haydn, Paesiello, Cimarosa, Hummel as well as secondary geniuses developed in them a thousand feelings that did not overstep the chaste bounds of their veiled hearts, but that penetrated into the creations to which they flew with outstretched wings. When they achieved perfection in performing several numbers, they clasped each other's hands and hugged each other, falling prey to lovely ecstasy. Their old teacher [Schmucke] would call them Saint Cecilias" (FE

67). In *L'Esprit des choses*, Saint-Martin had considered music the regulating instrument of life, the art of those whose goal it is to dissipate the "disharmonic" influences that surround us.[12] By permitting complete absorption into itself, the removal from current problems through temporary oblivion, and a return to reality with greater equanimity, music acts therapeutically as a tonic. No more seasoned example exists in Balzac's novels that in *Le Cousin Pons* when the good Schmucke, in order to satisfy his dying friend's last desire, sits at the piano and fills his final hours with musical enchantment. Pons requests:

> Now, play some music for me, regale me with one of your improvisations. . . . This will keep you busy, you'll forget your gloomy thoughts, and you'll fill this dark night with your poems. . . .
>
> Schmucke sat at the piano. After several moments of being thus in his element, musical inspiration, quickened by the trembling of sorrow and the irritation it caused him, carried the kindly German off, as was usual with him, into another world. . . . During that night in which Schmucke made Pons hear in advance the concerts of Heaven, that delightful music which Saint Cecilia's instruments trace from her hands, he was at once Beethoven and Paganini, the creator and the interpreter! Inexhaustible like the nightingale, sublime like the skies under which it sings, varied and folious like the forests it fills with its trills, Schmucke played as never before, and raised the old musician who was listening to him into a sphere of ecstasy such as Raphael once painted. . . . [CP 743]

The narrator in *La Peau de chagrin* says that God grants the musician the power to distribute sounds in a harmonious order whose prototype exists up above. There was no more fitting way for the candid musician to depart the murky world.

A Psyche of Inwardness

In an age like ours that is less focused on the norm than on deviations from it, *Massimilla Doni*'s and *Gambara*'s essays in eccentric psychology will catch our attention more readily than the comparatively homespun views illustrated by Balzac in his other works. Yet our sophistication (if this is what it is) ought not underrate the universal verities indicated by his examples. The fact that he gave music some kind of a psychological role to play in over twenty novels remains in itself a strong sign that he considered the art a significant phenomenon more than a pleasurable experience that gratifies the senses. In this he differed from many of his contemporaries who were at best sentimental music lovers and not more. Although Balzac relied heavily on amorous situations for his demonstrations, through them he did justice to the emotional stimulus that lies at the base of the musical experience.

Psychologists would agree that when Balzac reacts to a performance with phrases like "I was in Switzerland" or "I love with delight," he is proving that music is an expression of primitive dynamisms and of unconscious wishes which use scenes or objects to embody secret fantasies. At the origin of his reaction stands the theory of the sensuous construct, the postulate that whatever "meanings" were imparted to the novelist by tonal structures belong firstly to his sense perception. And this construct alone, one philosopher would say, is beautiful and contains all that contributes to music's beauty.[13]

Balzac's characters react like their creator. One might argue technically that there can be no specific change in an individual's disposition or intention by the agency of music, if one judged Balzac as a psychoanalyst. But as a novelist he was aware that, at least while the stimulus lasted, music could indeed affect Gambara's pulse rate, facilitate Louise's concentration, disturb Sarrasine's respiration, excite Raphaël's thoughts, and relax Pons' organism. He knew, too, that while music may temporarily influence more the musical than the unmusical person's behavior, its somatic powers could be felt by individuals not associated with the art in any performing or creative way. In such cases, their reactions are functions of sound rather than of music per se. When Massimilla says: "I see myself so well in the situation that that passage, which is too gay, for me is filled with sadness" (MD 365), she implies that when listening to music it is not always music we hear but ourselves through sounds, the sounds that quicken emotions to which we are predisposed. This is undoubtedly the case with an unmusical person like Castanier who finds himself catapulted into religious conversion by the sounds he hears from an organ. Balzac's assertion of the affective power of music was not arbitrary or gratuitous, fantastic or mythical. It was clear to him that people connect thoughts and feelings with it, and as a writer he portrayed characters who actually believed they experienced them.

Half a century before Balzac, musicologist and organist Charles Avison had said that "there are certain sounds natural to joy, others to grief or despondency, others to tenderness and love, and by hearing these, we naturally sympathize with those who either enjoy or suffer."[14] The statement reminds us of all the passages in *La Duchesse de Langeais* and *Béatrix* which fit it, especially of the one in the former novel where the nun modulates from major to minor to alter the meaning of her message. A modern analyst would want to distinguish between the composer, the original subject of the feelings involved, and the performer, who interprets them. While such a distinction was unnecessary for Balzac's purposes, he showed he was aware of it in Gambara's comment of La Pasta's rendering of Rossini, as well as in Schmucke's performance for the dying Pons. More often, and in a more comprehensive way, he was interested in music as an emotional catharsis whose essence is self-expression. In this sense, he would be corroborated in theory by Rousseau, Kierkegaard, and Croce, as well as by Beethoven, Schumann, and Liszt in practice. When Modeste, Ursule, Félicité, Schmucke, or Gambara perform, they seek and find self-expression. Even Eduard Hanslick, to whom emotional meanings in a composition where anathema, granted that execution may relieve one's feelings.[15] Sister Thérèse, Conti, Maximilien Longueville, and Julie d'Aiglemont choose their pieces because to them they express their conditions, and it should not surprise us if Massimilla goes to hear *Mosè in Egitto* for the same reason. Music gives convenient vent to their private experiences and often restores them to their personal balance. Whether music itself causes the release of real feelings, or, as psychoanalysts would have it, whether it produces some peculiar effects we mistake for them, was immaterial to Balzac. For him, musical energy extends in many directions, animates many principles of existence; the art may be derived from feelings (Modeste), it may be intended for them (Schmucke), or it may be about them (Raphaël). It may also stem from thought or give rise to it (Gambara). In every case, it results in a logical expression of common emotions of the heart, or of those less common emotions which for Gambara are synonymous with ideas. It relates to affects.

Because the forms of human feelings are much more congruent with musical forms than with the forms of language, Balzac intended music to reveal nuances of feeling, what he called unexplained affinities and involuntary sympathies, with a truth that language cannot approach. As such, it became a semantic of vital and emotional facts, in the sense that Marpurg had referred to it in *Historisch-Kritische Beiträge zur Aufnahme der Musik*. But to express this, the novelist used terms as simple as the emotions themselves, believing like Chopin that in the long run the beauty of music consists in capturing the heart or the imagination without being condemned to strict and pedantic rationalisation. While he enjoyed delving into the physical causes of the production of sounds, he avoided Fabre d'Olivet's vocabulary of "secret, sympathetic fluid" and of "unknown electricity" to describe their effects.[16] As the repertory of all subtleties of feeling, music's psychological phenomenon could best be translated by the trinity of dream-remembrance-love, and in this Balzac knew he had the backing of Plato and Plotinus. For the former had said that it is not difficult to recognize love in the very constitution of Harmony and Rhythm, and the latter had claimed that those who compose music are inspired by love unknowingly. If a single word could be used to describe the phenomenon, it would have to be "emanation" in the Saint-Martinian context (Senancour had referred to music's "invisible emanations")—a term which for the mystic represented the essence of creation. True emanation begins in the deepest, most inward recesses of our being, and music, which has an existence consonant with our most intimate feelings, is its analogy, perhaps even its substance. Balzac's enthusiasm for his century's musical productions from Beethoven forward made him summarize this tenet very unpretentiously: "Modern music . . . is the language of tender, loving souls inclined to a noble, inner exaltation" (MD 355). In the unpretentiousness, however, lay the profound recognition that music is a self-reflexive art, one that listens to itself, as it were, and thereby induces by transference similar introspection in the receiver. If it absorbs itself in itself so naturally, then it also facilitates and animates the listener's self-absorption. It pulses in tune with the inner being. Hence the perspicacious phrase in *Massimilla Doni*: "Only music has the power to make us enter ourselves" (G 436). And in Pascalian or Leopardian terms, within us stretches the true infinite, the one addressed by music, as Cataneo knows—"I know how to embrace the infinite" (MD 350)—and as Massimilla concludes about the "infinity" of the musical language which "contains everything" and "can explain everything" (MD 377).

CHAPTER XII

A DYNAMIC PHILOSOPHY

If music does not appear to stand out as saliently in *La Comédie humaine* as it does in the works of writers like Marcel Proust, Gabriele D'Annunzio, Thomas Mann, Alejo Carpentier, or Anthony Burgess, it does not because it is diffused into many novels rather than being concentrated into a few. As it is, it still assumes a commanding position when all of Balzac's uses of it are assembled and viewed aggregately. In its psychological animations, synaesthetic associations, physical and scientific sources, instrumental projections, demonic and mystic principles, religious promptings, and amorous and dramatic attributes, music gradually impresses us, in passing from one novel to another, as an energy of life, a universal power that can best be described as dynamic. The concept advances a vitalistic, rather than a mechanistic, aesthetics, whether applied to an *histoire psychique* like *Massimilla Doni*, a *vision mystique* like *Séraphita*, an *analyse matérielle* like *Gambara*, an *intrigue amoureuse* like *Béatrix*, or an *amitié humaine* like *Le Cousin Pons*.

To fathom music, he once declared to Zulma Carraud in discussing various arts, "one needs ten years of work before understanding the artistic synthesis as well as its material analysis."[1] The hard-pressed and compulsive author, however, could not behave accordingly and woo timidly the muse of music for a decade before obtaining the confidence to consort with her. She was rather a creative force to be captured by rapid degrees whenever invitations occurred. The total picture of Balzac's musical philosophy is therefore full but confused, a compilation of frequent but unsequenced ideas.

The Dualism of Matter and Spirit

Balzac expressed himself by way of a fundamental dualism, tersely described in *Le Lys dans la vallée*: "Man is composed of matter and spirit; the animal ends in him and the angel begins in him. Hence the struggle we all experience between a future destiny which we sense in advance and the remembrance of our past impulses from which we are not wholly detached: a carnal love and a divine love" (LV 948). Analogously, both the sensual and the mystical elements in music enticed him: opera and symphony, Rossini and Beethoven, the roulade and the pure tone, the romance and the hymn, just as in his life and works he reached for reality at the same time as he groped for dream. Onto the stem of Saint-Hilairian science he grafted the limbs of Hoffmannian fantasy and Swedenborgian vision. However fragmented, incomplete, and at times even artless, Balzac's musical dialectic took into account a network of complementary "emanations" that made him and his reader aware of the muse's emotional and rational, material and spiritual, human and divine configurations.

Cataneo and Capraja combine to embody the dualism Balzac felt within himself. One is subject to animalistic reactions, to "physical enjoyments": Genovese's voice "seized his fibers"; he "hangs in life by a thread" (MD 386, 351, 386). He is the materialist who penetrates being by dint of excessive pleasures. The other is subject to visions, "to ideas": "Tinti's [voice] attacked his blood"; he is "astride the roulade" (MD 351, 387). More a man of the spirit than his friend, he penetrates being through the power of thought. Balzac's autobiographical philosopher helps us to determine ontologically the realities involved when he asks himself "if . . . the blood circulation . . . corresponds to the transubstantiation of our Will, as the circulation of nerve fluid corresponds to that of thought" (LL 391).

The dualistic concept, along with the implied difficulty of arriving at a comprehensive understanding of music, is brought out in the two statements concerning the primacy of music over other creative endeavors: "Music is the first among the arts" (B 427), because it is the art which comes "closer to Heaven than the others" (MD 364). The words "art" and "Heaven" betray its human and divine impulses. While "we are forced to accept the poet's ideas, the painter's canvas, and the sculptor's statue," we are each accorded the privilege of private response to the composer's tones, which can thereby encompass "the whole of nature" and affect powerfully our "inner being." The first level of response concerns emotional, material, and human realities. Senancour had suggested how the olfactory sense occasions rapid, immense, but vague perceptions; how that of sight seems to interest the mind more than the heart; but how that of hearing impresses more profoundly and lastingly the whole human organism. "We admire what we see," wrote his Romantic hero, "but we feel what we hear."[2] Balzac thinks similarly. Whereas art, or the finished form of music, resides in the intellect, music itself is a language or principle of feeling, in the Kantian sense of *Gefühl* or *Empfindung*. In *Kritik der Urteilskraft*, the German philosopher calls it the art of the beautiful play of emotions. On this basis, a worshiper of reason would rate it the least significant of the art forms, and Romantics themselves, like Musset and Gautier, despite their affection for music, deemed it the most unstable of the arts and its value the most ephemeral. Balzac, like Nerval and Shelley, could not be satisfied with such one-sided conclusions. He felt that music, as a language without linguistic form, embraces more. The aesthetic idea is structured by a rational concept which in turn endows it with permanence. Because this concept is less conspicuous, it should not be considered an incidental or subsidiary by-product. The composer's "real struggle," as Frenhofer insisted for the painter (CI), is to relate the effect to its cause so as to appear an unmistakable reflection of it. Otherwise creation fails. Indeed, results should not turn out weaker than their generating stimuli, in love as in music, as the parables of *Massimilla Doni* and *Gambara* illustrate. Another Balzacian hero, Raphaël, declares that when the principle is stronger than the product, nothing is accomplished (PC) (also MD 371). Reason and feeling, then, while distinguishable, remain inseparable.

The author's world outlook espoused the materialism of a secret interplay of physical elements and the spiritualism of a divine emanation that gives matter its characteristic tonalities. Conscious of the Aristotelian distinction, the artist's task is to approach a suggestion of the universe by interpreting both forces. Art is a symbol, a reflection of the beyond, but also of the tension between the two forces.

"God made Form and Idea rivals," insists Massimilla, "otherwise nothing would live" (MD 369). Unfortunately, when Balzac speaks of "form" it is not always clear what he means. He uses the word often metaphysically, as we might expect, but then he talks about "inner meaning" shattering "Form," and of form that is always epistemologically "an interpreter" (CI 395), communicating knowledge, ideas, and sensations. In this case, form is appearance or effect rather than, metaphysically, being or cause. Massimilla tends to use the word in the non-metaphysical sense that Idea may seek expression and not find its Form, and conversely that a form readily found may house a worthless idea. For the apposition betrays paradoxically an intimate relation between the two. A certain idea can only be realized in a certain form, and vice versa.

Gambara is a victim of the opposition because of his unwillingness to come to terms with the fact that concrete idea, that which reaches the cognitive faculties of men, is a reluctant partner of abstract form for the communication of transcendence to the general public. An advocate of pure music, that is, of an autonomous, detached, artistic expression, he nonetheless attempts to communicate his dream not through a symphony but through the more plastic form of opera, though he remains a symphonist in theory and enthusiasm, a Hoffmannian Beethoven who has studied the mystics as well as the physical scientists. Like the poet (PC, Preface 1831), the composer must be endowed with "second sight," but his vision of a spiritual abstract, while always destined to leave the artist unsatisfied by virtue of its absolute uncommunicability, can hardly be realized through a medium relying heavily on words and finite scenic factors. The masses cannot rise to the height of pure feeling (as Cataneo envisions through the conjunction of two voices), a notion we find also in Schopenhauer. If music expresses the reality of the world in the essence of its phenomena,[3] its principles, or the "beyond," it is folly to think that its mysteriously remote and Heavenly substance could be imparted to all humans alike, as if Form and Idea could be fused perfectly by the stroke of a hand other than God's. By compelling reason to yield to the force of being—call it in Schopenhauerian terms the universal Will—and by exacting an extension of the self into the unexperienced dimensions of a superior life unknown to the rational world, Gambara's ideal music would have required of the listener a kind of depersonalization possible only for the happy few, and even then incomplete. No doubt the composer knew subconsciously that the faithful reconstruction of an aural dream, the integration of an ideal into reality, is an impossibility. Consciously however, like Frenhofer and Claës, he confused theory and method. But no contradiction is involved from Balzac's standpoint, who was demonstrating how overexacting analysis can lead to the ultimate incoherence of even the most admissible and reasonable premises. Balzac's marvel at Beethoven (a sensation more than an understanding, because Balzac felt strongly though never clearly recognized in him the identity of form and idea) stemmed from his philosophical assumption that a successful Gambara was impossible, or that his Grail resided beyond even the most heroic grasp. "When, in matters of moral nature, a man goes beyond the sphere in which plastic works are born through the process of imitation, and enters the wholly spiritual realm of abstractions where all is contemplated in its principle and is seen in the omnipotence of the results, such a man is no longer understood by ordinary intelligences" (MD 353).

Failure becomes a relative term for him who endeavors with elevated vision and a sense of mission. Thought, in its extreme exercise, shrinks the artist's ascendant vigor in *La Peau de chagrin*, disintegrating his strength and seemingly provoking the demise of Art. Yet, with disciplined handling—and for Balzac the masters were Rossini and Beethoven—human endeavor can use the tyrannical tension of analytic thought to create a superior tension, the spiritual firmness characteristic of plainchant and liturgical music: the metaphysical destiny of the phoenix whose permutation from consumption to creation may be considered metaphoric of the whole process. Only terminal consumption spells failure. The idealistic, unmaterialistic, creative disappointment does not. Emilio Memmi attempts to elevate the sensual to the spiritual in the context of sex ("You want to be Raphael in matters of love" [MD 369]) and fails through impotence; Gambara also fails to sublimate the material to the height of Idea, but in the context of artistic creation, of a visionary mission—hence in failure, if it must be called this, he walks in the end not pathetically but nobly.

If he could not extol Gambara's wisdom in his choice of means and methods, Balzac had to admire the sterling folly of his intentions. It is essential that music be analyzed in its causes. Only then can one hope to absorb it with finer understanding. Quantitatively, Balzac's illustrations showed a continuous preoccupation with the effects of music rather than with its principles. The novelist recognized certain fundamental, human temperaments, the conflicts resulting among them from various musical situations, and the way in which music disguises, exposes, and finally asserts an individual's character. Observing its influence, he assimilated it into his society's practical and imaginative life. Having listened voluptuously to music thinking of his Polish countess, he made of that process a kind of self-auscultation through which his characters understood themselves better. But as if to reproach himself for the quantitative imbalance, Balzac had Gambara complain of excessive reliance on appearances: "Up until now man has noted rather its effects than its causes! If he penetrated into its causes, music would become [for universal man] the greatest of all the arts" (G 435-436). Because Cataneo and Capraja are more melomaniacs than melophiles, they too (and Cataneo despite his premises) end by considering effects. Beyond appearances, which strike only the senses, there exists a vast zone of idea, approachable only by the mind, and an even vaster zone of principle open to intuition: sensory perception, understanding, and wisdom. Since principle, Swedenborg held in *De commercio animae et corporis*, moves into cause and both in turn into effect, thus establishing that the three coexist in the last, it is easy to justify Balzac's frequent application of music for purposes of sensual and psychological description.

Divested of all its applied aspects, music concerns essence. Wagner was to say this in Paris in 1841, hence during Balzac's lifetime but chronologically after Balzac's voicing of a similar idea. While the novelist did make music express what Wagner denied to it: "The passion, love, or longing of such-and-such an individual on such-and-such an occasion," it is clear from many statements by Balzac that he would have agreed with Wagner that music expresses "passion, love, or longing *in itself*, and this it presents through an unlimited variety of motivations—the exclusive and particular characteristic of music, foreign to and inexpressible in any other language." Therefore, "what music expresses is eternal, infinite, and ideal."[4] Balzac would also stress self-expression, to be sure, but more essentially a formulation and representation of emotions that constitute a picture of sentient, responsive life, a source of insight into things devoid of subjective involvement. For Gambara, music exists outside the orbit of the musician, independent of the effect it has on the listener, or on the composer himself. In this case, Frenhofer's aesthetic notion applies: "The effect by itself [the musician, the composition—in other words, the appearance] is an accident of life and not life itself [music]" (CI 394).

Here again, the proximity of Balzac's and Schopenhauer's views in *Die Welt als Wille und Vorstellung* is noticeable. By reproducing ideas—which are the objectification of Will—through objects, the other arts stand thereby once removed from essence, while music—which reproduces Will directly—emerges more powerful and penetratingly as the core art. And inasmuch as the same Will finds itself externalized in music and idea, there must exist a fundamental analogy between these two entities as they reflect the visible world. Harmony bears some relation to organic and inorganic existence, and melody to human and moral life, to human desire and its quality of movement (echoes of Mazzini). Does not the return of melody to the tonality of the one-chord symbolize the realization of desire? When Modeste Mignon instinctively composes her melodic ballads, she demonstrates what the German philosopher described as the most secret depths of Will, the essence of feeling that our imagination then associates with forms of the material world.[5] In this way is music "life itself."

If God "made Form and Idea enemies" (MD 369), He did not establish the same opposition between sensation and concept. Balzac could easily make a separation between the two entities which are not necessarily linked by a cause-effect relationship any more than psychology and metaphysics need be. The double nature of man, organic and immaterial, makes it possible for his intelligent principle to know through its own power, without borrowing anything from the senses except possibly the occasion or excuse for knowing. As if to dramatize the dichotomy, Balzac made even a singer, whose instrument by its very sensuous composition is closest to material reality, capable of translating the untranslatable, of expressing the superior sensitivities of nature, for the pleasure of the isolating mind: Conti's voice rose and "hurled [Calyste] into creation," having "removed its veil" (B 428), and Genovese's melody "penetrated the innermost mind, bringing it light" (MD 380). Such artists no longer express themselves in the human language, it would seem; speaking like the elements, they evoke supernatural impressions. Idea is its own stimulus, unassociated with human sensation. For this reason, music can become the expression of the great spectacles of nature, of those spectacles that assume majesty when perceived by the mind as examples of a magistral design.

The change from the rationalistic eighteenth century that placed music low on the scale of the arts, to the Romantic nineteenth whose tendency, as formulated by Schopenhauer (regardless of his lack of immediate influence in France), placed it in the center and related all arts to it, is evident in the importance Balzac gave to its autonomous manifestations. He could not conclude with Kant that music was enjoyment rather than a cultural agency high among the contributions to intellectual progress. He remained more Mazzinian. Even in its sensuous seductiveness, which Balzac along with most Romantics experienced fully, and in its dark orphic powers, which Hoffmann stressed and Balzac cultivated, it translates intangibles of nature's reality normally inaccessible to rational comprehension. It thrives on suggestion, and through it enlarges our cognitive faculties. In this respect, Balzac's attitude reflects more than the old theory of *imitatio naturae* dear to the ancients and to Rousseau, because it is a special nature, one recognized by Hoffmann in *Johannes Kreislers Lehrbrief*, a primarily suggestive and suprasensuous nature, to which he alludes. What Séraphita tells Wilfrid is indicative: "If you possessed the knowledge of nature, you would have made music for me" (S 480). If, in its consummate state, music—like her sister arts—is "the expression of the great spectacles of nature," or, as Genovese puts it, if instruments reproduce "more or less well the pure sound that nature has placed in all things," it is also true, in Massimilla's words about the choral number "O Nume d'Israël," that music provides a natural synthesis, "a . . . complete idealization of nature" (MD 377, 384, 358). To Gambara's "Music is an art woven into the very entrails of Nature," for "there exists in nature an eternal music, a suave melody, a perfect harmony, troubled only by the independent movements of Divine Will" (G 435, 442), Capraja adds conclusively his crowning valuation of the arts, among which music reigns: "through them man can bring external nature into agreement with [that] marvelous nature . . . called the inner life" (MD 353).

In his *Tableau naturel*, Saint-Martin indicated that when one produces a work of any kind, one merely makes visible the plan, the thought, or the design which he has formed. If all the laws of nature are uniform, we must also admit that all productions of general or particular creation are the visible expression of the principle that acts within them. To this postulate, Balzac queries that when we feel certain notions or dispositions develop in us like religion, justice, love, and music, are we not swayed by the superiority of such notions or dispositions and by their special mission, and is not their reproduction a dialectical form of continuous unveiling or discovering? Ballanche had pointed to the factor of sentiment, for while the goal of all art is the imitation of nature, the imitation would be useless in the absence of feeling.[6] The imitation of nature, therefore, does not consist in reproducing the objective aspect. Whether or not Gambara is serious when he implies that his music can describe some of the architectural details of the setting of *Mahomet*, the fact remains that he holds firmly to the belief that music is profound suggestion, that is, expressiveness rather than expression, and that we often attribute to it erroneously plastic qualities of description. Music may connote but not assert, permit inference but not calculation. Frenhofer concurs: "The mission of art is not to copy nature but to express it. An artist must not be a vile copyist, but a poet" (CI 394). Massimilla's doctor friend echoes him: "I am always revolted by the claim of certain enthusiasts who want to make us believe that music paints with sounds" (MD 376).[7] True reality being form (in the metaphysical sense of cause), imitating exterior nature (an effect) would mean missing the permanent and essential in favor of the transitory appearance. The question is one of mind rather than matter, of vision rather than photography. Genius consists not in "explaining what is," but in "casting [one's] eyes beyond the effects" (S 552), an idea found also in Ballanche. For the world of music exists outside ourselves as an ideal and is susceptible only to the poet's sensibility (if we use the term "poet" in the superior sense applied by Count Marcosini to Gambara). And the "poet," as Hoffmann says of a painter in *Die Jesuiterkirche* and *Signor Formica*, does not believe in his own reality *as such* but rather deems it a palpable projection of his vision. In music's movement is the consummate instance of himself, of his art, and of nature's eternity: "There exists in nature an eternal music" (G 442).

What Balzac approached was a mixture of Friedrich von Schelling's consideration that music is an art which to the greatest possible degree divests itself of corporeality and is borne aloft on invisible wings, and of Hans Christian Oersted's somewhat contrasting idea that music is a spiritually inspired sensuousness. The tension between mind and matter that juxtaposes *Gambara* and *Massimilla Dona* found Balzac strung between the two, but if his eventual opting for Beethoven over Rossini is to be trusted, as indeed his preference of religious to secular music must be, then we must see Balzac as swinging ultimately over to the side of mind, of "future destiny," and away from "anterior instincts." Pythagoras would have said that he preferred the muses to the sirens. As an intellectual, Louis Lambert heralds the choice.

Physics, Metaphysics, and Unity

As a mystic, Louis Lambert also strives toward the ultimate unity of creation, the Pythagorean instances of eventual fusion toward which all things and thoughts tend. That sensation and concept, matter and spirit, are separable does not preclude their final union, along with everything else, in the great All. By negating dualism, Saint-Martin had been able to declare matter "a representation and an image of what it is not,"[8] and in his *Essais de palingénésie sociale*, Ballanche had referred to the interpenetration of the material and spiritual worlds. Differently phrased, the expression of ideas "is possible only through material forms, and . . . when the idea rises, it divests itself in the artist's mind of its material substratum to the point of remaining only pure principle."[9] The question of where the human animal, or matter, is finally united with the divine movement of nature, or spirit, is a question of superaffinity, or transcendence, that Balzac finds best to express in musical terms. Philosophers of the ancient world called the whole of education "music"; Balzac would call the totality of being by the same name. In metaphoric language, the "dance" of stones is accompanied by organ tones and angelic voices (JCF 262). A hint of this coexistence comes in Cataneo's desire to confuse the sound of the human voice with that of a violin, that is, in his blurring of the boundary between material and spiritual. The Duke also takes the next step by declaring his love for the blending of two human voices—Genovese's and Tinti's—which might be called two thoughts, and which together as an "accord" symbolize what one voice alone could not symbolize: Unity.

A passage in Swedenborg's *Vera Christiana religio*, repeated by Balzac in *Séraphita*, concerns the angels who share the secret of the total harmony of creation, of its "spirit of sounds" that, as far as man's instruments go, can be only approximated by the harp and the organ. Balzac suggests and amplifies the same thought on several occasions, usually in a discussion of instruments because they serve him as vehicles through which to elaborate a physical analysis of music, the goal being a demonstration of mystic unity, the blending of the particular into the universal.

Improvised to express at least some degree of concordance with nature's "spirit of sounds," man's musical tools enjoy only incomplete success and require the cooperation of the soul, intelligence, heart, and nerves to supplement their inadequacies. Cataneo supplements by dreaming of sublime music which employs the pure sound that nature has put everywhere and that leads us to "the luminous spheres where man's thought can evoke the entire world" (MD 350). Hence the intellectual world merges with the spiritual through music's suggestion of the mysteries of transcendent nature. The intuition is only partial, inasmuch as music always functions on a level of suggestion rather than of revelation. Yet it is fitting that it function this way, because in a sense the former encompasses far more than the latter, and when Balzac attempts to explain the production of ideas through sounds, he is careful to describe sounds as affecting not thought itself but its ingredients, its "elements" which stir the "principles."[10] In other words, music penetrates beneath the confined structure of conscious sensitivity into the vast subconscious, which only reveals by suggestion.

To explain the intangible "elements" and "principles," Balzac had recourse to the realm of physics, ultimately to light. Methodologically, he followed the analytical procedure of the Ideologues, who began in Cartesian fashion *ab imo*, that is, with the senses—here meaning the basic fact of sound. Apart from Herschell's study, with which he was familiar, Balzac drew from different theories quoted at the time concerning the nature of light, which he extended to a consideration of sound: Newton's emanation theory whereby luminous corpuscles sent forth into space ("a fluid emanating from the sun" [FJP 551]) reach the human eye with infinite velocity, and Huyghens' undulation theory, brought to fruition by Flourens (continuing Herschell's concept) in 1822, whereby concentric ethereal patterns propagate like rippling waves in space. In a fragment concerning Herschell entitled "Traité de la lumière," Balzac, without choosing sides, alluded to the possibility of "an ethereal substance, weightless and spread all over space, where rapidly repeated *undulations* convey to our eyes the sensation of light, the way vibrations in the air produce sound for our ears" (FJP 551). Not content with the double theoretical possibility (today both structures obtain), the novelist turned atomist in analyzing that air with reference to sound: "Sound is modified air" (as Louis Lambert maintained [LL 448]); air is composed of analogous principles that respond to it, are sympathetic with it, and enlarge "through the power of thought." Therefore, air must contain as many "particles of varying elasticities," and be capable of as many vibrations of varying duration, "as there are sounds in sonorous bodies," and these particles, perceived by our ear and activated by the musician, "correspond to ideas" according to our make-up (G 434).

Physics clearly addresses physiology in Balzac's construct.

Descartes' notion of ether functions impellingly throughout creation. "All is the product of an ethereal substance," declares Lambert (LL 448), who in his Seventh Thought foresees the day in which light and air will be considered symbiotically. Balzac's scientific inquiry involves the molecular dimension, for instruments, while making use of "the same substances," that is to say, "gasses" that constitute the ether, sound dissimilar because of their chemical "decomposition" (G 435) as well as because of the known existence of overtones. This dispersal into multiple structures suggests a molecular—nearly mechanistic—concept of thought whereby each sound, each tonal quality, and each musical resonance evokes a certain sensation or idea. For this reason, opines Massimilla, a single phrase by Rossini can entail varied reactions. Hence the inner fingerkeys (*touches*) mentioned by Gambara, and hence, too, by virtue of the "analogous principles," his desire to scrutinize the physical laws of music in order to control the listener's response to his aesthetic.

The idea of light enables Balzac to move from the physical to the metaphysical. He referred to music as "light . . . [and] . . . gleams" (JP 13), "luminosity" (S 478, 558), "limpid with brilliance" (G 466), a "radiant fairy" (CB 463), a "resplendent goddess . . ., rays of the oriental sun . . ., sidereal light" (MD 351, 361, 352), "bundles of light" (DL 132), as if deliberately translating Senancour's "invisible emanations" into luminous rays. For light, we learn from Séraphita, is "the great nurturer of the globe" (S 556). A passage in *Les Amours de deux bêtes* stands out significantly: "It was . . . light that turned into music, as it had already turned into perfume, . . . a product of light that light engenders, . . . a light [that returns] to light" (ADB 326). Gambara claims the same. He is not speaking mercurially or demonstrating a lyrical faculty that evokes the world through images, as his creator did with ambiguous success when he verbalized Beethoven's Fifth Symphony at the end of the first section of *César Birotteau*. On the contrary, for the science-conscious Gambara, light is not an image; he is bathed in it as in an atmosphere that gives music relief. "[Music] relates to physics through the very essence of the substance it employs: sound is modified air . . . [and] the nature of sound is identical with that of light. . . . [Both] proceed by vibrations that end in man and that he transforms into thoughts (G 434-435). For this reason, music not only permeates but also penetrates creation. The importance of this passage may be assessed by the way it underpins Balzac's dynamic concept, linking together dialectically the physical world, that of sensations, and the spiritual, that of ideas. Indeed, the musical process acquires Hegelian hues, appearing as the objective, sensible side of the thought process.

Given his creed of Unity, Balzac was led to view music as both a science and an art derived from Number, through its physical and mathematical, imaginative and inspirational components. In *Gambara*, we read of the laws that mysteriously govern sound waves, and of the composer's advanced claim that harmony can be decomposed like light through a prism, and that scientific research could create harmony itself: "Music obeys physical and mathematical laws. . . . [If we discovered more about the former,] these new laws would arm a composer with fresh powers by offering him instruments superior to the current ones, and perhaps harmonic constructs that are grandiose by comparison with the kind that support music today" (G 435). And in *Massimilla Doni*, we pursue the composer's dream on a level of ecstasy: "[He] imagines a sublime creation where the marvels of the visible universe are reproduced with immeasurable grandeur, lightness, rapidity, and breadth, where sensations are infinite, and where only certain privileged natures possessing a divine power can penetrate" (MD 353). Balzac's concept advances to the point of envisaging indefinite perspectives for the world of music, which becomes therefore like the play of light on the infinite patterns of a kaleidoscope, an art of constant, self-generating luminous creation. At the same time, in Schopenhauerian terms, it remains an Absolute (Gambara's and Claës' quests are identical), enjoying a unity of substance, an "ethereal substance . . . that gives us music as well as light, the phenomena of vegetation as well as those of zoology" (G 435).

Similar to light, music resembles thought in that it is an emanation from whose creative centers radiate impulses that the imagination converts into visions and intuitions. Through the physiological world of sounds, then, Balzac arrived at the ideological world of thought. Séraphita claims: "Music, [this] celestial art . . ., is it not an ensemble of sounds harmonized by Number? Is not sound a modification of air, compressed, dilated, and repercussed? You know the composition of air: azote, oxygen, and carbon. Since you cannot obtain sound in a vacuum, it is clear that music and the human voice are organized chemical substances that fall into unison with the same substances prepared in us by our thought, and are coordinated by means of light" (S 556).[11]

The level on which the conversion and coordination take place is, as we have seen, that of synaesthesia. What the scientist's research cannot uncover, mystical vision finally opens up to Minna and Wilfrid: "They understood the invisible ties that bind the material and the spiritual worlds. In recalling the sublime efforts of the finest human minds, they found the principle of melody by hearing the songs of Heaven; it offered the sensations of colors, of perfumes, of thought, and recalled the countless details of all creation, the way a song of the earth animates infinite resemblances of love" (S 585). If music is the first of the arts, the one that penetrates deepest into the soul, then music and nature act as congruent concepts, since nature is the supreme art, *the* reflection of divine intellect. Saint-Martin saw the primeval golden age as light emitting tones, melody engendering light, colors moving because colors are alive. More than a purely associative or even rhetorical combination of sensory experiences, or a mere psychological experience as it had been for Hoffmann, synaesthesia was for Balzac a profound intellectual and aesthetic experience. With images of flowers singing, forms resounding, and music spreading "in the manner of perfumes" (MD 350), or of melodies and harmonies diminishing like dwindling flows of blue light, "waves of purple" sound, and "brown colors" (MD 359, 372) detaching themselves from a choral background, Balzac, too, bridges the outer and inner worlds, identifying the musical with the natural process. Like music—to repeat—colors are functions of light in varying intensities and permutations. Hence the elements unite: object, idea, emotion, and form correspond in the compendium and culmination of being. The dualism of mind and matter is resolved in a higher monism, the one represented by the music of the spheres where, implies Séraphita many times, melody exists without sounds. If Lavater, in discussing physiognomy, and Gall, in discussing organology, held that every grain of sand, every leaf, contains the infinite, Balzac, in concurring, envisioned an even broader synthesis through which all is spiritual harmony, a gigantic and poetic interpenetration of the supersensory with the sensory, thereby effecting a reconciliation of the "eternal enemies," Form and Idea, and distilling creation in a unitary vision. To use again Séraphita's words, music might be compared with those rarefied elements that "penetrate like an active cause . . ., sometimes like a dose of phosphorous that exalts life or accelerates its projection; sometimes like opium, that benumbs corporeal nature, frees the mind from its binds, lets it drift over the world, revealing it through a prism and drawing from it the nourishment it likes the most; sometimes, finally, the catalepsy, that annuls all faculties in favor of a single vision" (S 490-491).

By integrating music and philosophy, Balzac saw the possibility of giving the art a new vitality. By leaning toward the mystical, he may have diverted his thoughts from the more austere direction they had begun to take under the sway of Beethoven's genius: the consideration of theme as theme and the thematic interplays of a composition as music's proper content and context, of Form and Idea as one. But on the other hand, his visionary bent made him sense in music a life that could enjoin the most intimate life of man, his will. The idea that musical structures would cease to be "musical" if they should be found to possess an outer significance (the emotive-content theory) and relate or be part of anything beyond themselves was foreign to Balzac's way of thinking. In the scheme of totality, music could not exist without meaning. The novelist would have agreed with Moritz Hauptmann and Moritz Carrière[12] who, within a decade after his death, stressed the intellectual value of music, its close relation to concepts, its reality as a force in our mental life as well as in our affective experience.

Acting on will, music was like a creation or procreation in itself. Therefore, beautifully put, it could "enter the soul like another soul"—a formulation of true Virgilian sophistication (B 428). It is spirit asserting that its forms are unperishable, eternal like the world of nature that it permeates. It is energy scratching its mark upon the matter of our beings. Here Balzac joins Stendhal and Nietzsche, who found the essence of music's beauty in the excitement of the will and in the enhancement of being through ideas. More likely below the threshold of consciousness than above it, and certainly outside the pale of discursive thinking, music holds the imagination that is "personal and associative and logical, tinged with affect, tinged with bodily rhythm, tinged with dream, but concerned with a wealth of formulations for its wealth of wordless knowledge, its whole knowledge of emotional and organic experience, of vital impulse, balance, conflict, the ways of living and dying and feeling."[13] Balzac's intellectual pleasure in it related directly to the approach it paved toward the comprehension of Beauty, just as his aesthetic pleasure in it stemmed collaterally from the satisfaction of thinking he had discovered Truth. If music can be "true" to the life of feeling in a way language cannot, it can be no less "true" to the life of universal creation. "Music is to language as thought is to words" (LL 449). More than that, in fact, for language obscures, whereas music illumines. It can have not only a content but a metaphysical play of contents, connoting feelings and ideas like a prime mover without becoming, like words, wedded to them. The "rhythm" of life, the "harmony" of concepts, St. Augustine's view of human history as a "melody"—all of these expressions revert to the ancient Pythagorean notion of total Unity serving as a mystical key to universal understanding.

The mystical resonance, for Balzac, marked a great artistic conception. In conveying his profound impressions through it, he failed as much as he succeeded. His was a Romantic and literary mixture of occultist, spiritual, scientific, rational, and theriacal fascinations, characteristically made convincing, or at least impressive and thrilling, by the ardor of his enthusiasm. Mann's Leverkühn says: "Reason and magic may meet and become one in what one calls wisdom, initiation, in belief in the stars, in numbers. . . ."[14] But whatever their merit—and definitely there was some in them—Balzac's impressions were profound. Baldensperger conjectured that it must have been somewhat disturbing for an ambitious man of letters to think that another art was capable of realizing much more immediately "the hypostasis of being."[15] Here may lie secretly the reason for Balzac's "jealousy" of Beethoven. For the song of Ariel succeeds in washing away Caliban's sluggishness where the word of Prospero has failed.

CONCLUSION

Music became a literary vice during the ebullient Romantic years, when its fluidity and vague sensuous appeal elicited from writers responses that suggested a visual rather than an aural appreciation. Balzac was not free from the lyrical habits of his colleagues, but, as we have seen, he did not reduce his comments to those feelings and reveries within easy range of literary transcription. Characteristically, he ventured beyond, not always knowing to what extent his profession's tools adequately emulated Euterpe's lyre. Of one tool he felt confident, however: his imaginative mind, which could forge ideas from the raw material of feelings, and so like Gambara—or like Jacob—he too challenged the Angel.

Romain Rolland claimed that most men are too lacking in vitality to feel music deeply. On this basis alone, Balzac disqualifies from the category of most men. Though he was exposed to the art early, he came to it relatively late, and when he did, whether urged by social convention or intimate desire, he sensed a presence, sometimes a revelation. Presences of this kind, however, lend themselves scarcely to verbal translation, and revelations openly defy it. Yet, once having sipped the mystery of the great art, the cup had to be drained. The taste was a full one, rich and all-encompassing, and if the grand and profound was often diluted with the pretty and likable, the liquid nonetheless quenched Balzac's ready palate.

Where criticism exists, the claim invariably revolves around Balzac's unmusical reactions. Paul Dukas praised the page on Beethoven midway through *César Birotteau*, but felt constrained to conclude: "The realistical and mystical mind of the author of Séraphitus had to enjoy these 'correspondences' more than anyone else; toward them his visionary genius and thaumaturgical instincts incited him. His musical curiosity was probably and basically only a literary passion."[1] Otherwise stated, the novelist reacted *en littérateur*. But how else—ultimately—can a novelist react? Even prose masters who doubled as music critics, like Hoffmann and Diderot, wrote more *en littérateurs* than *en musiciens*. Besides, this method of listening to something out of which our training may not be able directly to make subjective and educated sense is not illegitimate. Crudely but successfully, an image magnetizes our feelings. The listener is not unmusical for employing this familiar crutch; he is merely insufficiently musical to react purely musically. Even so, Balzac's approach to the art often left the novelist behind the philosopher. Because translation and commentary mutilate, he chose to incorporate the suggestive energies of music into a context that outstripped analysis. The references to music in separate works end by embracing a broader concept, the way Balzac's individual novel becomes a chapter in the human epic. Although Gambara might have better served Balzac's purposes as a symphonist than as a musical dramatist, the distinction loses poignancy when we understand music as symbol. Music being connected with vision as well as with audition, the novelist logically used the sense of sight to impart his philosophy. Imparting it meant, as for the mystic, awakening affinities common to us all through images, comparisons, and correspondences, hopefully retaining at all times their role as approximations and analogies, and avoiding heavy imperatives or explications too rigidly declaimed.

Through *La Comédie humaine*, Balzac may well have brought Beethoven to as vast an audience of contemporaries as Rossini enjoyed in the theatres. And thanks to his visionary bent, he launched a new genre: the musical tale in a philosophical key. This satisfied his desires both as narrator and as thinker. In many respects, Mann's genial composer Adrian Leverkühn appears a descendant of Gambara, thus modernizing and intensifying conceptually the lineage which had begun with Diderot's Nephew of Rameau and Hoffmann's Knight Gluck. Says the narrator in *Doktor Faustus* "For [Adrian] did plunge into the infinite, which astrophysical science seeks to measure, only to arrive at measures, figures, orders of greatness with which the human spirit no longer has any relationship, and which lose themselves in the theoretic and abstract, in the completely non-sensory, not to say nonsensical."[2]

More than seeing himself as a literary amateur in music, which he was and honestly admitted, Balzac preferred to see himself as a musical amateur in literature. Whether or not he originally discovered in music utilizable material for literary conquest, the fact stands that he came to love the art very genuinely. We agree with Hucher who compares this love with his love of Touraine, about which he would say: "Do not ask me why I love it; I love it neither as one loves his cradle nor as one loves an oasis in the desert. I love it as an artist loves art. Without it, I perhaps couldn't live any more."[3] Necessarily, he resembled a brilliant but unmethodical schoolboy: initial insights, exciting intuitions of what is wonderful in music, but little time for homework. His seeking out Strunz points to more than a practical desire for technical knowledge. It points to a fondness. Fourcand relates the effect a musical conversation had upon him: "During the evening, Balzac had talked music with Strunz and he continued the conversation with himself. Never was the musical art illuminated with such splendor. In striking words that flashed forth like rockets, he evoked all the ideas, all the sensations that slumber at the bottom of symphonies; he depicted vividly—enough to give you chills—all the characters in all the operas. You felt you were in an imaginary world, but in a world that was amazingly grandiose, sparkling, tumultuous, formidable, where human truths were condensed into visions. His extraordinary words made reality out of myth, made you, so to speak, see the most subtle sensations."[4]

A sensitive and impassioned appreciator, then, and a visionary. Like anyone else not professionally involved, he confused loving with understanding. Music was more an experience than a culture. But not exclusively. He recognized the novelty of contemporary music, its discoveries and boldnesses in the field of harmony, and its aim toward a perfect balance of all the art's constituent elements. And he reached to grasp with words a future aesthetics before its implementation through sounds. Music enters *La Comédie humaine* on many levels, and he was involved with all of them. Sensation, idea, and sensitivity found translation in Rossini, Beethoven, and Gregorian chant respectively. Together they constituted a vision of total life through his often voiced trinities: melody, harmony, and form; love, music, and religion; matter, mind, and spirit. That he passed many hours in declared "voluptuousness" is no stigma. As Leverkühn remarked, "One must not blush for the sensual, or be afraid of it. . . . Idealism leaves out of count that the mind and spirit are by no means addressed by the spiritual alone. . . ."[5] In his undertaking to discover the total communion of man and nature, Balzac responded to every stage and function of reality and dream suggested to him by his various musical experiences.

Among other things, Balzac understood that music is a syntactic, formal art that connotes more than denotes, one that the untutored may very legitimately approach through inferences for enjoyment but not for understanding, which depends on a grasp of its processive relationships. These relationships he grasped feebly. On the other hand, he inferred richly and enjoyed genially. Above all, he understood that, like love, music is a performance of desire, and since through passion desire tends to overextend itself, of loss—as

Genovese, Gambara, and others experienced. Musical tension implodes, producing psychic results through imaginary emanations that shape a person's state of being; it also explodes, leading to philosophical concepts through abstract associations that form a viable world view. Such a view embraces Totality.

Since all persons have a role in Totality, the arts—its symbol—exist as everyone's patrimony. "I shall always be a member," he once wrote, "of the seditious and incorrigible party that proclaims the liberty of the eyes and ears in the republic of the arts; of the party that claims itself capable of enjoying works created by the brush, the score, the press; that irreligiously believes that paintings, operas, and books are made for everybody; and that thinks that artists would be quite embarrassed if they worked for themselves alone, and quite unhappy if they were judged only by themselves."[6] Gambara knew that his esoteric aesthetics could only be redeemed if he could communicate it to humans and if enlightened humans became his judges. Not that a composer ought not venture forth onto unexplored terrains of expression: "the liberty of the eyes and ears" suggests the contrary. Despite the need for analysis, for erudite scrutiny, his words also suggest caution in this regard. He had no use for cold and isolated intellectual investigation when such investigation becomes its own end or when it becomes a form of cryptology. Any work of art can never be divorced from man's *intelligence du coeur*. Theories remain insignificant when confronted with transcending presence. "Concerning music, theories do not cause the same pleasure as results. As for me, I have always been violently tempted to kick in the shins the connoisseur who, seeing me swooning with delight as I drink long draughts of an aria charged with melody, says to me: 'It's in F major!'"[7] Balzac did not read Dante to study the poet's grammar.

Rather than fossilizing music in any series of formulas, he wanted to comprehend more fluidly the share of life within it, savor the fullness of experience it affords. This experience lies scattered on or behind the pages of sixty-seven tales and novels in and out of *La Comédie humaine*. Hugo von Hofmannsthal has suggested a Balzac Encyclopedia,[8] each article of which would be drawn from the author's own words. Cooking recipes, chemical formulas, banking operations, future discoveries, and above all marriage, society, and politics would all fill long columns. Music, perhaps the least of his fortes, would turn out no less abundant, despite the shagreen-skin of time that always receded from his embrace and precluded a lengthier involvement. Did the hurried and untutored novelist feed his melomania with borrowings from Fétis,[9] Castil-Blaze, d'Ortigue, Blaze de Bury, Berlioz, and others? There is but the scantiest evidence of this, although he did read their comments. Or from

Hoffmann, Stendhal, Senancour, Sand, Nerval? There was influence, or what was "in the air," but nothing more. There was, of course, Strunz—more than Rossini, Liszt, and Chopin, or even Mme de Berny. Everyone of us has had a teacher. If one wishes, one can always find inheritances or adoptions. "Who can flatter himself on being an inventor," wrote Balzac to a friend,[10] recognizing how Hoffmann reflected Mesmer, Schelling, and Schubert. Was it not Brahms who, accused by pedants of stealing a theme from Walther's "Preislied" in Wagner's *Die Meistersinger* for his own Violin Sonata in A major snapped: "Any fool can see that!"? If Balzac put into his works a number of existing opinions, his overall utterances reflect his personal thoughts, revealing their development and fixing themselves on his private scale of values. His mind disaggregated and dissolved all influences in order to absorb them into his organism, incorporate them into his existing body of thought, and galvanize them into an independent expression of his personality. "Two kinds of men," wrote Ballanche, "according to their time march at the head of other men. Intuitive and spontaneous men, who create a priori, who are the tutors of the people. Assimilative men, who make themselves the representatives of an idea, of a period, of an opinion, of a system of ideas and beliefs, who are the expression of a general feeling."[11]

Leaning heavily toward the second category, Balzac cannot be denied his share of the first. Baudelaire, Manzoni, Tolstoy, and Proust, to all of whom *La Comédie humaine* bequeathed more than it stated, understood this. And let us add no less a figure than Richard Wagner, who while speaking with Judith Gautier asked her what the initial "H" represented in Balzac's name. Judith naturally replied: "Honoré." With thoughtful assurance Wagner corrected her: "No, Madame . . ., Homer."[12]

APPENDIX

OPERAS, COMPOSITIONS, AND THE ROMANCE

1. **Synopses of the Operas**

   a. Rossini's *Mosè in Egitto*

      Egypt is plunged in darkness. Pharaoh sends for Moses and swears he will release the people of Israel if he will free the country from this black plague. Moses does as he is asked; but Osiris, Pharaoh's son, who has contracted a secret marriage with a Jewish girl, Elcia, incites the Egyptians against the royal decision so as not to see his wife leave. The permission to depart is revoked. Moses calls down a hail of fire; in terror, Pharaoh renews his promise. Osiris tries to retain Elcia by leading her into an underground retreat, but is discovered. Once more Pharaoh, on the pretext that he is being threatened by neighboring peoples, breaks his word. Moses protests violently, and persuades Elcia to abandon Osiris. In despair the latter tries to kill her, but is struck down in the act by lightning. Pharaoh falls fainting on his son's body; Elcia is in tears, the Israelites are terror-stricken. Moses leads his people to the banks of the Red Sea, and Aaron announces the pursuit of the King with his army. The Red Sea divides, allowing the Israelites to pass, and the Egyptians are drowned in its closing waters.

   b. Meyerbeer's *Robert le Diable*

      The daughter of the Duke of Normandy, Berthe, has been

seduced by a diabolical creature, and the child born has shown himself to be so capable of horrors that he has been nicknamed "le Diable." Chased away to Sicily by his vassals, he becomes engaged to the beautiful Princess Isabelle. He offends her father, but is saved by one Bertram, who induces him to take up gambling. The night preceding the joust for Isabelle's hand, he loses everything and is forced to flee. Bertram advises him to procure a talisman, a magic branch lying on the tomb of St. Rosalie. In the cemetery, the tombs uncover and scores of nuns in black veils dance around Robert and convince him to leave the branch there. Through its special powers Robert wants to seduce Isabelle, but yielding to a moment of pity he breaks it and runs off. Now Bertram, the Devil, reveals himself as his father and attempts to form a pact with his son. Robert's horrified sister, Alice, shows him a warning testament left by their mother, and after a long effort succeeds in convincing her brother to pursue a virtuous course. He rejects the Devil.

c. Gambara's *Mahomet*

Mohammed and his wife, Cadhige, are talking about the persecution he faces from the magistrates, the soldiers, and the lords of the land. He is to possess Abdollah's daughter (Aiesha) and Omar's daughter (Hafsa). Cadhige has convinced the people of Mecca that her husband's epilepsy is the result of his commerce with the angels. Indeed, Mohammed communes with the angel Gabriel and receives his support, but is forced to flee. A small contingent of believers that remains by him succeeds in raising an army, and through it his militant religion conquers the three Arabias. During the general festivity, the leader, now a prophet, proclaims his polygamy, much to the sorrow of his faithful wife who has been instrumental in his attainment of glory. Eventually, however, having discovered the ills of polygamy, he regrets his first and unique love, Cadhige, and so confides in Abdollah and Omar. The price of greatness being too heavy to bear, Mohammed hopes for final consolation through death. A solemn prayer is offered before the holy casbah.

2. Musical Compositions Inspired by Balzac's Works

Balzac's interest in music and musicians is the subject of this book. A convenient table of musical references in *La Comédie humaine* is provided, in the Pléïade edition and under the appropriate heading, in volume XI, 1131-1292. In 1953, after the completion of my dissertation, *** Guillet, put together a similar index which takes into account, albeit without claiming completeness, writings not included in the Pléïade edition, namely the correspondence and sundry articles by Balzac. Guillet's overview, much of it in outline form, is "Balzac et la musique," presented for the *diplôme d'études supérieures* to the Faculté de Lettres de Grenoble. These listings are important because they are highly suggestive of Balzac's broad awareness of music. In turn, his own works have inspired a few musical compositions:

a. Daniel F. E. Auber: *Romance*

   Composition for voice and piano set to the lyrics found in *Modeste Mignon* (see Appendix III). At one time Auber contemplated writing an opera based on the same novel.

b. Ernest Chausson: *Réveil*

   Excellent art song (*mélodie*) for two voices based on a poem by Balzac. The voices enjoy complete independence, yet work together. The style is that of a simple romance, but is a hauntingly beautiful expression of it. *Réveil* is one of the composer's loveliest pieces for voice(s) and piano.

c. Jacques F. F. E. Halévy: *Le Shérif*

   A hurriedly written light opera in three acts on a libretto by Scribe based on *Maître Cornélius*. It shows the influence of Meyerbeer, is strangely Oriental in spots, and has sharply drawn characters, as befits Balzac's tale.

d. Ruggiero Leoncavallo: *Séraphita*

   A symphonic poem of uneven merit, yet interesting and at times exciting in the orchestral treatment of what one may surmise to be passages relating directly to the mystical atmosphere Balzac creates in his novel.

e. Hermann von Waltershausen: *Oberst Chabert*

   The composer's most successful opera. According to Grove's Dictionary, one of the most powerful specimens of German opera written under the influence of the Italian *verismo* of Mascagni and Leoncavallo. It was widely performed during the first quarter of the current century.

3. Auber's Music for the Romance in *Modeste Mignon*

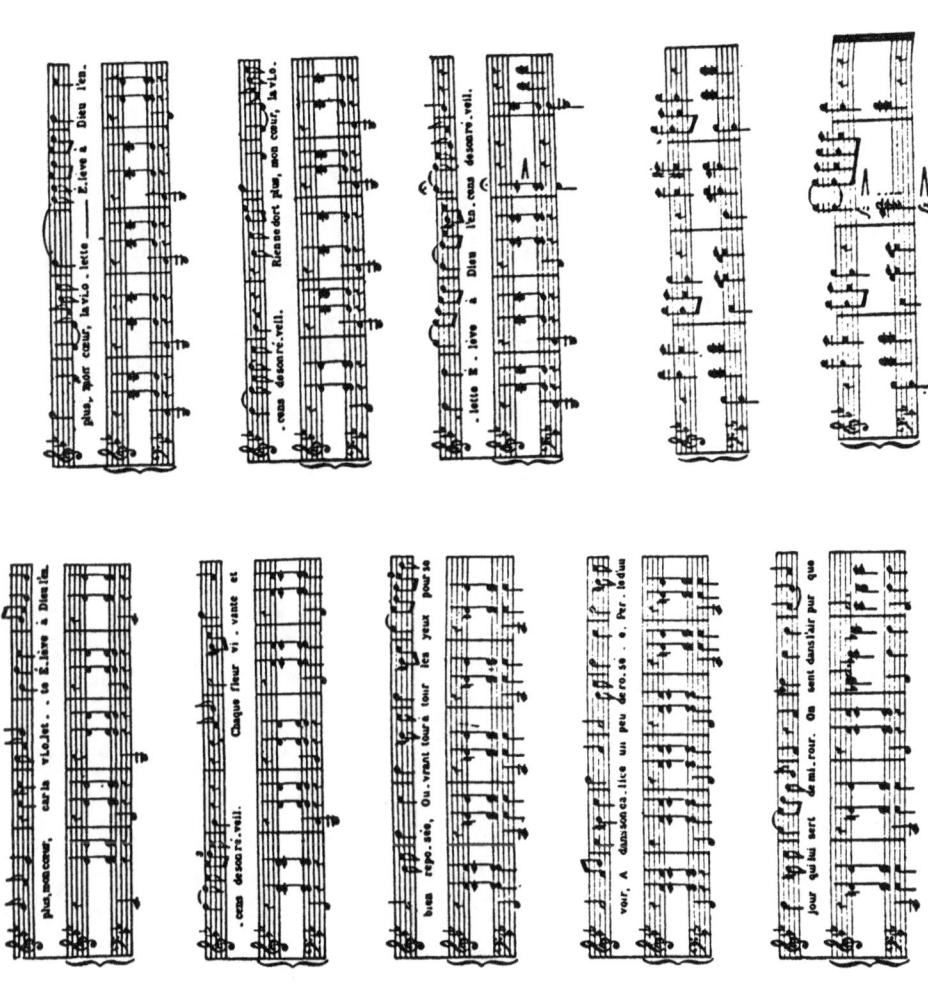

NOTES

Introduction

[1] Pierre Laubriet, *L'Intelligence de l'art chez Balzac* (Paris: Didier, 1961), 433.

[2] "Lettre à Maurice Schlesinger," *La Gazette musicale de Paris*, May 29, 1837, IV, 199.

[3] Gabriel Rouchès, "Le Sentiment musical chez les écrivains de 1830," *Le Courier musical*, January 15, 1905. See also January 1 of that same year, as well as December 1 and 15, 1904.

[4] See the 1862 conversation between Goncourt and Gautier reported by Romain Rolland, *Musiciens d'aujourd'hui* (Paris: Hechette, 1908), 213-214. We should remember, however, that in commenting on the divorce between music and literature in his day, Gautier exaggerated considerably his colleagues' lack of feeling for music and cannot be taken literally. In *Les Grotesques* (Paris, 1856), 158, for example, he claimed that "Lamartine runs at top speed when he sees someone opening a piano," something manifestly untrue, especially when at Saint-Point it was Liszt who "opened" the instrument.

[5] Louis de Fourcand, "La Musique dans Balzac," *Universal Review*, May, 1888, I, 113.

[6] Bernard Gavoty, *Revue de Paris*, July, 1951, 183. We cannot consider Stendhal's, Nerval's, and George Sand's musical opinions "disarming."

[7] Lila Maurice-Amour, "Balzac et la musique," *Mercure de France*, January 1, 1950, 87. See also "La Musique," *Balzac: le livre du centenaire* (Paris, 1952), 195-208.

[8] Herbert Hunt, *Balzac's Comédie Humaine* (London: Athlone Press, 1959), 144.

[9] Auguste Getteman, "Balzac et la musique," *Revue musicale*, June 1, 1922; Fernand Baldensperger, *Orientations étrangères chez Honoré de Balzac* (Paris: Champion, 1927), 13-14 and 219-227; Louis Laloy, "Le Goût musical," *Revue de Paris*, September 15, 1922; Rouchès, op. cit.; Camille Bellaigue, "Silhouettes de musiciens: Balzac," *Le Temps*, September 16, 1903, and "Balzac et la musique," *Revue des Deux Mondes*, October 1, 1924, XXIII. For example, for Laloy, only Balzac in the nineteenth century has a respect for music; for Bellaigue, Sand and Balzac are the only prose writers of the time to understand music; for Rouchès, Musset and Balzac are the only musicians among Romantic writers, although he prefers the former.

[10] Ernst R. Curtius, *Balzac* (Bern: A. Francke, 1951), 19. After quoting a statement by Gambara about his musical drama, Curtius adds: "Wagner, whose appearance has on the whole so much relationship with Balzac's, seems to be adumbrated here."

[11] Thérèse Marix-Spire, *Les Romantiques et la musique: le cas George Sand* (Paris: Nouvelles éditions latines, 1954), 45.

[12] *Gambara*, M. Regard, ed. (Paris: Corti, 1964), 7-49. *Massimilla Doni*, M. Milner, ed. (Paris: Corti, 1964), 7-82.

[13] *Correspondence*, ed. Calmann-Lévy (Paris: Calmann-Lévy, 1876), XXIV, 56-57.

[14] See Harry Zohn and Jean-Pierre Barricelli, "Music in Stefan Zweig's Last Years: Some Unpublished Letters," *The Juilliard Review*, III (1956), 3-11, reprinted in my *Melopoiesis: Approaches to the Study of Literature and Music* (New York: New York University Press, 1988), 13-20.

[15] E, I, 168, 170, 217, 355.

Chapter I: The Enticement of Sound

[1] Laure de Surville, *Balzac, sa vie et ses oeuvres d'après sa correspondance* (Paris: C. Lévy, 1858), 51.

[2] Léon Guichard, in his *La Musique et les lettres au temps du romantisme* (Paris: Presses universitaires de France, 1955), 297ff, would want to discard all such references.

[3] Surville, *Balzac*, 18-19.

[4] Philippe Bertault, *Balzac et la musique religieuse* (Paris: Naert, 1929), 13-14.

[5] *Les Etudes balzaciennes* (Paris, 1951), I, 52, fn 4.

[6] E. M., "Honoré de Balzac," *Gazette musicale de Paris*, Sept. 1, 1850, 292.

[7] Pianist and composer, born in Mannheim in 1771, died in London in 1838; author of piano etudes. In *Ursule Mirouët*, Balzac attributes the *Songe* to Hérold, just as in *Béatrix* he attributes Rossini's "Di tanti palpiti" from *Tancredi* to Zingarelli. His mistakes. It was Laure who was probably playing at some time numbers by Hérold in a similar style. The *Songe* contains an Introduction (*andante non tanto*) and a romance Aria (*moderato*) in ten variations, and figured later in piano anthologies of the then reputed great masters in 1869 and 1893.

[8] Surville, *Balzac*, 32-33.

[9] Théophile Gautier, *Honoré de Balzac* (Paris: Poulet-Malassis et de Broise, 1859), 26 and 119.

[10] Surville, *Balzac*, 32-33.

[11] See Léon Gozlan, *Balzac chez lui: souvenirs des Jardies* (Paris: M. Lévy, 1862), 36.

[12] Surville, *Balzac*, 38-39.

[13] Ibid., 40. In the throes of writing, he feared failure lest he would have to "renounce [his] furniture and even perhaps the piano." Quoted from Marix-Spire, *Les Romantiques et la musique*, 44. In 1819, he had written to Laure: "Are you still working at your piano? [I shall have my piano here] the first time you come." (*Lettres à sa famille*, Oct. 25, 1819, 16). There is no indication, however, that he ever got the piano.

[14] The adjective is of Berlioz.

[15] Surville, *Balzac*, 50.

[16] Ibid. Though for someone else, he had asked Laure for information about a composer-organist, Beauvarlet-Charpentier, but had correctly rejected him as mediocre: "You can improve, by practicing, the alacrity of your fingers. . . . To the devil with

mediocrity! The devil with the Pradons and the Beauvarlets. One must be Grétry and Racine" (21).

[17] *Correspondance*, 35.

[18] Philippe-Joseph Hinner, of German origin, pleased the queen who harbored a special fondness for German music.

[19] E, July 19, 1837, I, 418. Once he heard his brother-in-law sing "Que le jour me dure"; "Good Lord," he wrote to Mme de Berny, "he sings terribly, and how your singing, which I did not appreciate formerly, seemed charming." In Gabriel Hanotaux and Georges Vicaire, *La Jeunesse de Balzac* (Paris: A. Ferroud, 1921), 219.

[20] Baldensperger, *Orientations étrangères*, 220.

[21] *Lettres à sa famille*, June, 1821, 37. Urging Laure to study the piano was, by itself, nothing unusual. Stendhal, for instance, though in *De l'Amour* he made sport of a young lady's typical musical education, was not above telling his own sister: "In the century in which we live, a young lady must absolutely know music, otherwise she will not be credited with having any education. Therefore you must, of necessity, become good at the piano." See *Correspondance*, H. Martineau, ed. (Paris: Le Divan, 1933-1934), letters of Sept. 28, 1800, and Dec. 6, 1801.

[22] He saw that Laurence would stop with her marriage: "The piano will be compensated by diamond buttons" (*Lettres à sa famille*, July, 1821, 47), but Laure's ability meant more to him even if he sometimes teased her. "Laure-Dusseck-Balzac-Grétry-*charmante-soeur-riri-pan-pan-croque-note*" (ibid., Oct. 30, 1819, 21) was still the one he thought of when wrestling with the muse of poetry: ". . . having captured a fine thought, I put it in sonorous verses, I think I hear the voice that tells me: courage, go on; I listen to the tones of your piano and sit again to work with renewed vigor" (ibid., Sept. 6, 1819, 9).

[23] *Sténie* reflects strongly the influence of *La Nouvelle Héloïse*. It may not be pure coincidence that Job likes "Le Songe de Rousseau." Furthermore, Balzac was well acquainted with the Genevan's views on Italian and French music ("For the first time in his life he heard that music whose delights M. Jean-Jacques Rousseau had extolled to him so eloquently during an evening at Baron d'Holbach's" [Sa 95]). In *Les petits Bourgeois*, Balzac cites *Le Devin du village*.

[24] From L.-J. Arrigon, *Les Années romantiques* (Paris: Perrin, 1927), 259-260.

²⁵ From Marcel Bouteron, *Danse et musique romantiques* (Paris: Le Goupy, 1927), 161.

²⁶ E, July 1 and 15, 1834, I, 168 and 174.

²⁷ From Arrigon, *Les Années romantiques*, 107.

²⁸ E, Oct. 31, 1833, I, 70-71.

²⁹ *Correspondance*, 1831, 96-97; to Duchess d'Abrantès. Once he even fell stepping out of the carriage in front of the Opéra, so tired was he after his day's work. See "Voyage de Paris à Java," *Revue de Paris*, Nov. 25, 1832.

³⁰ E, April 28, 1834, I, 142.

³¹ E, July 1, 1834, I, 168.

³² See Edmond Werdet, *Portrait intime de Balzac: sa vie, son humeur et son caractère* (Paris: Dentu et Silvestre, 1859), 300-308, and specifically *Souvenirs de la vie littéraire* (Paris: Dentu, 1879), 74. In his *Petits mémoires de l'Opéra* (Paris: Librairie nouvelle, 1857), 151, Charles de Boigne says that Balzac appeared either "with hair a yard long down to his shoulders," or "shaven like a Capuchin."

³³ E, Oct. 18, 1834, I, 195.

³⁴ T. Gautier, *Souvenirs romantiques* (Paris: Garnier, 1929), ed. Garnier, 142.

³⁵Marquis de Podensac, Viscount Charles de Rastignac-Cadillac, Count de la Bastide-Florac, Vidame Nestor de Saint-André de Cubsac, Baron Emile de Barsac, Count de Grandignan-Preignac. For their real names, see Arrigon, *Les Années romantiques*, 183.

³⁶ Ironically, one of the "-ac" company, Nestor, a hard critic of the Opéra's administration, was to become its Director from 1847 to 1860.

³⁷ Werdet, *Portrait intime*, 305.

³⁸ Bouteron, *Les Cahiers balzaciens*, from Maurice-Amour, "Balzac et la musique," 87. A conversation during the course of an opera was, in Paris as in Milan and Rome, a "tolerated impertinence" (see Stendhal, *Rome, Naples et Florence* [Paris: Champion, n.d.], ed. Champion, 10, as well as chapter X of *Armance*). Balzac's behavior exceeded even this generous limit.

[39] E, July 13, 1834, I, 170.

[40] E, July 1, 1834, 168.

[41] "L'Opéra," *Les Etudes balzaciennes* (Paris: Garnier, 1958), V-VI, 189-190. Clearly, ahead of Wagner, Balzac saw opera as a *Gesamtkunstwerk*.

[42] E, July 1, 1834, I, 168. In this instance, his thought traveled to Poland, to the side of Mme Hanska.

[43] See René Bouvier and Edouard Maynial, *Les Comptes dramatiques de Balzac* (Paris: Sorlot, 1938), and Arrigon, *Les Années romantiques*, 180-183.

[44] E, Oct. 31, 1833, I, 70.

[45] E, Aug. 11, 1834, Oct. 19, 1834, Dec. 1, 1834, and Mar. 11, 1835, I, 179, 195, 209, and 237-238 respectively. At the beginning of this same year, he had also informed his mother: "I shall not renew my box either at the Opéra or at the Bouffons" (*Lettres à sa famille*, 171).

[46] E, Oct. 1 and Dec. 1, 1836, I, 348 and 367.

[47] "Lettre à Schlesinger," 200. Balzac, we know, visited Turin, Venice, and Milan, among other Italian cities. He visited the latter frequently, and La Scala assiduously. See Henry Prior, "Balzac à Turin," "Balzac à Milan," and "Balzac à Venise," *Revue de Paris*, Jan. 15, 1924, July 1, and Aug. 1, 1925, and Dec. 1, 1927, respectively.

[48] E, Nov. 22, 1835, Dec. 1, 1836, Oct. 1, 1836, and Oct. 22, 1836, I, 281, 367, 348, and 355 respectively.

[49] E, Apr. 7, 1843, II, 135.

[50] Surville, *Balzac*, 51.

[51] The relationship between Balzac and Rossini, Liszt, Berlioz, and Strunz will be discussed in chapters III and IV.

[52] "Lettre à Schlesinger," 200.

[53] E, Jan. 22, 1838, I, 457-458.

[54] Others frequently present were Sainte-Beuve, Heine, Mickiewicz, Princess Belgiojoso, and Berlioz, who first introduced

Liszt there. Balzac appeared often at Sand's home in Nohant after 1842.

[55] E, May 10, 1834, I, 156.

[56] From Rémy Montalée, *En lisant Balzac* (Paris: Figuière, 1925), 14.

[57] E, Nov. 7-14, 1837, I, 443.

[58] E, Mar. 30, 1835, I, 241.

[59] Bouteron, *Danse et musique romantiques*, 148.

[60] Werdet, *Portrait intime*, 307.

[61] Surville, 179.

[62] E, Feb. 2 and 27, 1847, IV, 243-244 and 246.

[63] *Correspondance*, June 25, 1849, 624.

[64] E, July 30, 1847, IV, 343.

[65] E, Aug. 19, 1846, III, 373.

[66] First given at the Conservatoire in 1844. See E, Feb. 17, 1845, III, 26. While the desire is there to attract Mme Hanska to Paris, he also felt strongly enough about the symphony to declare: "This is the first time that Parisian vogue is not mistaken and does not hoist a flag to some foolishness."

[67] In 1836, Count de Hanski had informed Balzac: "Anna . . . is getting more charming every day. She is already a little lady who has begun to play the piano, and promises to have a distinct talent" (E, I, 330 fn). From that day on, Balzac always inquired about Anna's progress. Thirteen years later, when he was able to witness her talent, he wrote to Laure: "I have sung [Sophie's and Anna's] praises so much here that Countess Anna dreams of nothing more than to make music with her rival Sophie when she will be in Paris, and to enjoy the Italiens and the Opéra. I say that Sophie is a fine musician . . ." (*Lettres à sa famille*, Oct. 20, 1849, 443). Anna, however, seems to have been a more accomplished pianist than her rival. Balzac had noted: "She has as much genius for music as she has love for it . . .; she plays everything at sight, exactly as Mozart would have done . . .," and her hands "have an iron fingering, like those of Liszt. . ." (ibid., 337 and 381).

[68] The way he had described his house in 1838 in a letter to Duchess de Castries (*Correspondance*, 317).

[69] See E, June 10, 1847, IV, 272.

[70] Balzac asked his sister to have Ambroise Thomas (her daughter Sophie was studying the piano under him), composer of *Mignon*, *Caïd*, and *Hamlet*, accompany her to the concertmaster of the Opéra, Sauvageot, for this acquisition. From Wierzchownia he wrote in 1849: "I hope that you have terminated the business of the violins, and that you have seen the superb collection [bric-à-brac] of M. Sauvageot, whom you will have met through the composer of *Caïd*. . . . I am waiting with great impatience for the reply concerning the violins, and, as things stand now, they must be relatively cheap. I await impatiently because I must have the money for the purchase transfered" (*Lettres à sa famille*, Feb. 9, 1849, 321). He refers to "the famous violin" in *Correspondance*, April 30, 1849, 621, and on June 21 of that year mentions "a veritable Stradivarius."

[71] E, May 15-16, 1843, II, 161.

Chapter II: Shallow Enchantments

[1] Claude Laforet, *La Vie musicale au temps romantique* (Paris: Peyronnet, 1929), 1.

[2] See Fétis, "Concert du Conservatoire," *La Revue musicale*, May 29, 1830.

[3] Quoted from Yves Hucher, "Balzac et les musiciens," *L'Information culturelle artistique*, Sept.-Oct., 1956, 112.

[4] Between 1828 and 1843, there was quantitatively an imposing list of premières: *La Muette de Portici*, *Le Comte d'Ory* (1828); *Guglielmo Tell* (1829); *Fra Diavolo* (1830); *Robert le Diable*, *Zampa*, *Le Philtre*, *La sonnambula*, *Norma* (1831); *Le Pré aux clercs*, *L'elisir d'amore* (1832); *Le Chalet* (1834); *La Juive*, *I puritani* (1835); *Les Huguenots*, *Le Postillon de Lonjumeau* (1836); *Le Domino noir*, *Lucia di Lammermoor* (1837); *Benvenuto Cellini* (1838); *Les Martyrs*, *La favorita*, *La figlia del regimento* (1840); *Don Pasquale* (1843).

[5] See Théophile Gautier, *Histoire de l'art dramatique en France depuis 25 ans* (Paris: Magnin et Blanchard, 1858-59), VI, 236.

[6] Only the works of composers dead for ten years or of young Conservatory composers could be performed at the Gymnase; it dated

from 1820. The Odéon, from 1824 to 1829, specialized in Rossini and Weber operas. The Nouveautés was, musically, on a lower echelon.

[7] *Correspondance*, to MM les Membres du Comité de la Société des Gens de Lettres, Composant la Commission dite du *Manifeste*, 351.

[8] The origins of this organization date back to the renewal of the *Concerts Spirituels* in 1805, but its real work as a regular concert society did not begin until 1828 when Habeneck became its director, a post he held until 1848.

[9] Other compositions by Beethoven that were performed at other times were: the Ninth Symphony (for the first time in Paris on March 27, 1831), the Septet in E-flat major, opus 20 (1830), the Finale from *Fidelio* (1831), the Overture to *Prometheus* (1831), the Fugue from the Ninth Quartet (1832), *Die Ruinen von Athen* (1841-42). Chopin, who had come to Paris in 1831, organized several Beethoven concerts with the aid of Kalkbrenner, Paër, and Norblin. At one of them, given at the Conservatoire, Mendelssohn performed a Beethoven piano concerto. The Fifth and Sixth Symphonies were the most popular among the symphonies.

[10] The usual Mozart selections included the Overture to *Die Zauberflöte*, *Ave Verum Corpus*, the Sextet from *Don Giovanni*, the *Davidde Penitente* cantata, *La clemenza di Tito*, *Les Mystères d'Isis* (a French adaptation of *Die Zauberflöte* by Lachnith and Morel), and various symphonies.

[11] Weber: Overtures to *Oberon* and *Der Freischütz*, and the chorus from *Euryanthe* in 1830; a Grand Concerto was performed by Liszt in 1835; again the Overture to *Der Freischütz* in 1841. Haydn: the first concert of the 1829 season was all Haydn. *Le Soir* and *La tempesta* (Symphony number 8 in G major), *Die Jahreszeiten*, the Finale from *Die Schöpfung*, a mass (a "First" mass, more likely the *Heiligmesse* Novello no. 1, than the *Missa brevis*, Haydn Society no. 1), *Die Sieben Worte des Erlösers am Kreuze*, received creditable performances. Gluck: mainly scenes from *Iphigénie en Aulide*, *Alceste*, *Armide*, and *Orfeo ed Euridice*.

[12] Bach: only an air from one of the Passions in 1840. Méhul: only a special and short memorial concert in 1830. Rameau: selections from *Les Indes galantes*. Berlioz was mainly performed at the Salle du Conservatoire and rarely at the Société des Concerts (which played his Overture to *Rob Roy* in 1833 and excerpts from *La Damnation de Faust* in 1849).

[13] Handel: selections from *Samson*. Hummel: Adagio and Finale from the *Fantasie* in E-flat major. Lulli: scenes from *Alceste*.

Mendelssohn: Overture to *The Hebrides* (his violin Concerto was not performed until 1848). Pergolesi: *Stabat Mater* and shorter selections of religious music. Spontini: selections from *La vestale*. Other composers whose names appeared on the programs include David, Onslow, Reber, Reicha, Deldevez, and Dancla. Chopin performed rarely at the Société, but in 1835 did accept to play one of his Polonaises.

[14] Ed(ouard) M(onnais), in *La Gazette musicale*, Nov. 20, 1836.

[15] We should note that sometimes such solliciting was done in order to overcome the ill will of certain dispensators of music. In 1828, for instance, M. de la Rochefoucauld, the top agent in the Ministry of Fine Arts, helped Berlioz to bypass Cherubini's objections to a concert of his works.

[16] Signed: "V. D." The comment may be found in II, no. 5.

[17] Jules Combarieu, *Histoire de la musique des origines à la mort de Beethoven* (Paris: Colin, 1913-1934), II, 254.

[18] Definition given by the composer and theoretician Henri Romagnesi, a master of the romance genre and the author of several works well known to his contemporaries: *L'Art de chanter les romances* (Paris: Duverger, 1846), and *Psychologie du chant* (Paris: Duverger, 1846). See Combarieu, III, 246 and 250, and Fétis, *Biographie universelle des musiciens* (Paris: Firmin Didot, 1865), VII, 300. The romance genre originated around the middle of the XVIIIth century with Moncrif.

[19] The following titles give some idea of the romances: "Le Bonheur de se revoir" (text by Guttinguer, music by Beauplan), "Belle pour lui" (Lemoine-Puget), "La Timide" (Richemont-Masini), "Loelia, mon bel ange" (Elwart-Delaporte), "Partir" and "Mon ange gardien" (text and music by Duchambge), "Que de diable emporte l'amour" (Lagoanère). Hortense put to music poems by Marot, Delphine Gay, and Béranger. Collections of such romances with piano accompaniments made favorite Christmas gifts. They usually contained only six pieces. When, in 1834, Amédée de Beauplan published a large album of accompanied romances, he endeared himself to the hearts of many. We should add here that there were, of course, serious composers who made fine use of some romances: Berlioz himself, for example, in *La Damnation de Faust* ("Il était un roi Thule"), and much later Verdi in *Otello* ("Il salce").

[20] In 1845, one Delaire wrote: "Publishers turn down quartets and other capital works as merchandise not in demand and without sale value, while they pay 500 francs for a romance and up to 6000

francs for a collection of six romances by a composer in vogue" (quoted from Laforet, *La Vie musicale au temps romantique*, 53).

[21] Auber had suggested to reverse the order of certain stanzas, to which Balzac agreed, thanking him for the music and apologizing for the trouble caused. He concluded his brief letter with: "I have at least the pleasure to express to you here my admiration for your fine talent." *Correspondance*, 404-405.

[22] A post scriptum adds that since Auber's music (see Appendix III) was already included in *La Comédie humaine*, he would not be able to use his (Chélard's) music, but that he would send him a copy of the novel. The letter is dated Paris, Oct. 4, 1844, and is reproduced in "Les Musiciens et la romance de Modeste Mignon," *L'Amateur d'autographes* (June, 1912), 177-178. The letter's dating may be incorrect, for Balzac had visited Mendelssohn in Berlin the year before. See E, Oct. 14, 1843, II, 196, as well as *Correspondance*, 366.

[23] Letter of 1822 to Mme de Berny in Hanotaux and Vicaire, *La Jeunesse de Balzac*, 194.

[24] Fernand Baldensperger, *Sensibilité musicale et romantisme* (Paris: Les Presses Françaises, 1925), 102.

[25] Julien Tiersot, "Balzac et la chanson populaire," *Revue des traditions populaires*, 1895, X, 334. See also his *La Chanson populaire et les écrivains romantiques* (Paris: Plon, 1931).

[26] We should also mention the interest in folk songs expressed by other writers, notably Dumas, Gautier, Stendhal, Lamartine, Mérimée (who cared only for the gay kind), and Musset (see poem "Chanson"), and call attention to Nerval's poem "Fantaisie": he "would give all Rossini, all Mozart, all Weber" for an old melancholy air.

[27] Tiersot found versions in Berri and Bresse, and Nerval, Max Buchon, and M. de Puymaigre found some in Valois, Franche-Comté, and Lorraine.

[28] Musset, too, appreciated the factor of simplicity in folk songs, as Deschamps did that of melody.

[29] Allusion is made to "Noces de Cana," a painting by Monnoye. Balzac's exactness could have resulted from his reading of texts on early XIXth century art in which instruments and their players were depicted in great detail.

[30] "O Richard. . ." is actually from the Grétry opera *Richard-Coeur-de-Lion*, but its style was considered popular.

[31] Jacques Barzun, *Berlioz and the Romantic Century* (Boston: Little, Brown, & Co., 1950), I, 26-27. *Le Médecin de campagne* was published the same year as a shorter work dedicated to Berlioz, *Ferragus*.

[32] E, Nov. 14, 1842, II, 80. Other popular songs used by Balzac include "A la première ville," "Sonament l'habille" (R), "Combien j'ai douce souvenance" (IP), "Dans les Gardes-Françaises" (EG), the plaintive ballad "Tualdes" (CV), "Gai, gai, gai, le tonnelier" (EG), "God save the King," attributed to Lulli (AS), "Partant pour la Syrie" (PG, MN, CP), "Ranz des Suisses" (St), "Toi qui connais les hussards de la garde" (Pa), "Va-t'en voir s'ils viennent" by Lamothe-Houdard (DF), "Veillons au salut de l'Empire" (C, R), and "Viens, aurore, je t'implore," attributed to Henry IV (EM).

[33] Hector Berlioz, *A travers chants* (Paris: Michel Lévy, 1862), 72.

[34] One of the publications of Balzac's press was *Henriette Sontag, histoire contemporaine, traduite de l'allemand, ornée d'un portrait* (Tome premier [et second], Paris, 1828). See Hanotaux and Vicaire, *La Jeunesse de Balzac*, 458.

[35] Quoted from Marcel Bouteron, "Le Culte de Balzac," *Revue des Deux Mondes*, May 15, 1924, 444.

[36] E, Oct. 26, 1837, I, 439.

[37] E, Mar. 30, 1835, I, 245.

[38] E, Apr. 7, 1843, II, 135. Such dreams always enthralled Balzac, as they enthralled his own Melmoth and Goethe's Faust.

[39] That is, until 1834, after which her voice began to deteriorate. The critical opinions regarding the singers' quality and range is corroborated in Grove's *Dictionary of Music and Musicians* (London: Macmillan, 1954-1961).

[40] E, Aug. 3, 1847, IV, 353.

[41] Alfred de Musset, "Débuts de Mlle P. Garcia" (Malibran), *Revue des Deux Mondes*, Nov. 1, 1839.

[42] See poem "A la Malibran," published in 1836.

⁴³ Quoted from Emile Bergerat, *Théophile Gautier, Entretiens, souvenirs et correspondance* (Paris: G. Charpentier, 1880), 83. Deschamps similarly made the voice and melody his aesthetic criterion: "For singers, one needs song first of all, and then more song." "Lettres sur la musique," in *Oeuvres complètes* (Paris: Lemerre, 1872-74), II, 34-35.

⁴⁴ Somewhat similarly, Mme de Staël, too, had delighted in the "delicious tenderness" induced by two perfectly accorded (Italian) voices (*Corinne*, book IX, chap. 2), but closer to Balzac's desire of expressing an ultimate in pure feeling had come Senancour's wish to hear melodies sung wordlessly, not with lingering chords of harmony, but by one voice or by two voices in unison. Words damage the sensation conveyed by pure music (*Obermann*, Letter XXXVI). Variations on the idea are found elsewhere in Balzac, as in *Le Lys dans la vallée* when Félix and Henriette listen with bucolic rapture to "the alternating song of two nightingales that repeated several times their single note" (LV 1013).

⁴⁵ Alfred de Vigny, "Première lettre parisienne: Moeurs et Beaux-arts," *L'Avenir*, Apr. 3, 1831: "They had attributed to him his little terrors, his mysteries, his dungeons, his incest, his murders; for here we always need a certain little perfume of crime and despair in order to be welcomed in society. He is pale, he is ravaged; he lacks nothing." Signed: "Y".

⁴⁶ Deschamps, "Lettres sur la musique," IV, 39.

⁴⁷ Gautier, *Histoire de l'art dramatique*, III, 181.

⁴⁸ Thalberg had been in Paris since 1835; his successes lasted until 1862. When Liszt left the capital with Countess d'Agoult, Thalberg succeeded him in the role of first pianist. On his return, however, Liszt felt he should regain his title. A formal contest was held at the home of Princess Belgiojoso where, as expected, Liszt triumphed. Mme de Girardin is to have declared, with typical neatness: "Thalberg is the first pianist of the world; Liszt is the only one."

⁴⁹ Only few, like the violinist Alard, limited their interests to serious chamber works.

⁵⁰ Batta was a Belgian 'cellist, in Paris since 1835. Gérard de Nerval (and of course George Sand) was one of the few Romantics not guilty of excessive misjudgments in his appraisal of performers. Apart from his unreserved praise of two mediocre artists (with whom he was in love at different times), pianist Marie Pleyel and singer Jenny Colon, he selected more carefully than Balzac. Yet, three of

Balzac's choices are unimpeachable, and his inclusion of Batta, a finer musician than either Pleyel or Colon but not in the category of Chopin, Liszt, and Paganini, at least reveals some independence of judgment.

[51] E, May 15-16, 1843, II, 160-161.

[52] E, Apr. 7, 1843, II, 135.

[53] E, May 28, 1843, II, 169.

[54] A similar comparison between Chopin and Raphael was voiced by Heine. But regardless of the possible source, it was certainly more acceptable than Deschamps' attempt to make Cimarosa the Shakespeare, and Mozart the Raphael, of music. Less selective than Balzac, Deschamps seemed to like everybody: Berlioz, Rossini, Meyerbeer, Halévy. . . . See Henri Girard, *Emile Deschamps dilettante* (Paris: Champion, 1921).

[55] "Charges," *La Caricature*, Mar. 17, 1831.

[56] Angelica Catalani, who managed the Théâtre-Italien, was truly a singer of "tremendous ability," with a voice of exquisite purity, force, and compass. Balzac's references to the "sou" and to the "good riddance" were undoubtedly prompted by the uncommonly high fees she demanded for her performances and by the tyranny, both artistic and financial, she exercised over the Italiens as she had done previously over the Opera of London.

[57] E, Nov. 18, 1833, I, 87.

[58] The guitar, another favorite instrument (Paganini was a master of it), evidently failed to impress Balzac (Huerta notwithstanding), in whose novels only the most insignificant references to it are made.

[59] The question of synaesthesia will be elaborated in Chapter VI.

[60] Victor Hugo, *William Shakespeare* (Paris: A. Lacroix, 1864), 29. Similarly, among others, Lamartine: "Music is the infinite," alone capable of translating the intangibles of life. See *Cours familier de littérature* (Paris: Chez l'auteur, 1856-1863), chap. IV, conversations 29 and 36.

[61] See Hugo's poem "Dans l'Eglise de ***," and Lamennais' *Esquisse d'une philosophie* (Paris: Pagnerre, 1840), III, 318-323.

[62] Father Castel, an XVIIIth century Jesuit mathematician and physicist, had published in 1735 in the *Mémoires de Trévoux* a study, "Nouvelles expériences d'optique et d'acoustique," in which he described a *clavecin oculaire* invented by him. The instrument would have provided the eye with a succession of colors, the way an ordinary clavier provides the ear with a succession of sounds.

[63] One of the finest examples of her musical intelligence may be found in her famous letter to Meyerbeer, in which she criticizes the abused conventions that stirred the "vulgar public" and the "unintelligent vocalists." It is quoted in Marix-Spire, *Les Romantiques et le musique*, 510 ff.

[64] Having tired of appearing to be outdone by the insuperable Rubini, Bordogni once broke forth in a resonant note which he sustained much longer than the score required. Rubini, surprised, deemed it necessary to reply with an incredible series of roulades. The public went wild.

[65] Quoted from Laforet, *La Vie musicale au temps romantique*, end of "Comment on aimait la musique."

[66] J.-G. Prod'homme, "Balzac et son musicien," address given to the Société de Musicologie on Nov. 22, 1949. See annals of the Société.

Chapter III: Celebrated Musician Friends

[1] Guichard, *La Musique et les lettres au temps du romantisme*, 229.

[2] Rossini was Director of the Théâtre Italien for about two years, and, until 1830, "compositeur du Roi et inspecteur général du chant."

[3] Coffee was a frequent subject of conversation. See *Lettres à sa famille*, Oct. 11/18, 1838, 202. During a typical chat, Rossini indicated that inspiration from the stimulation of coffee lasts fifteen days: "Such is the term that Rossini assigned to it, as far as he was concerned."

[4] E, Nov. 18, 1833, I, 87.

[5] E, Dec. 26, 1834, I, 213.

[6] E, Oct. 31, 1833, I, 70, and Dec. 15, 1834, I, 217.

[7] E, Nov. 17, 1833, I, 84.

[8] E, Nov. 18, 1834, I, 86-87.

[9] E, Nov. 20-24, 1833, I, 88.

[10] E, Nov. 17, 1833, I, 84.

[11] E, Dec. 26, 1834, I, 212. In *Voyage de Paris à Java*, Balzac speaks of Rossini's "eminently fine and witty words" and adds: "his conversation is worth his music" (VPJ 576).

[12] E, Nov. 18, 1833, I, 86; note dated Nov. 17 of that year.

[13] E, Oct. 26 and Dec. 26, 1834, I, 200 and 211.

[14] BS, ELV, PC, DL, FC, IP, G, B, MD, AS, H, MuD, CBe, CP, EHC; *Code des gens honnêtes, Le Bois de Boulogne et le Luxembourg, Lettre sur Paris, Voyage de Paris à Java.* E: letters especially between the years 1833 and 1838, 1842 and 1843, 1845, and 1846.

[15] E, Nov. 14, 1842, II, 81.

[16] E, Oct. 16 and Dec. 21, 1842, II, 68 and 93, and Apr. 7, 1843, II, 133.

[17] E, July 17, 1846, III, 320. He adds: "He saw that money gave independence and that independence was the first good. I shall act accordingly."

[18] *Lettre adressée aux écrivains français du XIXe siècle*, Nov. 1, 1834.

[19] A study of this relationship has been made by Thérèse Marix (-Spire), "Histoire d'une amitié: Fr. Liszt et H. de Balzac," *Bibliothèque de la revue des études hongroises*, Paris, 1934, X, 36-68. It relies on the *Correspondance de Liszt et de la comtesse d'Agoult* (Paris: B. Grasset, 1933-34), ed. Daniel Ollivier, and on Sophie de Korwin-Piotrowska, *Balzac et le monde slave* (Paris: Champion, 1933).

[20] *De la mode en littérature*, May 29, 1830.

[21] "Rondo brillant, mais facile," *La Caricature*, July 28, 1831.

[22] Augustin Challamel, *Souvenirs d'un Hugolâtre* (Paris: J. Levy, 1885), 637.

²³ E, II, fn 1, 79.

²⁴ Among them appear Chateaubriand, Ballanche, Senancour, Quinet, Mignet, Lamartine, Hugo, Sainte-Beuve, Nodier, Vigny, Musset, Heine, Dumas, Janin, and the brothers Deschamps.

²⁵ See Hucher, "Balzac et les musiciens," 114.

²⁶ E, Apr. 7, 1843, II, 135.

²⁷ See Thérèse Marix (-Spire), "Histoire d'une amitié," 40.

²⁸ *Correspondance*, 296, and E, May 20-June 5, 1838, I, 477.

²⁹ Marie d'Agoult visited George Sand at Nohant twice during this period, at the end of January and in July of 1837. She confided in her, solliciting suggestions to resolve her differences with her lover.

³⁰ E, Mar. 2, 1838, I, 464. Countess d'Agoult got her revenge in 1846 in her novel *Nélida*, published under the pseudonym of Daniel Stern. Despite the tacit rivalry between her and George Sand, the two women always remained close friends.

³¹ Quoted from Marix (-Spire), "Histoire d'une amitié," 44.

³² E, Apr. 23-24, 1843, II, 141.

³³ Quoted from Marix (-Spire), "Histoire d'une amitié," 45.

³⁴ Ibid., 46. See also *Les Nouvelles littéraires*, Aug. 6, 1930.

³⁵ E, May 15-16, 1843, II, 160.

³⁶ Idem.

³⁷ Quoted from Maurice-Amour, "Balzac et la musique," 99.

³⁸ Letter to George Sand, Dec. 15, 1837, in Marix-Spire, *Les Romantiques et la musique*, 618.

³⁹ E, Apr. 7, 1843, II, 135.

⁴⁰ E, May 18, 1843, II, 168-169.

⁴¹ E, Dec. 14, 1843, Jan. 13 and Mar. 1, 1844, II, 240, 268, and 320.

[42] E, Apr. 18 and June 3, 5, 10, and 23, 1844, II, 353, 368, 370, 371, and 381-382, and Feb. 15, 1845, III, 25. "Lara" alludes to the fatal hero of Byron.

[43] E, June 23 and Aug. 7, 1844, II, 379 and 417.

[44] E, Mar. 6 and Sept. 20, 1845, III, 40 and 107.

[45] Liszt was thirty-one at the time, and thirteen years younger than Balzac.

[46] Quoted from Korwin-Piotrowska, *Balzac et le monde slave*, 315.

[47] Franz Liszt, *Liszts Briefe* (Leipzig: Breitkopf und Härtel, 1893-1902), IV, 321, 377, and 399.

[48] Korwin-Piotrowska, *Balzac et le monde slave*, 315.

[49] *Lettres à sa famille*, 482. To Sophie and Valentine Surville, from Wierzchownia, Nov. 29, 1849.

[50] See Barzun, *Berlioz and the Romantic Century*, I, 559.

[51] Berlioz, *Les Années romantiques: 1819-1842* (Paris: Calmann Lévy, 1930), 408. Sometimes, however, his manner was open to question: Berlioz described to his sister Adèle one of his singular triumphs, which occurred on November 1, 1840: "At the end of the ["Dies Irae"], my dear enemy was stupid enough to blow a whistle, for which I would have paid a thousand francs if I could have bought it. In a flash, the whole hall stood up shouting madly, my performers joined their own applause to the audience's. The women applauded with their music books, the violins and basses with their bows, the tympanists with their sticks; you can say that it was a wild success" (422).

[52] Berlioz, *A travers chants*, 27.

[53] *La Revue bleue*, May 11, 1912, 578. Letter to Victor Hugo, possibly dated Dec. 10, 1831.

[54] Berlioz, *Les Grotesques de la musique* (Paris: C. Lévy, 1871), 17-18. The statement dates from 1859.

[55] Idem.

[56] It was performed again on July 22, 1828, at the Royal School of Music.

[57] *L'Artiste*, IV, 1832, 224. Getteman ("Balzac et la musique," 202), accepts as possible the influence of the disposition of little orchestras. Guillet ("Balzac et la musique," 60, fn 1) thinks of other connections, interesting but not as acceptable: namely, that the number of singers and their placement in the six side chapels recall the subject of the novel (*Histoire des Treize*), for 6 x 6 = 12, which is close to 13, which is the name of the secret organization and (by chance?) the number of priests who have come from different parishes. The thesis is a bit too ingenious; twelve is not thirteen.

[58] See Barzun, *Berlioz and the Romantic Century*, I, 262.

[59] In a letter dated June 22, 1842, to M. Pierret. It may be found in Hanotaux and Vicaire, *La Jeunesse de Balzac*, 146 fn.

[60] Edouard Ganche, *Frédéric Chopin, sa vie et ses oeuvres: 1810-1849* (Paris: Mercure de France, 1926), 331.

[61] Hucher, "Balzac et les musiciens," 116.

[62] E, Dec. 12, 1845, III, 148.

[63] E, Mar. 23, 1836, I, 309.

[64] See Montalée, *En lisant Balzac*, 20.

Chapter IV: An Otherwise Forgotten Teacher

[1] F. J. Fétis, *Biographie universelle des musiciens*, VIII, 162. Fétis being as unreliable a biographer as a musicologist, and statements from other sources describing Strunz's activities being largely conjectures, this account of the obscure composer's life makes no claim of accuracy. Sometimes he is called a violinist, other times a flutist, a composer, or simply an arranger; sometimes he is described as polite, but more often as temperamental; sometimes he appears modest, other times immodest; for some he is a fine and talented musician, for others a mediocre bohemian. We have tried to harmonize discordant details in an attempt to recreate at least the main elements of his biography and to infuse it with some feeling of the personality that attracted and influenced Balzac.

[2] June 15, 1834.

[3] July 6, 1834. See also the previous issue of May 15.

[4] January 18, 1835.

[5] Ibid. A mistake committed by Fétis, that Strunz had become "chef du bureau de copie à l'Opéra-Comique," is sometimes cited (e.g., Guichard, *La Musique et les lettres au temps du romantisme*, 302, fn. 24 from 301). This job, less important than that of singing master, may have been held by him at an earlier time. A singing master was someone who made piano reductions of scores, examined them, and smoothed their difficulties.

[6] Idem.

[7] George Sand describes something even more fantastic in "L'Orgue du Titan," in *Contes d'une grand'mère* (Paris: Calmann-Lévy, 1876), 143-181.

[8] It was eventually sold to an American magnate for $400,000!

[9] See André Coeuroy, Introduction to *Nouvelles musicales* (Paris: Stock, 1929). The *Harmoniphon* article refers to a work Balzac may have read: Révéroni-Saint-Cyr's *Essai sur le perfectionnement des beaux-arts par les sciences exactes* (Paris: C. Pougens, 1803).

[10] May we refer to *les ondes Martenot*, used by Messaien, for one, in his *Turangalila Symphonie*?

[11] It is appropriate to note that composer Félicien David, a Saint-Simonian apostle, adopted the same subject of Moses in an oratorio symbolic of the artist-priest leading his small flock of believers across the desert toward the Holy City. A similar idea underlies his symphony *Le Désert*, which Balzac admired in 1845. And, of course, we cannot forget Vigny's poem "Moïse." Balzac's high regard for Rossini's *Mosè in Egitto*, expressed through Massimilla's panegyric, grows therefore partly in a context of symbolism and social utopianism.

[12] See E, June 16 and July 8, 1846, III, 256-257 and 305.

[13] *Correspondance*, II, 366-367, 402, and 413.

[14] Balzac was not generally deceived by brilliant performance; he was aware of the cold professionalism that often marks the great artist. Conti and Tinti show he observed the Opéra not merely from a loge but from the wings as well.

Chapter V: From Beyond the Alps and Rhein

[1] Stendhal, *Vie de Rossini* (Paris: Champion, 1923), I, chap. 7.

[2] Quoted from Gustave Chouquet, *Histoire de la musique dramatique en France* (Paris: Didot, 1875), 133.

[3] See my "Romantic Writers and Music: The Case of Mazzini," *Studies in Romanticism*, XIV, 2, 1975, 95-117, reprinted in my *Melopoiesis*, 73-93.

[4] E, Oct. 15 and 20, 1843, II, pp. 200 and 205.

[5] Bellaigue, "Silhouettes des musiciens: Balzac."

[6] Stendhal, *Vie de Rossini*, I, 222.

[7] *Correspondance avec Zulma Carraud* (Paris: Gallimard, 1935), Mar. 1, 1833, 135.

[8] We might conjecture that, had Balzac lived to hear the Prelude to Wagner's *Parsifal*, he would have detected the opposite "meaning" of the music, which abandons the human pulse in favor of a mystical vision, harmonically realized. Very German, he would have concluded. Again conjecturing, had he lived longer, his ultimate idol would have been Giuseppe Verdi.

Chapter VI: Critical Estimates

[1] Baldensperger, "Orientations étrangères chez Balzac," 221.

[2] Laubriet, *L'Intelligence de l'art*, 418. Thérèse Marix-Spire, Camille Bellaigue, and Léon Guichard also bring out Balzac's arbitrariness in such matters.

[3] *Correspondance*, 1820, 18.

[4] We should remember, however, that he liked Weber, whatever he may have heard (perhaps Liszt's and Chopin's renderings of some *Konzertstücke*). As for the operas, it is understandable that Balzac makes no reference to them. In 1824, Castil-Blaze manufactured his *Robin des bois* from *Der Freischütz*, but it was not until 1841 when Pacini and Berlioz presented a new version that the Parisian public came to know the opera. As for *Euryanthe* and *Oberon*, they received no significant performances in the capital until 1857.

[5] "Lettre sur Paris," *Le Voleur*, Jan. 10, 1831. Not in Club de l'Honnête homme ed.

[6] "Un Pensionnat de jeunes-filles," *La Mode*, Apr 2, 1830. Not in Club de l'Honnête homme ed.

[7] E, Nov. 26, 1834, I, 213. See the review in *La Revue musicale*, 1834, VIII, 380-381.

[8] E, Feb. 7, 1844, II, 302.

[9] A summary of the story of *Robert le Diable* is contained in Appendix I.

[10] Laubriet (*L'Intelligence de l'art*, 415) refers to this but states that Gambara's reversal means nothing, coming at a time when "according to those who surround him he has returned to his folly." The fact to be stressed again is that what is folly for those surrounding him is not folly for him—or ideally for Balzac.

[11] See my "Autour de Gambara: Balzac et Meyerbeer," *L'Année balzacienne 1967*, 157-163, reprinted in my *Melopoiesis* as "A Case of Literary Diplomacy," A. Veylit trans., 97-102.

[12] Berlioz, *Les Années romantiques*, from Rome, Dec. 8, 1831, 180.

[13] Nov. 29, 1831; June 1, 1835; (many in 1835, in particular see *Revue musicale*, 1831, V, 347-348); Mar. 22, 1841; May 12-18, 1864; Mar. 20, 1870; Dec. 6, 1876; Nov. 27, 1831 respectively. In the last periodical, we read the following: "*Robert le Diable*, true child of the demon, is already causing much stir in the world. . . . The plot drags a little, and sometimes it lacks clarity, but all is forgotten before the thrilling charm of the music. The score is the principal part; here there are flights of inspiration, a variety of effects, an attracting force, the source of a score of different emotions. Are you looking for new sensations, for originality? Go and listen to this score, in which art deploys its most powerful resources, in which the composer has known how to master with able hand the ways of the Italian school and those of the German, how to modernize forms and discover new colors. This long and admirable score would deserve a volume of analysis; but it is difficult to give a detailed account of it after having heard it only once. . . . Meyerbeer's style is always sustained, broad, vigorous, bold, and with unexpected effects. Science and art cannot be pushed farther." The only reproaching voice seemed to be that of Schumann, who in the Musical Gazette of Leipzig wrote that Meyerbeer's signal coat-of-arms was stupefaction and flattery, techniques that are always

successful with the masses.

[14] See *La Revue musicale*, Dec. 3, 1831. Various issues in 1835 carried similar data.

[15] L. Dauriac, *Meyerbeer* (Paris: Alcan, 1913), 191.

[16] Friedrich Schiller, *Die Räuber*, Act I, scene 2.

[17] Alfred Einstein, *Music in the Romantic Era* (New York: Norton, 1947), 263.

[18] A summary of the story of *Mosè in Egitto* is contained in Appendix I.

[19] The passage reads:

> come di voce che si raccomanda,
> d'una gente che gema di duri stenti
> e de' perduti beni si rammenti. . .

("like an imploring voice of a people moaning under harsh privations, recalling their lost happiness. . .").

[20] In his *Vie de Rossini* (I, 21), Stendhal quoted a Dr. Cotugno who claimed "that the prayer of the Hebrews . . ., with its superb modulation, had caused more than forty attacks of nervous cerebral fever or of violent convulsions among young ladies too enamoured with music."

[21] The article is initialed "B. H." (Balzac Honoré?). It would be interesting, in this case, to note that a nucleus of ideas in 1834 was merely supplemented but not changed by the tutelage of Strunz (1837-1838).

[22] *Journal* (Paris, 1932), Mar. 4, 1824, I, 58.

[23] E, Dec. 15 and 26, 1834, I, 217 and 213.

[24] Charles Baudelaire, *L'Art romantique* (Paris: Conard, 1925), 219.

[25] Leo Schrade, *Beethoven in France: The Growth of an Idea* (New Haven: Yale University Press, 1942), 22.

[26] Guichard, *La Musique et les lettres*, 329.

Chapter VII: Religious Music—An Innate Affinity

[1] Philippe Bertault, *Balzac et la musique religieuse*, whose fine analysis should dispel any notion about Balzac's insensitivity to music.

[2] See the end of chapter II, "Paris à vol d'oiseau."

[3] E, Aug. 11, 1834, I, 180.

[4] Compare this to the description in part III, chap. 2 of Chateaubriand's work.

[5] See "Des artistes penseurs et des artistes creux," *L'Artiste* (1833), V, 257.

[6] Quoted in Bertault, *Balzac et la musique religieuse*, 93.

[7] Ibid., 54-55.

[8] Taken literally, the assumption of an incompatibility between musical sensitivity and any form of agnosticism or atheism is most questionable. Less rigidly stated, however, the assumption becomes more acceptable and still remains within the framework of Balzac's beliefs as expressed variously elsewhere: namely, that those persons unendowed with sensibility, religious or otherwise, are not likely to feel music deeply. In this there is an echo of Shakespeare's *Merchant of Venice* (see Chapter XI, note 7).

[9] Letter to Laure de Surville, Apr. 19-20, 1846, *Letters to His Family*, W. S. Hastings, ed. (Princeton: Princeton University Press, 1934), 226.

[10] E, Mar. 11, 1835, I, 240.

[11] Bertault, *Balzac et la musique religieuse*, 75.

Chapter VIII: Beethoven—The Growth of a Concept

[1] From an article by one Cambini, quoted from Leo Schrade, *Beethoven in France*, 3.

[2] Date of the first performance of the Ninth Symphony in Paris. We should note that the date 1828 may be advanced to 1826, if we accept a statement in *L'Artiste* in 1834 (vol. VIII, 303) which indicates that the Société was then in its "eighth" year, and another in 1837 (vol. XIX, 322) which recalls that "eleven years

ago" the Société was derided for performing Beethoven.

[3] For example, Deschamps' epithet: "the emperor of the symphony," and Hugo's "the mystic prophet of music."

[4] *L'Artiste* (1837), XIX, 322.

[5] *La Gazette musicale*, Jan., 1837.

[6] *Mémoires d'un touriste* (Paris, n.d.), 228.

[7] See *La Revue musicale* (1828-1829), IV, 515-519.

[8] In 1846, for example, *La Revue musicale* declared plainly that it loved music provided it was of Piccinni, Sacchini, Cimarosa, Paesiello, Paër, and Rossini.

[9] *La Revue des Deux Mondes* (Paris, 1854), XXIV, 310.

[10] "Charges," in *La Caricature*, Feb. 10, 1831. He called it an "admirable symphony," but little else, describing only a silence after a climax: "There's a moment when all the instruments stop suddenly. The effect is marvelous. You have no idea, unless you've heard it: it's a crescendo, crescendo, crescendo. . . . Then all of a sudden, complete silence" (not in Club de l'Honnête homme ed.; see Conard ed., 296-297).

[11] See Georges Guéroult, *Eugène Sauzay* (Mâcon: Protat frères, n.d.), 9.

[12] E, Nov. 7-14, 1837, I, 443.

[13] The letter continues: "I am living in such solitary fashion that I don't have to tell you about life in Paris. . ." etc. (443-444).

[14] Along with opera, Beethoven served as a distraction too: "At times I am weary. I find distraction only through the most extreme resources of thought—Beethoven, the Opéra." Quoted from L.-J. Arrigon, *Balzac et la "contessa"* (Paris: Editions des Portiques, 1932?), 35.

[15] *L'Artiste* (1834), VIII, 151.

[16] E, May 10, 1834, I, 156-157.

[17] E, Mar. 30, 1834, I, 245.

[18] See Anton Schindler's references to this and similar attitudes in his *Life of Beethoven* (London: Colbrun, 1841), "Musical Observations," II, 80-162. Also *Beethoven in Paris* (Münster: Aschendorff, 1842), 5, 7, 21, 40n.

[19] Edwin Evans' translation of Berlioz (*A travers chants*), *Beethoven's Nine Symphonies Fully Described and Analyzed* (New York: Scribner, 1923-1924), 123 and 56 respectively.

[20] Quoted from Schrade, *Beethoven in France*, 45.

[21] See, for example, d'Ortigue in *La Revue musicale*, May 11, 1833, and Berlioz in *Le Rénovateur* on the Fifth Symphony on Apr. 27 and May 11, and on the Sixth Symphony on Mar. 2, 1834. As for Hoffmann, his accounts of Beethoven's works (*Beethovens Instrumental-Musik* and the five chapters in *Musikalische Schriften*) are, to be sure, rich in technical analysis. He too, however, often gets "literary" (see, for example, his thoughts on Mozart in *Don Juan*).

[22] Marie d'Agoult, *Mémoires* (Paris: C. Lévy, 1927), 92.

[23] Quoted from Schrade, *Beethoven in France*, 74.

[24] E, May 10, 1836, I, 311-312.

[25] E, Nov. 7-14, 1837, I, 443 and 447.

[26] Ibid., 448-449.

[27] Lamennais, *Esquisse d'une philosophie* (Paris: Pagnerre, 1840-46), III, 342.

[28] Ignorance or carelessness? Did he consider the Ninth a work apart, not having heard it and being aware merely of its title, "Symphony with Chorus"? Or does this represent the kind of oversight or *lapsus calami* that made him attribute his favorite romance, Cramer's "Le Songe de Rousseau," to Hérold? Both suppositions are possible. Many people were ignorant of the Ninth in Balzac's day. The mistake is explainable, if not excusable.

[29] E, Nov. 7-14, 1837, I, 443.

[30] Berlioz, *A travers chants*, 30-35.

[31] Guichard, for example, believes that the Beethoven sections only serve the function of comparisons (*La Musique et les lettres*, 312).

[32] Gautier, *Histoire de l'art dramatique en France*, Nov. 14, 1840, II, 63-64.

[33] Marix-Spire, *Les Romantiques et la musique*, 36.

[34] The last sentence is a free translation, based on Balzac's analogy in the passage with a literary technique of Sir Walter Scott.

[35] Alfred Einstein, *Music in the Romantic Era*, 33.

[36] Hoffmann, *Beethovens Instrumental-Musik*, in *Werke* (Berlin-Leipzig: Bong, n.d.), I, 48.

[37] Guichard (*La Musique et les lettres*, 106) considers 1837 a termination, and rejects Mme Amour's argument (in "Balzac et la musique") that it is a commencement, a year in which Balzac's "ignorance . . . burned to become knowledge."

[38] *Correspondance*, 343.

[39] E, Apr. 9, 1842, II, 27.

[40] In his study on Stendhal and music, Francis Claudon singles out this passage as being quite "pertinent," and we agree: *L'Idée et l'influence de la musique chez quelques romantiques français et notamment Stendhal* (Paris: Champion, 1979), 98.

[41] E, Feb. 17, 1845, III, 26.

[42] E, Sept. 6, 1845, III, 92.

[43] *L'Artiste* (1834), VIII, 151.

[44] E, Dec. 12, 1845, III, 149.

[45] Léon Emery, *Harmonies* (Lyon: Les Cahiers Libres, 1954), 90.

[46] See my "Balzac and Beethoven: The Growth of a Concept," *Modern Language Quarterly*, XV, 4, 1964, 412-424, reprinted in my *Melopoiesis*, 21-32.

[47] Marix-Spire, *Les Romantiques et la musique*, 38.

[48] E, Feb. 24, 1833, I, 13. Baldensperger also remarked on this (*Orientations étrangères chez Balzac*, 221). We know from Berlioz that there had been a fine performance of *Fidelio* in Paris in 1827, but have no indication of Balzac's having attended it.

Chapter IX: *Gambara*—Preserving Idealism

[1] Reported by Maurice Regard, "Balzac est-il l'auteur de 'Gambara'?," *Revue d'histoire littéraire*, Oct.-Dec., 1953, 498. It seems that the protagonist's name comes from Carlo Antonio Gambara, a Venetian musician born in 1774, and from Giovanni-Battista Gambaro, born in Genoa in 1775. But let us not forget Countess Clara Maffei, whose salon Balzac visited in Milan, and whose mother was Ottavia Gambara. It is a common Italian name (Stendhal records several in Brescia in 1801). The identification has, however, no significance to the story. Writing *Massimilla Doni* simultaneously, Balzac crossed titles and names several times, Gambara becoming Genovese, Marianna appearing as Massimilla Geremei, before reverting to their original forms. For a more detailed account of the genesis of *Gambara*, see the Introduction to the edition by Maurice Regard, *Gambara* (Paris: José Corti, 1964).

[2] *Correspondance*, 269-270.

[3] From Regard, "Balzac est-il l'auteur de 'Gambara'?," 502.

[4] Both because the action of *Massimilla Doni* precedes that of *Gambara* (1820 and 1831-37 respectively), and because the end of the latter relates to the former, *Massimilla Doni* should be read before *Gambara*. *L'Etrangère*, years 1837 and 1838, contains many references to the various delays which plagued the two works.

[5] "You have created GAMBARA, I have merely dressed him" (Dedication of *Gambara* [G 415]). Another possible "aide" was Vicount de Ginestet, who corrected the galley proofs of *Gambara* in 1837 (see Lovenjoul, A 314, folio 66, dated June 26, 1837).

[6] See Regard, "Balzac est-il l'auteur de 'Gambara'?." Schlesinger, whom Balzac asked to convey his message to Meyerbeer, happened to be the publisher of *Robert le Diable* and *Les Huguenots*.

[7] E, May 24, 1837, I, 398-399.

[8] Maurice-Amour, "Balzac et la musique," 94.

[9] See Pierre-Georges Castex, *Le Conte fantastique en France* (Paris: J. Corti, 1951), 54. *La Revue de Paris*, *Le Mercure du dix-neuvième siècle*, and *La Mode* all published translations of Hoffmann in 1829, as well as Loewe-Veimar's adaptations of the *Phantasiestücke* and the *Nachtstücke*. It is likely, however, that Balzac had read Hoffmann before 1828. On this, see Pierre Laubriet, *Un Catéchisme esthétique: Le Chef-d'oeuvre inconnu* (Paris: Didier, 1961), 33.

[10] E, Nov. 2, 1833, I, 72.

[11] Idem.

[12] Grétry, *Mémoires* (Brussels: L'Académie de Musique, 1829), II, VIII.

[13] Hoffmann, *Der Dichter und der Komponist*, in *Werke*, V, 121.

[14] Many of his key signatures coincide with what Grétry had noted to be their special expressive character; for example, C major: open nobility; B-flat major and F major: nobility too, but less grand than C major; G major: warrior quality; C minor: pathétique or melancholy (D minor is better for this, according to Grétry); D major: brilliance. Bach, Rameau, and Chopin (*Préludes*) would not have disagreed. A summary of the story of *Mahomet* is contained in Appendix I.

[15] Maurice-Amour criticizes Balzac for this, when, as Guichard (*La Musique et les lettres*, 328) correctly rebuts, she should have praised him for it on the grounds that Balzac's strongest affinity with Wagner lies here.

[16] Wagner first exposed the French public to his theories on September 15, 1860, in his *Lettre sur la musique* to Frédéric Villot.

[17] To Tiennet, in George Sand's *Les Maîtres Sonneurs*, Joset's inventive music, too, is ununderstandable, "bedeviled." Sand expresses beautifully the simple idea that music is a language and that a discoverable truth exists in what one hears and in what one sees.

[18] Quoted from Gustave Robert, "Balzac musicien," *L'Ermitage*, Dec., 1896, VII, no. 12, 346.

[19] James Huneker was convinced that Wagner had read *Gambara*: "Balzac the Musician," *New York Times*, Mar. 16, 1919.

[20] Olin Downes, "Balzac and Music," *Harvard Musical Review*, July 13 (no year), I, 6.

[21] Léon Emery, *Balzac en sa création* (Lyon: Les Cahiers Libres, n.d.), 59. Herbert Hunt, too (*Balzac's Comédie Humaine*, 143) subscribes to the opinion that "Balzac may have been writing with his tongue in his cheek," and finds support for it in the fact that when Gambara is drunk he is alive to the sensations and emotions to which he seems impervious when sober. This point of view, we feel, is fundamentally incorrect because it does not take into account

both the Hoffmannian background of the tale and Balzac's serious fascination with the occult. Besides, if the whole matter were a hoax, why include *Gambara* among the *contes philosophiques*? We should like to stress far more strongly than Hunt that Balzac "accorded some basic sympathy to Gambara's crazy dreams."

[22] G. de Nerval, *OEuvres* (Paris: Pléïade, 1984), I, 1193-1194.

[23] Curtius, *Balzac*, 25.

[24] Maurice Bardèche, *Balzac romancier* (Paris: Plon, 1940), 208.

[25] See Samuel Rogers, *Balzac and the Novel* (Madison: University of Wisconsin Press, 1953), 88.

[26] *Paradise Lost*, IV, vv. 121-122.

[27] E, May 24, 1837, I, 399.

[28] Quoted from Rogers, *Balzac and the Novel*, 88-89.

[29] Letter to Laure de Berny, July 30, 1822, in Hanotaux and Vicaire, *La Jeunesse de Balzac*, 217.

[30] Albert Béguin, *Balzac visionnaire* (Geneva: A. Skira, 1946), 85. See my "Gambara: The Temptation of Genius," in my *Demonic Souls: Three Essays on Balzac*, EDDA (Oslo: Universitetsvorlaget, 1964), LI, 3 & 4, 209-213 & 292-315 (223-233).

[31] Count Andrea implies to the cook Giardini that Gambara's two sides indicate that what he really seeks is infinitely greater than music itself; he calls it poetry, if by music one means what lies within human reach, and by poetry what pertains only to divinity: "That man's intelligence has two windows, one shut to the world, the other open to Heaven: the first is music, the second is poetry" (G 453). The word "poet" for Balzac meant a consummate artist, a creator of forms in any field of endeavor (see *Aux Artistes*). Andrea's use of "poetry" in no way implies a superiority of the art of versification over that of notation.

[32] Béguin, *Balzac visionnaire*, 183. Emery (*Balzac en sa création*, 59) states that in *Gambara* Balzac "lets speak . . . the Mephistophelian character he carries inside himself."

[33] Hoffmann, *Höchst zerstreute Gedanken*, in *Werke*, 46.

[34] Quoted from Hucher, "Balzac et les musiciens," 114.

[35] Mann, *Doktor Faustus* (Frankfurt am Mein: S. Fischer, 1951), 419. See also 557-558.

[36] In his Introduction to Kierkegaard's *Don Juan* (*Don Giovanni*, Milan, 1944), Remigio Cantoni concurs in the demonic essence of music: "If music as such represents the immediate and the erotic, Mozart, with his Don Giovanni, expresses the essence of music, a Dionysiac and demonic essence repellent to any logical definition and to every ethical delimitation."

[37] Quoted from Giorgio Vigolo, "Il Risveglio del Vesuvio," *Il Mondo*, July 14, 1951, II. Drawing a distinction between the mysterious factors of rhythm and sound, and the purely aesthetic nature of music, Massimo Mila, in *L'Esperienza musicale e l'estetica* (Turin: G. Einaudi, 1950), states emphatically: "Rhythm and timbre are the elements through which the magic, sorcerous character of music reveals itself, a character upon which one has much insisted and which—we repeat—we do not intend to contest in any way. But we must state precisely, without the possibility of ambiguities, that it is foreign to the aesthetic nature of music and as such is accessory, not essential. Therefore, we put aside definitely the theories of music and 'musical aesthetics' that are based on the concept of magic, like those of Combarieu" (64).

[38] How can it be said that Balzac "definitely condemns Gambara by making him fail"? Laubriet (*L'Intelligence de l'art*, 417) claims this, implying veritable disapproval on the author's part, yet makes simultaneously a reference to Balzac's "secret sympathy" for his composer. Either Balzac admired him for his idealism or rejected him for his lack of realistic proportion. The ending of the tale makes it clear that he admired him. The failure in no way suggests the author's rejection on grounds that Gambara should have limited himself, in Andrea's words, "simply to awaken sensations in us" (G 467). That he did when drunk, and his cavatinas did not make him great. Like Don Quijote's anomalies, Gambara's were excesses, but neither Cervantes nor Balzac were only "secretly" sympathetic to their characters' intentions. Cervantes may have condemned the Don's method without impugning his motivation; Balzac could not even find fault with the method, of which, on the contrary, he speaks very earnestly.

[39] Mann, *Doktor Faustus*, 156.

Chapter X: *Massimilla Doni*—Transcending Sensualism

[1] E, May 24, 1837, I, 398. The name Doni, well known in Italy, came to Balzac probably in the form of a reminiscence of Raphael's

portrait of Margherita Doni which he had seen in Milan. For a useful commentary on the main themes of *Massimilla Doni*, see the Introduction to the edition by Max Milner, *Massimilla Doni* (Paris: José Corti, 1964).

[2] E, Oct. 26, 1837 and Jan. 22, 1838, I, 437 and 458.

[3] See Ginette Fainas, "Jules Janin inspirateur de Balzac: une source inattendue de *Massimilla Doni*," *L'Année balzacienne* (Paris: Gallimard, 1961), 223-226.

[4] E, Oct. 12, 1837, I, 434.

[5] Quoted from Bouvier and Maynial, *Les Comptes dramatiques de Balzac*, 299.

[6] Gambara—not only because of his several manners, but also because of a trace of epilepsy hinted by Balzac: "The slight spew that whitened the composer's lips made Andrea tremble" (G 446). His Mohammed, we are told, was an epileptic; Memmi and Genovese show only too obviously schizoid tendencies.

[7] Hoffmann, *Werke*, X, 64-65.

[8] Hoffmann, *Johannes Kreislers Lehrbrief*, in *Werke*, I, 309.

[9] C. P. E. Bach, *Versuch über die wahre Art, das Klavier zu spielen* (Leipzig: D. F. Kahnt, 1925), I, 85, as quoted in Langer, *Philosophy in a New Key* (Cambridge: Harvard University Press, 1942), 180.

[10] Ferruccio Busoni, *Abozzo di una nuova estetica della musica*, (Trieste: Schmidl, 1907), quoted in Langer, loc. cit.

[11] E. Bullough, "'Psychical Distance' as a Factor in Art and as an Aesthetic Principle," *British Journal of Psychology*, V (1912), part II, 91.

[12] Oscar Wilde, *A Portrait of Dorian Gray*, chap. 7.

[13] Max Milner, Introduction to *Massimilla Doni*, 81.

[14] Hoffmann, *Johannes Kreislers Lehrbrief*, 310.

[15] See Hunt, *Balzac's Comédie Humaine*, 145. The essential unity of all sense perceptions was a natural corollary of Romantic thinking from its inception (Novalis, Tieck). Balzac's originality lay in expanding the area of interchange from one sensation to

another. Another surprised critic is Milner, who sees Balzac mistaking metaphor for synaesthesia (Introduction, *Massimilla Doni*, 41).

[16] Baudelaire's poem is "Correspondances," v. 8. Balzac read Hoffmann in the Loewe-Veimars translation, and in this edition (Paris: Ronduel, 1832), the reference is to *Contes et fantaisies*, XVIII, 45. Hoffmann, who saw correspondences everywhere, bought a suit he said was colored in F-flat, to which he added a D major colored collar (harmonically, a dissonant second interval). On a more serious side, he claimed that orchestration equals coloration (see 63).

[17] Hoffmann, *Johannes Kreislers Lehrbrief*, 309. See also *Höchst zerstreute Gedanken*, in *Werke*, I, 56.

[18] "Lettre à Maurice Schlesinger," May 29, 1837.

[19] Hoffmann, *Höchst zerstreute Gedanken*, 56.

[20] Laubriet, Pierre, "Influences chez Balzac," *Les Etudes balzaciennes*, N.S., 5-6, Dec., 1958, 177.

[21] The names further serve to unify the work, inasmuch as some of them are also used in describing the erotic passions of Memmi and Genovese, and provide a cultural setting for the story (the opening pages on Italian art and the Prince's galleries).

[22] Swedenborg, *Heaven and its Wonders, and Hell* (*De Coelo et Terra*, par. 89, chap. XII) (New York: Swedenborg Foundation, 1937), 65.

[23] See ibid., pars. 104, 106, 110-112, 114. See also *Arcana Coelestia*, pars. 1563, 1568, 2763, 3484, 3493, 3636, 3643, 4215, 4222-24, 4403-20, 5131, 8615, 10030, and *Angelic Wisdom*, pars. 324, 347, 377, 399.

[24] Laubriet, "Influences chez Balzac," 178 and 180.

Chapter XI: An Animating Psychology

[1] L. de Fourcand, "La Musique dans Balzac," *Universal Review*, I, May 1888, 115.

[2] See my "From the Sublime to the Subliminal: The Proust-Balzac Musical Connection," in my *Melopoiesis*, 118-132.

[3] Respectively: E, July 1 and 13, 1834, I, 168 and 170; Nov. 22, 1835 and Nov. 15, 1838, I, 281 and 501.

[4] Swedenborg, *De Coelo et ejus mirabilius*, par. 241.

[5] Barzun, *Berlioz and the Romantic Century*, I, 131. In this context, of course, the incidence of love retards or even destroys the musical career because of the impossibility of maintaining a balance between the two. But this argument, in which Balzac believed and which he related to his life and to Hoffmann's (the latter's love of Cora Hatt and Minna Doerffer), should not be confused with his equally strong belief in the psychological effect of music or any art on love and vice versa where not the great creator but merely the sensitive individual is concerned.

[6] Par. 700. See also par. 326, as well as *Apocalypsis rivelata*, pars. 276 and 792.

[7] Act V, sc. 1, ll. 83-85, 88.

[8] Par. 5807.

[9] *Revue musicale*, Feb. 25, 1832: "A musical idea is not unique: each one of us translates it for himself according to his own impressions. Once launched, it bends to everyone's will; interpreted a thousand ways by a thousand listeners, it still remains equally true, sweet for some, violent for others."

[10] Bertault, *Balzac et la musique religieuse*, 34.

[11] Pars. 903 to 907.

[12] Closely associated with music, Nature, according to the Philosophe Inconnu, had once been charged with containing and absorbing disorder (I, 133).

[13] Suzanne Langer, *Philosophy in a New Key*, 208.

[14] Charles Avison, *An Essay on Musical Expression* (London: L. Davis, 1775), 5.

[15] Eduard Hanslick, *Vom Musikalisch-Schönen* (Leipzig: Breitkopf und Härtel, 1876), 78-79.

[16] See his "Conseils aux jeunes compositeurs" in *La Musique* (Paris, 1928).

Chapter XII: A Dynamic Philosophy

[1] *Correspondance*, Nov., 1834, 210.

[2] Senancour, *Obermann* (*Troisième fragment: De l'expression romantique et du Ranz des vaches*), ed. Monglond, Arthaud (1947), II, 164. In *L'Artiste* of 1833 (199-200), Pétrus Borel expressed ideas similar to those of Balzac concerning the definiteness of architecture, sculpture, and painting, and the unseizability, nebulousness, and indefiniteness of music. Balzac certainly was not alone in his views.

[3] See note 5.

[4] Richard Wagner, "Ein glücklicher Abend," *La Gazette musicale*, nos. 56-58, 1841.

[5] While nothing points to Balzac's having read Schopenhauer, we must not forget that he associated with many Germans or with people who were versed in German thinking, above all Strunz and Liszt. For both Schopenhauer and Balzac, music differs *essentially* from the other arts. Laubriet correctly brings out the similarity (*L'Intelligence de l'art*, 410, fn. 289). Whereas other arts are mere reproductions of Ideas through particular objects (Ideas being a multiple objectification of Will, the divine essence of the world), music is a direct reproduction of this Will, having more power and penetration than the others by virtue of the fact that it expresses not the shadow of being but being itself. The same Will is objectified in Idea as in music, and despite the exterior differences between the two, some parallelism or analogy *must* exist between them. The visible world is formed of their many and imperfect phenomena. Harmony relates to the organic and inorganic worlds, melody to the moral and human worlds, as Mazzini posited. And in its continuous movement, melody represents human desire, whose realization is symbolized by its return to the fundamental tone or basic chord. To compose a melody, therefore, means to cast light on the most intimate human feelings and will. Music expresses the essence of these feelings, not the feelings themselves; the imagination gives body to the abstract sounds by relating them to forms found in the physical world. We find no arguments by which Balzac's "system" differs from that of the author of *Die Welt als Wille und Vorstellung*.

[6] Pierre-Simon Ballanche, *Du Sentiment considéré dans ses rapports avec la littérature et les arts* (Lyon-Paris, Ballanche et Barret/C. Volland, 1801), 44.

[7] The word "paints" here is not understood synaesthetically

but simply as meaning "copies."

⁸ Saint-Martin, *L'Homme de désir*, quoted from Auguste Viatte, *Les Sources occultes du romantisme* (Paris: Champion, 1928), I, 276.

⁹ See Henri Evans, *Louis Lambert et la philosophie de Balzac* (Paris: Corti, 1951), 251.

¹⁰ It is important to realize that while Balzac speaks of ideas in terms of remembrances, images, thoughts, and fixed meanings like those inherent in the literary drama of *Mahomet*, he usually uses the word in a broader sense; the "elements" do not denote but connote remembrances or thoughts through their expressive movement. Had he used "idea" in music to signify the quivalent of a pre-established verbal image, then he would have declared, like Hegel, that as a sensory projection of an idea music ranks inferior to literature. But, like Hegel, he believed music too intellectual for such a verbal function.

¹¹ It is often difficult to determine how much Balzac owed to occult speculations and how much to scientific knowledge. Hence our fascination with him, because ultimately we marvel at the one quality that made him a superior writer: his vast imagination.

¹² In *Die Natur der Harmonik und Metrik* (Leipzig: Breitkopf und Härtel, 1853) and *Aesthetik* (Leipzig: Brockhaus, 1859), respectively.

¹³ Langer, *Philosophy in a New Key*, 244.

¹⁴ Mann, *Doktor Faustus*, 291.

¹⁵ Baldensperger, *Orientations étrangères*, 225-226.

Conclusion

¹ *Revue hebdomadaire*, V, Nov., 1896, 472.

² Mann, *Doktor Faustus*, 398.

³ From Hucher, "Balzac et les musiciens," 114.

⁴ Fourcand, "La Musique dans Balzac," 114.

⁵ Mann, *Doktor Faustus*, 618.

⁶ Quoted from Getteman, "Balzac et la musique," 202.

[7] "Lettre à Maurice Schlesinger," May 29, 1837.

[8] Hofmannsthal, "L'Univers de *La Comédie humaine*," *Les Etudes balzaciennes*, N.S. I, May-June, 1951, 21-22.

[9] Maurice Regard (Introduction to *Gambara*, 505) claims Balzac made use of "large borrowings" from Fétis' *La Musique mise à la portée de tous*. On page 104 we find Gambara's idea: "Sound . . . is merely the vibration of a sonorous body transmitted and modified by air." Later we meet another of his ideas: "Music is both an art and a science." And in the *Gazette musicale* of February 25, 1832, E. F(étis) wrote that a symphony of Beethoven was "a pitched battle. The concussion of cavalry masses, cannons belching forth grape-shot, nothing was lacking . . .," in short, according to Regard, Gambara's suggestion of Beethoven's order of battle. True, but these are not "large borrowings"; they are, in fact, unimportant, even where Balzac happily improves on Fétis' concussions and grape-shots.

[10] To Charles de Bernard, *Correspondance*, Aug. 25, 1831, 91.

[11] Ballanche, *Orphée*, in *Essais de palingénésie sociale* (Paris: Didot, 1827-29), 402.

[12] Paul Edmond, "Wagner et Balzac," *L'Intermédiaire des chercheurs et des curieux*, Dec. 20-30, 1919 and Jan. 10, 1920. Edmond quotes from a report of a conversation made by Paul Flat in his *Souvenirs*.

BIBLIOGRAPHY

PRIMARY SOURCES

General Publications

    Anderson, John P. "Bibliography" (appended to Frederick Wedmore, *Life of Honoré de Balzac*). London, W. Scott, 1890.
    Cerfberr, Anatole & Christophe, Jules. *Répertoire de la Comédie humaine*. Paris, C. Lévy, 1893.
    Ducourneau, Jean; Pierrot, Roger; Rancoeur, René. "Bibliographie balzacienne." *L'Année balzacienne*, 1960 to present.
    Lotte, Fernand. *Dictionnaire biographique des personnages fictifs de La Comédie humaine*. Paris, Corti, 1952.
    Royce, William Hobart. *A Balzac Bibliography*. Chicago, Chicago Univ. Press, 1929.
    _____. *Indexes to a Balzac Bibliography*. Chicago, Chicago Univ. Press, 1929.

Complete Works of Balzac

    Michel Lévy, ed. *Oeuvres illustrées de Balzac*, 8 vols. Paris, Lévy, 1851-1852.
    _____, ed. *Oeuvres de jeunesse de Balzac*, 2 vols. Paris, Lévy, 1868.
    Marcel Bouteron, ed. *La Comédie humaine*. Paris, Gallimard, 1949-1955, 10 vols. Vol. 11 (1959) includes *Les Contes drolatiques* and other writings, among them *Le Prêtre catholique*. "Pléiade" edition.
    Conard, ed. *Oeuvres complètes de Honoré de Balzac*, 40 vols. Paris, 1912-1940.
    ***. *Oeuvres complètes de Balzac*, 24 vols. Paris, Club de l'Honnête homme, 1956.

Correspondence

M. Bouteron, ed. *Balzac et Madame de Berny: Une correspondance inédite*. Revue des Deux Mondes, May 15, 1924, 440-456.
W. S. Hastings, ed. *Balzac and Souverain: An Unpublished Correspondence*. Garden City, Doubleday, Page, 1927.
Correspondance avec Mme de Castries. Les Cahiers balzaciens, no. 6, 1928.
M. Bouteron, ed. *Correspondance avec Zulma Carraud*. Paris, Gallimard, 1951.
Correspondance, 2 vols. Paris, C. Lévy, 1876.
Correspondance. XXIV of *Oeuvres complètes*, 24 vols. Paris, M. Lévy, 1876.
M. Bouteron, ed. *Lettres à l'Etrangère*, 4 vols. Paris, C. Lévy, 1899-1950. Also: *Revue de Paris*, Nov. 1949, Aug. 1950, Aug. 1952, Sept. and Oct. 1954, Nov. 1956; *Année balzacienne* 1960; *Revue des sciences humaines*, Oct.-Dec. 1959.
W. S. Hastings, ed. *Lettres à sa famille*. Paris, A. Michel, 1950. Trans. from *Letters to his Family*, Princeton, Princeton Univ. Press, 1934.
Hanotaux, Gabriel and Vicaire, Georges. *La Jeunesse de Balzac: Balzac imprimeur; Balzac et Madame de Berny*, incl. correspondence Balzac-Mme de Berny. Paris, A. Ferroud, 1921.
Surville, Laure de. *Balzac, sa vie et ses oeuvres, d'après sa correspondance*. Paris, Librairie Nouvelle, 1858.

Special Sources

Bouteron, Marcel. *Balzaciana*, 2 vols. Paris, La Cité des livres, Lapina, 1925, 1927 (resp.).
_____. *Bibliothèque balzacienne*. Paris, La Cité des livres, 1926.
Lovenjoul, Spoelberch de: collection. A 157 (Fols. 68-92) and A 158, notes on philosophy and religion, including material for the *Contes philosophiques*.

Separate Editions

L'Eglise. J. Pommier, ed., Paris, Droz, 1947.
Falthurne. P.-G. Castex, ed., Paris, Corti, 1950.
Sténie, ou les Erreurs philosophiques. A. Prioult, ed., Paris, Jouve, 1936.
Traité de la prière. P. Bertault, ed., Paris, Boivin, 1942.

Periodicals and Reviews of the Period (as both primary and secondary sources)

    Ariel
    L'Artiste, journal de la littérature et des beaux-arts
    Bibliographie de la France
    La Caricature
    La Chronique de Paris
    Le Constitutionnel
    Le Corsaire, Journal des spectacles, de la littérature, des arts, moeurs et modes
    Le Courrier des théâtres, de la littérature, des arts, des modes
    La France musicale
    La Gazette musicale de Paris (see La Revue et gazette musicale de Paris)
    L'Intermédiaire des chercheurs et des curieux
    Le Journal des débats
    Le Journal des spectacles
    Le Ménestrel, hebdomadaire, musique et théâtres
    Le Messager de l'assemblée
    La Mode, revue des modes, galerie des moeurs, album des salons
    Le Monde
    Le Monde illustré
    Le Moniteur universel
    Le Mousquetaire
    La Nouvelle revue
    La Presse
    La Quotidienne
    La Réforme
    Le Rénovateur
    La Revue bleue
    La Revue de Paris
    La Revue des Deux Mondes
    La Revue hebdomadaire
    La Revue indépendante
    La Revue musicale (see La Revue et gazette musicale de Paris)
    La Revue et gazette musicale de Paris: M. Schlesinger, ed., represents the fusion in November, 1835, of La Revue musicale, founded by Fétis (1827-Dec., 1835) with La Gazette musicale de Paris, founded by Schlesinger in 1834.
    La Revue parisienne
    La Silhouette
    Les Tablettes de Polymnie
    Le Temps

SECONDARY SOURCES

Abraham, Pierre. *Créatures chez Balzac*. Paris, Gallimard, 1931.
Adam, Adolphe. *Souvenirs d'un musicien*. Paris, Michel Lévy, 1857.
Adamson, Donald, and Lorant, André. "L' 'Histoire de deux bassons de l'Opéra' et 'Le Cousin Pons.'" *L'Année balzacienne*, 1963, 185-194.
Adhemar, Jean. "Balzac et la peinture." *Revue des sciences humaines*, April-June, 1953, 149-162.
Agoult, Marie d'. *Autour de Mme d'Agoult et de Liszt*, Daniel Ollivier, ed. Paris, Grasset, 1941.
_____. *Correspondance de Liszt et de la comtesse d'Agoult, 1833-1840*, 2 vols. Daniel Ollivier, ed., Paris, Grasset, 1933-1934.
_____. *Mémoires, 1833-1854*. Paris, C. Lévy, 1927.
_____. "Meyerbeer." *La Presse*, Oct. 16, 1842, (n.p.).
Aldrich, Richard. *Musical Discourse*. London, Milford, Oxford Univ. Press, 1928.
Amadou, Robert. *Louis-Claude de Saint-Martin et le martinisme*. Paris, Editions du Griffon d'Or, 1946.
Année balzacienne, L'. Paris, Garnier, 1960-present.
Apponyi, Rodolphe. *Vingt-cinq ans à Paris: 1826-1850*, 4 vols. Ernest Daudet ed. Paris, Plon, 1913-1926.
Arrigon, Louis-Jules. *Les Années romantiques de Balzac*. Paris, Perrin, 1927.
_____. *Balzac et la "contessa."* Paris, Editions des Portiques, 1932(?).
Atkinson, Geoffroy. *Les Idées de Balzac d'après La Comédie Humaine*, 5 vols. Geneva: Droz, and Lille, Giard, 1949-50.
Avison, Charles. *An Essay on Musical Expression*, 3rd ed. London, L. Davis, 1775.
Bach, Carl Ph. Em. *Versuch über die wahre Art, das Klavier zu spielen*. Leipzig, C. F. Kahnt, 1925, originally in two parts, 1753 and 1762.
Baldensperger, Fernand. *Orientations étrangères chez Honoré de Balzac*. Paris, Champion, 1927.
_____. *Sensibilité musicale et romantisme*. Paris, Les Presses Françaises, 1925.
Ballanche, Pierre-Simon. *Essais de Palingénésie sociale*, 2 vols., incl. Orphée. Paris, Didot, 1827-29.
_____. *Du Sentiment considéré dans ses rapports avec la littérature et les arts*. Lyon-Paris, Ballanche and Barret/C. Volland, year IX, 1801.
Barbier, Patrick. *La Vie quotidienne à l'Opéra du temps de Balzac et Rossini, 1800-1850*. Paris, Hachette, 1987.

Bardèche, Maurice. "Autour des 'Etudes Philosophiques.'" *L'Année balzacienne*. Paris, Garnier, 1960, 109-124.
Barrault, Emile. *Aux Artistes du passé et de l'avenir des Beaux-Arts*. Paris, Mesnier, 1830.
Barrelli, E. *Estetica wagneriana*. Florence, 1940.
Barricelli, Jean-Pierre. "Autour de 'Gambara': Balzac et Meyerbeer." *L'Année balzacienne*. Paris, Garnier, 1967, 157-163. See also *Melopoiesis*, 97-102.
_____. *Demonic Souls: Three Essays on Balzac*. EDDA (Oslo), LXIV, 1964, 209-233 and 293-315.
_____. "Balzac and Beethoven: The Growth of a Concept." *Modern Language Quarterly*, XXV, 4, Dec. 1964, 412-424. See also *Melopoiesis*, 21-32.
_____. "From the Sublime to the Subliminal: The Proust-Balzac Connection." In *Melopoiesis*, 118-132.
_____. *Melopoiesis: Approaches to the Study of Literature and Music*. New York, New York University Press, 1988.
_____ and Zohn, Harry. "Music in Stefan Zweig's Last Years: Some Unpublished Letters." *The Juilliard Revue*, III, 2, 1956, 3-11. See also *Melopoiesis*, 13-20.
_____. "Romantic Writers and Music: The Case of Mazzini." *Studies in Romanticism*, XIV, 2, 1975, 95-117. See also *Melopoiesis*, 73-93.
Barzun, Jacques. *Berlioz and the Romantic Century*, 2 vols. Boston, Little, Brown and Co., 1950.
Bassanville, Comtesse de. *Les Salons d'autrefois: souvenirs intimes*, 4 vols. Paris: P. Brunet, 1862-[66?].
Baudelaire, Charles. *L'Art romantique*. Paris, Conard, 1925.
Beauquier, Charles. *Philosophie de la musique*. Paris, Germer Baillère. New York, Baillère bros., 1865.
Béguin, Albert. *Balzac visionnaire*. Geneva, A. Skira, 1946.
Bellaigue, Camille. "Balzac et la musique." *Revue des Deux Mondes*. Oct. 1, 1924, 682-697.
_____. "Silhouettes de musiciens: Balzac." *Le Temps*. Sept. 16, 1903, (n.p.).
Bergerat, Emile. *Théophile Gautier-Entretiens, souvenirs et correspondance*. Paris, G. Charpentier, 1880.
Berlioz, Hector. *Les Années romantiques, 1819-1842*, Julien Tiersot ed. Paris, C. Lévy, 1930.
_____. *A travers chants*. Paris, Michel Lévy, 1862.
_____. *Correspondance inédite, 1819-1868*, Daniel Bernard ed. Paris, C Lévy, 1878.
_____. "De l'imitation en musique." *Revue et Gazette musicale de Paris*, IV, 1837, 9-11 and 15-17.
_____. *Les Grotesques de la musique*. Paris, C. Lévy, 1871.
_____. "Lettre d'un enthousiaste sur l'état actuel de la musique en Italie." *Revue musicale*, VI, 1832, 65-68 and

73-75.

———. *Mémoires: 1803-1865*, 2 vols. Paris, C. Lévy, 1896-97.

———. *Voyage musical en Allemagne et en Italie: études sur Beethoven, Gluck et Weber: mélanges et nouvelles*, 2 vols. Paris, J. Laffitte, 1844.

Bernheim, Pauline. *Balzac und Swedenborg: Einfluss der Mystik Swedenborgs und Saint-Martins auf die Romandichtung Balzacs*. Berlin, E. Ebring, 1914.

Bertault, Philippe. *Balzac et la musique religieuse*. Paris, Naert, 1929.

Billy, André. *Vie de Balzac*, 2 vols. Paris, Flammarion, 1944.

Blaze de Bury, Henri. "Idées sur le romantisme et les romantiques." *Revue des Deux Mondes*, XLVI, July 1, 1881, 5-50.

———. *Meyerbeer et son temps*. Paris, M. Lévy, 1865.

———. *Les Musiciens contemporains*. Paris, M. Lévy, 1865.

———. "Le Poète Grillparzer et Beethoven." *Revue des Deux Mondes*, LXXIV, 1886, 337-364.

———. "Mes souvenirs de la 'Revue des Deux Mondes.'" *Revue internationale*, 1888, XVII, 5-37, 161-182, 317-341, 477-498, 629-653, 841-853; XVIII, 197-209, 322-333, 437-453.

Böhme, Jakob. *De Tribus principiis, oder Beschreibung der drei Prinzipien Göttlichen Wesens*. 1730, (n.p.).

Boigne, Charles de. *Petits mémoires de l'Opéra*. Paris, Librairie nouvelle, 1857.

Bonhoure, G. *Le Collège et le lycée de Vendôme*. Paris, Picard, 1912.

Borel, Pétrus. "Des Artistes penseurs et des artistes creux." *L'Artiste*, V, 1833, 252-254.

———. "Le Balcon de l'Opéra, par Joseph d'Ortigue." *L'Artiste*, V, 1833, 199-201.

Boschot, Adolphe. *Une vie romantique: Hector Berlioz*. Paris, Plon, 1920.

Bourgault-Ducoudray, L.-A. "Meyerbeer: Souvenirs d'autrefois." *Revue musicale*, IV, 1904, 452-455.

Bouteron, Marcel. "Balzac et le médecin de campagne." *Revue des cours et conférences*, Feb. 15, 1936, 393-410.

———. *Danse et musique romantiques*. Paris, Le Goupy, 1927.

———. "La véritable Duchesse de Langeais." *Revue des Deux Mondes*, XLVI, July 1, 1928, 164-186.

Boutet de Monvel, Etienne. *Un artiste d'autrefois: Adolphe Nourrit*. Paris, Plon, 1903.

Bouvier, René, and Maynial, eds. *Les Comptes dramatiques* de Balzac. Paris, Sorlot, 1938.

Bouyer, Raymond. *Un contemporain de Beethoven: Obermann*,

précurseur et musicien. Paris, Fischbacher, 1907. Originally in *Le Menestrel*, beginning Jan. 28, 1906.

Brancour, R. "Le Rôle social de la musique dans le saint-simonisme." *Le Ménestrel*, 88, 1926, 409-412.

Brenet, Michel. *Les Concerts en France sous l'Ancien Régime*. Paris, Fischbacher, 1900.

Breuillac, Marcel. "Hoffmann en France." *Revue d'histoire littéraire de la France*, XIII, 1906, 427-457, and XIV, 1907, 74-105.

Bullough, Edward. "'Psychical Distance' as a Factor in Art and as an Aesthetic Principle." *British Journal of Psychology*, V, part 2, 1912, 87-118.

Busoni, Ferruccio. *Abozzo di una nuova estetica della musica* [*Entwurf einer neuen Aesthetik der Tonkunst*]. Trieste, Schmidl, 1907.

Cahiers balzaciens, Les, 8 vols., Marcel Bouteron, ed. Paris, La Cité des Livres, 1923-25, 4 vols., and Lapina, 1927-28, 4 vols.

Calzabigi, Ranieri. Dedication of C. W. Gluck's *Alceste*, in Oliver Strunk, *Source Readings in Music History*. New York, Norton, 1950.

Cantoni, Remigio. Introduction to Kierkegaard's *Don Juan [Don Giovanni]*. Milan, 1944.

Carrière, Mori(t)z. *Aesthetik: die Idee des Schönen und ihre Wirklung durch Natur, Geist und Kunst*, 2 vols. Leipzig, Brockhaus, 1859.

Castex, Pierre-Georges. "Balzac et Baudelaire." *Revue des sciences humaines*, Jan.-Mar., 1958, 139-151.

_____. *Le Conte fantastique en France de Nodier à Maupassant*. Paris, J. Corti, 1951.

Castil-Blaze, F. H. J., reports on Beethoven symphonies in *Le Journal des débats*, now in J.-G. Prod'homme, *Les Symphonies de Beethoven*. Paris, 1906.

_____. *Théâtres lyriques de Paris: l'Académie impériale de musique de 1645 à 1855*, 2 vols. Paris, Castil-Blaze, 1855.

_____. *Théâtres lyriques de Paris: l'Opéra-Italien de 1548 à 1856*. Paris, Castil-Blaze, 1856.

Cellier, Alexandre. "Un chapitre musical de la Comédie Humaine." *Le Ménestrel*, Aug. 27, 1926, 369-371.

Challamel, Augustin. *Souvenirs d'un hugolâtre*. Paris, J. Levy, 1885.

Chantavoine, Jean. *Liszt*. Paris, Alcan, 1910.

Chasles, Philarète. *Mémoires*, 2nd ed., 2 vols. Paris, Charpentier, 1877.

Chauchard, Paul. *La Chimie du cerveau*. "*Que sais-je?*" *Le point des connaissances actuelles*, no. 94: Paris: Presses universitaires de France, 1943.

Chopin, Fréderic. *Lettres*. Henri Opienski, ed. New York: Knopf, 1931.
Choron, A., and Fayolle, F.. *Dictionnaire historique des musiciens*, 2 vols. Paris, Valade, 1810-11.
Chouquet, Gustave. *Histoire de la musique dramatique en France*. Paris, Didot, 1873.
Claudon, Francis. *L'Idée et l'influence de la musique chez quelques romantiques français et notamment Stendhal*. Paris, Champion, 1979.
Coeuroy, André. *Appels d'Orphée*. Paris, Editions de la Nouvelle Revue Critique, 1928.
_____. *Musique et littérature*. Paris, Bloud et Gay, 1923.
_____. "La Musique, vice littéraire." *Journal de psychologie*, XXIII, 1926, 230-238.
_____. "Gérard de Nerval critique musical." *Revue musicale*, Oct. 1, 1924, 205-218.
_____. Introduction to Hoffmann's *Nouvelles Musicales*. Paris, Stock, 1929.
Colombiani, A. *Le Nove Sinfonie di Beethoven*. Milan: Bocca, 1947.
Combarieu, Jules. *Histoire de la musique des origines à la mort de Beethoven*, 3 vols. Paris, Colin, 1913-1924.
Courrier blazacien, Le. J. A. Ducourneau and Léon Gédéon ed., 10 numbers. Jan. 1949-Dec. 1950.
Cristal, Maurice. "Madame George Sand musicienne et librettiste d'opéra." *Le Ménestrel*, 1882, 204-5, 212-3.
Curtius, Ernst Robert. *Balzac*. Bern, A. Francke, 1951.
Dandelot, A. *La Société des Concerts du Conservatoire de 1828 à 1897: les grands concerts symphoniques de Paris*. Paris, G. Havard, 1898.
D[anjou], F. "Concert donné par M. Berlioz." *Revue musicale*, Nov. 30, 1833, (n.p.).
Dauriac, Lionel. *Meyerbeer*. Paris, Alcan, 1913.
Davenson, H. *Le Livre des chansons, ou Introduction à la chanson populaire française*. Neuchâtel, Collection des Cahiers du Rhône, 1944.
Delacroix, Eugène. *Journal: 1823-1863*, 3 vols. Paris, Plon, 1932.
_____. *Oeuvres littéraires*. Paris, Crès, 1923.
Della Corte and Pannian. *Storia della Musica*, 3 vols. Turin, Unione Tipografico-Editrice Torinese, 1944.
Denis, Ferdinand. "Des origines de la musique." *L'Artiste*, VI, 1833, 306-309.
Derwent, Lord. *Rossini*. London, Duckworth, 1934.
Deschamps, Emile. "Lettres sur la musique." II, 22-42, of *Oeuvres complètes*, 6 vols. Paris, Lemerre, 1872-74.
Donnard, Jean-Hervé. "Deux aspects inconnus du saint-simonisme de Balzac." *L'Année balzacienne*. Paris, Garnier, 1961,

139-147.
Downes, Olin. "Balzac and Music." *Harvard Musical Review*, I, July, 1913, 3-6.
Dukas, Paul. "Chronique musicale." *Revue hebdomadaire*, V, Nov., 1896, 467-472.
Duprez, G.-L. *Souvenirs d'un chanteur*. Paris, C. Lévy, 1880.
Edmond, Paul. "Wagner et Balzac." *L'Intermédiaire des chercheurs et des curieux*, Dec. 20-30, 1919 and Jan. 10, 1920.
Eigeldinger, Marc. *La Philosophie de l'art chez Balzac*. Geneva, P. Cailler, 1957.
Einstein, Alfred. *Music in the Romantic Era*. New York, Norton, 1947.
Elst, J. van der. "Autour du livre mystique: Balzac et Swedenborg." *Revue de littérature comparée*, X, Jan., 1930, 88-123.
Elster, Alexander Nikolaus. *Musik und Erotik*. Bonn, A. Marcus und E. Weber, 1925.
Elwart, A. *Histoire de la Société des Concerts du Conservatoire impérial de musique*. Paris, Castel, 1860.
Emery, Léon. *Balzac en sa création*. Lyon, Les Cahiers Libres, (n.d.).
_____. *Harmonies*. Lyon, Les Cahiers Libres, 1954.
Escholier, Raymond. "Romantisme et musique: Balzac." *Les Nouvelles littéraires*, Apr. 14, 1928, 9.
Escudier, Léon. *Littérature musicale. Mes Souvenirs. Les virtuoses*. Paris, Dentu, 1868.
Escudier, Marie and Léon. *Etudes biographiques sur les chanteurs contemporains*. Paris, Tessier, 1840.
Etudes balzaciennes, Les, J. A. Ducourneau (and Léon Gédéon) ed., 4 numbers. Mar. 1951-June-Dec. 1952.
Evans, Edwin. *Beethoven's Nine Symphonies Fully Described and Analyzed*, 2 vols. New York, Scribner, 1923-24.
Evans, Henri. *Louis Lambert et la philosophie de Balzac*. Paris, Corti, 1951.
_____. Introduction to *Massimilla Doni*. Club Français du Livre, II, (n.d.).
Evans, Raymond Leslie. *Les Romantiques français et la musique*. Paris, Champion, 1934.
Fabre d'Olivet. *La Musique*. Paris, Pinasseau, 1928.
Fainas, Ginette. "Jules Janin inspirateur de Balzac: une source inattendue de *Massimilla Doni*." *L'Année balzacienne*. Paris, Garnier, 1961, 223-226.
Fayolle, F.: see Choron.
Fétis, François Joseph. *Biographie universelle des musiciens et bibliographie générale de la musique*, 8 vols. Paris, Firmin Didot, 1860-65. Supplement, A. Pougin ed., 2 vols. Paris, Firmin Didot, 1878-80.

_____. "Concert." *Gazette musicale*, Feb. 25, 1832, (n.p.).

_____. "Concert du Conservatoire." *Revue musicale*, May 29, 1830, (n.p.).

_____. "Les Derniers quatuors de Beethoven." *Revue musicale*, VII, 1830, 279-286.

_____. *La Musique mise à la portée de tout le monde. Exposé succinct de tout ce qui est nécessaire pour juger de cet art, et pour en parler sans l'avoir étudié*, 2nd ed. Paris, Paulin, 1834.

_____. "Nouvelles de Paris. Académie royale de musique. Concerts spirituels." *Revue musicale*, III, 1828, 248-255.

_____. "Nouvelles de Paris. Académie royale de musique. Première représentation d'*Eurianthe*." *Revue musicale*, V, 1831, 77-78.

_____. "Sur la philosophie et sur la poétique de la musique." *Revue musicale*, III, 1828, (n.p.).

_____. "MM. Thalberg et Liszt." *Gazette musicale*, Apr. 23, 1837, (n.p.).

Flat, Paul. *Essais sur Balzac*. Paris, Plon, 1893.

_____. *Seconds essais sur Balzac*. Paris, Plon, 1893.

Fleuriot de Langle, Paul. "Franz Liszt et Daniel Stern ou les galériens de l'amour." *Mercure de France*, Feb. 1, 1929, 513-548.

Floran, Juan. "Soirées musicales de MM. Liszt, Batta et Uhran." *Le Monde*, Feb. 5, 1837, (n.p.).

Fortoul, Hippolyte. "Dernier concert de M. Liszt." *Le Monde*, Apr. 11, 1837, (n.p.).

_____. "Dernière représentation de M. Adolphe Nourrit: Gluck, Meyerbeer." *Le Monde*, Apr. 3, 1837, (n.p.).

Fosca, François. "Les Artistes dans les romans de Balzac." *Revue critique des idées et des livres*. Mar. 1922.

Fourcand (also Fourcauld), Louis de. "La Musique dans Balzac." *Universal Review*, I, May, 1888, 111-122.

Fourcand, E. de. "Le Musicien de Balzac." *L'Echo de Paris*, Sept. 30, 1910.

Gall, Franz Josef. *Neue Entdeckungen in den Gehirn-, Schedel- und Organenlehre*, trans. into French. Paris, Nicolle, 1807.

Ganche, Edouard. *Frédéric Chopin, sa vie et ses oeuvres: 1810-1849*. Paris, Mercure de France, 1926.

Gatz, F. M. *Musik-Aesthetik*. Stuttgart, F. Encke, 1929.

Gautier, Théophile. *Les Grotesques*. Paris: M. Levy frères, 1856.

_____. *Histoire de l'art dramatique en France depuis vingt-cinq ans*, 6 vols. Paris, Magnin et Blanchard, 1858-59.

_____. *Histoire du romantisme*. Paris, Charpentier, 1874.
_____. *Honoré de Balzac, sa vie et ses oeuvres*, 2nd ed. Paris, Poulet-Malassis et de Broise, 1859.
_____. *La Musique*. Paris, Fasquelle, 1911.
_____. *Portraits contemporains*. Paris, Charpentier, 1874.
_____. *Souvenirs romantiques*. Paris, Garnier, 1929.
Gavoty, Bernard. "La Musique." *Revue de Paris*, July, 1951.
Gehring, A. *The Basis of Musical Pleasure*. New York, G. P. Putnam's Sons, 1910.
George, A.-J. *Pierre-Simon Ballanche, Precursor of Romanticism*. Syracuse, N.Y., Syracuse University Press, 1945.
Getteman, Auguste. "Balzac et la musique." *Revue musicale*, June 1, 1922, III-IV, 199-222.
Girard, Henri. *Emile Deschamps dilettante*. Paris, Champion, 1921.
Gozlan, Léon. *Balzac chez lui: souvenirs des Jardies*. Paris, M. Lévy, 1862.
_____. *Balzac en pantoufles*, 3rd. ed. Paris, M. Lévy, 1865.
_____. *Balzac intime*. Paris, Librairie illustrée, 1886.
Grétry, André E. M. *Mémoires ou essais sur la musique*, J. H. Mees, ed., 3 vols. Brussels, L'Académie de Musique, 1829.
Grove, Sir George. *Dictionary of Music and Musicians*, 5th ed. Eric Blom ed., 10 vols. London, Macmillan, 1954-61.
Guéroult, Adolphe. "Concert des Champs-Elysées." *Le Temps*, Aug. 3, 1833, (n.p.).
_____. "Concert historique donné par M. Fétis." *La Temps*, Jan. 15, 1833, (n.p.).
_____. "L'Eglise et l'Opéra." *L'Artiste*, IV, 1832, 76-79.
Guéroult, Georges. *Eugène Sauzay, 1809-1901*. Mâcon, Protat frères, (n.d.).
Guichard, Léon. *La Musique et les lettres au temps du romantisme*. Paris, Presses universitaires de France, 1955.
Guillet, ***, *Balzac et la musique* (thesis). Grenoble, Faculté des lettres, 1953.
Guyon, Bernard. *La Création littéraire chez Balzac: La genèse du Médecin de campagne*. Paris, Colin, 1947.
_____. Introduction to *Le Cousin Pons*. Club Français du Livre, X.
Hanslick, Eduard. *Vom Musikalisch-Schönen*, 5th ed. Leipzig, Breitkopf und Härtel, 1876.
Hauptmann, Moritz. *Die Natur der Harmonik und Metrik*. Leipzig, Breitkopf und Härtel, 1853.
Hervesy, André de. "Liszt et les romantiques." *Revue de Paris*,

Nov. 1, 1911, 124-148.
Hewett-Thayer, Harvey W. *Hoffmann: Author of Tales*. Princeton Univ. Press, 1948.
Hoffmann, Ernst Theodor Amadeus. *Werke*, 15 vols. Berlin-Leipzig, Bong, n.d.
Hofmannsthal, Hugo von. "L'Univers de la Comédie Humaine." A. Béguin, trans., *Les Etudes balzaciennes*, May-June, 1951, 17-29.
Hommage à Balzac. UNESCO. Paris, Mercure de France, 1950.
Huber, Kurt. *Der Ausdruck musikalischer Elementarmotive: eine experimental-psychologische Untersuchung*. Leipzig, J. A. Barth, 1923.
Hucher, Yves. "Balzac et les musiciens." *L'Information culturelle artistique*, I, 1, Sept.-Oct., 1956, 112-118.
Huneker, James C. "Balzac the Musician." *New York Times*, Mar. 16, 1919.
_____. *Melomaniacs*. New York, Scribner, 1902.
_____. *Overtones: A Book of Temperaments*. New York, Scribner, 1904.
Hugo, Victor. William Shakespeare. Paris, Flammarion, 1973.
Hunt, Herbert J. *Balzac's Comédie Humaine*. London, Athlone Press, 1959.
Jaeckel, Kurt. *Richard Wagner in der französischen Literatur*, 2 vols. Breslau, Priebatsch, 1931-32.
Janin, Jules. "Théâtre de l'Opéra." *Journal des débats*, Feb. 25, 1835, 1-2.
Jansen, Albert. *Jean-Jacques Rousseau als Musiker*. Berlin, G. Reimer, 1884.
Jullien, Adolphe. *Musique. Mélanges d'histoire et de critique musicale et dramatique*. Paris, Librairie de l'Art, 1896.
_____. *Paris dilettante au commencement du siècle*. Paris, Didot, 1884.
Kelkel, Manfred. *Naturelisme, vérisme et réalisme dans l'Opéra (1850-1900)*. Paris, Vrin, 1984.
Klein, John W. "Stendhal as Music Critic." *Musical Quarterly*, XXIX, 1943, 18-31.
Korwin-Piotrowska, Sophie de. *Balzac en Pologne*. Paris, Champion, 1933.
_____. *Balzac et le monde slave: Mme Hanska et l'oeuvre balzacienne*. Paris, Champion, 1933.
Kurth, Ernst. *Musikpsychologie*. Berlin, M. Hesse, 1931.
Laforet, Claude. *La Vie musicale au temps romantique*. Paris, Peyronnet, 1929.
Laloy, Louis. "Le Goût musical." *Revue de Paris*, Sept. 15, 1922, 428-437.
Lamartine, Alphonse de. *Cours familier de littérature*. Paris, Chez l'auteur, 1856-1863.
Lamennais, Félicité de. *De l'art et du beau*. Paris, Garnier,

(n.d.).

_____. *Esquisse d'une philosophie*, 4 vols. Paris, Pagnerre, 1840-46.

Lamm, Martin. *Swedenborg*. Paris, Stock, 1936.

Langer, Susanne K. *Philosophy in a New Key: A Study in the Symbolism of Reason, Rite, and Art*. Harvard Univ. Press, 1942. Also Mentor Books, New York, The New American Library of World Literature, 1955.

Lasserre, Pierre. *Le Romantisme français: essai sur la révolution dans les sentiments et dans les idées au XIXe siècle*. Paris, Mercure de France, 1907.

Laubriet, Pierre. *Un catéchisme esthétique: Le Chef-d'oeuvre inconnu*. Paris, Didier, 1961.

_____. "Influences chez Balzac: Swedenborg, Hoffmann." *Les Etudes balzaciennes*, Dec., 1958, 160-180.

_____. *L'Intelligence de l'art chez Balzac: d'une esthétique balzacienne*. Paris, Didier, 1961.

Lavater, Johann Casper. *Physionomische Fragmente*. Vienna, J. P. Sollinger, 1829.

Lawton, Frederick. *Balzac*. London, Richards, 1910.

Leclerc, Ed. "Une soirée chez Liszt." *Mercure de France*, June 15, 1835, 70-71.

Lecomte, Jules. *L'Italie des gens du monde. Venise: un coup d'oeil littéraire, artistique, historique, poétique et pittoresque*. Paris, H. Souverain, 1844.

Legouvé, E. "Concert de M. Liszt, à l'Opéra." *Revue et gazette musicale de Paris*, IV, 1837, 103-104.

_____. "Les Concerts de MM. Liszt, Batta et Urhan." *Revue et gazette musicale de Paris*, IV, 1837, 81-82.

_____. *Soixante ans de souvenirs*. Paris, Hetzel, 1886.

Leichtentritt, Hugo. *Music, History, and Ideas*. Cambridge, Harvard Univ. Press, 1947.

Lethève, Jacques. "Balzac et la phrénologie." *AEsculape*, Mar., 1951.

Le Yaouanc, Moïse. "La Chimie de l'intelligence d'après 'La Recherche de l'Absolu.'" *Revue d'histoire littéraire de la France*, LIII, 1953, 519-525.

Lhopital, M. *La Notion d'artiste chez George Sand*. Paris, Boivin, 1946.

Liszt, Franz. *Briefe*, La Mara, ed., 8 vols. Leipzig, Breitkopf und Härtel, 1894-1919.

_____. "Concert de M. Berlioz." *Le Monde*, Dec. 11, 1836, (n.p.).

_____. Correspondence with Countess d'Agoult: see Agoult.

_____. "De la situation des artistes et de leur condition dans la société." Ms., British Museum, Add 33965, Fol. 237-242.

_____. *Gesammelte Schriften*, L. Ramann, ed., 6 vols. in

  4. Leipzig, Breitkopf und Härtel, 1880-1883.

  _____. "Sur Paganini." *Revue et gazette musicale de Paris*, VII, 1840, 431-432.

***. *Littérature et Opéra*, P. Berthier & K. Ringger, eds. Grenoble, Presses Universitaires de Grenoble, 1987. See Pierre Michot, "Le Spectacle dans la salle" (Balzac et l'opéra), 45-54.

Lorant, André: see Adamson.

Locke, Arthur Ware. *Music and the Romantic Movement in France*. London: K. Paul, Trench, Trubner & Co.; New York: Dutton, 1920.

Lovenjoul, Spoelberch de. *Autour de Balzac*. Paris, C. Lévy, 1897.

_____. "Les 'Etudes philosophiques' de Honoré de Balzac." *Revue d'histoire littéraire de la France*, XIV, 1907, 393-441.

Mainzer, J. "Influence du chant sur l'éducation morale." *Gazette musicale de Paris*, II, 1835, 207-208.

Malvezzi, Aldobrandi. *La Principessa Cristina di Belgiojoso*, 3 vols. Milan, S. A. Fratelli, 1936-37.

Mann, Thomas. *Doktor Faustus*. Frankfurt-am-Main, S. Fischer, 1951.

Marcello, Benedetto. *Il Teatro alla Moda o sia Metodo sicuro e facile per ben comporre, ed eseguire l'Opere Italiane in Musica all'uso moderno*. Venice, Belisania per Aldiviva Licante, c. 1720.

Marix, Thérèse: see Marix-Spire.

Marix-Spire, Thérèse. "Bataille de dames: George Sand et Madame d'Agoult." *Revue des sciences humaines*, Apr.-Sept., 1951, 224-243.

_____. "George Sand: la musique naturelle et la musique populaire." *Revue musicale*, July 1, 1926, 33-45.

_____. "Histoire d'une amitié: Fr. Liszt et H. de Balzac." *Revue des études hongroises*, XII, 1934, 36-68, 323-329.

_____. *Les Romantiques et la musique: le cas George Sand, 1804-1838*. Paris, Nouvelles éditions latines, 1954.

Marpurg, F. W. *Historisch-kritische Beyträge zur Aufnahme der Musik*, 5 vols. Berlin: G. A. Lange, 1754-60.

Massias, Baron. *Rapports de la nature à l'homme et de l'homme à la nature*, 2 vols. Paris, F. Didot, 1814.

Masson, Paul-Marie. "Les Idées de Rousseau sur la musique." *Revue musicale*, VIII, 6 and 7, 1912, 1-17 and 23-32.

_____. "Lullistes et Ramistes: 1733-1752." *L'Année musicale*, I, 1911, 187-211.

Matoré, Georges. "La Notion d'art et d'artiste à l'époque romantique." *Revue des sciences humaines*, Apr.-Sept., 1951, 120-136.

Maurice-Amour, Lila. "Balzac et la musique." *Mercure de France*, Jan. 1, 1950, 84-102.

_____. "La Musique." In *Balzac: Le Livre du centenaire*, Paris, Flammarion, 1952, 195-208.

_____. "La Musique que Balzac aimait." in *Balzac et la Touraine. Rapports lus au congrès d'histoire littéraire*, Tours, Gibert-Clarey, 1950.

Maurois, André. Introduction to *César Birotteau*. Club Français du Livre, II, (n.d.).

Maynial, Ed.: see Bouvier.

Mazzini, Giuseppe, *Filosofia della Musica*. Adriano Lualdi ed., Milan, Bocca, 1943.

Mengin, Urbain. *L'Italie des romantiques*. Paris, Plon-Nourrit, 1902.

Meyer, Gilbert. Introduction to *La Duchesse de Langeais* and *Un Début dans la vie*. Paris, Nizet, 1949.

_____. *La Qualification affective dans les romans de Balzac*. Paris, Droz, 1940.

Meylan, Pierre. *Les Ecrivains et la musique*. Lausanne, Concorde, 1944.

_____. "Le Rôle joué par Rossini dans la vie de Balzac." *La Tribune de Genève*, Aug. 10, 1948.

Michaud, Régis. "Baudelaire, Balzac et les correspondances." *The Romanic Review*, XXIX, Oct., 1938, 253-261.

Mila, Massimo. *L'Esperienza musicale e l'estetica*. Turin, G. Einaudi, 1950.

Milner, Max, ed. *Massimilla Doni*. Paris, José Corti, 1964.

M[onnais], E[douard], "Honoré de Balzac." *Revue et gazette musicale de Paris*, Sept. 1, 1850, (n.p.).

_____. ***. *Revue et gazette musicale de Paris*, Nov. 20, 1836.

Montalée, Rémy. *En lisant Balzac*. Paris, Figuière, 1925.

Moore, W. G. "Vers une édition critique de 'César Birotteau.'" *Revue d'histoire littéraire de la France*, LVI, Oct.-Dec., 1956, 506-515.

Moos, Paul. *Die Philosophie der Musik*. Stuttgart, Deutsche Verlags-Anstalt, 1922.

Nerval, Gérard de. *Oeuvres*, 2 vols. Paris, Pléïade, 1984.

Nicholls, F. *The Language of Music, or, Musical Expression and Characterization*. London, Paul, Trench and Trubner, 1924.

Noli, R. *Les Romantiques français et l'Italie*. Dijon, Bernigaud et Privat, 1928.

Ortigue, Joseph-Louis d'. *Le Balcon de l'Opéra*. Paris, E. Renduel, 1833.

_____. "Etudes biographiques, I: Franz Liszt." *Gazette musicale de Paris*, II, 1835, 197-204.

_____. ***. *La Quotidienne*, Mar. 23 and Apr. 16, 1833.

_____. ***. *Revue musicale*, May 11, 1833.
Pannain: see Della Corte.
Parker, D. C. "Balzac the Musician." *Musical Quarterly*, V, April, 1919, 160-168.
Photiadès, Constantin. "Liszt et la comtesse d'Agoult." *Revue des Deux Mondes*, Mar. 1, 1933, 79-109.
Pommier, Jean. "Comment Balzac a nommé ses personnages." *Cahiers de l'Association internationale des Études françaises*, July, 1953.
_____. Introduction to *Modeste Mignon*. Club Français du Livre, VII, (n.d.).
_____. "Notes balzaciennes." *Revue des sciences humaines*, Apr.-Sept., 1951, 156-176.
Pontmartin, A. de. *Mes mémoires*, 2 vols. Paris, Dentu, 1882-86.
Portnoy, Julius. *The Philosopher and Music: A Historical Outline*. New York, The Humanities Press, 1954.
Pougin, Arthur. *Jean-Jacques Rousseau musicien*. Paris, Fischbacher, 1901.
_____. *Marie Malibran: histoire d'une cantatrice*. Paris, Plon-Nourrit, 1911.
Pourtalès, Guy de. *La Vie de Franz Liszt*. Paris, Gallimard, 1927.
Pratt, Carroll C. *The Meaning of Music*. New York-London, McGraw-Hill, 1931.
Prior, Henry. "Balzac à Turin." *Revue de Paris*, Jan. 15, 1924.
_____. "Balzac à Milan." *Revue de Paris*, July 15 and Aug. 1, 1925, 283-302 and 602-620 respectively.
_____. "Balzac à Venise." *Revue de Paris*, Dec. 1, 1927.
Prod'homme, J.-G., "Balzac et son musicien." Address made to the Société de Musicologie, Paris, Nov. 22, 1949.
_____. "Die Entdecker Beethovens in Frankreich." *Die Musik*, XIX, 1927, 400-411.
_____. "Meyerbeer à Paris avant 'Robert le Diable' (1831), d'après son journal inédit." *Mercure de France*, Apr. 15, 1936, 275-304.
_____. *Les Symphonies de Beethoven*. See Castil-Blaze.
Pugh, Anthony. "Balzac's Beethoven: A Note on *Gambara*." *Romance Notes*, VIII, 1, 1966, 1-4.
Quicherat, Louis-Marie. *Adolphe Nourrit, sa vie, son talent, son caractère, sa correspondance*, 3 vols. Paris, Hachette, 1867.
Regard, Maurice. "Balzac est-il l'auteur de 'Gambara'?" *Revue d'histoire littéraire de la France*, LV, Oct.-Dec., 1955, 6-12.
_____, ed. *Gambara*, Paris, José Corti, 1964.
Regnard, Charles. "Une erreur de Balzac." *Chronique médicale*, X, Feb. 1, 1903, 90.

Révéroni-Saint-Cyr. *Essai sur le perfectionnement des beaux-arts par les sciences exactes*. Paris, C. Pougens, 1803.
Revue des sciences humaines (see CCV, 1, 1987: "Musique et Littérature").
Ricci, Jean F.-A. *E. T. A. Hoffmann, l'homme et l'oeuvre*. Paris, Corti, 1947.
Robert, Gustave. "Balzac musicien." *L'Ermitage*, VII, Dec., 1896, 338-346.
_____. *La Musique à Paris*. Paris, Fischbacher, 1896.
Roche, M. *Balzac et le philosophe inconnu*. Tours, L'Imprimerie Gilbert-Clarey, 1951.
Rogers, Samuel. *Balzac and the Novel*. Madison, Univ. of Wisconsin Press, 1953.
Rolland, Romain. *Musiciens d'autrefois*. Paris, Hachette, (n.d.).
_____. *Musiciens d'aujourd'hui*. Paris, Hachette, 1908.
Romagnesi, Henri. *L'Art de chanter les romances, les chansonnettes, les nocturnes, et généralement toute la musique de salon, accompagné de quelques exercices de vocalisation, et suivi de dix romances pour servir d'application à la méthode*. Paris, Duverger, 1846.
_____. *Psychologie du chant: méthode abrégée de l'art de chanter contenant des exercises de vocalisation et de Mélodie de genres différents*. Paris, Duverger, 1846.
Roncaglia, G. *Rossini l'Olimpico*. Milan, Bocca, 1946.
Rouchès, Gabriel. "Le Sentiment musical chez les écrivains de 1830." *Le Courrier musical*, VII, 1904, 424-427, 441-446; "Honoré de Balzac": 636-639, 669-671; VII, 1904, "Honoré de Balzac": 5-7, 37-40.
S***. "Concert de MM. Berlioz et Liszt." *Revue et gazette musicale de Paris*, III, 1836, 464.
Sacy, S. de. Introduction to *La Duchesse de Langeais*. Club Français du Livre, II, (n.d.).
_____. Introduction to *Ursule Mirouët*. Club Français du Livre, VIII, (n.d.).
Sainte-Beuve, C.-A. *Portraits contemporains*, 3 vols. Paris, Didier, 1846.
Saint-Martin, Louis-Claude de. *Le Cocodrile*. Paris, year VII (c. 1799).
_____. "Des erreurs et de la vérité." *Journal des débats*, 14 Brumaire year XII (Nov. 6, 1803), 1-2.
_____. *L'Esprit des choses*, 2 vols. Paris, year VIII (c. 1800).
_____. *Tableau universel des rapports qui existent entre Dieu, l'homme et l'univers*. Lyon, Edimbourg, 1782.
Saint-Simon, Claude Henri de. *Selected Writings*. F. M. H. Markham, trans., Oxford, Blackwell, 1952.
Sand, George. *Contes d'une grand'mère*, 2 vols. Paris, Editions

d'Aujourd'hui, 1976.

_____. "Une correspondance inédite de G. Sand avec Balzac." *Les Nouvelles littéraires*, July 19-Aug.30, 1930, (n.p.).

_____. *Journal intime*. Paris, C. Lévy, 1926.

_____. "Lettre à Giacomo Meyerbeer." *Revue des Deux Mondes*, ser. 4, VIII, 1836, 444-462.

_____. "Lettres à Mme d'Agoult et à Liszt, 1835-1862." *La Nouvelle Revue*, X, 1881, 257-259.

Saussine, Renée de. *Paganini le magicien*. Paris, Gallimard, 1938.

Schelling, F. W. J. von. *Philosophie der Kunst*. Darmstadt, Wissenschaftliche Buchgesellschaft, 1960.

Schindler, Anton. *Biographie von Ludwig van Beethoven*, Münster, Aschendorff, 1842. Trans. *Life of Beethoven*, 2 vols. London, Colbrun, 1841.

Schlesinger, Maurice. "D'une critique musicale rétrospective et de son utilité." *Revue et gazette musicale de Paris*, III, 1836, 105-106.

Schneiderbauer, Anna Maria. *Das Element des Daemonischen in Honoré de Balzacs Comédie Humaine* (dissertation). Augsburg, Blasaditsch, 1967.

Schoen, Max. *The Effects of Music*. London, Paul, Trench and Trubner, and New York, Harcourt, Brace, 1927.

Schönherre, K. *Die Bedeutung E. T. A. Hoffmanns für die Entwicklung des musikalischen Gefühls in der französischen Romantik* (dissertation). Munich, Mundruck, 1931.

Schopenhauer, Arthur. *Schriften über Musik*. Regensburg, Bosse, c. 1922.

Schrade, Leo. *Beethoven in France: The Growth of an Idea*. New Haven, Yale University Press, 1942.

Scudo, Paul. *Critique et littérature musicales*. Paris, Amyot, 1850.

Seashore, Carl. *Psychology of Music*. New York and London, McGraw-Hill, 1938.

Séché, Léon. "Balzac et Madame de Girardin." *Mercure de France*, June 1, 1910, (n.p.).

Serval, Maurice. "Autour de Balzac: 'César Birotteau.'" *Revue d'histoire littéraire de la France*, XXXVII, Apr.-June and July-Sept., 1930, 196-226 and 368-392.

_____. "Autour d'un roman de Balzac: 'Le Lys dans la vallée." *Revue d'histoire littéraire de la France*, XXXIII, July-Sept. and Oct.-Dec., 1926, 370-389 and 565-594.

_____. "Les Sources d'un roman de Balzac: 'La Recherche de l'Absolu.'" *Revue bleue*, May 18 and ff., 1929, 303-306, 331-334.

Sjödén, K.-E. "Balzac et Swedenborg." *Cahiers de l'association internationale des études françaises*, no. 15, Mar., 1963, 295-307.
Stendhal. *Correspondance*, Henri Martineau, ed. Paris, Le Divan, 1933-1934.
_____. *Journal*. H. Debraye and L. Royer, eds., 5 vols. Paris, Champion, 1932.
_____. *Rome, Naples et Florence*. Paris, Champion, (n.d.).
_____. *Vie de Rossini. Notes d'un dilettante*, 2 vols. H. Prunières, ed., Paris, Champion, 1923.
_____. *Vies de Haydn, de Mozart et de Métastase*. D. Muller, ed., Paris, Champion, 1914.
Sucher, Paul. *Les Sources du merveilleux chez E. T. A. Hoffmann*. Paris, Alcan, 1912.
Surville, Laure de. *A une amie de province. Lettres de Laure de Surville de Balzac, 1831-1837*. A. Chancerel and J.-N. Faure-Biguet, eds., Paris, Plon, 1932.
_____. *Balzac, sa vie et ses oeuvres*. New ed., OEuvres complètes, Paris: C. Lévy, 1878, XXIV. Originally, *Balzac, sa vie et ses oeuvres d'après sa correspondance*. Paris: C. Lévy, 1858.
Swedenborg, Emanuel. *Complete Works*, 36 vols., London, Swedenborg Society British and Foreign, 1880.
_____. *Heaven and Its Wonders, and Hell*. New York, Swedenborg Foundation, 1937.
Tardel, H. *Die Sage von Robert dem Teufel*. Berlin, Duncker, 1900.
Thibert, Marguerite. *Le Rôle social de l'art d'après Saint-Simon*. Paris, Rivière, 1925.
Thomas, Ernest. "Lamartine et Mozart." *Le Guide musical*, 42nd yr., 1896, 683-686.
Thouvenin, G. "La Composition de 'La Duchesse de Langeais." *Revue d'histoire littéraire de la France*, XLVII, Oct.-Dec., 1947, 331-347.
_____. "La Genèse d'un roman de Balzac: La Recherche de l'Absolu." *Revue d'histoire littéraire de la France*, Oct.-Dec., 1911, 865-884.
Tiersot, Julien. "Balzac et la chanson populaire." *Revue des traditions populaires*, X, 1895, 334-337.
_____. *Berlioz et la société de son temps*. Paris, Hachette, 1904.
_____. *La Chanson populaire et les écrivains romantiques*. Paris, Plon, 1931.
_____. *Jean-Jacques Rousseau*. Paris, Alcan, 1912.
_____. *La Musique aux temps romantiques*. Paris, Alcan, 1930.
_____. "Victor Hugo musicien." *Revue musicale*, Sept.-Oct., 1935, 167-196.

Tild, Jean. *Gautier et Balzac*. Paris, A. Michel, 1951.
Viatte, Auguste. "Saint-Martin théosophe et théocrate." *Revue de littérature comparée*, XLVI-XLVII, 1928, 270-292. Also in 2 vols., Paris, Champion, 1931.
_____. *Les Sources occultes du romantisme*. Paris, Champion, 1931.
_____. "Les Swedenborgiens en France." *Revue de littérature comparée*, XI, July-Sept., 1931, 416-450.
Vicaire, Georges. See Hanotaux, Gabriel.
Vier, Jacques. "Comment Balzac composait un roman: l'affaire 'Béatrix.'" *L'Ecole*, Feb. 5, 1955, (n.p.).
Vigny, Alfred de. *Correspondance. Première série (1816-1835)*. F. Baldensperger, ed., Paris, Conard, 1933.
_____. "Première lettre parisienne: Moeurs et Beaux-arts." *L'Avenir*, Apr. 3, 1851, (n.p.).
Vigolo, Giorgio. "Il Risveglio del Vesuvio." *Il Mondo*, July 14, 1951, (n.p.).
Wagner, Richard. *Gesammelte Schriften und Dichtungen*, 9 vols. Leipzig, C. F. W. Siegel and R. Linnemann, 1911.
_____. "Ein glücklicher Abend." *La Gazette musicale*, nos. 56-58, 1841, (n.p.).
Werdet, Edmond. *Portrait intime de Balzac. Sa vie, son humeur et son caractère*. Paris, Dentu et Silvestre, 1859.
_____. *Souvenirs de la vie littéraire: portraits intimes*. Paris, Dentu, 1879.
Worthington, Hugh S. "The Beethoven Symphony in Balzac's 'César Birotteau.'" *Modern Language Notes*, XXXIX, Nov., 1924, 414-419.
Zohn, Harry. See Barricelli.
Zweig, Stefan. *Balzac; sein Weltbild aus den Werken*. Stuttgart, R. Lutz, 1908.
***. "Balzac et le phosphore." *La Chronique médicale*, Jan. 1, 1901, 5.
***. "Balzac et les Swedenborgiens." *L'Intermédiaire des chercheurs et des curieux*, Oct. 10-Nov.20, 1896.
***. "Les Musiciens et la romance de Modeste Mignon." *L'Amateur d'autographes*, June, 1912, 315.
***. "Honoré de Balzac." *Revue et gazette musicale*, Sept. 1, 1850, (n.p.).

DESCRIPTIVE OUTLINE OF THE CHAPTERS

Introduction (1).

1. **The Enticement of Sound.** The formative years [1799-1819] (9); First decade in Paris [1819-1829] (12); Great musical exaltations [1829-1837] (17); Years of maturation [1837-1839] (29); The final years [1839-1850] (24); Epilogue (27).

2. **Shallow Enchantments.** Paris, its organizations and salons (29); Balzac, romances, and folksongs (33); The great singers (37); Styles of singing (39); Instrumental virtuosity (43); Favored instruments (47); [Conclusion] (49).

3. **Celebrated Musician Friends.** Introduction (51); Gioacchino Rossini (51); Franz Liszt (55); Hector Berlioz (61); Frédéric Chopin (65); [Conclusion] (67).

4. **An Otherwise Forgotten Teacher.** The life of Jacques Strunz (68); The panharmonicon (72); The social mission of music (73); Musicians and society (75).

5. **From Beyond the Alps and Rhine.** Melody versus harmony (87); Italian and French music (89); The unity of melody and harmony (91).

6. **Critical Estimates.** Startling conjunctions (96); Historical lacunae (98); Balzac, Meyerbeer, and diplomacy (102); Balzac, Rossini, and adulation (109); Advice to young composers (117).

7. **Religious Music: An Innate Affinity.** Introduction (123); Early exposure to religious music (123); The sacred hymns (124); The organ (129); Mystical essences (130).

8. **Beethoven: The Growth Of a Concept.** Beethoven's reception in France (133); Beethoven's gradual ascendancy (135); Beethoven's Fifth and *César Birotteau* (138); Beethoven's presence in *Gambara* (141); Denouement of a concept (143).

9. *Gambara*: **Preserving Idealism.** Genesis of the tale (149); The Hoffmannian dimension (151); Gambara's *Mahomet* (154); Pre-Wagnerian visions (158); Demonic visions (163).

10. *Massimilla Doni*: **Transcending Sensualism.** Introduction (173); The problem of the fiasco (175); The process of synaesthesia (180).

11. **An Animating Psychology.** Music as inner force (188); Music to dream, remember, and love (190); A psyche of inwardness (199).

12. **A Dynamic Philosophy.** Introduction (203); The dualism of matter and spirit (204); Physics, metaphysics, and unity (211).

Conclusion (219).

INDEX

INDEX

Abencérages, Les (Cherubini), 31
Abrantès, Duchess Laure, 3, 15
Adam, Adolphe, 30, 67, 89, 124
Adieu (Balzac), 151
AEneid (Virgil), 108
Africaine, L' (Meyerbeer), 110
Agoult, Countess Marie, 16, 32, 55, 56, 57, 58, 124
"Agrafia" (Hoffmann), 151
"Ah, se puoi così lasciarmi" (Rossini), 111
"Air de la ballade du capitaine, L'," 35
Albéniz, Isaac, 36
Albert Savarus (Balzac), 38, 79, 80
Alceste (Gluck), 159
Alfieri, Vittorio, 178
Ambrose, St., 99
"Amours de deux bêtes, Les" (Balzac), 62, 183
"Amours forcés, Les" (Balzac), 56
Ancelot, Mme Jacques, 15
"Andiamo mio ben" (Mozart), 21, 198
Andrea del Sarto, 183
Anerio, Felice, 127, 128
Anna Bolena (Donizetti), 15, 30

Antiphonaire (St.Bernard), 99
Apocalipsis explicata (Swedenborg), 192
Apponyi, Count Antoine-Rodolphe, 16
Arcana coelestia (Swedenborg), 194
Argow le pirate (Balzac), 125, 127, 189
Armance (Stendhal), 179
Arnim, Bettina von, 59
"Art, L'" (Méry), 107
"Artushof, Der" (Hoffmann), 151
Asola, Andrea d', 128
A travers chants (Berlioz), 62
Auber, Daniel, 16, 24, 30, 34, 51, 66, 67, 89, 90, 101, 107, 115
Auberge rouge, L' (Balzac), 151
Augustine, St., 42, 216
"Automate, Die" (Hoffmann), 72, 154
Aux Artistes: Du présent et de l'avenir des beaux-arts (Barrault), 73, 74
"Ave Maria" (Schubert), 31
"Ave Maria" (Verdi), 93
Aventures du dernier Abencérage, Les (Chateaubriand), 31
Avison, Charles, 200

Baader, Francis Xavier de, 177
Bach, Johann Sebastian, 31, 42, 44, 55, 66, 90, 98, 107, 168
Bach, Karl Philipp Emanuel, 179
Baillot, Pierre Marie, 44
Baldensperger, Fernand, 3, 14, 96, 216
Bal de Sceaux, Le, (Balzac), 21, 193-194
Baldi (singer), 37
Ballanche, Pierre, 55, 73, 164, 210, 223
Balocchi (librettist), 110
Balzac, Bernard-François, 9, 11
Balzac, Laure [see Surville]
Balzac, Laurence, 11
Balzac, Mme [see Sallambier]
Barbiere di Siviglia, Il, (Rossini), 21, 30, 54, 100, 109, 189, 191
Bardèche, Maurice, 164
Bardes, Les (Lesueur), 30
Barilli, Luigi, 37
Barrault, Emile, 73
Barrès, Maurice, 127
Baron von B., Der (Hoffmann), 152
Batta, Alexandre, 44
Battle of Vittoria, The (Beethoven) [see *Battle Symphony*]
Battle Symphony (Beethoven), 72
Baudelaire, Charles, 25, 117, 172, 181, 187, 223
Béatrix (Balzac), 14, 24, 38, 45, 46, 56, 57, 58, 75-76, 79, 100, 101, 109, 125, 175, 190, 192, 193, 194, 196, 201, 203, 204, 209
Beaumarchais, Pierre-Augustin Caron de, 36
Beauplan, Amédée de, 32, 33

Beethoven, Ludwig van, 2, 10, 13, 17, 21, 22, 24, 25, 26, 27, 31, 42, 44, 45, 46, 48, 49, 55, 56, 60, 61, 64, 67, 72, 73, 81, 87, 89, 90, 91, 92, 96, 100, 101, 102, 103, 105, 107, 108, 109, 112, 113, 115, 118, 123, 131, 142, 150, 160, 161, 162, 182, 185, 187, 192, 193, 195, 198, 199, 201, 202, 204, 206, 207, 210, 213, 215, 217, 219, 220, 221
Begnio (singer), 37
Béguin, Albert, 166
Belgiojoso, Princess Cristina [Trivulzio], 15, 59
Bellaigue, Camille, 3, 90
Bellini, Giovanni, 183
Bellini, Vincenzo, 17, 30, 31, 38, 66
Belloy, Marquis Auguste de, 67, 149, 151
Benevoli, Orazio, 127
Benvenuto Cellini (Berlioz), 61
Béranger, Pierre-Jean de, 37
"Berceuse" (Chopin), 66
Berg, Alban, 160
Bériot, Charles-Auguste de, 44
Berlioz, Hector, 16, 22, 24, 25, 29, 31, 32, 34, 37, 40, 42, 44, 48, 50, 51, 55, 60, 61-65, 66, 67, 68, 73, 77, 87, 88, 89, 101, 105, 106, 114, 128, 132, 151, 158, 159, 161, 162, 164, 168, 183, 192, 222
Berlioz (père), Dr., 63
Bernard de Clairvaux, St., 99
Berny, Emma de, 14
Berny, Emmanuelle de, 14
Berny, Laure de, 14, 223

Bertault, Fr. Philippe, 10, 98, 117, 125, 126, 128, 130, 132, 198
Berthoud, Samuel-Henri, 16
Bertini, Jérôme-Henri, 31
Beschreibung der drei Prinzipien göttlichen Wesens (Böhme), 165
Bettina (Bettina von Arnim), 60
Bettina von Arnim, 60
Blanche de Provence (Cherubini), 31
Blangini, Giuseppe, 31, 32
Blasio (singer), 37
Blaze de Bury, Ange-Henri, 39, 50, 222
Boeufs, Les (singer), 26
Bohain (Director of *L'Encyclopédie Littéraire*), 53, 150
Bohème galante, La (Nerval), 35
Böhme, Jakob, 165
Boieldieu, François-Adrien, 13, 30, 89, 100
Boïto, Arrigo, 106
Bonald, Vicount Louis de, 36
Bordogni (singer), 37, 49
Borel, Pétrus, 87, 129
Boschi (singer), 37
Bossuet, Jacques-Bénigne, 130
Bouffarelli (Strunz), 69
Bourget, Paul, 117
Brahms, Johannes, 223
Brod, Henri, 44
Brunswick, Duke Karl-Friedrich, 19
Buisson (jeweler), 18
Bullough, Edward, 179
Burgess, Anthony, 203
Busoni, Ferruccio, 179
Buxtehude, Dietrich, 98
Byron, George Gordon Lord, 12, 60, 96, 97

Cabinet des antiques, Le (Balzac), 21, 97, 100, 193
Calife de Bagdad, Le (Boieldieu), 100
"Calunnia, La" (Rossini), 54, 109
Calzabigi (musicologist), 159
Cambiale di matrimonio, La (Rossini), 54
Carissimi, Giacomo, 98
Carlone, Giovanni Battista, 75
Carpentier, Alejo, 203
Carraud, Zulma, 17, 27, 93
Carrière, Moritz, 216
Castel, Fr. Louis-Bertrand, 48, 73, 182
Castil-Blaze (François-Blaze), 13, 100, 222
Castries, Duchess Henriette Claudine de, 15, 16, 51, 129
Catalani, Angela, 46
Cavalli, Pietro Francesco, 98
Cazaux (singer), 37
Celano, Tommaso di, 128
"Celeste man placata" (Rossini), 111
Cenerentola, La (Rossini), 25
Cervantes, Miguel de, 152
"C'est la faute à Voltaire, c'est la faute à Rousseau" (Béranger), 37
Challamel, Augustin, 55
"Chanson de la mariée, La," 35
Chansonnier des Grâces (Strunz), 76
"Chant d'une jeune-fille" (Auber-Balzac), 31-32
Chardin, Pierre, 25
Chateaubriand, Vicount René de, 1, 15, 32, 34, 59, 60, 99, 125, 126
Chef-d'oeuvre inconnu, Le (Balzac), 3, 21, 150, 151, 163, 205, 208, 210
Chélard, Hippolyte, 32
Cherubini, Luigi, 13, 31, 67

Chopin, Frédéric, 16, 25, 26, 32, 33, 44, 45, 46, 47, 48, 49, 51, 65-66, 68, 81, 101, 106, 123, 201, 223
Choron, Alexandre-Etienne, 98, 124
Chouans, Les (Balzac), 15, 16, 35, 47, 125
Cimarosa, Domenico, 13, 30, 40, 87, 100, 101, 115, 193, 194, 198
Cinti (Cinthie Montalant), 37
Ciro di Babilonia (Rossini), 194
"Code des gens honnêtes" (Balzac), 53
Collé, Charles, 13
Colonnel Chabert, Le (Balzac), 21
Combarieu, Jules, 32
Comédie du Diable, La (Balzac), 14, 125, 151
Comédiens sans le savoir, Les (Balzac), 40, 109
Confessions of an Opium Eater (De Quincey), 180
Constant, Benjamin, 15
Consuelo (Sand), 40, 165, 190
Contrat de mariage, Le (Balzac), 54
Copland, Aaron, 36
Coradori (singer), 37
Corbet (critic), 123
Corneille, Pierre, 13
Corsair, The (Byron), 12
Courses de New-Market, Les (Strunz), 69
Cousine Bette, La (Balzac), 38, 46, 47, 80, 109, 117, 164, 165
Cousin Pons, Le (Balzac), 24, 76, 77, 79, 80, 101, 129, 131, 152, 174, 190, 198, 203
Cramer, Johann-B., 11, 12, 33, 101, 196
Crescentini, Girolamo, 99

Croce, Benedetto, 201
Cromwell (Balzac), 13
Curé de village, Le (Balzac), 125
Curtius, Ernst Robert, 3, 164
Cuzzoni, Francesca, 37
Czartoryska, Princess Marie, 15

"Dal tuo stellato soglio" (Rossini), 10, 43, 92, 93, 113, 115, 123
Dalvimare (composer), 32
Dame blanche, La (Boieldieu), 100, 108
Damnation de Faust, La (Berlioz), 61
D'Annunzio, Gabriele, 189, 203
Danrémont, Count/Gen. Charles de, 64
Dante Alighieri, 45, 83, 90, 132, 165, 180, 222
Dante Sympyony (Liszt), 60
Darwin, Charles, 36, 77
d'Aurevilly, Barbey, 26-27
David, Félicien, 27, 101, 156
Debussy, Claude, 3, 73, 160, 162
Début dans la vie, Un (Balzac), 37
Decazes, Duke Elie, 15
De commercio animae et corporis (Swedenborg), 207
Delacroix, Eugène, 29, 65, 115
Delavigne, Casimir, 107
Delloye (editor and publisher), 150
Delphine (de Staël), 34
"De profundis," 125, 192
Député d'Arcis, Le (Balzac), 38, 79, 80
De Quincey, Thomas, 180
"Dernière pensée de Weber, La" (Strunz), 33, 69
"Des Artistes" (Balzac), 72-

73, 81-82, 89, 118, 166-167, 173
Descartes, René, 212
Deschamps, Emile, 49, 65, 87, 101
"Des chevaliers de ma patrie" (Meyerbeer), 105
Désert, Le (David), 27, 100, 156
Dessaignes, Victor, 177
Destouches (Philippe Néricault), 13
Destutt de Tracy, 13
Deux musiciens, Les [*Le Cousin Pons*] (Balzac), 76
"Deux rêves, Les" (Balzac), 151
Diarium spirituale (Swedenborg), 198
Dichter und der Komponist, Der (Hoffmann), 152, 154
Dickens, Charles, 11, 184
Dictionnaire historique des musiciens (Choron), 98
Diderot, Denis, 2, 24, 87, 152, 153, 159, 170, 177, 179, 220
"Dies Irae," 64, 99, 125, 127, 128, 129
Dieu (Hugo), 162
Dinorah (Meyerbeer), 110
Divina Commedia, La (Dante), 132
Doctor Faustus (Mann), 169, 220
Dolci, Carlo, 183
d'Olivet, Fabre, 201
Don Giovanni (Mozart), 19, 30, 88, 93, 97, 100, 103, 106, 112, 116, 161, 167, 193
Donizetti, Gaetano, 17, 30, 31, 40
Don Juan (Hoffmann), 152, 154
Don Juan (Kierkegaard), 169
Don Juan (Molière), 97

Donna del lago, La (Donizetti), 28
Don Quijote de la Mancha (Cervantes), 172
"Dormez, dormez, mes chères amours" (Beauplan), 33
Dorus (Vincent-Joseph van Steenkiste), 44
Dostoievsky, Fyodor, 172
Dotti (singer), 37
"Dov'è mai quel core amante" (Rossini), 111
Downes, Olin, 163
Drame au bord de la mer, Un (Balzac), 21, 100, 198, 161, 167, 193
Duchambge, Dame Antoinette Pauline de Montet, 32
Duchesse de Langeais, La (Balzac), 2, 14, 21, 33, 48-49, 58, 64, 92, 99, 110, 123, 125-126, 130, 189-190, 192, 194-195, 201, 213
"Dunque il mio bene tu mia sarai" (Zingarelli), 101
Duprez, Gilbert-Louis, 37, 190
Duras, Duchess Claire de, 15
Dvořák, Antonin, 36

"Ein bel endroi de sainé," 36
Elixiere des Teufels, Die (Hoffmann), 151
Elixir de longue vie, L' (Balzac), 21, 125, 126-127 151
Emery, Léon, 164
Employés, Les (Balzac), 152
Enfance du Christ, L' (Berlioz), 158
Enfant maudit, L' (Balzac), 99, 125, 131, 152, 192, 195, 197
English Suites (Bach), 42
Envers de l'histoire contemporaine, L'

(Balzac), 36
Erard, Sébastien, 16, 17, 22, 24, 25, 55
"Erlkönig, Der" (Schubert), 56
Ernani (Gabussi), 101
Esprit des choses, L' (Saint-Martin), 199
Esquisse d'une philosophie (Lamennais), 99
Essais (Grétry), 189
Essais de palingénésie sociale (Ballanche), 211
Etoile du nord, L' (Meyerbeer), 110
Eugénie Grandet (Balzac), 125, 131
Euripides, 90
Euryanthe (Weber), 70, 106

Facino Cane (Balzac), 21, 38, 79, 83, 109, 115, 125
Faguet, Emile, 33
Falcon, Marie-Cornélia, 37
"Fantasia" XVIII (Mozart), 104
"Fantaisie-impromptu" (Chopin), 67
Fantasiestücke (Hoffmann), 152
Fantasio (Musset), 68
Farinelli (Carlo Broschi), 13, 46, 82
Fausse maîtresse, La (Balzac), 100, 125
Faust (Goethe), 97 171
Faust (Gounod), 106
Faustina (singer), 37
Faust Symphony (Liszt), 60
Fay, Léontine, 55
Federici, Vincenzo, 13
Femme de trente ans, La (Balzac), 126, 196
"Fermate, Die" (Hoffmann), 152
Ferragus (Balzac), 1, 61, 63, 64, 99, 123, 125, 127-128, 184
Fétis, François-Joseph, 16, 17, 22, 24, 25, 29, 44, 55, 65, 68, 70, 98, 158, 197, 222
Feuilletons de journal politique (Balzac), 212
Fidelio (Beethoven), 19, 46, 70, 112
Fille aux yeux d'or, La (Balzac), 83, 190
Fille d'Eve, Une (Balzac), 76, 78, 81, 95, 152, 198
Filles du feu, Les (Nerval), 35
Filosofia della musica (Mazzini), 74, 88
Fin de Satan, La (Hugo), 162
Fioravanti, Valentino, 31, 131
Flaubert, Gustave, 130
Fleur des pois [*Le Contrat de mariage*] (Balzac), 54
Fleurs du mal, Les (Baudelaire), 181
"Fleuve du Tage" (Pollet), 33, 194, 195
Florine (singer), 37, 38
Flotow, Count Friedrich von, 31
Flourens, Pierre, 212
Fodor, Joséphine, 37, 38, 39, 81
Forza del destino, La (Verdi), 93
Fourcand, Louis de, 2, 221
Fourier, Charles, 73
Fra Diavolo (Auber), 19, 90, 100
Franchomme, Auguste-Joseph, 44, 65, 106
Franck, César, 124
Freischütz, Der (Weber), 69

Gabrielli (Janin), 174
Gabussi, Vincenzo, 31, 101
Galériens, Les [*Béatrix*]

(Balzac), 56
Gall, François Joseph, 215
Gallay (musician), 46
Galli (singer), 37
"Gallop chromatique" (Liszt), 44
Galuppi, Baldassare, 52
Gambara (Balzac), 2, 3, 4, 13, 19, 22, 23, 24, 60, 64, 65, 66, 67, 70, 72, 73, 74, 79, 80, 87, 88, 89, 90-91, 93, 94, 96, 97, 98, 100, 102-109, 117, 118, 125, 131, 132, 149-172, 173, 176, 177, 185-186, 188-189, 199, 203, 205, 207, 209, 210, 212, 213, 214
Gardano, Antonio (Gardane), 127
Gautier, Judith, 223
Gautier, Théophile, 2, 3, 11, 18, 40, 44, 52, 65, 87, 88, 205
Gavoty, Bernard, 3
Gay, Delphine, 15
Gay, Sophie, 15
Gazza ladra, La (Rossini), 16, 19, 30, 52
"Gelübde, Das" (Hoffmann), 151
Génie du Christianisme, Le (Chateaubriand), 99, 126
Gérard, Baron François, 16, 26, 37, 55
Gespräche mit Eckermann (Goethe), 168
Gettemann, Auguste, 3
Gide, André, 184
Girardin, Delphine de, 16, 31, 49, 55
Giotto (Angiolotto di Bondone), 48, 96, 97, 183
Giusti, Giuseppe, 114
"Gloire à la Providence" (Meyerbeer), 106

"Gloria in excelsis," 124
Gluck, Christoph Willibald, 31, 81, 88, 89, 96, 97, 99, 100, 104, 109, 110, 115, 152, 153, 155, 159, 182, 190
Goethe, Johann Wolfgang, 60, 168, 170, 171
Gosslin, Charles, 16
Götterdämmerung (Wagner), 156, 161, 162
Gounod, Charles, 106
"Grâce pour toi" (Meyerbeer), 106, 193
Gradual (St. Bernard), 99
"Grand Duo for Piano and 'Cello" (Chopin-Franchomme), 106
Grassini (singer), 15, 37
Graziani (singer), 37
Gregorian chant, 42, 98, 99, 118, 124, 221
Gregory I (pope), St., 99
Grétry, André, 13, 21, 42, 96, 97, 98, 154, 159, 189, 193
Greuze, Jean-Baptiste, 25
Grieg, Edvard, 36
Grillparzer, Franz, 65
Grimm, Baron Friedrich Melchior von, 87
Grisar (composer), 32
Grisi, Giuditta, 37
Grisi, Giulia, 16, 17, 32, 37, 38
Guichard, Léon, 118
Guidoboni-Visconti, signora (Sarah Lowell), 16, 20, 57
Guglielmi, Pietro, 13, 131
Guglielmo Tell (Rossini), 19, 20, 31, 38, 45, 52, 69, 80

Habeneck, François Antoine, 22, 24, 25, 26, 31, 50, 67
Halévy, Jacques-Fromental-

Elie, 30, 32, 66, 67, 89
Handel, Georg Friedrich, 31, 90, 99, 108, 124, 127
Hanska, Anna de, 26, 27, 58, 59
Hanska, Countess Eveline, 18, 19, 20, 23, 24, 25, 26, 27, 28, 38, 52, 53, 56, 57, 58, 59, 60, 61, 80, 116, 131, 151, 173, 190, 207
Hanski, Count Wenceslas, 52, 58, 67
Hanslick, Edvard, 201
Harold en Italie (Berlioz), 65, 161
Hauptmann, Moritz, 216
Haydn, Franz Joseph, 27, 31, 92, 99, 100, 152, 182, 185, 198
Hegel, Georg Wilhelm Friedrich, 170, 172, 213
Heine, Heinrich, 44
Henry IV, King of France, 99
Hérold, Louis, 27, 30, 67, 77, 89, 101, 131
Herschell, John, 182, 212
Herz, Heinrich, 44
Histoire de la grandeur et de la décadence de César Birotteau (Balzac), 22, 25, 33, 55, 79, 193, 213, 219
Histoire des Treize (Balzac), 49
Historisch-Kritische Beiträge zur Aufnahme der Musik (Marpurg), 201
Höchst zerstreute Dedanken (Hoffmann), 152, 167
Hoffmann, Ernst Theodor Amadeus, 2, 40, 72, 108, 149, 151-154, 158, 163, 164, 167, 168, 169, 177, 178, 181, 182, 183, 184, 186, 187, 206, 209, 210, 215, 220, 223
Hofmannsthal, Hugo von, 222
Holbach, Baron Paul-Henri d', 87
Homer, 96, 97, 110, 223
Homme d'affaires, Un (Balzac), 66
Honorine (Balzac), 23, 53
Horace, 164
Hortense de Beaumarchais, Queen of Holland, 32
Hucher, Yves, 67, 220
Huerta (musician), 46
Hugo, Victor, 29, 32, 33, 48, 49, 51, 59, 61, 73, 98, 100, 125, 129, 162
Huguenots, Les (Meyerbeer), 19, 110
Hummel, Johann N., 31, 198
Hunt, Herbert, 3
Huyghens, Christian, 212

Iliad (Homer), 97
Illusions perdues, Les (Balzac), 30, 34, 37, 76, 79, 81, 99, 164
"Il mio cor si divide" (Rossini), 101, 196
"In exitu," 125
"In manus," 125
"In Paradisium," 129
Israélite, L' (Balzac), 100, 125
Isouard, Nicolas [Nicolo], 30
Italiana in Algeri, L' (Rossini), 30
Italian Classical School, 2

"J'ai longtemps parcouru le monde" (Grétry), 36-37
Jane la Pâle (Balzac), 14, 81, 193, 213
Janin, Jules, 174
Jean de Paris (Boieldieu), 30
Jean Sgobar (Nerval), 195
"Je lui dus la victoire et perdis le bonheur"

(Meyerbeer), 104
"Je me suis engagé—pour l'amour d'une brune" (Mürger), 35
"Jesuiterkirche, Die" (Hoffmann), 154, 310
Jésus-Christ en Flandre (Balzac), 14, 48, 99, 125, 151-152, 211
Joconde (Isouard), 30
Johannes Kreislers Lehrbrief (Hoffmann), 178, 182, 209
Joseph (Méhul), 30
Josquin des Prés, 98
Journal (Stendhal), 189
Jouy, Victor Joseph Etienne de, 13, 110

Labarre, Théodore, 32
Lablache, Luigi, 15, 37, 38
Laloy, Louis, 3
Lamartine, Alfonse de, 32, 33, 52, 54, 59, 130
Lamennais, Félicité de, 60 74, 87, 99, 123, 199, 130
Lasso, Orlando di (Roland Delattre), 98
Latour-Mézeray (writer), 53
Laubriet, Pierre, 1, 3, 96, 187
"Lauda Sion," 125, 127
Lavater, Jean-Gaspard, 193, 215
Lecou (editor), 150
Lefèbvre, Fr., 11
Légende des siècles, La (Hugo), 162
Leibniz, Gottfried Wilhelm, 168
Lejay, Sulpice-Philippe, 124
Leonardo da Vinci, 183
Leopardi, Giacomo, 127, 202
Lesueur, Jean-François, 30, 88
'Lettre aux écrivains français" (Balzac), 99

"Lettre sur Kiev" (Balzac), 60, 62
Levasseur, Nicolas-Prosper, 37
"Libera me," 125
Lieder (Schubert), 33, 56
Lind, Jenny, 37, 39
Lipinski, Karl Josef, 34
Liszt, Franz, 16, 22, 24, 25, 31, 32, 33, 34, 43-44, 45, 46, 47, 49, 51, 55-60, 61, 62, 64, 66, 67, 68, 73, 75, 81, 101, 106, 124, 129, 132, 155, 158, 161, 201, 223
Locke, John, 184
Lombardi, I (Verdi), 175
Lope de Vega Carpio, Feliz, 190
Louis XIV, King of France, 87
Louis Lambert (Balzac), 10, 81, 150, 159, 163, 172, 182, 185, 204, 212, 213, 216
Louis-Philippe, King of France, 107
Lovenjoul, Count Spoelberch de, 56
Lucia di Lammermoor (Donizetti), 30, 40, 42
Lulli, Giambattista, 31, 87, 89, 98, 100
Lys dans la vallée, Le (Balzac), 1, 14, 21, 48, 59, 125, 126, 129, 204

Machiavelli, Niccolò, 3, 176
Madame Firmiani (Balzac), 14
Maelzel, Johann Nepomuk, 72
Maffei, Countess Clara, 16
"Ma Franchette est charmante dans sa simplicité," 33
Magdale, Lady, 128
"Magnificat," 1, 125, 130, 194, 195
Maillart, Louis [Aimé], 30
Maison Nucingen, La (Balzac), 54, 100, 109

Maître Cornélius (Balzac), 19, 36, 125
Maître de chapelle, Le (S. Gay), 15
Maîtres sonneurs, Les (Sand), 165, 195
"Malbrough s'en va-t-en guerre" [John Churchill, Duke of Marlborough], 36
Malibran (Dame María-Felícia-García), 17, 27, 37, 38, 39, 50, 81
Mandragola, La (Machiavelli), 176
Manfred (Byron), 97
Mann, Thomas, 28, 169, 171, 203, 216, 220
Manzoni, Alessandro, 223
Marcello, Benedetto, 48, 87, 90, 96, 97
Marie-Antoinette, Queen of France, 14
Marino Faliero (Delavigne), 30
Mario, Giuseppe (Count of Candia), 37
Marix-Spire, Thérèse, 3, 57
Martini (Johann Schwarzendorf), 88
Marpurg, Friedrich Wilhelm, 201
Marx, Karl, 172
Masini (composer), 32
Massé, Félix-Marie (Victor), 30
Massimilla Doni (Balzac), 2, 3, 4, 19, 22, 23, 24, 36, 38, 40-41, 42-43, 45, 46, 47, 48, 54, 70, 71, 74, 79, 80, 87, 88, 89, 90, 91, 92-93, 94, 96, 100, 102, 109, 110-115, 116, 117, 118, 125, 131, 149, 150, 159, 161, 169, 173-187, 189, 190, 191, 192, 196, 199, 200, 202, 203, 204, 205, 206, 207, 208, 209, 210, 212, 213, 214, 215
Matrimonio segreto, Il (Cimarosa), 30, 40, 42, 101
Maurice-Amour, Lola, 3
Mazzini, Giuseppe, 2, 74, 88, 89, 90, 92, 93, 115, 162, 208, 209
Medea (Euripides), 90
Médecin de campagne, Le (Balzac), 37, 63, 129, 131
Mefistofele (Boïto), 106
Meifred (composer), 31
Meistersinger von Nürenberg, Die (Wagner), 223
Melmoth réconcilié (Balzac), 64, 123, 125, 128, 129, 171, 198
Mémoires (Berlioz), 62
Mémoires (d'Agoult), 124
Mémoires de deux jeunes mariées (Balzac), 1, 196, 197
Mendelssohn, Felix, 31, 34, 39, 66
Mercadante, Giuseppe Valerio Raffaele, 67
Méhul, Etienne-Nicolas, 30, 31, 88
Merchant of Venice, The (Shakespeare), 193
Mérimée, Prosper, 49, 53, 87, 91
Merlin, Countess (María de las Mercedes de Jaruco), 15, 55
Merkwürdige musikalische Leben des Tonkünstlers Joseph Berglinger, Das (Wackenroder), 153
Méry, Joseph, 107
Mesmer, Friedrich Anton, 96, 97, 223
Messe de l'athée, La (Balzac), 21

Messe de Sacre (Cherubini), 31
Messe solennelle (Berlioz), 64
Messe solennelle (Strunz), 69
Meyerbeer, Giacomo, 2, 13, 16, 23, 24, 30, 31, 39, 65, 66, 67, 68, 75, 88, 93, 94, 96, 97, 100, 102-109, 110, 114, 149, 162, 163, 167
Michaut (singer), 37
Michelangelo Buonarroti, 46, 48, 169
Michelet, Jules, 36
Mickiewicz, Adam, 65
Midsummer's Night's Dream, A (Shakespeare), 90
Milner, Max, 3
Milton, John, 165
"Mi manca la voce" (Rossini), 79, 112
Miroir, Eloi-Nicolas-Marie, 79
Miroir, François-Marie, 79
"Miserere nobis" (Fioravanti), 131
"Miserere nobis" (Guglielmi), 131
Modeste Mignon (Balzac), 24, 33, 34, 35, 38, 46, 59, 67, 74, 79, 95, 100, 101, 109, 115, 168, 169, 192, 198
Mohammed, 10
Molière (Jean-Baptiste Poquelin), 13, 20, 96, 97
Monpou, Hippolyte, 31
Monsigny, Pierre Alexandre, 98
Montet, Pauline de, 32
Monteverdi, Claudio, 160
Moreau (decorator), 53
Moschelès, Ignaz, 46, 81
Mosè in Egitto (Rossini), 10, 19, 23, 30, 43, 52, 74, 90, 92, 93, 110, 117, 123, 149, 158, 173, 174, 175, 181, 183, 186, 197, 201
Moses, 89
Moussorgsky, Modest Petrovich, 160
Mozart, Wolfgang Amadeus, 2, 11, 13, 17, 21, 26, 31, 42, 49, 66, 81, 88, 92, 93, 96, 97, 99, 100, 102, 103, 104, 115, 124, 152, 153, 159, 161, 167, 182, 185, 192, 193, 198
Muette de Portici, La (Auber), 100
Mürger, Henri, 35
Murillo (Bartolomeo Esteban), 183
Muse du département, La (Balzac), 47, 61
Musset, Alfred de, 15, 32, 37, 40, 49, 52, 54, 68, 87, 91, 205

Nabucco, Il (Verdi), 175
Napoleon(e) B(u)onaparte, 12, 45, 69, 76
Nerval, Gérard de, 2, 35, 54, 99, 101, 159, 195, 205, 223
Neveu de Rameau, Le (Diderot), 170
Newton, Sir Isaac, 212
Niebelungenlied, Das (Wagner), 158
Niedermeyer, Louis, 124
Nietzsche, Friedrich, 162, 168, 216
Nodier, Charles, 15, 53
Noël (Adam), 124
"Nonnes, qui reposez sous cette froide pierre" (Meyerbeer), 105
Norma (Bellini), 15, 19, 30, 38
Notre-Dame de Paris (Hugo), 125

Nourrit, Adolphe, 32, 37, 38
Novalis (Friedrich, Baron von Hardenberg), 172
Nozze di Figaro, Le (Mozart), 100

Odyssey (Homer), 97
Oestead, Hans Christian, 210
"O filii et filae," 21, 99, 125, 126, 129
"Ombra adorata" (Hoffmann), 154
Ondines, Les (Strunz), 69
"O nume d'Israel" (Rossini), 110
Oper und Drama (Wagner), 159, 161
Optique des couleurs, L' (Castel), 182
Orcagna, Andrea, 183
Orfeo ed Euridice (Gluck), 153
"O Richard, ô mon roi" (Grétry), 21, 36
Ortigue, Joseph-Louis d', 123, 222
Otello (Rossini), 19, 26, 30, 38, 40, 42, 101, 109, 196
Otello (Verdi), 93

"Pace mia smarrita" (Rossini), 112
"Pace, mio Dio" (Verdi), 93
Paër, Ferdinand, 13, 15, 31
Paesiello, Giovanni, 13, 75, 88, 100, 115, 198
Paganini, Niccolò, 16, 21, 26, 32, 43, 44, 45, 46, 55, 58, 60, 67, 68, 81, 101, 199
Palestrina (Giovanni Pierluigi), 98, 127, 129
Palmerini (singer), 37
Panseron, Auguste-Mathieu, 32
Paradoxe sur le comédien (Diderot), 177

"Parisienne, La" (Auber), 100
Pascal, Blaise, 202
Pasta, Giuditta, 15, 17, 37, 38, 39, 81, 101, 169, 188, 201
Paysans, Les (Balzac), 35, 36, 79
Peau de chagrin, La (Balzac), 11, 12, 14, 17, 30, 54, 55, 80, 101, 109, 116, 129, 151, 152, 166, 168, 172, 173, 192, 193, 194, 197, 198, 205, 206-207
Pélissier, Olympe, 16, 20, 51, 52, 53, 80
Pelléas et Mélisande (Debussy), 160
Pellegrini, Felice, 37
Père Goriot, Le (Balzac), 21, 33, 37, 53, 109, 116-117, 125
Persiani, Fanny (Tacchinardi), 15, 37, 40, 101
Pergolesi, Giovanni Battista, 31, 87, 99, 194
Perro del hortelano, El (Lope de Vega), 190
Petites misères de la vie conjugale (Balzac), 28
Petits bourgeois, Les (Balzac), 78
Petrarch (Francesco Petrarca), 180
Phantasien über die Kunst (Tieck), 153
Philosophie der Kunst (Schelling), 157
Physiologie du mariage (Balzac), 15, 16, 19, 54, 152
Piccini, Nicola, 88
Pierrette (Balzac), 35, 100, 131
Pindar, 110
Piola, Pellegro or Pellegrino, 75

Pirandello, Luigi, 175
Pirata, Il (Bellini), 30
Pisaroni (singer), 37
Pitoni, Giuseppe Ottavio, 128
Pius X (pope), 99
Planche, Gustave, 56, 57, 62, 63, 87
Plato, 43, 202
Pleyel, Marie, 44
Plotinus, 202
Polmartin, Mme (salon hostess), 31
Pontus de Tyard, 15
"Porgi la destra amata" (Rossini), 113
Poussin, Nicolas, 183
Préault, Antoine-Auguste, 32, 55
"Preislied" (Wagner), 223
Prêtre catholique, Le (Balzac), 125
"Pria che spunti l'aurora" (Cimarosa), 101, 194
"Prinzessin Brambilla" (Hoffmann), 178
Prod'homme, J.-G., 50
Prophète, Le (Meyerbeer), 110
Proscrits, Les (Balzac), 90
Proust, Marcel, 189, 190, 203, 223
Prova d'un'opera seria, La (Gnecco), 30
Psalms (Marcello), 96
Puccini, Giacomo, 159
Pucitta (composer), 13
Puget, Louise-Françoise (Loïsa), 32
Puritani della Scozia, I (Bellini), 19, 26, 30, 197
Pythagoras, 211, 216

"Quand j'ai quitté la Normandie" (Meyerbeer), 105
"Que la musique date du XVIe siècle" (Hugo), 48

Racine, Jean, 13, 96, 97, 98, 178
Rameau, Jean-Philippe, 31, 87, 89, 100, 153
"Ranz des Suisses," 14
Raphael (Raffaello Sanzio), 41, 45, 46, 47, 48, 66, 169, 183, 199
"Rat Krespel" (Hoffmann), 152
Raüber, Die (Schiller), 108
Rauzan, Duchess de (salon hostess), 15, 55
Recherche de l'Absolu, La (Balzac), 163, 172
Regard, Maurice, 13
Regnard, Jean-François, 13
Regondi, Jules, 55
"Reine Mab" scherzo (Berlioz), 61
Reinken, Johann Adam, 98
Requiem: Messe des morts (Berlioz), 32, 63, 64, 124
Réquisitionnaire, Le (Balzac), 152
Respighi, Ottorino, 72
Rheingold, Das (Wagner), 162
Ricci, Luigi, 31
Rigoletto (Verdi), 112
Rimbaud, Artur, 190
"Ritter Gluck" (Hoffmann), 152
Robert le Diable (Meyerbeer), 19, 23, 26, 30, 38, 65, 66, 80, 88, 93, 97, 100, 102-109, 110, 112, 117, 123, 132, 149, 155, 158, 163, 167, 168, 170, 171, 193
Rode, Pierre, Joseph, 31, 44
Roger, Gustave Hippolyte, 37
Rolland, Romain, 219
Romagnesi, Henri, 32
Rome, Dr. Aimable, 63
Romeo e Giulietta (Zingarelli), 101, 196
Roméo et Juliette symphony (Berlioz), 61

"Rondo brillant mais facile" (Balzac), 47, 100
Ronsard, Pierre de, 15
Roques, Mario, 1, 2
Rossi, Luigi, 98
Rossini, Gioacchino, 10, 13, 15, 16, 17, 19, 21, 22, 23, 24, 26, 27, 30, 31, 32, 34, 39, 40, 42, 45, 46, 47, 51-52, 56, 62, 63, 66, 67, 68, 70, 76, 77, 80, 81, 87, 88, 89, 91, 92, 93, 100, 101, 103, 107, 109-117, 118, 124, 126, 152, 156, 162, 169, 175, 176, 178, 183, 185, 186, 188, 193, 194, 196, 197, 201, 204, 207, 210, 213, 220, 221, 223
Rothschild, James de, 15
Rouchès, Gabriel, 3
Rousseau, Jean-Jacques, 2, 14, 36, 87, 89, 159, 172, 201, 209
Roze, Fr. Nicolas, 124
Rubini, Giovanni Battista, 15, 17, 26, 37, 38, 40, 46, 49, 76, 82, 101, 194, 196
Ruth (Franck), 124
Ruy Blas (Hugo), 70

Sacchini, Antonio Maria Gasparo, 88
Saint-Aulaire, Count Louis-Clair de Beaupoil de, 15
Sainte-Beuve, Charles Augustin, 40, 58
Saint, Hilaire, Geoffroy, 204
Saint-Martin, Louis-Claude de, 189, 199, 202, 209, 211, 215
Saint-Simon, Count Claude Henri de, 73, 74, 123
Salieri, Antonio, 13, 88
Sallambier, Anne Charlotte Laure (Mme Balzac), 9
Sand, George, 23, 25, 26, 34, 35, 40, 42, 49, 56, 57, 60, 65, 74, 87, 101, 150, 165, 190, 195, 223
Sandeau, Jules, 53, 56, 57, 75
"Sandmann, Der" (Hoffmann), 154
"Santa Cecilia" (Raphael), 41, 47
"Sant'Ambrogio" (Giusti), 114
Sarrasine (Balzac), 14, 37, 38, 39, 80, 151, 196
"Saule, Le," 50
Sauvageot, Charles, 67, 76, 77, 78
Scarlatti, Alessandro, 87, 98
Scève, Maurice, 15
Schiller, Friedrich, 108
Schira (composer), 31
Schönberg, Arnold, 3, 160
Schopenhauer, Arthur, 161, 206, 208, 209, 214
Schroeder, Wilhelmina, 37
Schubert, Franz, 26, 31, 33, 56, 60, 223
"Schüler Tartinis, Der" (Hoffmann), 152
Schumann, Robert, 26, 27, 44, 66, 169, 201
Scott, Sir Walter, 96
Scribe, Eugène, 107
Scudo, Paul, 65
Secrets de la princesse de Cadignan, Les (Balzac), 47
"Se il padre m'abbandona" (Rossini), 40
Semiramide (Rossini), 19, 30, 31, 52, 109, 116, 196
Senancour, Etienne Pivert de, 60, 87, 202, 204, 213, 223
Senesino (singer), 37
Septet in E-flat (Beethoven), 31
Séraphita (Balzac), 21, 47,

48, 55, 124, 130, 131, 132, 165, 169, 185, 203, 209, 210, 211, 213, 214
"Serenade in D minor" (Schubert), 31
Sextet (Bertini), 31
Shakespeare, William, 90, 193, 217
Shelley, Percy Bysshe, 205
Siegfried (Wagner), 162
"Signor Formica - Salvador Rosa" (Hoffmann), 154, 210
"Si je le promets" (Meyerbeer), 104
Siméon, Vicount Joseph-Balthazar, 15
Sirènes (Debussy), 162
Smetana, Bedrich, 36
Socrates, 43
"Soleil, soleil, divin soleil," 33
Sonata for Violin in A major (Brahms), 223
"Songe de Rousseau, Le" (Cramer), 11, 12, 14, 27, 47, 100, 193, 196
Sonnambula, La (Bellini), 15, 19, 30, 197
"Son regina, son guerriera" (Rossini), 196
Sontag, Henriette, 37, 38, 39, 81
Souverain (publisher), 174
Splendeurs et misères des courtisanes (Balzac), 30, 78, 80, 100, 164
Spontini, Luigi, 13, 30, 31, 88, 115
"Stabat Mater," 124
Stabat Mater (Rossini), 124
Staël, Mme de (Germaine Necker), 34, 159, 194
Steibelt, Daniel, 33, 44
Stendhal (Henri Beyle), 2, 29, 30, 37, 39, 42, 49, 51, 54, 62, 87, 89, 92,
110, 115, 118, 119, 151, 176, 179, 189, 190, 196, 216, 223
Sténie (Balzac), 14, 15, 124-125, 193
Stolz, Rosine, 37
Straniera, La (Bellini), 30
Strauss, Richard, 73, 160
Stravinsky, Igor, 3, 73, 160
Strunz, Jacques, 22, 23, 24, 43, 67, 68-83, 87, 102, 132, 149, 151, 157, 158, 161, 174, 221
Sue, Eugène, 16, 59
"Super flumina Babylonis," 124, 125
Surville, Laure de, 9, 10, 12, 13, 14, 20, 21, 155
Surville, Sophie, 27
Swedenborg, Emmanuel, 56, 131, 165, 181, 182, 184, 186, 187, 189, 191, 192, 194, 198, 204, 207, 211
Symphonie fantastique (Berlioz), 64, 65, 128
Symphony No. 3 in E-flat major (Beethoven), 31
Symphony No. 5 in C minor (Beethoven), 22, 24, 25, 67, 100, 105, 107, 161, 162, 193, 213
Symphony No. 6 in F major (Beethoven), 25
Symphony No. 7 in A major (Beethoven), 195-196
Symphony No. 9 in D minor (Beethoven), 106, 162
Symphony No. 41 in C major (Mozart), 102

Tableau de la France (Michelet), 36
Tableau naturel (Saint-Martin), 209
Taglioni, Maria, 46, 106
Tamburini, Antonio, 17, 26, 37, 38

Tancredi (Rossini), 30
"Te Deum," 33, 125, 126, 127, 130
Teissier (decorator), 53
Telemann, Georg Philipp, 98
Thalberg, Sigismund, 32, 44, 49
Theophrastus, 76
"Théorie de la démarche" (Balzac), 46
Thiers, Louis-Adolphe, 59
Thomas, Ambroise, 30, 67
Tieck, Ludwig, 152
Tiepolo, Giovanni Battista 183
Tiersot, Julien, 34
Tintoretto (Jacopo Robusti), 183
Titian (Tiziano Vecelli), 183
Tolstoy, Lev, 223
Tommaso di Calano, 99
"Tormenti! affanni! smanie!" (Rossini), 113
Toscanini, Arturo, 4
Tottola (librettist), 110
Tournier (decorator), 53
"Traité de la lumière" (Balzac), [see *Feuilletons des journaux politiques*]
Traité de la lumière (Herschell), 182
Troyens, Les (Berlioz), 158
Tulou, Jean-Louis, 12, 44, 47
"Tu ne sauras à quel excès je t'aime"(Meyerbeer), 104

Ursule Mirouët, 14, 24, 33, 46, 78, 79, 95, 97, 125, 131, 191, 193, 195, 196, 198
"Ut queant laxis," 125

Vacances de Camille, Les (Mürger), 35
Vaet (composer), 127
Valentino, Henri-Justin, 26, 64
Vecchi, Orazio, 128
Veluti, Giovanni Battista, 99
"Veni Creator," 125
"Venite, adoremus," 125, 129
Vera (composer), 31
Vera Christiana religio (Swedenborg), 211
Verdi, Giuseppe, 93, 112, 115, 158, 160, 175
Vestale, La (Spontini), 13, 30
Viardot, Pauline (García), 37
Vicaire des Ardennes, Le (Balzac), 14
Vieux musicien, Le (*Le Cousin Pons*) (Balzac), 24, 76
Vieuxtemps, Henri, 44
Vigano, signora (singer), 16, 37
Vigny, Count Alfred de, 32, 43, 49, 59, 74, 87, 98, 129
Villa-Lobos, Heitor, 36
Violin Concerto (Rode), 31
Violin Concerto (Strunz), 69
Virgil, 108, 216
Vittoria (Tomás Luís de Victoria), 98
"Voci di giubilo" (Rossini), 111, 183
Vogt (musician), 44
Voltaire (François Arouet), 73
Voyage de Paris à Java (Balzac), 99, 108

Wackenroder, Wilhelm Heinrich, 153, 168
Wagner, Richard, 2, 3, 25, 55, 65, 111, 154, 158-163, 207, 208, 223
Walküre, Die (Wagner), 162
Wann-Chlore (Balzac), 125
Warens, Baroness Louise-Elénore de la Tour du Pil, 14
Weber, Carl Maria von, 17, 25, 26, 31, 39, 42, 49,

55, 56, 60, 66, 69, 87, 99, 115, 131, 158, 161, 162
Welt als Wille und Vorstellung, Die (Schopenhauer), 208
Werdet, Edmond, 18, 25, 53
Wieck, Clara (Schumann), 27, 65
Wilde, Oscar, 179

Wolff, Edvard/August, 16
Wozzeck (Berg), 160

Zimmermann, Pierre, 31, 32
Zingarelli, Nicola Antonio, 101, 193, 196
Zola, Emile, 4
Zurbarán, Francisco, 183
Zur Stellung der Künstler (Liszt), 73
Zweig, Stefan, 4

For Product Safety Concerns and Information please contact our EU
representative GPSR@taylorandfrancis.com
Taylor & Francis Verlag GmbH, Kaufingerstraße 24, 80331 München, Germany

www.ingramcontent.com/pod-product-compliance
Lightning Source LLC
Chambersburg PA
CBHW061427300426
44114CB00014B/1578